Third World
Liberation Theologies

A Reader

THIRD WORLD
LIBERATION THEOLOGIES

A Reader

Edited by
Deane William Ferm

ORBIS BOOKS

Maryknoll, New York 10545

The Catholic Foreign Mission Society of America (Maryknoll) recruits and trains people for overseas missionary service. Through Orbis Books Maryknoll aims to foster the international dialogue that is essential to mission. The books published, however, reflect the opinions of their authors and are not meant to represent the official position of the society.

Library of Congress Cataloging in Publication Data

Main entry under title:

Third World liberation theologies.

   Includes bibliographical references.
   1. Liberation theology—Addresses, essays,
lectures.   I. Ferm, Deane William, 1927-
BT83.57.T48   1985   230   85-15302
ISBN 0-88344-516-6 (pbk.)

Third World Liberation Theologies Set
ISBN 0-88344-517-4

Contents

PART 3
ASIA

Preface

This book of readings has two purposes: to be the companion to my *Third World Liberation Theologies: An Introductory Survey*, and to serve as a sampling of the work of the foremost Third World liberation theologians. The primary aim of the survey is to summarize the views of major theologians and trends in Third World liberation theology while offering also a guide to references to significant books and articles that illustrate these trends. The present book contains selections that allow the theologians to speak for themselves.

A recurring theme in the survey is the plurality of perspectives within Third World liberation theology; theologians from Latin America, Africa, and Asia display their own distinctive approaches. In the present volume I have included readings that illustrate this distinctiveness and diversity. Although significant, the final statements of the six meetings of the Ecumenical Association of Third World Theologians (EATWOT) have not been included—they will be published by Orbis Books in a forthcoming volume.

Obviously one cannot do justice to every theologian and trend in an anthology the length of this one. However, I believe that this collection provides readers with a balanced presentation of the most significant development in contemporary theology.

With the exception of the Medellín Document on Peace, selections have been edited for exclusive language.

PART 1

LATIN AMERICA

1

Latin American Episcopal Council (CELAM)

Medellín Document on Peace

The Medellín Conference (Second General Conference of Latin American Bishops) in 1968 provided the setting and stimulus for the emergence of Latin American liberation theology. This selection is the document on peace, taken from The Church in the Present-day Transformation of Latin America in the Light of the Council, II, Conclusions *(Bogotá: General Secretariat of CE-LAM, 1970), pp. 71–82.* © *1970 by the General Secretariat of CELAM.*

I. THE LATIN AMERICAN SITUATION AND PEACE

1. "If development is the new name for peace,"[1] Latin American underdevelopment, with its own characteristics in the different countries, is an unjust situation which promotes tensions that conspire against peace.

We can divide these tensions into three major groups, selecting, in each of these, those variables which constitute a positive menace to the peace of our countries by manifesting an unjust situation.

When speaking of injustice, we refer to those realities that constitute a sinful situation; this does not mean, however, that we are overlooking the fact that at times the misery in our countries can have natural causes which are difficult to overcome.

In making this analysis, we do not ignore or fail to give credit to the positive efforts made at every level to build a more just society. We do not include this here because our purpose is to call attention to those aspects which constitute a menace or negation of peace.

3

Tensions between Classes and Internal Colonialism

2. *Different forms of marginality.* Socio-economic, cultural, political, racial, religious, in urban as well as rural sectors;

3. *Extreme inequality among social classes.* Especially, though not exclusively, in those countries which are characterized by a marked bi-classism, where a few have much (culture, wealth, power, prestige) while the majority has very little. The Holy Father describes this situation when directing himself to the Colombian rural workers: "Social and economic development has not been equitable in the great continent of Latin America; and while it has favored those who helped establish it in the beginning, it has neglected the masses of native population, which are almost always left at a subsistence level and at times are mistreated and exploited harshly."[2]

4. *Growing frustrations.* The universal phenomenon of rising expectations assumes a particularly aggressive dimension in Latin America. The reason is obvious: excessive inequalities systematically prevent the satisfaction of the legitimate aspirations of the ignored sectors and breed increasing frustrations.

The same low morale is obtained in those middle classes which, when confronting grave crises, enter into a process of disintegration and proletarization.

5. *Forms of oppression of dominant groups and sectors.* Without excluding the eventuality of willful oppression, these forms manifest themselves most frequently in a lamentable insensitivity of the privileged sectors to the misery of the marginated sectors. Thus the words of the Pope to the leaders: "That your ears and heart be sensitive to the voices of those who ask for bread, concern, justice. . . ."[3]

It is not unusual to find that these groups, with the exception of some enlightened minorities, characterize as subversive activities all attempts to change the social system which favors the permanence of their privileges.

6. *Power unjustly exercised by certain dominant sectors.* As a natural consequence of the above-mentioned attitudes, some members of the dominant sectors occasionally resort to the use of force to repress drastically any attempt at opposition. It is easy for them to find apparent ideological justifications (anticommunism) or practical ones (keeping "order") to give their action an honest appearance.

7. *Growing awareness of the oppressed sectors.* All the above results are even more intolerable as the oppressed sectors become increasingly aware of their situation. The Holy Father referred to them when he said to the rural workers: "But today the problem has worsened because you have become more aware of your needs and suffering, and you cannot tolerate the persistence of these conditions without applying a careful remedy."[4]

The static picture described in the above paragraphs is worsened when it is projected into the future: basic education will increase awareness, and the demographic explosion will multiply problems and tensions. One must not forget the existence of movements of all types interested in taking advantage of and irritating these tensions. Therefore, if today peace seems seriously endangered, the automatic aggravation of the problems will produce explosive consequences.

International Tensions and External Neocolonialism

8. We refer here, particularly, to the implications for our countries of dependence on a center of economic power, around which they gravitate. For this reason, our nations frequently do not own their goods or have a say in economic decisions affecting them. It is obvious that this will not fail to have political consequences given the interdependence of these two fields.

We are interested in emphasizing two aspects of this phenomenon.

9. *Economic aspect*. We only analyze those factors having greater influence on the global and relative impoverishment of our countries, and which constitute a source of internal and external tensions.

a) *Growing distortion of international commerce*. Because of the relative depreciation of the terms of exchange, the value of raw materials is increasingly less in relation to the cost of manufactured products. This means that the countries which produce raw materials—especially if they are dependent upon one major export—always remain poor, while the industrialized countries enrich themselves. This injustice, clearly denounced by *Populorum progressio*,[5] nullifies the eventual positive effect of external aid and constitutes a permanent menace against peace, because our countries sense that "one hand takes away what the other hand gives."[6]

b) *Rapid flight of economic and human capital*. The search for security and individual gain leads many members of the more comfortable sectors of our countries to invest their money in foreign countries. The injustice of such procedures has already been denounced categorically by the encyclical *Populorum progressio*.[7] To this can be added the loss of technicians and competent personnel, which is at least as serious and perhaps more so than the loss of capital because of the high cost of training these people and because of their ability to teach others.

c) *Tax evasion and loss of gains and dividends*. Some foreign companies working in our country (also some national firms) often evade the established tax system by subterfuge. We are also aware that at times they send their profits and dividends abroad without contributing adequate reinvestments to the progressive development of our countries.

d) *Progressive debt*. It is not surprising to find that in the system of international credits, the true needs and capabilities of our countries are not taken into account. We thus run the risk of encumbering ourselves with debts whose payment absorbs the greater part of our profits.[8]

e) *International monopolies and international imperialism of money*. We wish to emphasize that the principal guilt for economic dependence of our countries rests with powers, inspired by uncontrolled desire for gain, which leads to economic dictatorship and the "international imperialism of money"[9] condemned by Pope Pius XI in *Quadragesimo anno* and by Pope Paul VI in *Populorum progressio*.

10. *Political aspect*. We here denounce the imperialism of any ideological bias that is exercised in Latin America either indirectly or through direct intervention.

Tensions among the Countries of Latin America

11. We here denounce the particular phenomenon of historico-political origin that continues to disturb cordial relations among some countries and impedes truly constructive collaboration. Nevertheless, the integration process, well understood, presents itself as a commanding necessity for Latin America. Without pretending to set norms of a truly complex, technical nature, governing integration, we deem it opportune to point out this multi-dimensional character. Integration, in effect, is not solely an economic process; it has a broader dimension reflected in the way in which it embraces man in his total situation: social, political, cultural, religious, racial.

Among the factors that increase the tensions among our countries we underline:

12. An *exacerbated nationalism* in some countries. The Holy Father has already denounced the unwholesomeness of this attitude, especially on a matter where the weakness of the national economies requires a union of efforts.[10]

13. *Armaments*. In certain countries an arms race is under way that surpasses the limits of reason. It frequently stems from a fictitious need to respond to diverse interests rather than to a true need of the national community. In that respect, a phrase of *Populorum progressio* is particularly pertinent: "When so many communities are hungry, when so many homes suffer misery, when so many men live submerged in ignorance, . . . any arms race becomes an intolerable scandal."[11]

II. DOCTRINAL REFLEXION

Christian View of Peace

14. The above-mentioned Christian viewpoint on peace adds up to a negation of peace such as Christian tradition understands it.

Three factors characterize the Christian concept of peace:

a) Peace is, above all, a work of justice.[12] It presupposes and requires the establishment of a just order[13] in which men can fulfill themselves as men, where their dignity is respected, their legitimate aspirations satisfied, their access to truth recognized, their personal freedom guaranteed; an order where man is not an object, but an agent of his own history. Therefore, there will be attempts against peace where unjust inequalities among men and nations prevail.[14]

Peace in Latin America, therefore, is not the simple absence of violence and bloodshed. Oppression by the power groups may give the impression of maintaining peace and order, but in truth it is nothing but the "continuous and inevitable seed of rebellion and war."[15]

"Peace can only be obtained by creating a new order which carries with it a more perfect justice among men."[16] It is in this sense that the integral development of man, the path to more human conditions, becomes the symbol of peace.

b) Secondly, peace is a permanent task.[17] A community becomes a reality in time and is subject to a movement that implies constant change in structures, transformation of attitudes, and conversion of hearts.

The "tranquility of order," according to the Augustinian definition of peace, is neither passivity nor conformity. It is not something that is acquired once and for all. It is the result of continuous effort and adaptation to new circumstances, to new demands and challenges of a changing history. A static and apparent peace may be obtained with the use of force; an authentic peace implies struggle, creative abilities, and permanent conquest.[18]

Peace is not found, it is built. The Christian man is the artisan of peace (see Matt. 5:9). This task, given the above circumstances, has a special character in our continent; thus, the People of God in Latin America, following the example of Christ, must resist personal and collective injustice with unselfish courage and fearlessness.

c) Finally, peace is the fruit of love.[19] It is the expression of true fraternity among men, a fraternity given by Christ, Prince of Peace, in reconciling all men with the Father. Human solidarity cannot truly take effect unless it is done in Christ, who gives peace that the world cannot give (see John 14:27). Love is the soul of justice. The Christian who works for social justice should always cultivate peace and love in his heart.

Peace with God is the basic foundation of internal and social peace. Therefore, where this social peace does not exist there will we find social, political, economic, and cultural inequalities, there will we find the rejection of the peace of the Lord, and a rejection of God (see Matt. 25:31–46).

The Problem of Violence in Latin America

15. Violence constitutes one of the gravest problems in Latin America. A decision on which the future of the countries of the continent will depend should not be left to the impulses of emotion and passion. We would be failing in our pastoral duty if we were not to remind the conscience, caught in this dramatic dilemma, of the criteria derived from the Christian doctrine of evangelical love.

No one should be surprised if we forcefully reaffirm our faith in the productiveness of peace. This is our Christian ideal. "Violence is neither Christian nor evangelical."[20] The Christian man is peaceful and not ashamed of it. He is not simply a pacifist, for he can fight,[21] but he prefers peace to war. He knows that "violent changes in structures would be fallacious, ineffectual in themselves and not conforming to the dignity of man, which demands that the necessary changes take place from within, that is to say, through a fitting awakening of conscience, adequate preparation and effective participation of all, which the ignorance and often inhuman conditions of life make it impossible to assure at this time."[22]

16. As the Christian believes in the productiveness of peace in order to achieve justice, he also believes that justice is a prerequisite for peace. He recognizes that in many instances Latin America finds itself faced with a situation of injustice that can be called institutionalized violence, when, because of a structural deficiency of industry and agriculture, of national and international economy, of cultural and political life, "whole towns lack necessities, live in such dependence as hinders all initiative and responsibility as well as every possibility for cultural promotion and participation in social and political life,"[23] thus violating fundamental rights. This situation demands all-embracing, courageous, urgent, and profoundly renovating transformations. We should not be surprised, therefore, that the "temptation to violence" is surfacing in Latin America. One should not abuse the patience of a people that for years has borne a situation that would not be acceptable to any one with any degree of awareness of human rights.

Facing a situation which works so seriously against the dignity of man and against peace, we address ourselves, as pastors, to all the members of the Christian community, asking them to assume their responsibility in the promotion of peace in Latin America.

17. We would like to direct our call, in the first place, to those who have a greater share of wealth, culture, and power. We know that there are leaders in Latin America who are sensitive to the needs of the people and try to remedy them. They recognize that the privileged many times join together and with all the means at their disposal pressure those who govern, thus obstructing necessary changes. In some instances, this pressure takes on drastic proportions which result in the destruction of life and property.

Therefore, we urge them not to take advantage of the pacifist position of the church in order to oppose, either actively or passively, the profound transformations that are so necessary. If they jealously retain their privileges and defend them through violence, they are responsible to history for provoking "explosive revolutions of despair."[24] The peaceful future of the countries of Latin America depends to a large extent on their attitude.

18. Also responsible for injustice are those who remain passive for fear of the sacrifice and personal risk implied by any courageous and effective action. Justice, and therefore peace, conquer by means of a dynamic action of awakening (*concientización*) and organization of the popular sectors, which are capable of pressing public officials who are often impotent in their social projects without popular support.

19. We address ourselves finally to those who, in the face of injustice and illegitimate resistance to change, put their hopes in violence. With Paul VI we

realize that their attitude "frequently finds its ultimate motivation in noble impulses of justice and solidarity."[25] Let us not speak here of empty words which do not imply personal responsibility and which isolate from the fruitful nonviolent actions that are immediately possible.

If it is true that revolutionary insurrection can be legitimate in the case of evident and prolonged "tyranny that seriously works against the fundamental rights of man, and which damages the common good of the country,"[26] whether it proceeds from one person or from clearly unjust structures, it is also certain that violence or "armed revolution" generally "generates new injustices, introduces new imbalances and causes new disasters; one cannot combat a real evil at the price of a greater evil."[27]

If we consider, then, the totality of the circumstances of our countries and if we take into account the Christian preference for peace, the enormous difficulty of a civil war, the logic of violence, the atrocities it engenders, the risk of provoking foreign intervention, illegitimate as it may be, the difficulty of building a regime of justice and freedom while participating in a process of violence, we earnestly desire that the dynamism of the awakened and organzied community be put to the service of justice and peace.

Finally, we would like to make ours the words of our Holy Father to the newly ordained priests and deacons in Bogotá, when he referred to all the suffering and said to them: "We will be able to understand their afflictions and change them, not into hate and violence, but into the strong and peaceful energy of constructive works."[28]

III. PASTORAL CONCLUSIONS

20. In the face of the tensions which conspire against peace, and even present the temptation of violence; in the face of the Christian concept of peace which has been described, we believe that the Latin American Episcopate cannot avoid assuming very concrete responsibilities, because to create a just social order, without which peace is illusory, is an eminently Christian task.

To us, the pastors of the church, belongs the duty to educate the Christian conscience, to inspire, stimulate, and help orient all of the initiatives that contribute to the formation of man. It is also up to us to denounce everything which, opposing justice, destroys peace.

In this spirit we feel it opportune to bring up the following pastoral points:

21. To awaken in individuals and communities, principally through mass media, a living awareness of justice, infusing in them a dynamic sense of responsibility and solidarity.

22. To defend the rights of the poor and oppressed according to the gospel commandment, urging our governments and upper classes to eliminate anything which might destroy social peace: injustice, inertia, venality, insensibility.

23. To favor integration, energetically denouncing the abuses and unjust consequences of the excessive inequalities between poor and rich, weak and powerful.

24. To be certain that our preaching, liturgy, and catechesis take into account the social and community dimensions of Christianity, forming men committed to world peace.

25. To achieve in our schools, seminaries, and universities a healthy critical sense of the social situation and foster the vocation of service. We also consider very efficacious the diocesan and national campaigns that mobilize the faithful and social organizations, leading them to a similar reflection.

26. To invite various Christian and non-Christian communities to collaborate in this fundamental task of our times.

27. To encourage and favor the efforts of the people to create and develop their own grass-roots organizations for the redress and consolidation of their rights and the search for true justice.

28. To request the perfecting of the administration of justice, whose deficiencies often cause serious ills.

29. To urge a halt and revision in many of our countries of the arms race that at times constitutes a burden excessively disproportionate to the legitimate demands of the common good, to the detriment of desperate social necessities. The struggle against misery is the true war that our nations should face.

30. To invite the bishops, the leaders of different churches, and all men of good will of the developed nations to promote in their respective spheres of influence, especially among the political and financial leaders, a consciousness of greater solidarity facing our underdeveloped nations, obtaining, among other things, just prices for our raw materials.

31. On the occasion of the twentieth anniversary of the solemn declaration of Human Rights, to interest universities in Latin America to undertake investigations to verify the degree of its implementation in our countries.

32. To denounce the unjust action of world powers that works against self-determination of weaker nations who must suffer the bloody consequences of war and invasion, and to ask competent international organizations for effective and decisive procedures.

33. To encourage and praise the initiatives and works of all those who in the diverse areas of action contribute to the creation of a new order which will assure peace in our midst.

NOTES

1. Paul VI, *Populorum progressio*, 87.
2. Paul VI, Address to the Peasants (Mosquera, Colombia, Aug. 23, 1968).
3. Paul VI, Homily of the Mass on Development Day (Bogotá, Aug. 23, 1968).
4. Paul VI, Address to the Peasants.
5. See Paul VI, *Populorum progressio*, 56–61.
6. Ibid., 56.
7. Ibid., 24.
8. See ibid., 54.

9. Ibid., 26.

10. See ibid., 62.

11. Ibid., 53.

12. See Vatican Council II, *Gaudium et spes*, 78.

13. See John XXIII, *Pacem in terris*, 167, and Paul VI, *Populorum progressio*, 76.

14. See Paul VI, Message of January 1, 1968.

15. Ibid.

16. Paul VI, *Populorum progressio*, 76.

17. See Vatican Council II, *Guadium et spes*, 78.

18. See Paul VI, Christmas Message, 1967.

19. See Vatican Council II, *Gaudium et spes*, 78.

20. Paul VI, Homily of the Mass on Development Day; cf. Paul VI, Opening Address at the Second General Conference of Latin American Bishops (Bogotá, Aug. 24, 1968).

21. See Paul VI, Message of January 1, 1968.

22. Paul VI, Homily of the Mass on Development Day.

23. Paul VI, *Populorum progressio*, 30.

24. Paul VI, Homily of the Mass on Development Day.

25. Ibid.

26. Paul VI, *Populorum progressio*, 31.

27. Ibid.

28. Paul VI, Address to New Priests and Deacons (Bogotá, Aug. 22, 1968).

2

Christians for Socialism

Declaration of the 80

The Christians for Socialism movement was a vanguard Christian group active in Chile in the early 1970s. This selection was issued by a group of priests who met in Santiago, Chile, in 1971. It is taken from John Eagleson, ed., Christians and Socialism *(Maryknoll, N.Y.: Orbis Books, 1975), pp. 3–6.*

We are a group of 80 priests who live and work with people of the working class. We came together to analyze the present situation of Chile as it begins to develop and implement socialism.

The working class is still subject to exploitation and its attendant conditions: that is, malnutrition, lack of housing, unemployment, and limited possibilities for futher education and cultural development. The cause of this situation is specific and clear. It is the capitalist system, resulting from domination by foreign imperialism and maintained by the ruling classes of this country.

This system is characterized by private ownership of the means of production and by ever-growing inequality in the distribution of income. It turns the worker into a mere cog in the production system, stimulates an irrational distribution of economic resources, and causes an improper transferal of surplus goods to foreign lands. The result is stagnation, which prevents our country from escaping its situation of underdevelopment.

Such a situation cannot be tolerated any longer. It is clear to us that the working masses found great hope in the accession of the People's Government to power and in this respect they were not mistaken.

Socialism, which is characterized by social appropriation of the means of production, paves the way for a new economy which makes possible autonomous development at a more accelerated pace and which overcomes the division of society into antagonistic classes. But socialism is not just a new economy. It should also generate new values which will pave the way for a society that evinces more fellowship and solidarity. In this society the workers will shoulder their proper role with new dignity.

We feel committed to the process that is now under way, and we want to contribute to its success. The underlying reason for our commitment is our faith in Jesus Christ, which takes on depth and vitality and concrete shape in accordance with historical circumstances. To be a Christian is to be in solidarity, in fellowship, with other human beings. And at this moment in Chile fellowship means participation in the historical project that its people have set for themselves.

As Christians we do not see any incompatibility between Christianity and socialism. Quite the contrary is true. As the Cardinal of Santiago said last November: "There are more evangelical values in socialism than there are in capitalism." The fact is that socialism offers new hope that persons can be more complete, and hence more evangelical: that is, more conformed to Jesus Christ, who came to liberate us from any and every sort of bondage.

Thus it is necessary to destroy the prejudice and mistrust that exist between Christians and Marxists.

To Marxists we say that authentic religion is not the opiate of the people. It is, on the contrary, a liberating stimulus to revivify and renew the world constantly. To Christians we offer a reminder that our God has been and is committed personally to the history of human beings. And we say that at this present moment loving one's neighbor basically means struggling to make this world resemble as closely as possible the future world that we hope for and that we are already in the process of constructing.

We are not unaware of the difficulties and the suspicions on both sides. In large measure they have been caused by past historical circumstances that no longer prevail in Chile today. There is a long road ahead for both Christians and Marxists. But the evolution that has taken place in Christian and Marxist circles permits them to engage in a joint effort on behalf of the historical project that the country has set for itself.

This collaboration will be facilitated to the extent that two things are done: (1) to the extent that Marxism presents itself more and more as an instrument for analyzing and transforming society; (2) to the extent that we Christians proceed to purify our faith of everything that prevents us from shouldering real and effective commitment.

Hence we support the measures aimed at social appropriation of the means of production: for example, the nationalization of mineral resources, the socialization of banks and monopoly industries, the expansion and acceleration of agrarian reform, and so forth.

We feel that much sacrifice will be entailed in the implementation of socialism, that it will involve a constructive and united effort if we are to overcome our underdevelopment and to create a new society. Obviously enough this will provoke strong resistance from those who will be deprived of their special privileges. Hence the mobilization of the people is absolutely necessary. With some concern we note that this mobilization has not been achieved as had been hoped.

We also believe that it is indispensable to lay the foundations for the creation of a new culture. This new culture must not be the mirror image of capitalist concerns and interests; it must be the real-life expression of the genuine values of our people. Only then can we see the emergence of the New Person, who will create a societal life that is truly one of fellowship and solidarity.

We note that there are large groups of workers who are in favor of the changes taking place and who are benefiting from them but who are not actively involving themselves in the process that has already been initiated. The union of all workers, whatever their party loyalty may be, is critical at this juncture. Our country is being offered a unique opportunity to replace the existing system of dependent capitalism and to promote the cause of the laboring class throughout Latin America.

Lack of class consciousness among these workers is being encouraged and fostered by the ruling groups, primarily through the communications media and party activities. They are inculcating suspicions and fears, which ultimately lead to resistance and passivity.

We must recognize and admit that not everything being done is necessarily positive and effective. But at the same time we insist that criticism should be formulated from within the revolutionary process, not from outside it.

It is a time full of risk, but a time full of hope also. We priests, like each and every Christian, must do what we can to make our own modest contribution. That is why we have come together to reflect and to prepare ourselves in this workshop on the participation of Christians in the implementation of socialism.

3

Gustavo Gutiérrez

The Meaning of the Term *Liberation*

Gustavo Gutiérrez has consistently insisted that liberation involves the total person and embraces three different interrelated levels of meaning. This selection is from A Theology of Liberation *(Maryknoll, N.Y.: Orbis Books, 1973), pp. 36–37. The book was originally published in Peru in 1971.*

We can distinguish three reciprocally interpenetrating levels of meaning of the term *liberation*, or, in other words, three approaches to the process of liberation.

In the first place, *liberation* expresses the aspirations of oppressed peoples and social classes, emphasizing the conflictual aspect of the economic, social, and political process which puts them at odds with wealthy nations and oppressive classes. In contrast, the word *development*, and above all the policies characterized as developmentalist [*desarrollista*], appear somewhat aseptic, giving a false picture of a tragic and conflictual reality. The issue of development does in fact find its true place in the more universal, profound, and radical perspective of liberation. It is only within this framework that *development* finds its true meaning and possibilities of accomplishing something worthwhile.

At a deeper level, *liberation* can be applied to an understanding of history. Humankind is seen as assuming conscious responsibility for its own destiny. This understanding provides a dynamic context and broadens the horizons of the desired social changes. In this perspective the unfolding of all the dimensions of human persons is demanded—persons who make themselves throughout their lives and throughout history. The gradual conquest of true freedom

15

leads to the creation of new women and men and a qualitatively different society. This vision provides, therefore, a better understanding of what in fact is at stake in our times.

Finally, the word *development* to a certain extent limits and obscures the theological problems implied in the process designated by this term. On the contrary, the word *liberation* allows for another approach leading to the biblical sources which inspire the presence and action of humankind in history. In the Bible, Christ is presented as the one who brings us liberation. Christ the Savior liberates humankind from sin, which is the ultimate root of all disruption of friendship and of all injustice and oppression. Christ makes persons truly free, that is to say, he enables persons to live in communion with him; and this is the basis for all human solidarity.

This is not a matter of three parallel or chronologically successive processes, however. These are three levels of meaning of a single, complex process, which finds its deepest sense and its full realization in the saving work of Christ. These levels of meaning, therefore, are interdependent. A comprehensive view of the matter presupposes that all three aspects can be considered together. In this way two pitfalls will be avoided: first, *idealist* or *spiritualist* approaches, which are nothing but ways of evading a harsh and demanding reality, and, second, shallow analyses and programs of short-term effect initiated under the pretext of meeting immediate needs.

4

Gustavo Gutiérrez

A Spirituality of Liberation

In this excerpt Gutiérrez argues that true spirituality is inextricably bound to praxis: spirituality that is primarily interiorist or isolationist is incomplete. True spirituality can develop only when a person is engaged in the struggle for justice and liberation—the struggle to transform unjust social, political, and economic structures. The excerpt is from A Theology of Liberation *(Maryknoll, N.Y.: Orbis Books, 1973), pp. 203–8.*

To place oneself in the perspective of the kingdom means to participate in the struggle for the liberation of those oppressed by others. This is what many Christians who have committed themselves to the Latin American revolutionary process have begun to experience. If this option seems to separate them from the Christian community, it is because many Christians, intent on domesticating the good news, see them as wayward and perhaps even dangerous. If they are not always able to express in appropriate terms the profound reasons for their commitment, it is because the theology in which they were formed—and which they share with other Christians—has not produced the categories necessary to express this option, which seeks to respond creatively to the new demands of the gospel and of the oppressed and exploited peoples of this continent. But in their commitments, and even in their attempts to explain them, there is a greater understanding of the faith, greater faith, greater fidelity to the Lord than in the "orthodox" doctrine (some prefer to call it by this name) of reputable Christian circles. This doctrine is supported by authority and much publicized because of access to social communications media, but it is so static and devitalized that it is not even strong enough to abandon the gospel. It is the gospel which is disowning it.

But theological categories are not enough. We need a vital attitude, all-embracing and synthesizing, informing the totality as well as every detail of our lives; we need a "spirituality." Spirituality, in the strict and profound sense of the word, is the dominion of the Spirit. If "the truth will set you free" (John 8:32), the Spirit "will guide you into all the truth" (John 16:13) and will lead us to complete freedom, the freedom from everything that hinders us from fulfilling ourselves as human persons and as daughters and sons of God and the freedom to love and to enter into communion with God and with others. It will lead us along the path of liberation because "where the Spirit of the Lord is, there is liberty" (2 Cor. 3:17).

A spirituality is a concrete manner, inspired by the Spirit, of living the gospel; it is a definite way of living "before the Lord," in solidarity with all persons, "with the Lord," and before humankind. It arises from an intense spiritual experience, which is later explicated and witnessed to. Some Christians are beginning to live this experience as a result of their commitment to the process of liberation. The experiences of previous generations are there to support it and, above all, to remind them that they must discover their own way. Not only is there a contemporary history and a contemporary gospel; there is also a contemporary spiritual experience which cannot be overlooked. A spirituality means a reordering of the great axes of the Christian life in terms of this contemporary experience. What is new is the synthesis that this reordering brings out, in stimulating a deepened understanding of various ideas, in bringing to the surface unknown or forgotten aspects of the Christian life, and, above all, in the way in which these things are converted into life, prayer, commitment, and action.

The truth is that a Christianity lived in commitment to the process of liberation presents its own problems which cannot be ignored and meets obstacles which must be overcome. For many, the encounter with the Lord under these conditions can disappear by giving way to what God brings forth and nourishes: love for humanity. This love, however, does not know the fullness of its potential. This is a real difficulty, but the solution must come from the heart of the problem itself. Otherwise, it would be just one more patchwork remedy, a new impasse. This is the challenge confronting a spirituality of liberation. Where oppression and the liberation of humankind seem to make God irrelevant—a God filtered by our longtime indifference to these problems—there must blossom faith and hope in God who comes to root out injustice and to offer, in an unforeseen way, total liberation. This is a spirituality which dares to sink roots in the soil of oppression-liberation.

A spirituality of liberation will center on a *conversion* to the neighbor, the oppressed person, the exploited social class, the despised race, the dominated country. Our conversion to the Lord implies this conversion to the neighbor. Evangelical conversion is indeed the touchstone of all spirituality. Conversion means a radical transformation of ourselves; it means thinking, feeling, and living as Christ—present in exploited and alienated humankind. To be converted is to commit oneself to the process of the liberation of the poor and oppressed, to commit oneself lucidly, realistically, and concretely. It means to commit oneself not only generously, but also with an analysis of the situation and a strategy of action. To be converted is to know and experience the fact that, contrary to the laws of physics, we can stand straight, according to the gospel, only when our center of gravity is outside ourselves.

Conversion is a permanent process in which very often the obstacles we meet make us lose all we had gained and start anew. The fruitfulness of our conversion depends on our openness to doing this, our spiritual childhood. All conversion implies a break. To wish to accomplish it without conflict is to deceive oneself and others: "No man is worthy of me who cares more for father or mother than for me." But it is not a question of a withdrawn and pious attitude. Our conversion process is affected by the socio-economic, political, cultural, and human environment in which it occurs. Without a change in these structures, there is not authentic conversion. We have to break with our mental categories, with the way we relate to others, with our way of identifying with the Lord, with our cultural milieu, with our social class, in other words, with all that can stand in the way of a real, profound solidarity with those who suffer, in the first place, from misery and injustice. Only thus, and not through purely interior and spiritual attitudes, will the "new man and woman" arise from the ashes of the "old."

Christians have not done enough in this area of conversion to the neighbor, to social justice, to history. They have not perceived clearly enough yet that to know God *is* to do justice. They still do not live *in one sole action* with both God and all persons. They still do not situate themselves in Christ without attempting to avoid concrete human history. They have yet to tread the path which will lead them to seek effectively the peace of the Lord in the heart of the social struggle.

A spirituality of liberation must be filled with a living sense of *gratuitousness*. Communion with the Lord and with all persons is more than anything else a gift. Hence the universality and the radicalness of the liberation which it affords. This gift, far from being a call to passivity, demands a vigilant attitude. This is one of the most constant biblical themes: the encounter with the Lord presupposes attention, active disposition, work, fidelty to God's will, the good use of talents received. But the knowledge that at the root of our personal and community existence lies the gift of the self-communication of God, the grace of God's friendship, fills our life with gratitude. It allows us to see our encounters with others, our loves, everything that happens in our life as a gift. There is a real love only when there is free giving—without conditions or coercion. Only gratuitous love goes to our very roots and elicits true love.

Prayer is an experience of gratuitousness. This "leisure" action, this "wasted" time, reminds us that the Lord is beyond the categories of useful and useless. God is not of this world. The gratuitousness of God's gift, creating profound needs, frees us from all religious alienation and, in the last instance, from all alienation. The Christian committed to the Latin American revolutionary process has to find the way to real prayer, not evasion. It cannot be denied that a crisis exists in this area and that we can easily slide into dead ends. There are many who—nostalgically and in "exile," recalling earlier years of their life—can say with the psalmist: "As I pour out my soul in distress, I call to mind how I marched in the ranks of the great to the house of God, among exultant shouts of praise, the clamor of the pilgrims" (Ps. 42:4). But the point is not to backtrack; new experiences, new demands have made heretofore familiar and comfortable paths impassable and have made us undertake new itineraries on which we hope it might be possible to say with Job to the Lord, "I knew of thee then only by report, but now I see thee with my own eyes" (42:5). Bonhoeffer was right when he said that the only credible God is the God of the mystics. But this is not a God unrelated to human history. On the contrary, if it is true, as we recalled above, that one must go through people to reach God, it is equally certain that the "passing through" to that gratuitous God strips me, leaves me naked, and universalizes my love for others and makes it gratuitous. Both movements need each other dialectically and move toward a synthesis. This synthesis is found in Christ; in the God who became human we encounter God and humankind. In Christ humankind gives God a human countenance and God gives humanity a divine countenance. Only in this perspective will we be able to understand that the "union with the Lord," which all spirituality proclaims, is not a separation from humankind; to attain this union, I must go through others and the union, in turn, enables me to encounter them more fully. Our purpose here is not to "balance" what has been said before, but rather to deepen it and see it in all of its meaning.

The conversion to the neighbor, and in the neighbor to the Lord, the gratuitousness which allows me to encounter others fully, the unique encounter which is the foundation of communion of persons among themselves and of persons with God, these are the source of Christian *joy*. This joy is born of the gift already received yet still awaited and is expressed in the present despite the difficulties and tensions of the struggle for the construction of a just society. Every prophetic proclamation of total liberation is accompanied by an invitation to participate in eschatological joy: "I will take delight in Jerusalem and rejoice in my people" (Isa. 65:19). This joy ought to fill our entire existence, making us attentive both to the gift of integral liberation of humanity and history as well as to the detail of our life and the lives of others. This joy ought not to lessen our commitment to humankind that lives in an unjust world, nor should it lead us to a facile, low-cost conciliation. On the contrary, our joy is paschal, guaranteed by the Spirit (Gal. 5:22; 1 Tim. 1:6; Rom. 14:17); it passes through the conflict with the great ones of this world and through the cross in order to enter into life. This is why we celebrate our joy in the present by recalling the passover of the Lord. To recall Christ is to believe in this Lord. And this celebration is a feast (Rev. 19:7), a feast of the Christian community, those who explicitly confess Christ to be the Lord of history, the liberator of the oppressed. This community has been referred to as the small temple in contradistinction to the large temple of human history. Without community support neither the emergence nor the continued existence of a new spirituality is possible.

The Magnificat expresses well this spirituality of liberation. A song of thanksgiving for the gifts of the Lord, it expresses humbly the joy of being loved by God: "Rejoice, my spirit, in God my Savior; so tenderly has he looked upon his servant, humble as she is. . . . So wonderfully has he dealt with me, the Lord, the Mighty One" (Luke 1:47–49). But at the same time it is one of the New Testament texts which contains great implications both as regards liberation and the political sphere. This thanksgiving and joy are closely linked to the action of God who liberates the oppressed and humbles the powerful. "The hungry he has satisfied with good things, the rich sent empty away" (52–53). The future of history belongs to the poor and exploited. True liberation will be the work of the oppressed themselves; in them, the Lord saves history. The spirituality of liberation will have as its basis the spirituality of the *anawim*.

Living witnesses rather than theological speculation will point out, are already pointing out, the direction of a spirituality of liberation. This is the task which has been undertaken in Latin America by those referred to above as a "first Christian generation."

5

Gustavo Gutiérrez

Liberation and the Poor:
The Puebla Perspective

Gutiérrez believes the Puebla Conference (Third General Conference of Latin American Bishops) in 1979 was a reaffirmation of the Medellín Conference. The following essay shows not only the link between the two conferences but also provides a broad summary of Latin American liberation theology. "Liberation and the Poor: The Puebla Perspective" is taken from The Power of The Poor in History *(Maryknoll, N.Y.: Orbis Books, 1983), pp. 125–65. The article was originally published in 1979.*

The reality of poverty, misery, and exploitation in the life of the vast majority of Latin Americans doubtless constitutes the most radical challenge to the proclamation of the gospel. After all, as Puebla repeatedly stressed, this is a society that is supposed to be Christian. But the gospel reveals to us a God who—as Karl Barth put it, echoing the message of Scripture—takes sides with the poor.[1]

It should be scant cause for astonishment that the matter of poverty came up as a key one in the preparation for Puebla. It was a matter the bishops would very possibly themselves wish to raise, it was thought, in witness to the authenticity of a church that ought to be laying itself open to questioning by the word of God, as well as by the concrete situation of the poor and oppressed in whom it ought to be recognizing the countenance of its Lord. The general theme selected by the bishops for Puebla made the subject of poverty even more pressing: "Evangelization in Latin America's Present and Future."

But there was another factor at work here as well. Over and above any empty words of compliance and conformity that might be pronounced—apart from all the courtesy nods—what about real continuity with Medellín? After all, Medellín had made a clear option of solidarity with the poor and their liberation. Nor was anyone ignorant of the fact that the perspective of the poor had been a central theme in Latin American theological reflection on liberation for at least ten years, and this was another bone of contention.

All this occasioned heated discussions during Puebla's preparatory stage. In the judgment of many, the subject was being slanted away from its raw, massive reality and radical evangelical demand. Basic Christian communities, the *comunidades de base,* were crying out against what they considered to be efforts to skirt the question by giving it a spiritualistic focus, foreign both to the Christian message and to the concrete circumstances of Latin America's poor.[2] These pressures, admittedly, had been brought to bear by a minority, but that minority played an important role in Puebla's preparatory stage.

Then there was the opposite fear: that if the grass-roots protests won out, everything would be so simplified that the rich, complex gospel theme of poverty would be reduced to merely one of its many dimensions. Hence the bishops were rightly asked to take a clear stand on the matter at Puebla. And indeed Puebla did hotly debate the subject, and it is no secret that the document "A Preferential Option for the Poor" encountered heavy weather.[3] Nevertheless, the life of a poor people, and the experiences of the church in Latin America over the preceding years, finally worked their way into this capital question.

Some points were settled; others were left as a task to be undertaken. But the subject of poverty is very much to the fore in the documents of Puebla, and not only in the one especially devoted to it (which without a doubt constitutes one of the better and more homogeneous of the Puebla texts) but in others as well. This must be kept in mind when attempting to analyze the treatment of poverty in that episcopal conference.

The pages that follow make no pretense of an exhaustive analysis of all the Puebla documents. Indeed, a chapter-length piece could scarcely hope to accomplish a like task. Let me make this clear at the outset, lest there be any misunderstanding. We shall limit our considerations here to the question of poverty itself, along with some points concerning liberation where it touches the question of the poor as such. These have been matters of harsh debate over the past years and are critical for the church's practice and reflection in Latin America. And of course they provide a point of departure for the examination of other themes, taken up in Puebla.[4]

IN THE FOOTSTEPS OF MEDELLÍN

Puebla explicitly asserts its continuity with Medellín, and it does so with a straightforwardness that we do not find in the preparatory texts. Nor is this continuity limited to express declarations; in fact it is found mainly in Puebla's manner of approach to certain central themes.

A Clear and Prophetic Option

In its exordium as in its conclusion, the document on the "preferential option" clearly states Puebla's intention of following in the footsteps of Medellín. Such a frame for the presentation of the text is significant in itself. Chapter 1 opens:

> With renewed hope in the vivifying power of the Spirit, we are going to take up once again the position of the Second General Conference of the Latin American episcopate in Medellín, which adopted a clear and prophetic option expressing preference for, and solidarity with, the poor. We do this despite the distortions and interpretations of some, who vitiate the spirit of Medellín, and despite the disregard and even hostility of others [§ 1134].[5]

The intention, then, is to resume the position Medellín takes regarding the poor. This option is unhesitatingly qualified as *prophetic*. And this is indeed the impression left on the Latin American people by Medellín, in spite of all efforts since then to consider the whole thing to have been just a matter of euphoria and romanticism, and in spite of all the complicated distinctions brought to bear on this prophetic stance in an effort to divest it of its original meaning—which was the proclamation of the word of God from a point of departure in the reality of the poor person, a judgment rendered upon the offense committed against the Lord in the outrage and spoliation of the oppressed.[6]

Furthemore, Puebla here takes up a key term used by Medellín to concretize its option for the poor: *solidarity.* The document before us repeats the word several times—once quoting Pope John Paul II—thereby specifying what is meant by this "option," and precluding its investiture with the ambiguities and tenor of paternalistic condescension toward the poor, which some would have liked to attribute to it. In this wise the accent falls rather on a real involvement with the sufferings and the joys, the struggles against injustice and the longing for liberation, of the poor, as will be stated in texts we shall cite below.

In the same context, Puebla adopts, with certain precisions of its own, the "three meanings of poverty" as presented in Medellín, thereby stating its position with respect to it:

> The gospel demand for poverty, understood as solidarity with the poor and as a rejection of the situation in which most people on this continent live, frees the poor person from being individualistic in life, and from being attracted and seduced by the false ideals of a consumer society [§ 1156].

The option for the poor, as Puebla says more than once, is preferential and not exclusive. The pope had already emphasized this in various discourses he had pronounced on his visit to Mexico.[7] Let us be clear about this. Some have wished to see a criticism here of the practice and reflection that have been under way in Latin America over these last years. They are mistaken. There is nothing to be gained by beating about the bush here. There are distorted interpretations abroad, insistently repeated, and we may as well come right out and tell the truth of the matter.

This alleged exclusivity would be an evident mutilation of the gospel message. That message is directed to every human being, as someone loved by God and redeemed by God's Son. The gospel is not anyone's private property, to do with as one might wish. *Preference* for the poor is written into the gospel message itself. But this alleged exclusivity, if it gained the upper hand, would— paradoxically—deprive that very preference of its historical "bite."

Precisely what so many find insupportable in the preferential option for the poor is its claim to announce the gospel within the dialectic of a universality that moves from and through the particular, from and through a preference. But it is precisely this preference that makes the gospel so hard and demanding for the privileged members of an unjust social order. An "exclusivity" would rather leave them on the sidelines, where this proclamation denouncing whatever despoils and oppresses the poor would go right on by them.

No, the gospel is addressed to every human being; only it has a predilection for the poor, and therefore makes its proclamation from a position of solidarity with the oppressed. This is what gives it such a precise tone in Latin America, where the majority are exploited and oppressed. No one is excluded from the proclamation of the good news, or from the concerns of the church, especially if it is to continue in solidarity with the life, sufferings, and aspirations of the ones the pope called "God's favorites."

For it is in just such terms that Medellín had couched its own preference for the poor. For example in the Medellín Document on Poverty, under "Solidarity and Preference for Poor," the episcopal conference says:

> The Lord's mandate is to preach the gospel to the poor. We must therefore distribute our apostolic personnel and efforts so as to give a preference to the poorest and neediest, and to those who are segregated for any reason. We must encourage and step up the studies and initiatives that are directed to this end [§ 9].[8]

Then this document adds:

> We wish to heighten our awareness of the obligation to have solidarity with the poor, an obligation that is prompted by charity. This means that we shall make their problems and struggles our own, that we shall find ways of talking to them.

This must be fleshed out by our denunciation of injustice and oppression, by a Christian struggle against the intolerable situation of many poor people, and by a process of dialogue with the groups responsible for this situation that will help them to appreciate their obligations [§ 10].

Puebla speaks in the same sense. Hence after reaffirming the meaning of gospel poverty as solidarity with the poor and protest against poverty (as in the text cited above), Puebla continues:

In like manner the witness of a poor Church can evangelize the rich whose hearts are attached to wealth, thus converting and freeing them from this bondage and their own egotism [§ 1156].

This is what the theology of liberation had attempted to do, both before Medellín and after. For the reasons noted, no exclusivity is ever affirmed. Instead, Puebla emphasizes a preference, stressing the special place the poor have in the message of the Bible and in the life and teaching of Jesus and the position they ought therefore to occupy among those who consider themselves his disciples.

From this point of departure it is possible to proclaim the gospel to *every* human being. Solidarity with the poor, with their struggles and their hopes, is the condition of an authentic solidarity with everyone—the condition of a universal love that makes no attempt to gloss over the social oppositions that obtain in the concrete history of peoples, but strides straight through the middle of them to a kingdom of justice and love.

Thus the assertions of John Paul II to the effect that it is a matter of preference, not exclusivity, far from being a criticism—as was claimed by international news agencies that seemed to have taken it upon themselves to dispel illusions about Puebla, and as was even thought with a great deal of good will by persons simply unfamiliar with the matter—actually corroborate precisely what is clearest and sanest in recent Latin American theological experience and reflection.

Of course another reason to rejoice in these assertions of the pope's is that they had the effect of promoting the option for the poor into one of the key themes of the Puebla conference. It was to enjoy an importance in the texts that perhaps it would not have had had it not been for the pope's insistence. And indeed the theme is missing from the preparatory documents.

There is one more matter deserving of our attention here with regard to Puebla's avowed effort to follow the lead of Medellín. The Puebla text recognizes and admits that, in spite of Medellín's clear option, that conference had afterward not been spared a number of "deviations and interpretations" that had been enjoying great currency in the years between Medellín and Puebla. But it also emphasizes the disregard and even hostility that Medellín's prophetic voice had encountered, as other texts will lament, in the dominant sectors of Latin American society. These circles had countered the teachings of Medellín with a studied neglect, on the pretext that its denunciations of social injustice suffered by the popular classes amounted to an abandonment of the true "spiritual" mission of the church.

We shall return to this point later on. For the moment let us simply observe that there could scarcely have been anything naive about Puebla's announcement that it was resuming the position of Medellín.

A Specifically Christian Concept of Poverty?

Puebla's continuity with Medellín is even more striking if we take into account the distance between Puebla and its own Preparatory Document on the subject of the poor. It would be superfluous to detail here the elements of this discrepancy.[9] Suffice it simply to note that the Preparatory Document does not even refer to Medellín, either explicitly or implicitly, and bypasses the subject of the preferential option for the poor in favor of an examination of what it calls the "deeper meaning" of poverty—a poverty it terms "specifically Christian." Such an approach, regardless of its framers' intentions, resulted in a de facto refinement and spiritualization of the notion of poverty to the point where it no longer had any direct reference to actual poverty.

This is another point to which we shall have to return. For the moment, however, let us merely observe that Puebla made a clean break with the approach taken in the preparatory texts and, as we have just seen, resumed the Medellín approach. The retrenchment attempt had been nipped in the bud.

A note that the Working Draft devoted to the topic ("The Poor and Poverty"), although timid and not altogether bereft of ambiguities, is a noticeable improvement over the Preparatory Document. The change had been provoked by the contributions of the national episcopates, many of which bore the mark of the experience and reflection of their basic Christian communities. Among these contributions the Peruvian document is outstanding on this point, as the note just referred to clearly shows. Peru's contribution had in turn been worked out on the basis of the contributions of regional bishops' assemblies, at which different sectors of the Peruvian church had had the opportunity to express themselves. Thus in the note we have a return to the three meanings of the notion of poverty that appear in Medellín, together with a sketch of certain points that Puebla would adopt and clarify, and of which we shall be speaking below.

Here we merely wish to point out that the note seeks to adjoin what it calls a "fourth type" of poverty, which Puebla did not adopt as such. (Medellín, by the way, does not speak of types of poverty but of different meanings of the *notion* of poverty.) The Working Draft reads, "He [also] is poor who remains open to the community." The reason for the exclusion, for that matter, is advanced in the Working Draft itself: the "fourth type" would be only one aspect of the second meaning delineated by Medellín. Hence the appendage would only have created confusion.

The "preferential option document" closed, as we have indicated, by ratifying its continuity with Medellín:

With its preferential but not exclusive love for the poor, the Church present in Medellín was a summons to hope for more Christian and humane goals, as the Holy Father pointed out. . . . This Third Episcopal Conference in Puebla wishes to keep this summons alive and to open up new horizons of hope[§1165].

A clear conclusion can be drawn from this reaffirmation of fidelity to Medellín. It is a conclusion that is valid not just for the "preferential option" document, but for all Puebla texts together. This episcopal conference had no intention of substituting itself for Medellín. Medellín retains all its validity. Its clear, prophetic option for the poor and for solidarity with them, in intimate nexus with Puebla, will continue to be demanded by "fidelity to the poor Christ"—to use the document's own expression.

THE POOR

The most significant fact in the political and church life of Latin America in recent years is the active presence that the poor are coming to assume in it. As can be imagined, this does not fail to provoke fear and hostility. Thus some actually went so far as to accuse Medellín (or interpretations of its texts characterized by them as capricious and irresponsible) of having itself created the problems and questions, and hence the aspirations and hopes.

What an incredible denial—from our point of view—of such a massive reality! Of course it stemmed from private interests. And so a polemic arose, eventually entrapping even the well-intentioned. The point at issue was the true meaning of real poverty—"material" poverty, it came to be called—for Christian faith. It was feared that all the insistence on material poverty was going to cause the spiritual and genuinely evangelical sense of poverty to drop out of view.

On a terrain so long crisscrossed by blind alleys and wrong ways, where Medellín had sought to map out some clear paths, it was no great matter to kick up a few dust clouds that would send persons scurrying back to the old accustomed routes, especially persons having little understanding of biblical questions, or fearful of the radical conversion demanded by raw reality. On the other side, the need for immediate action led some persons to use expressions that oversimplified a complex situation. And so Puebla had some precisions to contribute on the matter.

The Reality of the Poor

In Puebla, a commission, the first, was given the assignment of presenting a survey of the real situation in Latin America from a pastoral point of view. This did not prevent many other documents from framing their subjects in reference to the concrete situation in which they were to be found. But poverty, as a total question and the greatest challenge to the task of evangelization, naturally found its place in the text presented by this first commission. Examination of the reality of poverty thus occurs in the introductory text of the Puebla document, as part of the first commission's overview of Latin American reality as a whole. This can only underscore the importance of this analysis.

Right from the start, Puebla proclaims its continuity with Medellín:

So we place ourselves within the dynamic thrust of the Medellín Conference . . ., adopting its vision of reality that served as the inspiration for so many pastoral documents of ours in the past decade [§25].

When one thinks of the attacks leveled at Medellín for its analysis of the social reality of Latin America, the full validity of this language can be appreciated. But the case was not closed with this verbal declaration of loyalty and continuity. Puebla now proceeded with content, in the form of a description of the situation, an examination of its causes, and the judgment in faith that all of this merits.

Institutionalized Injustice

Repeatedly, the Puebla bishops declare that we in Latin America live in a situation they call "institutionalized injustice." The expression is forcefully reminiscent of one of the boldest and most embattled assertions of Medellín— that our situation in Latin America is one of "institutionalized violence." (Puebla uses the latter expression as well—for example, in the document entitled "Church Activity on Behalf of the Person in National and International Society" [§1259].)[10] But there is a difference. Medellín mentions "institutionalized injustice" only once, and of course two long documents dealing with the same kinds of topics will inevitably employ similar terminology. (Medellín's use of these words is especially powerful, of course, because its immediate context is concretely topical.) But Puebla uses it on various occasions[11]—either in so many words, or in synonymous phraseology such as "in the position of permanently violating the dignity of the person"(§41).

The Puebla documents seek to define precisely what is meant. Thus the situation of poverty is identified as the result of a prevailing social order, of a structure, indeed of a "structural conflict." The document cites "two clear tendencies" in Latin America: "a thrust toward modernization, entailing strong economic growth," and "on the other hand the tendency . . . toward the pauperization and growing exclusion of the vast majority of Latin Americans from production" (§1207). Then it goes on:

These contradictory tendencies favor the appropriation by a privileged minority of a large part of the wealth as well as the benefits created by science and culture. On the other hand they are responsible for the poverty of a large majority of our people, who are aware of being left out and of having their growing aspirations for justice and participation blocked [§1208].

The passage concludes:

So there arises a grave structural conflict: "The growing affluence of a few people parallels the growing poverty of the masses" (Pope John Paul II, Opening Address, III, 4) [§1209].[12]

That is the only sort of statement a serious examination of the social situation in Latin America can lead to. Indeed, as the pope says:

Analyzing this situation more deeply, we discover that this poverty is not a passing phase. Instead it is the product of economic, social, and political situations and structures, though there are also other causes for the state of misery. In many instances this state of poverty within our countries finds its origin and support in mechanisms which, because they are impregnated with materialism rather than any authentic humanism, create a situation on the international level where the rich get richer at the expense of the poor, who get even poorer [Opening Addresss, III, 3].

For that matter, the pope had insisted on these structural factors in the mechanisms that generate poverty when he told the Amerindians of Oaxaca and Chiapas that they have "a right to have the barricades of exploitation removed." In turn, the "preferential option document" denounces "the grave injustices stemming from mechanisms of oppression" (§1136) and demands "the required change in unjust social, political, and economic structures" (§1155; cf. §1264). This is all groundwork for a denunciation of the capitalistic system prevailing in Latin America and of the presence of multinational corporations (e.g., §§47, 312, 342, 1277).

Puebla offers us a vivid description of the poverty of the great majority of Latin Americans, in a sketch accompanied by a demanding pastoral and theological focus. (Let us not forget that Puebla proposed to offer "a pastoral view of the real Latin American situation." It achieved its aim admirably.) This situation of poverty is said to "take on very concrete faces in real life. In these faces we ought to recognize the suffering features of Christ the Lord, who questions and challenges us" (§31). Then come the faces, group by group. In spite of the length of the description, we think it will be helpful to reproduce it in its entirety:

[They include]
—the faces of young children, struck down by poverty before they are born, their chance for self-development blocked by irreparable mental and physical deficiencies; and of the vagrant children in our cities who

are so often exploited, products of poverty and the moral disorganization of the family;

—the faces of young people, who are disoriented because they cannot find their place in society, and who are frustrated, particularly in marginal rural and urban areas, by the lack of opportunity to obtain training and work;

—the faces of the indigenous peoples, and frequently of the Afro-Americans as well; living marginalized lives in inhuman situations, they can be considered the poorest of the poor;

—the faces of the peasants; as a social group, they live in exile almost everywhere on our continent, deprived of land, caught in a situation of internal and external dependence, and subjected to systems of commercialization that exploit them;

—the faces of laborers, who frequently are ill-paid and who have difficulty in organizing themselves and defending their rights;

—the faces of the underemployed and the unemployed, who are dismissed because of the harsh exigencies of economic crises, and often because of development-models that subject workers and their families to cold economic calculations;

—the faces of marginalized and overcrowded urban dwellers, whose lack of material goods is matched by the ostentatious display of wealth by other segments of society;

—the faces of old people, who are growing more numerous every day, and who are frequently marginalized in a progress-oriented society that totally disregards people not engaged in production.

We share other anxieties of our people that stem from a lack of respect for their dignity as human beings, made in the image and likeness of God, and for their inalienable rights as children of God [§§31–40].

In speaking of institutionalized injustice, Puebla does not restrict itself to calling attention to the situation of *oppression* in which we live in Latin America. It also refers to the *repression* present here. And it is well aware of the connection between the two. Immediately following the long text just cited, Puebla denounces the "permanent violation of the dignity of the person," and then goes on:

To this there are added other anxieties that stem from abuses of power, which are typical of regimes based on force. There are the anxieties based on systematic or selective repression; it is accompanied by accusations, violations of privacy, improper pressures, tortures, and exiles. There are the anxieties produced in many families by the disappearance of their loved ones, about whom they cannot get any news. There is the total insecurity bound up with arrest and detention without judicial consent. There are the anxieties felt in the face of a system of justice that has been suborned or cowed. As the Supreme Pontiffs point out, the Church, by virtue of "an authentically evangelical commitment" (John Paul II, Opening Address at Puebla, III, 3), must raise its voice to denounce and condemn these situations, particularly when the responsible officials or rulers call themselves Christians [§42].

A "pastoral view" should make a deeper analysis of this situation, and that is what the document now proceeds to do, examining this poverty and this misery from the viewpoint of the faith.

A Situation of Sin

Many were those who, in the years following Medellín, rent their garments over another of that conferences' bold expressions: that we in Latin America are in a "situation of sin."[13] Even at Puebla there were those who, though in full retreat before the use of the expression "structure of sin" by the Holy Father himself in his addresses, performed the same hypocritical ritual, decrying the "problems of conscience" aroused by such terms for the "children of good families" or for sisters who belonged to wealthy religious congregations.

But the only thing the protesters managed to achieve by their protests was that they themselves were left standing before the eyes of all in stark theological nakedness. For the expression "situation of sin," besides having such extensive biblical roots, unmasked a lacerating Latin American reality. But it is true that this expression is incompatible with a bourgeois, individualistic conception of friendship with God and with one another, and consequently of the breach of this friendship, which is what we call sin.

Echoing Medellín and the discourses of John Paul II, Puebla now pronounced its theological judgment, calling the institutionalized injustice in which we live in Latin America "social sinfulness"—and noting that the sin is all the more grave for the fact that this pernicious social order exists in countries calling themselves Catholic:

> Viewing it in the light of faith, we see the growing gap between rich and poor as a scandal and a contradiction to Christian existence (cf. John Paul II, Opening Address, III, 2). The luxury of a few becomes an insult to the wretched poverty of the vast masses (cf. Paul VI, *Populorum Progressio,* 3). This is contrary to the plan of the Creator and to the honor that is due him. In this anxiety and sorrow the Church sees a situation of social sinfulness, all the more serious because it exists in countries that call themselves Catholic and are capable of changing the situation: "[The exploited] have a right to have the barriers of exploitation removed, . . . against which their best efforts at advancement are dashed" (John Paul II, Address to the Indians of Oaxaca and Chiapas) [§28].

The statement is a clear one. It places the responsibility for the misery at the door of a society that claims to be Christian. Nor are we dealing with an isolated text. The same phraseology is repeated in various places, with different nuances, as social dimensions of sin are cited and described as "very broad"(§73), or in a context of sin at once individual and social.[14]

The same idea, the same judgment, rings out in other expressions as well. In the "preferential option document," for example, the bishops declare: "Committed to the poor, we condemn as anti-evangelical the extreme poverty that affects an extremely large segment of the population on our continent" (§1159).[15] In "Church Activity on Behalf of the Person in National and International Society" the bishops resume a point on which Puebla is most sensitive—the scandal of social injustice in a society claiming to be Christian:

> The people of Latin America continue to live in a social situation that contradicts the fact that they inhabit a continent which is Christian for the most part. The contradictions existing between unjust social structures and the demands of the Gospel are quite evident [§1257].

The poverty—the "inhuman poverty" (§29)—in which Latin America is living represents an "anti-evangelical situation," a situation contrary to the gospel, and cries out against the guilty. The breach of friendship with God, and among persons—that is to say, sin—is the true root of the institutionalized injustice. Puebla says this with all the frankness one could wish for. There are the guilty, and there are victims. This must be denounced. The denunciation refuses to whitewash the facts, and turns into a challenge:

> Faced with the situation of sin, the Church has a duty to engage in denunciation. Such denunciation must be objective, courageous, and evangelical. Rather than condemning, it attempts to save both the guilty party and the victim. Such denunciation, made after prior agreement has been reached between pastors, appeals to the internal solidarity of the Church and the exercise of collegiality [§1269].[16]

As in Medellín, a structural analysis of a social order that oppresses and despoils the poor is accompanied by a judgment and a denunciation from the standpoint of faith that leave no loopholes. Both the analysis and the judgment have been objects of practice and theological reflection during recent years on the part of Christians committed to the process of liberation of the exploited masses of Latin America.

"Avenger of the Lowly"

Reinforcing the thinking of Medellín and the theology of liberation, Puebla understands the gospel demand for poverty in terms of solidarity with Latin America's poor, and protest against the situation of spoilation and oppression that prevents them from living as human beings. This solidarity and rejection are set forth as the indispensable condition for authentically living and proclaiming that central aspect of the gospel constituted by spiritual childlikeness—understood as availability in the sight of the Lord.

After all, to become as little children is a condition for entry into the kingdom of God, and, as Puebla reminds us, "the poorest sometimes seem to intuit this Kingdom in a privileged and forceful way" (§132). For "many of the poor incarnate in their lives the evangelical values of solidarity, service, simplicity, and openness to accepting the gift of God" (§1147). For some persons, as we have already noted, emphasis on the concrete situation of the poor and oppressed meant a neglect of the spiritual perspective they considered essential to the genuine notion of evangelical poverty. They were mistaken. Let us examine Puebla on this point.

The Reason for a Preference

To which "poor" do the documents refer when they speak of their "preferential option"? Clearly, the poor as they actually exist in Latin America and as rendered poor by the prevailing "mechanisms of oppression." Of this there cannot be the slightest doubt. In order to set the correct tone and preclude the possibility of any misunderstanding, the document on the "preferential option" tells us right at the start which poor are meant: "the vast majority of our fellow humans continue to live in a situation of poverty and even wretchedness that has grown more acute" (§1135).

A footnote, which in the document actually approved in Puebla had formed part of the main text, explains what is meant:

[The] vast majority of our people lack the most elementary material goods. This is in contrast to the accumulation of wealth in the hands of a small minority, frequently the price being poverty for the majority. The poor do not lack simply material goods. They also miss, on the level of human dignity, full participation in sociopolitical life. Those found in this category are principally our indigenous peoples, peasants, manual laborers, marginalized urban dwellers, and, in particular, the women of these social groups. The women are doubly oppressed and marginalized [§1135, footnote].

The list is unequivocal. May we be allowed to call the reader's attention to the appearance in the list of the native peoples, the Indians—elsewhere described as "the poorest of the poor" (§34)—and the special concern of the conference for the women of each of these social sectors—"doubly oppressed and marginalized," because they are not only poor, but poor women.[17]

A little further on, after indicating that the gospel commitment of the church should be like that of Christ, who took on full solidarity with humanity, and therefore should be a commitment to those most in need (§1141), the explanation appears: "When we draw near to the poor in order to accompany them and serve them, we are doing what Christ taught us to do when he became our brother, poor like us" (§1145).

Between these last two texts comes the forthright statement that "the poor merit preferential attention, whatever may be the moral or personal situation in which they find themselves" (§1142).[18] The preference for the poor is based on the fact that God, as Christ shows us, loves them for their concrete, real condition of poverty, "whatever may be" their moral or spiritual disposition. The text reveals its source admirably, and the latter helps us understand it better. The note "The Poor and Poverty" in the Working Document had said:

> It is our brothers' and sisters' indigence as such, without regard for their moral or personal situation, which creates the right they have to our attention . . . for, independently of their faith or goodness, Jesus Christ took all weaknesses upon himself in order to heal them [§187].

The source of the Working Document, in turn (and explicitly recognized as such), is the material contributed by the Peruvian episcopate, which expresses the same idea with all desirable clarity and with a solid basis in theology:

> The privilege of the poor, then, has its theological basis in God. The poor are "blessed" not because of the mere fact that they are poor, but because the kingdom of God is expressed in the manifestation of his justice and love in their favor.[19]

The conclusion is unmistakable. The preferential option is for the poor as such, the poor as poor. The value of their attitude of openness toward God is not neglected, and we shall return to this point below. But this does not constitute the primary motive of the privilege of the poor, as is clear from our Puebla document when it says:

> This central feature of evangelization was stressed by Pope John Paul II: "I have earnestly desired this meeting because I feel solidarity with you, and because you, being poor, have a right to my special concern and attention. I will tell you the reason: the pope loves you because you are God's favorites. In founding his family, the Church, God had in mind poor and needy humanity. To redeem it, he sent his Son specifically, who was born poor and lived among the poor to make us rich with his poverty (2 Cor. 8:9)" (Address in the Barrio of Santa Cecilia, Jan. 30, 1979) [§1143].

The barrio of Santa Cecilia is a poor neighborhood of the city of Guadalajara. The pope maintains that, in their quality as poor and marginalized persons, and independently of their spiritual dispositions, those who live in this neighborhood are "God's favorites." The quotation from the pope in the next paragraph, again from a homily delivered during his Latin American visit, reinforces this perspective. It is an important statement, and Puebla introduces it with another assertion charged with meaning:

> In her Magnificat (Luke 1:46–55), Mary proclaims that God's salvation has to do with justice for the poor. From her, too, "stems authentic commitment to other human beings, our brothers and sisters, especially to the poorest and neediest, and to the necessary transformation of society" (Homily in Zapopán,4) [§1144].

This interpretation of the Magnificat has been a favorite element in the life and reflection of Christians committed to the process of liberation in Latin America.[20] It receives further papal encouragement later on in the Zapopán address:

> As my predecessor, Paul VI, states in his Apostolic Exhortation *Marialis Cultus* (37), Mary is also the model, as faithful handmaid of the will of God, of those who refuse passively to accept the adverse circumstances of their personal and social life, who refuse to be victims of "alienation, " as you say today, but who proclaim with her that God is the "avenger of the lowly," and that if need be he "pulls down the mighty from their thrones"—to use the words of her Magnificat once more.

Then, too, there are innumerable occasions when the Puebla documents cite—and denounce—the situation of the poor, who lack "the most elementary material goods." The conference leaves no room for doubt as to the character of this poverty—so frequently modifying "poor" with expressions such as "oppressed," "most needy," "suffering," "forgotten," and so on.[21]

I have already cited passages where this concrete situation of the poor is referred to. Here let me simply call attention to the fact that Puebla considers it to be just this aspect of their poverty that occasions the "preferential option" constituting one of the central aspects of its message. The language is clear as day:

> This option, demanded by the scandalous reality of economic imbalances in Latin America, should lead us to establish a dignified, fraternal way of life together as human beings and to construct a just and free society [§1154].

The option is demanded by the scandalous reality of poverty. There is no way to think that the scandal may have been provoked by "poverty of spirit."

The Anti-Evangelical Nature of Poverty in Latin America

There is something that has to be added to what we have said so far about the reason for Puebla's preference for the poor. We have emphasized the concrete, material nature of the poverty motivating Puebla to make a preferential option for the subject of that poverty. And we have based our stance on text and context, as Puebla luminously propounds its view. If one does not grasp this, then "Blessed are the poor" loses its meaning.

But Puebla puts us on the track of further implications when it characterizes poverty here and now in Latin America as "anti-evangelical." There is no abstraction going on here; there is no playing with the gospel and with human beings, after the fashion of those who make poverty a sweet and tender ideal (which they are at great pains to avoid striving for).

Puebla, like Medellín, not only does not use this ambiguous language about an "ideal," but explicitly rejects it, and continues to stress material poverty. The poverty in which the poor and oppressed of Latin America are living is contrary to the Christian message, and a denial of the God who is revealed in the Bible. As a Bolivian *campesino,* Paz Jiménez, put it in a press conference on February 2, 1979, with an insight that is profoundly biblical: "an atheist is someone who fails to practice justice toward the poor."

It is knocking on the wrong door to wish to salvage the spiritual nature of the Christian message by trying to rid it of the clear and direct meaning of material poverty in the Bible as a determinate, concrete, human, social condition. On the contrary, a heightened consciousness of it is what most lucidly reveals the meaning of the proclamation of the kingdom of God.

The Beatitudes are a proclamation of Jesus' central message: "the kingdom of God is at hand." Hence they have in the first instance a *theological* character: they tell us who God is. Secondly, they are *anthropological.* That is, they emphasize the importance of spiritual dispositions in those who hear the word. These two aspects are not opposed; they are complementary. But the theological aspect—the emphasis on God and God's goodness toward the poor—is the primary.

What does this mean? All exegetes agree that the message of the Beatitudes is a genuinely religious message. But those who have studied them in greater depth contradict those who think the way to maintain the religious nature of the Beatitudes is to assert that they refer exclusively, or at least primarily, to somebody "spiritually poor," lest they canonize any determinate social group.[22] This is not only faulty biblical interpretation, it is ignorance of the texts themselves.

To assert that the proper, original message of the Beatitudes refers first of all to the "material poor" is not a "humanization" or politicization of their meaning. It is a recognition that God is God and that God loves the poor with all freedom and gratuity—and that God does so not because the poor are good, or better than others, but just because they are poor. That is, they are afflicted, they are hungry, and this situation is a slap in the face of God's sovereignty, God being the Go'el ("Savior, Redeemer"), the Defender of the poor, the "Avenger of the lowly."

The Beatitudes are, before all else, a revelation about God. Their theological perspective is primary. Only if we recognize and accept this fact will we be able to understand the Beatitudes as a declaration of the dispositions that human beings must have in order to hear the word—which is their secondary, anthropological, perspective.

Once the primary notion is appreciated, we can address the secondary. To be sure, the "blessedness" of the poor is constituted by the fact that the God of the Bible is a God of justice, and hence a God of the poor. There is a consequence to be drawn here—in complementarity, not in contradiction, with its theological antecedent. Spiritual poverty—that is, spiritual childlikeness—is the condition for being able to hear the revelation of the kingdom. At the same time it remains clear that if we forget that the Beatitudes are talking about the materially poor, and therefore are talking about God, we will not understand what they tell us about the spiritually poor, the "poor in spirit."

It must likewise be understood that the religious character, the authentically spiritual nature of the message, is not limited to discourse about spiritual poverty. The religious nature of the Beatitudes is apparent mainly in their first meaning: blessed are those who are caught in a position of social inferiority, for God is God. As the document from the Peruvian episcopate put it, "the privilege of the poor . . . has its theological basis in God."

Viewed in this light, our insistence that it is the materially poor who are blessed is not reductionist in the least. The kingdom is at hand, and the kingdom is contrary to all injustice. What we are dealing with is a *paradox:* If we "spiritualize" the poor too early, before the proper moment in the dialectic, we "humanize" God. We make God more accessible to human understanding by attempting to fit God into bourgeois categories and a middle-class mentality. But the theology of the Beatitudes must always come before their anthropology. God, one could think, would surely have a preferential love for the good. After all, the good have more merits. But if instead we maintain that God prefers the poor just because they are poor (again, materially poor)—then we may be flying in the face of logic, but we are standing point-blank before the mystery of God's revelation and the gratuitous gift of God's kingdom of love and justice.

We are in the presence of something that defies our human categories. We are before the mystery of a God who is irreducible to our mode of thinking. But does this not deprive spiritual poverty (spiritual childlikeness) of its meaning and thereby contradict the gospel and the Christian tradition? On the contrary, it affords us a better understanding of it. Spiritual "childhood," or childlikeness, as Medellín said repeatedly, is one of the central elements of the gospel message. Hence Puebla says:

> For the Christian, the term "poverty" does not designate simply a privation and marginalization from which we ought to free ourselves. It also designates a model of living that was already in evidence in the Old Testament, in the type known as "the poor of Yahweh" (Zeph. 2:3, 3:12–20; Isa. 49:13, 66:2; Ps. 74:19, 149:4) [§1148].

Here we have the first two senses of the term "poverty," as distinguished in Medellín, and the necessary premise for understanding the gospel demand of poverty as "solidarity with the poor and as a rejection of the situation in which most people on this continent live" (§1156). Spiritual poverty permits one to live this solidarity, and all its consequences, in the insecurity of quest, and confidence in the Lord.

The Poor Christ

Medellín sought to base its vigorous summons to the witness of poverty and the reflection that accompanies it on the example of Christ.[23] Puebla also appeals to the Christological foundation.

Here the nub is in Christ's identification with the poor as we find it in Matthew 25:31–46, that key text for Puebla and for the pope's addresses in Mexico. It is also a central passage, as we know, for the basic Christian communities, as well as for theological reflection on the commitment to liberation in Latin America. In a passage cited above, Puebla speaks of the "suffering features of Christ," and then goes on to enumerate the concrete form these features take in the faces of the poor of Latin America (§§31–40).[24] As a consequence of this identification, Puebla tells us:

[This] Christian message . . . will also be lived by those who renounce a life of ready pleasure and dedicate themselves to serving others in a realistic way in today's world. For that is the criterion and gauge that Christ is going to use in passing judgment on human beings, even on those who had not known him (Matt. 25)[§339].

Puebla repeats the idea that service to the poor, and involvement with them and commitment to their cause, are the "privileged . . . gauge of our following of Christ" (§1145). And this service demands "constant conversion and purification among all Christians. That must be done if we are to achieve fuller identification each day with the poor Christ and our own poor" (§1140).

"The poor Christ" is an expression that has been acquiring more and more meaning and power among the poor of Latin America.[25] In it they see expressed their faith in the Son of God become a human being, become poor—"poor like us," as the "preferential option document" phrases it. In this expression, which is so closely linked with that of "Christ the Liberator" (of whom Puebla speaks in its "Message"), Jesus is seen as the word made flesh, the one who "pitched his tent in our midst," as John's Gospel puts it (1:14).

Yes, in the midst of his people—a people poor and exploited, but believing and hoping in him.

One must be very far removed from the life of the people to fail to be able to perceive—here in this profession of faith in Christ's nearness as manifested in the expression "the poor Christ"—a profession of the presence of God in the concrete history of humanity, a profession that Jesus is the Son of God. I do not mean an external profession, with the lips, but one that springs from the everyday sufferings, struggles, and hopes of the poor; not an "orthodoxy" that exhausts itself within itself, but the affirmation of a vital, extremely intimate, and yet conscious and reflective truth. The masses receive but very little from those obsessed with the formal theses of the Christian faith. For Christ's poor in Latin America, these professions are part of daily life, prayerful practice, and of authentic theological reflection.

The term "following of Christ," in the text above, is a classic expression from the annals of ascetical literature, and one become current again today in Latin American theology.[26] It means walking the road Christ himself walked. That road, of course, is the one of "commitment to those most in need," according to the program mapped out in Luke 4:18–21 (§1141; cf. §190). Here Puebla strikes root in the fertile Christological soil of solidarity with the poor. Another text says, concerning members of religious orders:

> Radically denying themselves, they accept the Lord's cross as their own (Matt. 16:24) and shoulder it. They accompany those who are suffering from injustice. . . . Sharing in the death of those who suffer, they joyously rise with them to newness of life. Becoming all things to all human beings, they regard the poor as privileged beings, as the Lord's favorites [§743].[27]

Here I should like to make an observation. Puebla published a document devoted to Christology. It was well-intentioned. But its general, basic statements are calculated to assure a broad and pacific consensus. It avoids major questions and fails to afford any stimulus for practice and reflection. Still it would be mistaken to see Puebla's doctrine on Christ as limited to this one document. There are rich Christological observations scattered throughout the Puebla texts, and sometimes they touch on concrete problems, even disputed ones, facing the people of Latin America. Puebla sought fertile inspiration in the deeds and words of the Lord—and therefore it manifested a creativity abundantly deserving of our attention.

LIBERATION AND EVANGELIZATION

From a number of points of view, evangelization and liberation are closely connected in the life of the Latin American church. But this link runs the risk of taking off for the blue sky of the abstract unless it maintains its orientation toward the concrete poor. This is a point that had been made with precision and force in Latin American practice and reflection for a number of years. Then it was taken over by Medellín, and now we find it in Puebla.

Poverty and Integral Liberation

A Polemical Question

Liberation has been a key term in the experience of the Latin American people for some years now. At the economic and political level, it expresses a breach with compromise and reformism.[28] But the term "liberation" also means, at the theological level, an effort to cut to the very roots of the social injustice rampant in our part of the world—to go all the way to an understanding of the notion of salvation in present historical conditions, as a free gift of the Lord who becomes flesh in the life of a people fighting for its human dignity, and its status as offspring of God.

The synthetic, complete—and demanding—perspective expressed in this term immediately gave rise to a lively polemics. At first it was said we were running the risk of reducing Christ's liberation to its historical and social implications. Then it was said, without batting an eyelash and without taking the trouble to read what was actually written, that these historical and social consequences were the only thing in which the Christians involved in the liberation process were interested. Finally, with all the foregoing as a self-evident premise, the term "integral liberation" came into currency, as a "response" to this alleged reductionism. What was curious in all this was that "integral liberation," as understood by the proponents of the new term, was no more integral, for all its vaunting, than the reductionism they were themselves alleging. For they were *reducing* liberation to the so-called religious or spiritual—spiritualistic—plane.

As had happened with the preferential/nonexclusive option for the poor, now too the only aim was to win the argument by dint of sheer insistence, with little concern for the truth. One had the impression these guardians of the spiritual might even be seeking to convince themselves. At best, they began with ambiguous and sporadic assertions, and then generalized from them without attention to the complexity of the subject. Here again, then, putting aside any false sense of shame, we must energetically confront and belie these declarations. For they twist and distort the truth.

One of the oldest themes in the theology of liberation is the totality and complexity of the liberation process. This theology conceives total liberation as a single process, within which it is necessary to distinguish different dimensions or levels: economic liberation, social liberation, political liberation, liberation of the human being from all manner of servitude, liberation from sin, and communion with God as the ultimate basis of a human community of brothers and sisters. As I have written elsewhere:

This is not a matter of three parallel or chronologically successive processes, however. These are three levels of meaning of a single, complex process, which finds its deepest sense and its full realization in the saving work of Christ. These levels of meaning, therefore, are interdependent. A comprehensive view of the matter presupposes that all three aspects can be considered together. In this way two pitfalls will be avoided: first, *idealist* or *spiritualist* approaches, which are nothing but ways of evading a harsh and demanding reality, and, second, shallow analyses and programs of short-term effect initiated under the pretext of meeting immediate needs.[29]

Paradoxically, then, integral or total liberation, presented in this polemic as an alternative to its supposedly lopsided antithesis in the theology of liberation, is actually one of the latter's most classic themes. But—and this is important— one must be careful to conceive of it as *really integral*. That is, one must keep account of the complexity of the subject, avoid sidetracking any of its dimensions, and understand it in conjunction with all the exigencies and demands from which it cannot be divorced. This, at bottom, is what those who deny that they see the historical implications of Christ's salvation have refused to do, and will so continue.

The Cry for Liberation: A Threat

Medellín had spoken of the mute cry for liberation of millions of Latin Americans (Document on Poverty, §2). Puebla asserts that, ten years later, things have changed: "The cry might well have seemed muted back then. Today it is loud and clear, increasing in volume and intensity, and at times full of menace" (§89).

Puebla recognizes that the yearning for liberation in Latin America has become even more urgent and demanding than before. In his addresses in Santo Domingo and Mexico, the pope had already spoken in this vein more than once, and now Puebla takes up the theme—frequently employing the adjective "integral." Hence it is important to see what Puebla means by "integral." One text is especially interesting. It expatiates on the integral character of true liberation and makes some important precisions. This passage, part of the contribution of the Commission of Human Dignity, is so long (§§321–29) that we can cite only a few extracts, paraphrasing and condensing the rest.

After asserting that freedom is a gift and a task, which "cannot be truly achieved without integral liberation (John 8:36)," and which "in a real sense . . . is the goal of human beings, according to our faith," Puebla cites a text from St. Paul that has played an important role in our reflection on liberation—Galatians 5:1. The apostle says, "When Christ freed us, he meant us to remain free" (§321). Puebla goes on to say that fashioning a community, a participation, having its roots in the freedom that is the capacity to dispose of ourselves—fashioning our lives in their concrete reality—is something that must be done "on three inseparable planes: our relationship to the world as its master, to other persons as brothers or sisters, and to God as God's children"

(§322). There follows a detailed presentation of these three planes (§§323-25). Finally, their intimate links with one another are expounded, as based upon a profound unity:

> Through the indissoluble unity of these three planes, the exigencies of communion and participation flowing from human dignity appear more clearly. If our freedom is fully realized on the transcendent plane by our faithful and filial acceptance of God, then we enter into loving communion with the divine mystery and share its very life (*Gaudium et Spes,* 18). The opposite alternative is to break with filial love, to reject and despise the Father. These are the two extreme possibilities, which Christian revelation calls grace and sin respectively. But these two possibilities do not occur without simultaneously extending to the other two planes and having enormous consequences for human dignity [§326].

The last two points are an effort to identify the relationship between the third plane—one's relationship with God—and the other two: the relationship among persons and the relationship between persons and the material world (§323). The link between the third and second planes will be "first and foremost a labor of justice":

> The love of God, which is the root of our dignity, necessarily becomes loving communion with other human beings and fraternal participation. For us today it must become first and foremost a labor of justice on behalf of the oppressed. The fact is that "one who has no love for the brother he has seen cannot love the God he has not seen" (1 John 4:20)[§327].

This "labor of justice," then, means the effort of liberation. The link with the first plane is expressed in a transformation of the material world with a view to the construction of a just lordship there—one that will consist in a true communion of sisters and brothers:

> Authentic communion and participation can exist in this life only if they are projected on to the very concrete plane of temporal realities, so that mastery, use, and transformation of the goods of this earth and those of culture, science, and technology find embodiment in humanity's just and fraternal lordship over the world—which would include respect for ecology[§327].

Next, the document reaffirms the inseparability of the planes, following the schema of grace and sin indicated above. First, grace: the document sets forth the concrete social and historical demands of the love of God, of friendship with God:

Confronted with the realities that are part of our lives today, we must learn from the Gospel that in Latin America we cannot truly love our fellow human beings, and hence God, unless we commit ourselves on the personal level, and in many cases on the structural level as well, to serving and promoting the most dispossessed and downtrodden human groups and social classes, with all the consequences that will entail on the plane of temporal realities [§327].

There is no love for God without love for one's brothers and sisters, particularly those who are most poor, and this means—the document could not be clearer—a commitment on the level of social structures, "with all the consequences that will entail on the plane of temporal realities."

Now the document looks at what happens in the other half of the schema: sin. Of course the picture just presented is only reinforced. The concrete, historical consequences of sin—breach of friendship with God—are inevitable:

Sinfulness on the personal level, the break with God that debases the human being, is always mirrored on the level of interpersonal relations in a corresponding egotism, haughtiness, ambition, and envy. These traits produce injustice, domination, violence at every level, and conflicts between individuals, groups, social classes, and peoples. They also produce corruption, hedonism, aggravated sexuality, and superficiality in mutual relations (cf. Gal. 5:19–21)[§328].

All this is a description of the creation of a situation of sin, a notion that, as we have already mentioned, was central in Medellín, and which Puebla here resumes with greater force and insistence: "thus they establish sinful situations which, at the worldwide level, enslave countless human beings and adversely affect the freedom of all" (§328).

Sin, the breach with God, is not something that occurs only within some intimate sanctuary of the heart. It "always" translates into interpersonal relationships, the document says, and hence is the ultimate root of all injustice and oppresssion—as well as of the social confrontations and conflicts of concrete history, whose existence among us the document makes no attempt to sidestep.

This is how far one must go if one wishes to grasp the meaning of Christ's liberation and all its implications. As Medellín says, in a now familiar passage:

It is the same God who, in the fullness of time, sends his Son in the flesh, so that He might come to liberate all men from the slavery to which sin has subjected them: hunger, misery, oppression, and ignorance, in a word, that injustice and hatred which have their origin in human selfishness [Justice, §3; CELAM-LAB trans.]

Puebla takes up the same idea, in the conclusion of this long passage on the manner of understanding the expression "integral liberation"—and reasserts from this viewpoint the inseparability of the three planes that have now been so carefully expounded:

> It is from this sin, sin as the destroyer of human dignity, that we all must be liberated. We are liberated by our participation in the new life brought to us by Jesus Christ, and by communion with him in the mystery of his death and resurrection. But this is true only on the condition that we live out his mystery on the three planes described above, without focusing exclusively on any one of them. Only in this way will we avoid reducing the mystery to the verticalism of a disembodied spirtual union with God, to the mere existential personalism of individual or small-group ties, or to one or another form of social, economic, or political horizontalism (John Paul II, Opening Address at Puebla, III, 6) [§329].[30]

Puebla has the perspicacity to insist on the pope's integral focus—which condemns not only horizontal reductionism (the shibboleth of the polemicists) but the vertical as well, so frequently passed over in silence.

The passage is crystal clear. And the precision of its language recaptures the best of Latin American reflection on the point at issue. Puebla does not fall prey to the terrorist attitudes of those who undertake to ignore the complex, rich meaning of the term "liberation" as it has been used during recent years— years of increasing commitment, in the form of Christian practice and reflection, to the struggles of an exploited community of believers to build a humane and just society. Their communion with the death and resurrection of Jesus Christ, at the heart of this battle, is the magnificent witness of this people during these years.

To live the love of Christ to the point of giving one's life for one's sisters and brothers, affirming one's hope in the life of the resurrected Christ who vanquishes all death and injustice, is the central element of the power of the poor in history. This is why the aspirations and struggles of the poor for liberation are a threat to the great ones of this world, those who reap the benefits of a social order where they sow death—but fail to stifle hope.[31]

This long passage, then, is the key to the correct understanding of the term "integral liberation," so frequently used in Puebla.[32] It is in light of this notion of integral liberation that the whole series of Puebla documents on the subject should be read.[33]

The Evangelizing Potential of the Poor

When Puebla was in preparation, there was a great deal of searching to identify the primary and most urgent challenge to the task of evangelization in the church. After all, this would be the theme of the conference itself. But when the conference convened, there was no hesitation. Puebla stated its position at the very beginning. Hence we too may enter at once upon the point that interests us here—the relationship between gospel and liberation, from the perspective of the poor:

> The situation of injustice described in the previous section forces us to reflect on the great challenge our pastoral work faces in trying to help human beings to move from less human to more human conditions. The deep-rooted social differences, the extreme poverty, and the violation of human rights found in many areas pose challenges to evangelization. Our mission to bring God to human beings, and human beings to God, also entails the task of fashioning a more fraternal society here [§90].

Bringing God to human beings presupposes the building of a society of brothers and sisters. A dominant theme in Puebla will be this relationship between the proclamation of the gospel and the struggle for justice—the relationship between salvation, and that "justice for the poor" that is the teaching of the Magnificat (§1144).[34]

Puebla takes up a position from one of the richest gospel perspectives when it recalls:

> The poor are the first ones to whom Jesus' mission is directed (Luke 4:18-21), and . . . the evangelization of the poor is the supreme sign and proof of his mission (Luke 7:21–23) [§1142].

But given the concrete situation of the poor in Latin America, this evangelization will make an option for liberation. This is why, after pointing out that service rendered to the poor is the "privileged gauge" of the following of Christ, Puebla asserts:

> The best service to our fellows is evangelization, which disposes them to fulfill themselves as children of God, liberates them from injustices, and fosters their integral advancement [§1145].

The passage is brief but precise. It explains the meaning of a liberating evangelization by placing it within the context of the three planes of integral liberation, which we saw above and which we saw to be inseparable. This is the context in which the preferential option for the poor is situated:

> The objective of our preferential option for the poor is to proclaim Christ the Savior. This will enlighten them about their dignity, help them in their efforts to liberate themselves from all their wants, and lead them to communion with the Father and their fellow human beings through a life lived in evangelical poverty [§1153].

The option is demanded by the "scandalous reality of . . . Latin America," as we saw (§1154). It "should lead us to establish a dignified, fraternal way of life together as human beings and to construct a just and free society" (§1154). The proclamation of the gospel is a contribution to liberation from whatever oppresses the poor in the here and now of the social injustice in which they live. It summons them to live as children of God and to enter into communion with God. The condition for this proclamation of the gospel is "the lived experience of evangelical poverty" (§1157)—which we now know to be solidarity with the poor and rejection of the situation of spoliation in which the vast majority in Latin America live.

But Puebla goes a step further along these lines, echoing the rich experience of the Latin American church in recent years. In the document "The People of God Are in the Service of Communion," the conference asserts that the postconciliar years have been marked in Latin America "by a rising awareness of the masses of the common people" (§233). This and other considerations lead the Puebla bishops to demand in another document that the Latin American poor "be taken into account as responsible people and subjects of history, who can freely participate in political options, labor-union choices, and the election of rulers" (§135).

Accordingly, conscious of the fact that "the common people . . . construct the pluralistic society through their own organizations," the church must contribute to the construction of "a new society for and with the common people" (§1220). These observations and demands, concerning the poeple as agent of its own history, are also expressed in a most meaningful way in a context of evangelization. The "preferential option document" says:

> Commitment to the poor and oppressed and the rise of grass-roots communities have helped the Church to discover the evangelizing potential of the poor. For the poor challenge the Church constantly, summoning it to conversion; and many of the poor incarnate in their lives the evangelical values of solidarity, service, simplicity, and openness to accepting the gift of God [§1147].

This notion had been expressed with great lucidity in the contribution of the Peruvian episcopate to Puebla's preparatory phase, in a section devoted to "the poor in Latin America as addressees and agents of evangelization" (§§435-41). There we find a discussion of the "evangelizing charism of the poor":

> The church's commitment to the poor and oppressed, and the growing importance of the basic church communities among the masses, from Medellín on, have led it to discover, and recognize the value of, the evangelizing charism of which the poor and oppressed are the bearers. For they constantly call the church to conversion, and many of them live a life of evangelical values themselves—solidarity, service, simplicity, and openness to receive the gift of God.[35]

The similarity of the two texts speak for itself. The Peruvian statement helps us better understand what Puebla means. What is being reflected here is a deep and fertile experience of the Latin American church, proceeding, as the text says, from a practice that intimately intertwines two elements: a commitment to the poor and oppressed, and the growth of the grass-roots church communities. It had been in this solidarity, and in the rise of active and responsible Christian communities in the popular sectors, that the church had had the experience of the poor actually evangelizing—proclaiming the gospel themselves. To them, and not to the learned and prudent, is the love of God revealed (cf. Matt. 11:25). It is the poor who receive it, understand it, and announce it, in their own distinctive, demanding way. This is what Puebla means when it says that the ones the Bible calls the poor are not only the privileged recipients of the gospel; they are also, by that very fact, its messengers.[36]

Puebla's conviction is the fruit of praxis. Here we have an expression of the life of the Latin American church that bureaucracy and fear did not succeed in suffocating.

In this same connection, some observations on the basic Christian communities, the grass-roots Christian communities, will not be out of place.[37] This was a bone of contention in Puebla. Persons unfamiliar with concrete pastoral work, and perhaps influenced by connotations that certain terms have in other parts of the world, looked on this phenomenon—one of the most fertile in the life of the church in recent years—with a certain diffidence at first. But, here again, life is not easily ignored.

There is nothing more massive and bruising than reality itself, and any effort to conjure it away or counterfeit it eventually ends up in smithereens. This is what happened at Puebla. And here the Brazilian bishops—without a doubt one of the most outstanding delegations present—along with others (both bishops and nonbishops—members of the Latin American Conference of Religious [CLAR], for example) gave the doubters to understand the meaning of these Christian groups. They are groups born in, and committed to, the world of the common people. By whatever name they are called, they express a gospel experience, in communion with the church, of great wealth and promise for the presence of the church of Jesus Christ in Latin America. Hence Puebla notes with approval: "The poor, too, have been encouraged by the church. They have begun to organize themselves and to live their faith in an integral way, and hence to reclaim their rights" (§1137).

Latin Americans have found, in their grass-roots community life, a rich vein of faith and vitality, and have found a way to carry forward their combat against social injustice, their struggle for liberation, and their experience of the gospel. And they have done so with ability, courage, and a sense of realism. The Puebla bishops declare their approval and patronage in a passage from the document "Evangelization and the People's Religiosity":

The gap between rich and poor, the menacing situation faced by the weakest, the injustices, and the humiliating disregard and subjection endured by them radically contradict the values of personal dignity and brotherly solidarity. Yet the people of Latin America carry these values in their hearts as imperatives received from the Gospel. That is why the religiosity of the Latin American people is often turned into a cry for true liberation. It is an exigency that is still unmet. Motivated by their religiosity, however, the people create or utilize space for the practice of brotherhood in the more intimate areas of their lives together: e.g., the neighborhood, the village, their labor unions, and their recreational activities. Rather than giving way to despair, they confidently and shrewdly wait for the right opportunities to move forward toward the liberation they so ardently desire [§452].

Puebla's viewpoint—the evangelizing potential of the poor—constitutes a definite advance over that of Medellín. Puebla has sought out a stance in creative continuity with its predecessor, and this position enables us to comprehend better the meaning of the liberating evangelization so much insisted upon, in recent years, by Medellín, by Puebla, and especially by the praxis of the Latin American church.[38]

CONVERSION FOR EVANGELIZATION

In order to receive the kingdom of God one must undergo what the gospel calls "conversion." But conversion is also a prerequisite for the proclamation of the good news without telling a lie. Puebla is sensitive to this tandem of truths, and hence demands, on more than one occasion, the conversion of the church itself.

From the very beginning, in their opening "Message" (§2), the bishops ask themselves, "Are we really living the Gospel of Christ on our continent? . . . We are still far from living all that we preach." Then they frankly beg forgiveness: "For all our faults and limitations we pastors, too, ask pardon of God, our brothers and sisters in the faith, and humanity."

Acknowledgment of one's faults, and contrition for them, is an important element in conversion. It implies the desire to take a new path. This exordium establishes a theme whose thread is woven all through the Puebla texts—the conversion of the church and the reform of its structures.

"This Witness, Nascent but Real"

The bishops' opening question is concretized in terms of their commitment to the poor. What is done for the poor will witness to the authenticity of a life according to the gospel:

We wish to take note of all that the Church in Latin America has done, or has failed to do, for the poor since the Medellín Conference. This will serve as a starting point for seeking out effective channels to implement our option in our evangelizing work in Latin America's present and future [§1135].

The church's commitment to the poor has a connection with the efficacy of the activity of evangelization. Significant sectors of the church—with a might and a sense of reality that will always seem illusory to the defenders of a situation advantageous to themselves—have begun to take on a solidarity with the poor, and to denounce the unjust structures that make and keep them poor:

> We see that national episcopates and many segments of lay people, religious men and women, and priests have made their commitment to the poor a deeper and more realistic one. This witness, nascent but real, led the Latin American Church to denounce the grave injustices stemming from mechanisms of oppression [§1136].[39]

We have already seen that, along the lines traced by Medellín and the discourses of John Paul II, Puebla underscored the structural causes of Latin American poverty. It is on account of these structural causes that involvement with the poor must go beyond good-heartedness and social work. It must now become denunciation and battle. For it is the *social order* that is unjust.[40]

This has been the experience of numerous Christians in Latin America; this has been their involvement, during these years. It is an involvement, a commitment, that has brought many of them slander, prison, torture, and even death. These are the martyrs—the witnesses to the faith in God in the hearts of the poor—of recent Latin American history. Puebla does not give this the attention it deserves. Nevertheless there are some clear allusions. The "preferential option document" says:

> The Church's prophetic denunciations and its concrete commitments to the poor have, in not a few instances, brought down persecution and oppression of various kinds upon it. The poor themselves have been the victims of this oppression [§1138].

This last bears repeated emphasis. Puebla is certainly to the point when it says that it is the poor themselves who have been the first victims of these reprisals on the part of those who hold economic and political power in Latin American society. This is important. These persons—"history's anonymous ones"—often pass by unnoticed.

Another text comes right out and says that the church has had "to endure the persecution and at times death of its members in witness to its prophetic mission" (§92)—a profound recognition of the reason for the murder of so many sisters and brothers of ours in witness to the faith. Puebla also makes allusion to the reservations entertained in the dominant sectors toward the stance the church has taken regarding service to the poor.[41]

Latin America today is full of manifestations of these reservations. They are by no means divorced from the anxieties aroused by the prospect of an episcopal conference in Puebla in the first place. Fearing a "second Medellín," elements in the dominant sectors undertook harsh attacks upon the sectors most committed to the process of Latin American liberation. They also sought in various ways to bring pressure to bear on the course of the conference itself. In this sense Puebla's day was both painful and instructive. Conservative groups, many of them calling themselves Catholics, carried out a campaign of defamation before and during the conference. When the conference was in progress, even bishops of great pastoral experience, who were playing an important role at Puebla, were attacked and calumniated.[42]

With great lucidity, Puebla itself gives the profound reason for this attitude:

> The enormously positive activity of the Church in defense of human rights and its dealings with the poor have led groups with economic power, who thought they were the front ranks of Catholicism, to feel that they have been abandoned by the Church. As they see it, the Church has forsaken its "spiritual" mission [§79].

The analysis is clear. There is no mistaking the bishops' meaning. By "spiritual mission" the dominant sectors mean something that not only does not call their interests into question but actually protects them.[43]

Solidarity with a People Organizing Itself

Resistance encountered in the privileged sectors was thus due to the church's involvement with the poor. And it had been long in brewing. The church had been expressing great interest in organization of the people, in defense of legitimate interests, as far back as Medellín. It was not a matter of a sudden turn toward the poor on the part of the Latin American church.

Traditional Christian circles often have a concern for the poor, provided always that it not raise any questions. What was novel in Medellín and Puebla was the concrete nature of their interest. In a text we have cited above, the Puebla bishops express their satisfaction with the attempts the poor have made to organize themselves, in recent years, so as "to live their faith in an integral way, and hence to reclaim their rights" (§1137).

The preferential option, then, is not in favor of one or another individual poor person, nor again of the poor who are "grateful and good," as one is wont to hear in affluent social circles. Poverty as we have it in Latin America has a collective dimension, and leads ineluctably to a situation of social conflict.

We have seen this in our examination of the Puebla texts on the situation of poverty in Latin America. It is the result of unjust structures, which have created broad strata of poverty, broad strata of poor. Hence the "preferential option document" will say that the church should "understand and denounce the mechanisms that generate this poverty" (§1160). Only thus, by uniting its efforts to those of other churches and "with those of people of good will," will the Catholic Church be able "to uproot poverty and create a more just and fraternal world" (§1161). Indeed this is what the whole discussion is about— doing away with a poverty that dehumanizes, that tramples underfoot these persons' condition as children of God.

But, then, the people must organize. The pope stressed this point powerfully on his visit to Mexico, and Puebla echoes him:

> We support the aspirations of laborers and peasants, who wish to be treated as free, responsible human beings. They are called to share in the decisions that affect their lives and their future, and we encourage all to improve themselves [§1162].

To this end it is essential that they defend "their fundamental right 'to freely create organizations to defend and promote their interests, and to make a responsible contribution to the common good' " (§1163; cf. John Paul II's Address to the Workers at Monterrey, 3). The Puebla document will repeat the pope on this point. The workers of Latin America, it will say, "should not forget what Pope John Paul II told them in his talk. It is the right of workers 'to freely create organizations to defend and promote their interests, and to contribute to the common good in a responsible way' " (§1244). This is a repeated concern of Puebla, and the conference denounces every obstacle to these efforts of the popular classes to organize themselves:

> In many places labor legislation is either applied arbitrarily or not taken into account at all. This is particularly true in countries where the government is based on the use of force. There they look askance at the organizing efforts of laborers, peasants, and the common people; and they adopt repressive measures to prevent such organizing [§44].

In contrast with these preventive measures, and this hostility to such popular organizations, Puelba now unmasks the type of social order prevailing in our region of the world and denounces the present state of affairs: "But this type of control over, or limitation on, activity is not applied to employer organizations, which can exercise their full power to protect their interests" (§44).

The first step toward authentic resolution of social confrontations resulting from an unjust socioeconomic system is not to hide them.

And so the commitment to which Puebla, in the footsteps of Medellín, summons us is hard and demanding. Nor therefore is it to be wondered at that, in these years:

> All this has produced tensions and conflicts both inside and outside the Church. The Church has frequently been the butt of accusations, either of being on the side of those with political or socioeconomic power, or of propounding a dangerous and erroneous Marxist ideology [§1139].

For we already know that if the church were to take seriously what John Paul II said about the defense of human rights being "an authentically *evangelical commitment* which, like that of Christ, is primarily a commitment to those most in need" (Opening Address at Puebla, III, 3), if we were to concretize the "preferential concern to defend and promote the rights of the poor, the marginalized, and the oppressed" (§1217), the church would be accused, as we saw, of forsaking its "spiritual" mission. It would even be accused, as we saw just a few lines above, of "a dangerous and erroneous Marxist ideology." This is exactly what has occurred in recent years. The accusations have come from those who see any denunciation of the *fact* of misery and exploitation as motivated by *ideology*. They would have liked to see preparation for Puebla take the form of an ideological dispute. They were crestfallen when it dealt instead with the massive facts. "How wonderful things would be," someone has ironically claimed they said, "if it weren't for reality."[44]

In addition to these "tensions and conflicts" outside the church, Puebla is not afraid to admit their existence inside the church as well. Once again we find ourselves reading language that is clear and outspoken, not afraid to call a spade a spade. What is happening is that the demands made on Christians in solidarity with the poor and oppressed are so serious that they are leading the whole church to a radical change in its way of life—to a conversion. Efforts along the lines of an involvement with the despoiled, marginalized sectors of society are vitally in evidence today, in the on-going history of the Latin American people as well as in that of a church with such deep roots in that people. And yet the Puebla conference does not declare itself satisfied with this initial solidarity with the poor.

Inadequate Identification with the Poor Christ and a Poor People

Nascent and real, our commitment to the poor is insufficient, in the eyes of the bishops gathered in Puebla. "Not all of us in the Latin American Church have committed ourselves sufficiently to the poor. We are not always concerned about them or in solidarity with them." Medellín's call was answered by important sectors of the church, but much remains to be done. The "preferential option document" has already referred to the "disregard and even hostility" (§1134) of many toward Medellín. Puebla now seeks to reaffirm its predecessor's demands of solidarity with the poor and oppressed. This is obviously one of its key themes. Hence Puebla notes: "Service to them really calls for constant conversion and purification among all Christians. That must be done if we are to achieve fuller identification each day with the poor Christ and our own poor" (§1140).

This conversion is presented as the means par excellence for concretizing the preferential option (§§1157–58). The criterion by which the evangelizing activity of the church is to be judged will be its similarity to Christ's own proclamation of his gospel:

As the Pope has told us, the evangelical commitment of the Church, like that of Christ, should be a commitment to those most in need (cf. Luke 4:18–21; Opening Address, III, 3). Hence the Church must look to Christ when it wants to find out what its evangelizing activity should be like [§1141].

The conversion that arises out of this comparison will permit the church to acquit itself of its task of witness and proclaim the gospel. This conversion involves two things.

First, it requires a reexamination of the church's own structures and of the life of its members:

To live out and proclaim the requirement of Christian poverty, the Church must re-examine its structures and the life of its members, particularly that of its pastoral agents, with the goal of effective conversion in mind [§1157].[45]

Effective conversion is a demand of an efficacious evangelization, a condition of the authenticity of the pastoral word. "Without the witness of a converted Church, our word as pastors would be futile" (§1221; cf. Paul VI, *Evangelii nuntiandi,* 41). If the church is defined by its proper task, that of evangelization (§4), it need not fear to reexamine its structures, in order the more efficaciously to place them at the service of the proclamation of the message. The reexamination of these structures is therefore presented in the Puebla documents as a facet of the conversion of the church.

The dynamic standpoint taken here by Puebla is an expression of *parrhesia*—the Christian audacity of the Acts of the Apostles. It contrasts with the zealous defense of particular historical forms and structures, a defense undertaken rather in the service of one's vested securities than in view of a true sense of the presence of the Spirit in the church. The gospel tells us that the Spirit will lead us to the full truth (John 14:26), but there are those who cannot resign themselves to not knowing in advance which road to the truth will be the one to take.

Secondly, the Puebla document emphasizes the demands of an authentic lifestyle:

Such conversion entails the demand for an austere lifestyle and a total confidence in the Lord, because in its evangelizing activity the Church will rely more on the being and power of God and his grace than on "having more" and secular authority [§1158].

Reliance on the strength of the gospel, rather than on the powers of this world, for the accomplishment of the church's mission is one of Puebla's deep concerns. For example:

The Church must become more and more independent of the powers in this world. Only thus can it enjoy a broad area of freedom that will enable it to carry out its apostolic work without interference. That work includes the practice of cultic worship, education in the faith, and the fostering of those many and varied activites that lead the faithful to implement the moral imperatives deriving from the faith in their private, family, and social life. Thus, free of compromising and vested only with its wintness and teaching, the Church will be more credible and better heard [§144].

Independence from vested interests is a condition of credibility for the proclamation of the gospel. To have said this of Latin American society, where there are still so many different modes of intimacy between "the powers of this world" and important sectors of the church, was an act of courage. And a commitment. A commitment made before the Lord, and before the poor of Latin America.[46] Finally, it is an act of confidence and faith. As the bishops say in their profession of faith at the end of their "Message to the Peoples of Latin America": "We believe in the power of the Gospel."

A church free of these entanglements will be a church that is poor and open to the poor and oppressed:

In this way [the church] will present an image of being authentically poor, open to God and fellow human beings, ever at their disposal, and providing a place where the poor have a real chance for participation and where their worth is recognized [§1158].

This was one of Medellín's great concerns, and the motive of some of its best and most courageous statements. After recognizing with honesty and Christian humility the reasons that "have helped create this image of a rich official Church" (§2), the Medellín Document on Poverty continues:

The poverty of the Church and her members in Latin America should be a sign and a commitment: a sign of the inestimable value of poverty in God's eyes, and a commitment to solidarity with those who are suffering [§7].

This is the church that will be both "sign and commitment." This is the church that will strike root in the world of poverty, the world of those who "intuit . . . in a privileged and forceful way" that "Kingdom brought to us by Christ" Puebla, (§132). In order to open itself to them the church need only recognize them, see them already present—with "their poverty on their backs," as Bartolomé de las Casas described them. For the church in Latin America, to be poor means to take on the life, the struggles, the sufferings, and the aspirations of the majority of its own members—the poor who are within that church indeed, but whose voice, especially if they are claiming their rights, sounds foreign to many within the same church.

Puebla, like Medellín, is neither a beginning nor an end. It is a stage along the historic march of the people of God in Latin America, an important moment in a life where, as Puebla itself says, the spirit must not be quenched or prophecy killed. Without this life of the church community, so evident in the preparation of the conference as well as during the course of its deliberations, there is no understanding the fact of Puebla. Its documents are an expression of every-thing within that church community at that time, including the nuances, the tensions, and the differences in perception on many a matter that are always present in a complex reality. But withal there is that solid, unshakable core, that basic, total option, maintained with courage and energy in spite of all the fears and calumnies.

Nor can the next stage be understood without first understanding the life of this Christian community. A meeting of pastors produces texts. But it also, and especially, creates attitudes and involvements—without which the texts would be a dead letter. What is important now, more than anxiously to defend the documents and argue over this passage or that one, is to do an exegesis of them within the actual praxis of the Latin American church. A facile "war of texts" must be avoided. Any passages brought into confrontation with one another should be examined against a background of authentic commitment to the poor of Latin America, in whom we are called to discover the face of the Lord. Otherwise we will only have a kind of "star wars."

No, if we want to step down to earth from outer space—where perhaps some have mounted in the hope that the silence reigning there will allow their voice, drowned out in the din of the earth, to be heard at last—we must take up the great options of Puebla in our everyday practice. With our feet firmly on the earth, and amid the tumult of our daily round, we must accept the fact that our voice is but one among many in Latin America. The documents of Puebla have not changed things in Latin America. Our hope is that they change things in the church.[47]

Puebla has allowed us to see that Medellín's program has not been com-pletely carried out. And this is one of Puebla's great demands. In placing itself in continuity with Medellín, Puebla has reissued Medellín's call and challenge. For that call and challenge have not been sufficiently heard, and the Puebla documents remind us of this repeatedly. The new subjects taken up serve only to render the demand more urgent. It is a demand that must be answered with creativity—the creativity to which John Paul II exhorted us at the close of his opening address at Puebla. What precise and particular paths will be taken in carrying forward this resolution will depend on the decisions and work of the Christian community as a whole. The rich pastoral experiences of these past years—our experience of solidarity with the poor and oppressed—have opened a furrow that we must now continue to plow, with might and imagin-ation.

Puebla addressed itself to many topics. It opened many promising paths. Other points are left for the future. In these pages we have sought only to shed light on two great themes: the perspective of the *poor,* and, in relationship with it, the subject of *liberation*. This is why we took the document "A Preferential Option for the Poor" as our guide. We have left many other themes out of consideration here. We trust that the points selected will afford access to what is fundamental in Puebla's option and thereby shed light on other important and controverted questions as well.

In solidarity, then, with the poor and oppressed of Latin America in their life, their sufferings, their struggles to break free of an unjust social order, and their longing for liberation, let us now address ourselves to a task that we shall surely find to be rigorously demanding: that of entering into, taking upon ourselves, the reality of the misery and exploitation in which the great majority of our people live. But we shall also find in it a communion—communion in the profound hope of the people in God as their Liberator, as the "Avenger of the Lowly," Rescuer and Vindicator of this exploited Christian people. This is what Puebla meant when it said that with a preferential option for the poor, and in the footsteps of Medellín, it was opening "new horizons of hope."

NOTES

1. "God always takes his stand unconditionally and passionately on this side and on this side alone: against the lofty and on behalf of the lowly; against those who already enjoy right and privilege and on behalf of those who are denied it and deprived of it" (Karl Barth, *Church Dogmatics* [New York: Scribner's], vol. 2/1 [1957], p. 386).

2. This is the same viewpoint as that expressed in a widely distributed brochure (March 1978) in defense of the Preparatory Document by A. López Trujillo, "Los pobres—¿olvido o rescate?"

3. An earlier draft, whose wording was very close to that of the final text, although approved, received forty-three negative votes—making this document, along with those of the First Commission (on the Latin American situation), the ones most heavily opposed in the balloting. (For precise data, see *CELAM* 135 [Feb. 1979]:48.) It is common knowledge that "A Preferential Option for the Poor" encountered further difficulties as well, at the hands of certain members of the conference, even after approval by the conference.

4. The present article will incorporate extensive citations from the Puebla documents. The advantages are evident. The version I cite [in the Spanish original of this article—ed.] is the *Texto Oficial,* which is known to contain numerous variant readings as compared with the text actually approved by the bishops in Puebla. English quotations are from *Puebla and Beyond,* John Eagleson and Philip Scharper, eds. (Maryknoll, N.Y.: Orbis, 1979), a collection of documents including the NCCB-authorized translation of the Final Document from Puebla, as well as the major addresses of Pope John Paul II in Mexico, together with commentaries by specialists on Puebla.

5. A good many other texts in the same vein declare Puebla's fidelity to Medellín. See, for example, §§ 24, 88, 142, 143, 235, 480, 1165.

6. The "Message to the Peoples of Latin America," introducing all the other Puebla documents, recalls this classic biblical theme: "all that infringes upon human dignity somehow wounds God too" (*Puebla and Beyond,* p.118). Puebla speaks more than

once of the charism of prophecy, in the sense in which we have just used the term. For example, the document "The People of God Are in the Service of Communion" states: "[The people of God] are sent out as a prophetic People to announce the Gospel or discern the Lord's calls in history. They are to announce where the presence of the Lord's Spirit is manifested; and they are to denounce where the mystery of iniquity is at work through deeds and structures that prevent more fraternal participation in the construction of society and in the enjoyment of the goods that God created for all" (§267). Then this document adds (contradicting an opinion commonly held in conservative circles in Latin America): "In the last ten years we have seen a definite increase in the function of prophecy" (§268).

7. The pope explicitly asserts that Medellín itself understood the privilege of the poor in this way. See his "Homily at the Basilica of Guadalupe" on the occasion of the solemn opening of the Puebla conference, Jan. 27, 1979, in *Puebla and Beyond,* pp. 72–76.

8. Unless otherwise noted, English quotations from the Medellín documents are taken from *Between Honesty and Hope* (Maryknoll, N.Y.: Orbis, 1970).

9. For a comprehensive study of this document, see chap. 5, "The Preparatory Document for Puebla: A Retreat from Commitment," in *The Power of the Poor in History* (Ed.).

10. The *Texto Oficial* seems to have missed the meaning of the text actually approved in Puebla. The latter had said, "the situation of violence—institutionalized, subversive, and repressive. . . . " But the official text (and translation) reads, "the situation of violence—which can be called institutionalized violence (either as subversion or as repression). . . . " The wording softens the characterization of violence as the primary attribute of the overall situation in Latin America.

11. For example: "In recent years we have also seen deterioration in the political sphere. Much harm has been done to the participation of citizens in the conduct of their own affairs and destiny. We also frequently see a rise in what can be called institutionalized injustice" (§46; cf. §509). The expression "institutionalized injustice" had already been employed by Cardinal Lorscheider to describe the situation in Latin America (*Osservatore Romano,* Sept. 24, 1978).

12. Another passage runs in the same tenor: "But so long as huge segments of society cannot manage to satisfy these legitimate aspirations while others indulge themselves to excess, the tangible goods of the modern world will turn into a source of growing frustrations and tragic tensions. The blatant and striking contrast between those who possess nothing and those who show off their opulence is an insuperable obstacle to establishing the Reign of peace" (§138; cf. §§1260, 1264, 1269).

13. See the Homily in Zapopán.

14. See, for example, §§70, 185–86, 281, 452, 515, 1032, 1269.

15. The text approved by Puebla had said: "the extreme poverty that reigns on our continent."

16. The actual Puebla text had put it, expressively: "This denunciation is a summons to *(es convocadora de)* the church."

17. The condition of women is treated in several places in the Puebla documents, and the treatment constitutes without a doubt one of the conference's remarkable contributions. The passage cited here is one of the conference's clearest statements of the particularly oppressed condition of women in the despoiled and exploited populous sectors.

18. The actual Puebla text had said: "even before taking account of their moral or personal situation."

19. "Aporte de la conferencia episcopal peruana al documento de consulta del Celam para la tercera conferencia general del episcopado latinoamericano" (Lima, 1978), no. 421. Various regional assemblies of the Peruvian bishops had insisted on this perspective in their contributions to the preparation of this document.

20. See, for example, Leonardo Boff, "Maria, Mulher prophética libertadora: A piedade mariana na teologia da libertação," *Revista Eclesiástica Brasileira* 149 (March 1978): 59–78. See also my *Theology of Liberation,* pp. 207–8; and Edmundo Leon, *María y la Iglesia profética* (Lima: CEP, 1977).

21. See, for example, §§12, 196, 268, 385, 695, 696, 711, 965, 1143.

22. To cite but two authors: Jacques Dupont, *Les Béatitudes* (Paris: Gabalda) is exhaustive on the theme (vol. 1, *Les Béatitudes: le probléme littéraire* [1969]; vol. 2, *Les Béatitudes: la bonne nouvelle* [1969]; and vol. 3, *Les Béatitudes: les Evangélistes* [1973]); and the shorter work by Julio de Santa Ana, *Good News to the Poor: The Challenge of the Poor in the History of the Church* (Maryknoll, N.Y.: Orbis, 1979).

23. "Christ, our Savior, not only loved the poor but became poor" ("he was rich, but he became poor"—2 Cor. 8:9). He lived in poverty, focused his mission around proclaiming the liberation of the poor, and founded his Church as a sign of this poverty among men" (Medellín Document on Poverty, 7—*Honesty and Hope,* p. 213).

24. In his opening address at the Puebla conference, John Paul II stated: "There can be no doubt that all this imposes exacting demands on the attitude of any Christians who truly wish to serve the least of their brothers and sisters, the poor, the needy, the marginalized: i.e., all those whose lives reflect the suffering countenance of the Lord (*Lumen gentium,* 8)" (*Puebla and Beyond,* p. 60). And later he adds: "In the parable of the Good Samaritan, the Lord outlined the model way of attending to all human needs (Luke 10:30 ff.); and he said that in the last analysis he will identify himself with the disinherited—the imprisoned, the hungry, and the abandoned—to whom we have offered a helping hand (Matt. 25:31 ff.)" (ibid., p. 66). In the document entitled "The Truth about Jesus Christ, the Savior We Proclaim," Puebla says that, thanks to "the efforts at renewal that have taken place mainly since the Medellín Conference," there has been a "labor and growth" that has "brought many segments of the People of God closer to the Gospel and has prompted their search for the ever new face of Christ, who is the answer to their legitimate yearning for integral liberation" (§173). Matthew 25:31–46 is an important text in the pope's teaching. He appeals to it once more in his encyclical *Redemptor hominis* and reaches a demanding conclusion: "This eschatological scene must *always* be 'applied' to man's history; it must always be made the 'measure' for human acts as an essential outline for an examination of conscience by each and every one . . . " (§16; emphasis added). Just above, he had spoken of a "confrontation" and a "contrast" between "rich, highly developed societies" and "the remaining societies, or at least broad sectors of them," which suffer hunger, "with many people dying each day of starvation and malnutrition" (ibid.) According to the pope, this is owing to prevailing "mechanisms" and "structures," and the textual apparatus refers us to his addresses in Santo Domingo and Mexico. This analysis lends very concrete content to the passage we have referred to from Matthew 25.

25. An entire paragraph of the "Aporte de la conferencia episcopal peruana," the Peruvian bishops' document drawn up in preparation for Puebla, was devoted to the subject of "Christ Poor" (nos. 456–60).

26. See Leonardo Boff, *Jesus Christ Liberator: A Critical Theology for Our Times* (Maryknoll, N.Y.: Orbis, 1978); and Jon Sobrino, *Christology at the Crossroads: A Latin American Approach* (Orbis, 1978). See also J. I. González-Faus, *La humanidad nueva: Ensayo de cristología,* 2 vols. (Madrid, 1974).

27. The actual Puebla document had said, forcefully: "They, and those crucified by injustice, accept the Lord's cross as their own and shoulder it."

28. Puebla speaks of "changes" that "either have not taken place, or else they have been too slow in coming in the concrete life of Latin America" (§30). And elsewhere: "In particular we must note that since the decade of the fifties, and despite certain achievements, the ample hopes for development have come to nothing. The marginalization of the vast majority and the exploitation of the poor have increased" (§1260).

29. *Theology of Liberation,* p. 37. The importance for the theology of liberation, ever since it began, of understanding Christ's salvation to include these different dimensions has been very well pointed up by R. Oliveros, *Liberación y teología: Génesis y crecimiento de una reflexión* (1966–1976) (Lima: CEP, 1977), and Miguel Manzanero, *Teología y Salvación-Liberación* (Bilbao, 1978).

30. Elsewhere, resuming the old classic distinction between freedom *from* and freedom *for,* a distinction used in the theology of liberation as well, the bishops say: "There are two complementary and inseparable elements. The first is liberation from all the forms of bondage, from personal and social sin, and from everything that tears apart the human individual and society; all this finds its source to be in egotism, in the mystery of iniquity. The second element is liberation for progressive growth in being through communion with God and other human beings; this reaches its culmination in the perfect communion in heaven, where God is all in all and weeping forever ceases" (§482). And then, still in a perspective embracing all the various dimensions of a human being: "This liberation is gradually being realized in history, in our personal history and that of our peoples. It takes in all the different dimensions of life: the social, the political, the economic, the cultural, and all their interrelationships" (§483).

31. Puebla asserts: "From the depths of the countries that make up Latin America a cry is rising to heaven, growing louder and more alarming all the time. It is the cry of a suffering people who demand justice, freedom, and respect for the basic rights of human beings and peoples" (§87).

32. There are echoes here of a passage from *Evangelii nuntiandi,* which it will be worthwhile to reproduce in its entirety:

> It is well known in what terms numerous Bishops from all the continents spoke of this at the last synod, especially the Bishops from the Third World, with a pastoral accent resonant with the voice of the millions of sons and daughters of the church who make up those peoples. Peoples, as we know, engaged with all their energy in the effort and struggle to overcome everything which condemns them to remain on the margin of life: famine, chronic disease, illiteracy, poverty, injustices in international relations and especially in commercial exchanges, situations of economic and cultural neocolonialism sometimes as cruel as the old political colonialism. The Church, as the Bishops repeated, has the duty to proclaim the liberation of millions of human beings, many of whom are her own children—the duty of assisting the birth of this liberation, of giving witness to it, of ensuring that it is complete. This is not foreign to evangelization [no. 30].

33. The media made a great deal of what they liked to see as a "condemnation of the theology of liberation." Wishful thinking indeed. For one thing, as everyone knows, the magisterium of the church, and the papal magisterium especially, is not exercised in unverifiable oral statements made to journalists. Secondly, the pope certainly did not use the words "condemn" or "condemnation" in any of his addresses in Santo Domingo or Mexico. Thirdly, the imagined condemnation was denied on more than one occasion

by bishops in Puebla who had great influence at the conference. Finally, if any doubts remain, they must be dispelled by Pope John Paul II's catechetical address of Feb. 21, 1979, in which he spoke directly of the theology of liberation in terms calculated to put an end to a stubborn campaign that had only betrayed again what interests it represented. How uninformed the representatives of those interests are when it comes to knowing how such matters are dealt with in the church today!

34. See also the document "Evangelization, Liberation, and Human Promotion" (*Puebla and Beyond,* pp. 188–94). All these approaches frequently have as their backdrop the notion of "integral development" as presented in *Populorum progressio,* 21.

35. A timid, ambiguous anticipation of this text is to be found in the Working Document, in a position midway between the Preparatory Document and the Peruvian contribution: "The poor are the riches of the church. It is in relationship with them that one discovers the evangelizing charism of the church of Latin America for our time." Puebla itself stops beating about the bush and espouses the unadulterated Peruvian position.

36. It is a pity that the documents "The Hierarchial Ministry" and especially "Lay People" (*Puebla and Beyond,* pp. 215–27, 227–35) failed to profit by this rich perspective.

37. Several passages in the Puebla documents take note of the expansion and maturation of these communities since Medellín. Puebla emphasizes the promise they hold for the Latin American church: "In 1968 base-level ecclesial communities [CEBs: *comunidades eclesiales de base*] were just coming into being. Over the past ten years they have multiplied and matured, particularly in some countries, so that now they are one of the causes for joy and hope in the Church. In communion with their bishops, and in line with Medellín's request, they have become centers of evangelization and moving forces for liberating and development. The vitality of these CEBs is now beginning to bear fruit. They have been one of the sources for the increase in lay ministers, who are now acting as leaders and organizers of their communities, as catechists, and as missionaries" (§§96–97). See also, of course, the document "Base-Level Ecclesial Communities" itself (§§617–57), which has a great many worthwhile things to say about these grass-roots communities. Numerous other passages throughout the Puebla material make other contributions. It is this grass-roots experience that forms the basis for that bone of contention, the church as "born of the people under the influence of the Spirit." A Puebla text laments the use of the *expression* "people's church," or "church born of the people," as "rather unfortunate" (§263)—but then the very same passage goes on to endorse the actual *content* of these expressions (as the Working Document had already done, tenuously): "The problem of the 'people's Church,' the Church born of the People, has various aspects. The first obstacle is readily surmounted if it is interpreted as a Church that is trying to incarnate itself in the ranks of the common people on our continent, and that therefore arises out of their response in faith to the Lord. This rules out the seeming denial of a basic truth: i.e., that the Church always arises from a first initiative 'from above,' from the Spirit who raises it up and from the Lord who convokes it" (§263). Actually John Paul II himself had already opened up this approach when he said that one should not understand "people" here as a "mental category," and explicitly maintained that "the church is *born* of the faith response we make to Jesus Christ." And indeed the point is precisely the faith response that persons make to the convoking, summoning, message of Christ, of which they are the privileged addressees. A "church born of the people under the action of the Spirit," all arbitrary interpreta-

tions by its enthusiasts or its adversaries notwithstanding, is a challenging vocation for the whole church, not a sterile alternative to the church that already is. Viewed in this light, commitment along these lines becomes all the more urgent, given the conditions of the life of the Latin American church today.

38. This is Puebla's emphasis right from the start. After recalling that "evangelization is the very mission of the Church," the conference presents the evangelizing task as seeking "to contribute its services to a better future for the peoples of Latin America, to their liberation and growth in all of life's dimensions" (§4).

39. Concerning the involvement of members of religious orders in this area, Puebla had already stated: "Pastoral openness in one's labors and a preferential option for the poor represent the most noticeable tendency of religious life in Latin America. Indeed religious increasingly find themselves in difficult, marginalized areas; in missions to the indigenous peoples; and in silent, humble labors. This option does not imply exclusion of anyone, but it does imply a preference for the poor and a drawing closer to them. This had led to a re-examination of traditional works in order to respond better to the demands of evangelization. It has shed clearer light on their relationship with the poverty of the marginalized. Now this does not imply simply interior detachment and community austerity; it also implies solidarity with the poor, sharing with them, and in some cases living alongside them" (§§733–34). The activities of CLAR (*Conferencia Latinoamericana de Religiosos,* Latin American Conference of Religious) receive clear support in this passage. CLAR is known to have initiated, and courageously maintained, this involvement with the popular and marginalized sectors, while seeking to base it on solid theological reflection. See CLAR, *Pobreza y vida religiosa en América Latina* (Bogotá, 1970); and Equipos de Teólogos CLAR, *Vida religiosa en América Latina a partir de Medellín: Nueva situación* (Bogotá, 1976).

40. Underscoring this aspect of service to the poor, Puebla quotes Vatican Council II: "The demands of justice should first be satisfied, lest the giving of what is due in justice be represented as the offering of a charitable gift. Not only the effects but also the causes of various ills must be removed. Help should be given in such a way that the recipients may gradually be freed from dependence on others and become self-sufficient" (Decree on the Apostolate of the Laity, 8) (§1146). The document from the Peruvian episcopate makes the same citation.

41. "The collective voice of the bishops has been awakening a growing interest in public opinion; but frequently it also runs up against reservations in certain sectors with little social sensitivity. This is a sign that the Church is carrying out its role as Mother and Teacher of all" (§160).

42. Cardinals Juan Landázuri and Paulo Evaristo Arns, and bishops Hélder Câmara, Marcos McGrath, Leonidas Proaño, and Luis Bambarén, among others.

43. At bottom, the dominant groups understand very well what is at stake. A newspaper noted for its coarse and offensive campaigns against progressive elements during the Puebla conference ran this revealing headline over an article on a meeting of business executives: *"Dañina a la Empresa Teología de Liberación"* ("Theology of Liberation Business in Trouble") (*La Voz de Puebla,* Feb. 10, 1979)–not the gospel, not the Christian faith, but some "business" or other.

44. Puebla indicates one of the reasons for these accusations: "Fear of Marxism keeps many from facing up to the oppressive reality of liberal capitalism. One could say that some people, faced with the danger of one clearly sinful system, forget to denounce and combat the established reality of another equally sinful system (cf. Pope John Paul II's Homily in Zapopán)" (§92). This distinction between *existing reality* and *potential*

danger, and especially the importance of the poor and their liberation for an under-standing of the mission of the church—our subject in these pages—affords a better appreciation of what Puebla means when it talks about the thorny problems of the relationship between faith and politics, theology and the social sciences, or social reality and Marxist analysis. When these problems are handled on the doctrinal level they are subjected to more of an ideological approach, whereas they actually deserve an ad hoc examination in their own right.

45. The text actually approved in Puebla had spoken of a reexamination of the life of "all" of the members of the church, and had concluded: "Thus, once converted, it will be able efficaciously to evangelize the poor." The official text in the section entitled "Witness" reads: "This is our first pastoral option: the Christian community itself—its lay people, pastors, ministers, and religious—must be converted more and more to the Gospel so that they will be able to evangelize others" (§973).

46. This is actually a ratification of the commitment made in Medellín, where that conference had said: "We want our Church in Latin America to be free of worldly tie-ups, conniving relationships, and ambiguous hallmarks. We want her to be 'free in spirit from the bonds of wealth' (Paul VI, Opening Address to the Latin American Bishops' Conference, Aug. 24, 1968), to make her mission of service more transparent and solid, and to live in the world reflecting Christ's light and participating in its betterment. We wish to stress and acknowledge the value and legitimate autonomy of temporal tasks" (Medellín Document on Poverty, 18: *Honesty and Hope,* p. 216.).

47. Bishop Proaño, a prelate of broad pastoral experience, put it this way, both inside and outside the Puebla conference: "We are duty bound to submit this document to the faithful and see how they react. They will know whether we have interpreted them correctly or not."

6

Juan Luis Segundo

The Hermeneutic Circle

Juan Luis Segundo maintains that any authentic, contemporary attempt to interpret the Bible must employ a methodology that he calls the "hermeneutic circle." This selection is from The Liberation of Theology *(Maryknoll, N.Y.: Orbis Books, 1976), pp. 7–39. The book was originally published in 1975.*

We cannot start with the chicken and the egg, so let us start with the reality of everyday life and consider whether it is possible to differentiate the attitudes of a liberation theologian from those of some other theologian on that basis.

My past and present experience has taught me that theology, for all the changes that may have taken place, continues to be taught in an autonomous way. And this is true not only with respect to future professors of theology but also with respect to average people who will only use theology vis-à-vis the real-life problems that face ordinary people.

In mentioning this autonomy of theology I am referring to a long tradition in the Christian churches. Christianity is a *biblical* religion. It is the religion of a *book*, of various books if you will, for that is precisely what the word "bible" means. This means that theology for its part cannot swerve from its path in this respect. It must keep going back to its book and reinterpreting it. Theology is not an interpretation of humankind and society, not in the first place at least.

Attached as it is to a book, theology does not assert its independence from the past or from the sciences which help it to understand the past: for example, general history, the study of ancient languages and cultures, the history of biblical forms, and the history of biblical redaction. On the other hand theology does implicitly or explicitly assert its independence from the sciences that deal with the present.

For example, a theologian as progressive as Schillebeeckx can arrive at the conclusion that theology can never be ideological—in the Marxist sense of the term—because it is nothing but the application of the divine word to present-day reality.[1] He seems to hold the naive belief that the word of God is applied to human realities inside some antiseptic laboratory that is totally immune to the ideological tendencies and struggles of the present day.

Now a liberation theologian is one who starts from the opposite end. The liberation theologian's suspicion is that anything and everything involving ideas, including theology, is intimately bound up with the existing social situation in at least an unconscious way.

Thus the fundamental difference between the traditional academic theologian and the liberation theologian is that the latter feels compelled at every step to combine the disciplines that open up the past with the disciplines that help to explain the present. And he or she feels this necessity precisely in the task of working out and elaborating theology, that is to say, in the task of interpreting the word of God as it is addressed to us here and now.

Without this connection between past and present there is no theology of liberation in the long run. You might get a theology which *deals with* liberation, but its methodological naiveté would prove to be fatal somewhere along the line. It would eventually be reabsorbed by the deeper mechanisms of oppression—one of these being the tendency to incorporate the idiom of liberation into the prevailing language of the status quo.

In this book I am going to try to show that an approach which attempts to relate past and present in dealing with the word of God has to have its own special methodology. I shall give this special methodology a pretentious name and call it the *hermeneutic circle*. Here is a preliminary definition of the hermeneutic circle: it is the continuing change in our interpretation of the Bible which is dictated by the continuing changes in our present-day reality, both individual and societal. "Hermeneutic" means "having to do with interpretation." And the circular nature of this interpretation stems from the fact that each new reality obliges us to interpret the word of God afresh, to change reality accordingly, and then to go back and reinterpret the word of God again, and so on.

The term "hermeneutic circle" is used in a strict sense to designate the method used by Bultmann in interpreting the Scriptures, and the New Testament in particular. At first glance it might seem that my use of the term here is less rigorous. But I hope to show, and the reader will be able to judge this, that my "hermeneutic circle" deserves that designation far more strictly than does Bultmann's. But first I must spell out in greater detail what I am referring to in concrete terms.

I think that two preconditions must be met if we are to have a hermeneutic circle in theology. The first precondition is that the questions rising out of the present be rich enough, general enough, and basic enough to force us to change our customary conceptions of life, death, knowledge, society, politics, and the world in general. Only a change of this sort, or at the very least a pervasive suspicion about our ideas and value judgments concerning those things, will enable us to reach the theological level and force theology to come back down to reality and ask itself new and decisive questions.

The second precondition is intimately bound up with the first. If theology somehow assumes that it can respond to the new questions without changing its customary interpretation of the Scriptures, that immediately terminates the hermeneutic circle. Moreover, if our interpretation of Scripture does not change along with the problems, then the latter will go unanswered; or worse, they will receive old, conservative, unserviceable answers.

It is most important to realize that without a hermeneutic circle, in other words, in those instances where the two aforementioned preconditions are not accepted, theology is always a conservative way of thinking and acting. It is so not so much because of its content but because in such a case it lacks any *here-and-now* criteria for judging our real situation. It thus becomes a pretext for approving the existing situation or for disapproving of it because it does not dovetail with guidelines and canons that are even more ancient and outdated.

It is my feeling that the most progressive theology in Latin America is more interested in *being liberative* than in *talking about liberation*. In other words, liberation deals not so much with content as with the method used to theologize in the face of our real-life situation.

In this chapter I shall present four sample attempts at fashioning a hermeneutic circle. But first I think it would be wise for me to reiterate the two preconditions for such a circle. They are: (1) profound and enriching questions and suspicions about our real situation; (2) a new interpretation of the Bible that is equally profound and enriching. These two preconditions mean that there must in turn be four decisive factors in our circle. *Firstly* there is our way of experiencing reality, which leads us to ideological suspicion. *Secondly* there is the application of our ideological suspicion to the whole ideological superstructure in general and to theology in particular. *Thirdly* there comes a new way of experiencing theological reality that leads us to exegetical suspicion, that is, to the suspicion that the prevailing interpretation of the Bible has not taken important pieces of data into account. *Fourthly* we have our new hermeneutic, that is, our new way of interpreting the fountainhead of our faith (i.e., Scripture) with the new elements at our disposal.

The examples chosen in this chapter may or may not be good ones. But if we keep our attention focused on these four factors, I think the examples will be comprehensible and useful. At least that is my hope.

FIRST SAMPLE ATTEMPT:
COX AND THE SECULAR CITY

As I just indicated, the circle that I described above in theoretical terms begins with a special or particular way of experiencing and evaluating reality in general. It is a critical way of experiencing, almost by its very definition—at least if it is to be the start of a hermeneutic circle. A human being who is content with the world will not have the least interest in unmasking the mechanisms that conceal the authentic reality.

Karl Mannheim writes: "An increasing number of concrete cases makes it evident that (a) every formulation of a problem is made possible only by a *previous actual human experience* which involves such a problem; (b) in selection from the multiplicity of data there is involved an *act of will* on the part of the knower; and (c) forces arising out of living experience are significant in *the direction which the treatment of the problem* follows."[2]

Keeping this in mind about the starting point, let us consider our first sample attempt. Many examples could have been chosen, of course, but I have picked the well-known book of Harvey Cox entitled *The Secular City*. His starting point dovetails with Mannheim's description. It presupposes Cox's own personal experience of his secular society, and it also entails a meaningful selection from the multiplicity of data in that society. Cox is specifically interested in examining the difference between the old way of solving problems and the new way of solving problems that is characteristic of the technopolis. The old way was to appeal to the loftiest human values. The new way is to appeal to the values of technology, to efficiency: in a word, to pragmatic criteria.

One of the subheads in the book, "A Celebration of Its Liberties and an Invitation to Its Discipline," clearly indicates what Mannheim referred to as "an act of will" on the part of the investigator. Harvey Cox *chooses* to celebrate the liberty of the new pragmatic society and, at the same time, to speak to it of Christianity and its message. Thus, as Mannheim indicated, the author's act of will is significant in determining the way in which the problem will be treated. To be specific, Cox does not accept the way people like Tillich choose to deal with theological problems.

That brings us to the second point in our hermeneutic circle: secularization and urbanization provide an ideological basis for interpreting reality—including theological reality—in a new and presumably more correct way. This is clearly suggested by another subhead in the book: "Secularization and Urbanization in Theological Perspective." According to Cox, in other words, a "celebration" of the secular city's liberties and an "invitation" to its discipline should provide us with meaningful direction in our attempt to deal with the theological problems.

As I indicated, the direction in this case will separate Cox's way of dealing with pragmatism from Tillich's way of dealing with it. Cox says: "We should not be dismayed by the fact that fewer and fewer people are pressing what we have normally called 'religious' questions. The fact that urban-secular man is incurably and irreversibly pragmatic, that he is less and less concerned with religious questions, is in no sense a disaster."[3] Cox later says: "We begin by accepting pragmatic man *as he is*, and this means we must part company with Tillich."[4] Why exactly? Because "Tillich's approach has no place for pragmatic man. It is built on the assumption that man by his very nature *must* [Cox's italics too] ask these 'ultimate' or existential questions. . . . We must uncover and bring to consciousness this ultimate concern, Tillich argued, for it poses the question for which the Gospel is the answer."[5]

The real challenge posed to the theology of Cox is this: Can the gospel answer questions that are not even asked by the pragmatic person? In other words, can it answer questions in which ultimate concern is not present?

When we see that Cox gives an affirmative answer to these questions, we find ourselves at the third point of our hermeneutic circle. What exactly is the new theological experience that enables us to pose new questions to the Christian sources? Clearly enough the fundamental feature of this experience is the theologian's dialogue with the pragmatic person. Dialoguing with such a person, Cox finds a new light for interpreting many portions of the biblical message. He discovers the possibility for establishing what he himself calls "a viable theology of revolutionary social change."[6] Here we cannot analyze all the rich implications of his new interpretation. The only thing that is of crucial interest to us here is this question: Will this new theology reach the pragmatic person?

The answer to this question does not come easily. Cox's pragmatic person picks a new Miss America each year. Now if he or she looks to the theologian to find out the meaning of this sexual symbol, this is the answer the pragmatic person gets from Cox: "The Protestant objection to the present cult of The Girl must be based on the realization that the The Girl is an idol. . . . Like every idol she is *ultimately* a creation of our own hands and cannot save us. The values she represents as *ultimate* satisfactions—mechanical comfort, sexual success, unencumbered leisure—have no *ultimacy*."[7]

What has happened here? Well the fact is that Cox is responding to this particular question in exactly the same way that Tillich would. He is appealing to ultimate values instead of accepting pragmatic persons as they are, instead of dropping his concern for those ultimate values. This is clear from the fact that Cox states that pragmatic persons erected this idol because "The Girl is . . . the omnipresent icon of consumer society."[8]

Needless to say, Cox never claimed that the word of God has only the function of approving eveything that goes on in connection with the pragmatic person. His supposition is that Christianity should constitute a critical leaven for pragmatic persons. But what is to be the basis for this critical function if at the same time the theologian is supposed to accept pragmatic persons as they are? If this point is taken seriously, then pragmatic persons as they are must at the very least accept the *basis* of that criticism. And that basis cannot be an appeal to ultimate values because that is clearly not a common basis shared by both the theologian and the pragmatic person.

If we are going to take pragmatic persons as they are, then there is only one way we can be critical with regard to the point in question. We would have to show that the cult of The Girl is not *advantageous* to the interests of consumer society. But can we use Scripture for an argument of that sort? Cox does not seem to think so, since he retreats and takes refuge in arguments like those of Tillich. Those arguments may be valid, but they leave pragmatic persons cold if they truly are pragmatic.

But perhaps it would not be impossible to interpret the Bible and thereby dialogue with pragmatic persons as they are. When all is said and done, the word of God has always dialogued with human beings preoccupied with very practical problems. It has dialogued with people facing the pragmatic necessity of fleeing from bondage in Egypt, with people trying to establish themselves in the promised land, with people facing the task of returning from exile and restoring the kingdom of David. Jesus himself dialogued with disciples who were constantly preoccupied with the notion of trying to make sure that they would get the choice spots in the coming kingdom. Moreover, many portions of the Bible, including the Book of Proverbs and many counsels of Jesus, seem to be completely pragmatic and even downright shrewd. Jesus, for example, advises his disciples how to sneak up to the best places at a banquet table.

In any case Harvey Cox has no intention of formulating a new— pragmatic—interpretation of the Bible in order to continue his dialogue with the people of the secular city. The hermeneutic circle is interrupted when it seemed at the point of reaching its (provisional) terminus: that is, that of providing a new interpretation of Scripture.

Of course *The Secular City* is much more than an interrupted hermeneutic circle. But the latter is our interest here. We are not interested in enumerating all the interesting and fecund points in the book.

Now let us ask another question: Exactly why and where is the circle interrupted? At first glance the latter aspect of the question (where?) seems easy enough to answer. The circle is interrupted at the third point, just before it moves to the fourth point (a new interpretation of the Bible). But if we consider the first part of our question (why?), we arrive at the curious and interesting conclusion that the circle was doomed from the very *first* stage. We now know, albeit *a posteriori*, that Cox never really accepted pragmatic persons as they are or the consumer society as it is. He never really committed himself to them. Thus the "act of will" cited by Mannheim as an essential feature of the starting point was never fully present. And this lack of an enthusiastic base, in my opinion, will prevent Harvey Cox from completing his hermeneutic circle and thus revolutionizing theology in some way. That is true, at least, in the case of his book entitled *The Secular City*.

So let me sum up briefly. A hermeneutic circle in theology always presup- poses a profound human commitment, a *partiality* that is consciously accepted—not on the basis of theological criteria, of course, but on the basis of human criteria.[9]

The word "partiality" may cause surprise, since the common assumption is that a scholarly science starts out from a state of total impartiality. That is precisely the pretension of academic theology. But it is very important that we do not make the mistake of accepting this claim as valid. Academic theology may well be unaware of its unconscious partiality, but the very fact that it poses as something impartial is a sign of its conservative partiality from the very start. We must realize that there is no such thing as an autonomous, impartial, academic theology floating free above the realm of human options and biases. However academic it may be, theology is intimately bound up with the psychological, social, or political status quo though it may not be consciously aware of that fact.

SECOND SAMPLE ATTEMPT: MARX AND HIS CRITIQUE OF RELIGION

Our first example showed us how the hermeneutic circle can be interrupted in the absence of a clearcut and total commitment vis-à-vis some human alternative. As our second example we shall use an author whose partiality and commitment are beyond any shadow of a doubt, whatever one may think of the man or his work. I refer to Karl Marx.

It is not easy to include Marx among the theologians, of course. He himself would be the first to protest such inclusion. At the same time, however, there can be no doubt about his influence on contemporary theology, particularly on the most imaginative and creative types of it.[10]

The point of departure for Marx's thinking, and specifically for its relationship with religion, is the choice he made between interpreting the world and changing it. As Marx sees it, we must change the world, and we must do this with the proletariat and for the proletariat.

Marx tells us that "the history of all hitherto existing society is the history of class struggles."[11] Then he goes on to say: "Our epoch, the epoch of the bourgeoisie, possesses, however, this distinctive feature: it has simplified the class antagonisms. Society as a whole is more and more splitting up into two great hostile camps, into two great classes directly facing each other—bourgeoisie and proletariat."[12]

Thus thinking that intends to change the world means thinking from within this struggle, and of course thinking that will tip the scales in favor of the proletariat.

Nevertheless it is clear that Marx felt a real need throughout his life to explain, more or less implicitly, why it was that the proletariat—the vast majority of people in all the developed nations—were unable to win immediate victory over the minority forces of the bourgeoisie. In the manifesto cited above, Marx notes the fact that "with the development of industry the proletariat not only increases in number; it becomes concentrated in greater masses, its strength grows, and it feels that strength more."[13] All the more reason then to expect quick victory in such an unequal struggle. Despite countless attempts, however, the revolution did not come and Marx died waiting for it. From the start it would seem that Marx was keenly aware of the delay, felt the need to find some explanation for himself, and sought to find some solid basis for his hopes.

I believe that he found what he was looking for in the notion of *historical materialism*. And with this theory of historical materialism we come to the second stage or point of our hermeneutic circle. We now have a theory that enables us to discover the authentic face of reality in line with our own historical commitment.

For our purposes here we need only say that the theory of historical materialism can be summed up in one sentence from the *Manifesto of the Communist Party*: "The ruling ideas of each age have ever been the ideas of its ruling class."[14] This means two things: (1) even the proletariat itself must change its way of thinking about itself because this way of thinking, which seems *natural*, has been imposed on it by the ruling classes in order to conceal the mechanisms of the existing mode of production against which the proletariat must fight; (2) we must view the ideas of a given age—and that would include philosophical, religious, and political ideas among the rest—as more or less determined by the material mode of production peculiar to that age.

Historical materialism, in other words, teaches us two things: (1) the theoretical and practical superstructure depends unwittingly but in large measure on the economic structure of society; (2) even though one cannot possibly expect a profound change in the superstructure unless the economic structure is altered, nevertheless ideological changes are not only possible but also decisive if the proletarian class is to become consciously aware of its own true interests and possibilities, if it is to be revolutionary despite its oppressed condition.

Here we cannot discuss at length the well-known problem of determining the exact content of the term "historical materialism" in Marx's mind. First of all, Marx himself never defined the concept in rigorous terms that would serve to designate the relations between the ideological superstructure and the economic structure. He used different words in that connection and qualified them with different adjectives and adverbs to compound the problem. So it is easy to see why there are as many different explanations of historical materialism today as there are commentators on Marx. At times Marx seems to say that the economic structure *determines* the ideologies; at times he seems to say that it *produces* the ideologies; at times he seems to say that it *conditions* them; and sometimes he even seems to say that it *is conditioned* to some extent by them.

If we take Marx's work as a whole, it seems that we can say without fear of error that Marx never failed to include these two conditions in the revolutionary struggle of the proletariat: (1) economic change in the existing mode of production; (2) the theoretical liberation of human consciousness vis-à-vis the ideologies that conceal and sacralize the existing mode of production that is exploiting the proletariat.

Let us cite some passages from Marx that tend to confirm this. In the Prologue to *A Contribution to the Critique of Political Economy*, Marx says: "The mode of production in material life determines the *general* [here we have one of those qualifying words that modify a determinist statement] character of the social, political, and spiritual processes of life. It is not the consciousness of man that determines their existence, but, on the contrary, their social existence determines their consciousness." A little further on he elaborates:

"With the change of the economic foundation the entire immense superstructure is *more* or *less rapidly* transformed. In considering such transformations the distinction should always be made between the material transformation of the economic condition of production which can be determined with the precision of natural science, and the legal, political, religious, asthetic or philosophic—in short, ideological forms in which men *become conscious* of this conflict and fight it out."[15]

Now is this distinction designed to tell the proletariat that it should leave aside the *ideological* struggle or rely wholly on the economic process alone? While Marx's work as a whole clearly gives the lie to such an hypothesis, certain passages in his work do seem to point in that direction. In *The German Ideology*, for example, he writes: "Morality, religion, metaphysics, and other ideologies . . . no longer retain . . . their appearance of autonomous existence."[16] He goes on to say:

> It does not explain practice from the idea but explains the formation of ideas from material practice, and accordingly comes to the conclusion that all the forms of and products of consciousness can be dissolved, not by intellectual criticism . . . but only by the practical overthrow of the actual social relations, . . . that not criticism but revolution is the driving force of history, as well as of religion, philosophy, and all other types of theory.[17]

Now all this may be true, but Marx cannot forget the other side of the revolutionary process: that is, the necessity of creating a revolutionary class. In the same work he admits that "associated with this is the emergence of a class . . . which comprises the majority of the members of society and in which there develops a *consciousness* of the need for a fundamental revolution."[18]

In *Capital*, too, Marx stressed the necessity of using this approach to the study of ideological problems, implying that it represents a new and scientific way of dealing with these problems, particularly the religious ones:

> Any history of religion . . . that fails to take account of this material basis is uncritical. It is, in practice, much easier to discover by analysis the earthly core of the misty creations of religion, than, conversely, *to infer from the actual relations of life at any period the corresponding "spiritualized" forms of those relations*. But the latter method is the only materialistic, and therefore the only scientific one.[19]

Here Marx is claiming to detach himself from the approach that Darwin uses to disqualify religion, from the easy way out. The difficult but scientific approach to religious problems, the only one that Marx accepts in theory, involves three suppositions: (1) that each and every religious form has a specific place in the ideological superstructure of a given age; (2) that the prevailing religious forms of an age, including those accepted by the oppressed class, derive from the living experience of the dominant classes; and (3) that the process of discovering this connection abets the revolutionary forces of the proletariat.

This at least is what Marx affirms with regard to all the other levels of the social superstructure: legislation, political parties, labor unions, cultural forms, and so forth. So we find ourselves now at the third stage of the hermeneutic circle. When we view religion under the lens of ideological suspicion, it shows up as two things: (1) as a specific interpretation of Scripture imposed by the ruling classes in order to maintain their exploitation—though this intention may never be made explicit; and (2) as an opportunity for the proletariat to convert religion into their own weapon in the class struggle through a new and more faithful interpretation of the Scriptures.

But what happens at this point in the case of Marx? The circle stops because he goes against his own principles. Instead of examining the specific concrete and historical possibilities of religion and theology, he takes the easy way out of disqualifying religion in general insofar as he views it as an autonomous and a historical monolith. In the thought of Marx, religion is not viewed as belonging to an ambiguous superstructure. Instead it is viewed as belonging to a purely spiritual plane or, even worse, as being a merely ideal refutation of historical materialism.

At one point Marx writes: "Religious suffering is at the same time an expression of real suffering and *a protest against real suffering*."[20] Now if that is the case, one would assume that Marx would proceed to infer the exact nature of the concrete spiritualized form of this protest against real suffering in each age. But instead he goes on to say: "Religion . . . is the opium of the people. The *abolition* of religion, as the illusory happiness of men, is a demand for their real happiness."[21] Instead of "abolition," one would expect Marx to have talked about "changing" religion so that it might accentuate and eventually correct the situation being protested against.

Thus the hermeneutic circle of theology is interrupted. To be sure, we could cite various passages from Marx's writings in which his profound intuition spotlights the social influence of such dogmas as that of original sin and individual salvation. Marx, along with Freud and Nietzsche, is regarded by Paul Ricoeur as one of the great masters of "suspicion." But somehow Marx does not seem to have ever entertained the suspicion that ideology could have warped the thinking of the theologians and the interpreters of Scripture so that they ended up unwittingly interpreting it in a sense that served the interests of the ruling classes. Marx does not seem to have shown any interest in trying to find out whether distortion had crept into the Christian message and whether a new interpretation favoring the class struggle of the proletariat might be possible or even necessary.

From our standpoint, the important thing is to determine at what point the circle was interrupted. At the third point, it might seem. But it might be interesting and worthwhile to show that is was really interrupted at the second stage, and that Marx's hermeneutic circle was doomed to interruption from there on.

To fully appreciate the significance of the third point or stage in the herme-neutic circle of theology, we must realize that it is a repetition of the first stage in the more restricted area of theology proper. If the first stage assumes a commitment to change the world, the third stage assumes a commitment to change theology. The third stage, in other words, reproduces the three elements that Mannheim spelled out for the first stage: a concrete evaluational experi-ence of theology, an act of the will on the part of the theologian with respect to his theology, and a direction in treating new problems that derives from this act of the will.

Now while Marx made a personal commitment to change the world, he never had a personal experience of theology as a science tied to sources. A philosophy of religion cannot perform the same function as theology, since it does not feel bound to an interpretation of the biblical sources. Moreover, Marx's act of will to abolish religion is not an act of will from within theology itself, an act of will that could signify a change in the way of treating problems theologically. It is rather an abandonment of them.

We know for a fact that during the course of Marx's lifetime his thinking moved from a basic preoccupation with the problems of the ideological superstructure towards a deepening interest in the economic structure. The whole subject of ideology is still present in *Capital*, but that is due to the need to refute the ideas of the ruling class concerning economics—or, to be more specific, concerning the science of economics.

One can of course debate, as Althusser has done, the whole question as to whether there was one Marx or two. That debate makes little sense to me. But even if it were meaningful, it would have little import for our discussion here. The important point is that for some reason or another Marx never managed to carry out the scientific task he had proposed to do: that is, to infer the specific, spiritualized forms in the superstructure that correspond to the material pro-duction relationships. To put it a little better, he never managed to carry out that task at the level of the complex societies existing in his own day and ours, leaving that task for present-day Marxism. In *The German Ideology*, for example, we find a profound and powerful analysis of the relationship between culture and production in primitive societies. But his analysis becomes ever weaker and more superficial as it attempts to tackle industrial society—or even the feudal society of the Middle Ages.

This would seem to suggest, in principle at least, that the more or less developed social sciences should be able to carry through the analysis which Marx foresaw and described and set in motion but which he never carried through on certain decisive levels. In any case Marx's work was such a stimu-lus for theology that new methods and profound questions in present-day theology are an inheritance from him, even though Marx had rejected the-ology.

Let me sum up. The purpose of my second example is to make it clear that a general theory about our perception of reality is called upon to be incorporated into theological methodology. For insofar as it discovers a deeper or rich layer of reality, it enriches theology with new questions and obliges it to undertake a new interpretation of its own sources. Even if it did just that and nothing else, any general theory capable of providing a methodology for ideological analysis would deserve to be called liberative; for in doing that, it would keep biblical interpretation moving back and forth between its sources and present-day reality. It would thus free academic theology from its atavism and its ivory tower, toppling the naive self-conception it entertains at present: that is, that it is a simple, eternal, impartial interpretation, or authorized translation, of the word of God.

THIRD SAMPLE ATTEMPT: WEBER ON CALVINISM AND CAPITALISM

For our third example we shall use a thinker who certainly did make the move from the second to the third[22] stage of the hermeneutic circle. I refer to Max Weber.

Like Marx, Weber was not a theologian. But his work obliged him to engage in theological activity to the point where Weber styled himself an "amateur theologian." He was at least that, and a brilliant one. Let us consider a specific work of his.

In one of his most well-known works, Weber's sociological interest led him to study the principal dogmas of Calvinism in connection with the economic attitudes of Western captialism, using in the process a methodology whose roots can and must be traced back to Marx's historical materialism.

That statement might sound strange to some ears, for Weber has often been dubbed the *Anti-Marx*. Weber's more or less implicit commitment to Western capitalism would seem to place him at the opposite end of the spectrum from Marx and his commitment to the proletariat. But that is not the key reason why Max Weber is dubbed the *Anti-Marx*. The principal reason, in my opinion, is the supposition that Marx's historical materialism is a kind of economic determinism. This supposition is in fact bolstered by official Marxism. But if we recall Engel's famous disclaimer on this point, as well as many texts of Marx himself, then I do not think that one can maintain any radical opposition between the methodology of Weber and that of Marx.[23] It seems clear that Weber's intention was to complement rather than to correct Marx; or at most to correct an excessive emphasis on the economic structure.

In any case, both Marx and Weber base their sociological analysis on the necessary and inevitable relationship between economic and cultural forms, between structure and superstructure. In his analysis Weber concretely tries to point out both the *necessity* and the *possibilities* of carrying forward the analysis of the cultural superstructure of modern society. And in doing this he takes two things for granted: (1) the *relative* independence of the elements of a complex superstructure vis-à-vis the presently existing system of economic production; (2) the *relative* influence of these superstructural forms in adapting people's attitudes to a specific mode of production. I do not think that either of these two presuppositions is opposed to the underlying thought of Marx.

In the first part of the book in question, *The Protestant Ethic and the Spirit of Capitalism*, Weber defines his sociological intention very precisely: "We have no intention whatever of maintaining such a foolish and doctrinaire thesis as that the spirit of capitalism . . . could only have arisen as the result of certain effects of the Reformation, or even that capitalism as an economic system is a creation of the Reformation [theses that would be directly opposed to Marx's historical materialism]. . . . *On the contrary*, we only wish to ascertain whether and to what extent religious forces have taken part in the qualitative formation and the quantitative expansion of that spirit over the world."[24] In the realm of theory at least, it would be difficult to find a more genuine expression of Marx's thinking about ideological analysis in connection with historical materialism.

Weber's lack of social commitment immediately suggests that he too will fail to complete our hermeneutic circle. But because of what we have just said, we are going to take Weber as our third example here because we have reason to believe that he will make the move from the second to the third step. In other words, it is as if Marx had carried out his proposal to infer the spiritualized forms that correspond to the mode of production at the start of the capitalist era.

It would be futile to try to sum up Weber's detailed exposition of the principal dogmas of the earliest Calvinist era and their later versions among other practicing sects: that is, pietism, Methodism, and the Baptist sects. Amateur theologian Weber correctly expounds the dogmas in question and establishes their interrelationships in highly intelligent fashion. He also does a very good job of grasping the differences between the thought of Calvin and that of the two other major theologies of the period: that is, the Lutheran and the Catholic.

An academic theologian might well be put off by Weber's lack of interest in the fonts of theology. Weber certainly pays little attention to the connection between the dogmas he is examining and the internal logic of the Reformation. He is even less interested in some possible distortion of the biblical message— with the exception of two cases which we shall mention further on. His only interest is to find the relationship between really existing ideas, wherever they may come from, and attitudes really existing in the realm of ethical and economic praxis. Weber writes:

> We are naturally not concerned with the question of what was theoreti-
> cally and officially taught in the ethical compendia of the time, however
> much practical significance this may have had. . . . We are interested
> rather in something entirely different: the influence of those psychologi-
> cal sanctions which, *originating in religious belief* and the practice of
> religion, gave a direction to practical conduct and held the individual to
> it.[25]

Despite this pragmatic point of view regarding religious ideas, Max Weber carefully examines the complex structure of Calvin's thought and the reasons which forced his separation from both the Catholic Church and Martin Luther's thinking. He makes an in-depth study of many key doctrines and then compares them with the analogous doctrines in other theological systems. Among the doctrines he examines meticulously are: original sin, the grace of God, predestination to heaven and to damnation, the means for proving the state of grace, the desperate preoccupation with the signs of predestination to heaven, the glory of God as evidenced in natural and historical events, and the quest for some form of certainty outside one's own self.

Thus Max Weber does not take the easy way out of writing off the "earthly core" of religion—as Marx in fact does while censuring that approach. Instead he takes the difficult but scientific path of "inferring the spiritualized forms" that go hand in hand with the real conduct of human beings at that particular point in the process of material production.

To accomplish this, Weber builds a psychological bridge between economic attitudes and religious beliefs. For example, he asserts that it is not just logic that connects the religious superstructure to economic attitudes; many times there is an unexpected psychological connection between the two:

> The Calvinistic faith is one of the many examples in the history of religions of the relation between the logical and the *psychological* consequences for the practical religious attitude to be derived from certain religious ideas. Fatalism is, of course, the only logical consequence of predestination. But on account of the idea of proof [of predestination], the psychological result was precisely the opposite [of fatalism].[26]

Stressing the psychological relationship between the superstructure and economic attitudes does not mean that Weber is trying to evade the social and political consequences of ideas. On the contrary, psychology enables him to carry out the task that Marx had talked about. In the complex realm of the whole superstructure he is able to infer the "spiritualized forms" which often correspond to economic attitudes. Psychology, in short, is a decisive feature of any modern ideological analysis of a complex social superstructure.

Now when all is said and done, the reader must not forget that the relationship discovered by Weber between Protestant Calvinism and the spirit of Western capitalism has never been proved by any empirical sociology, much less by statistical studies. Recall Weber's statement of intent: "to ascertain whether and to what extent religious forces have taken part in *the qualitative formation and the quantitative expansion* of that spirit over the world." Well, then, how are we to evaluate the outcome of this twofold intention?

It does not seem probable that the second aspect (the "quantitative" expansion) could ever be proved by a *behaviorist* sociology such as that which prevails at present, nor by any other sociology with objective scientific methods. The part that might have been played by religious forces in the quantitative expansion of the capitalist spirit seems destined to remain a mystery forever. It is hard to explain how Max Weber, in his own day, could have imagined scientific or statistical verification of that sort.

The first aspect (the "qualitative" formation) is not really susceptible of empirical proof either. But if that is true, it is because it basically does not need any such proof. The probative force of Weber's hypothesis lies in a comparison of various concepts. And since it is a qualitative matter, it is hard to see how it could be proved with the quantitative methods of an empirical science. In that sense one can say that Weber's hypothesis is proved, since the conceptual relationship that he establishes by analogy between the two sets of phenomena is clear.

If one wanted to argue with Weber's thesis at all, it would be in connection with the point brought out by Talcott Parsons, the scholar who translated Weber's book into English. He says: "It is the temptation of one who expounds a new and fruitful idea to use it as a key to unlock all doors, and to explain by reference to a single principle phenomena which are, in reality, the result of several converging causes."[27] But it is not our task here to pass judgment on Weber. We are interested only in examining the methodology he uses to move from a general ideology to the specific analysis of theological ideas.

That brings us to the third point of our hermeneutic circle. We must ask ourselves: What is the real experience of Weber himself vis-à-vis the theological reality which he has just discovered, and which he has seen to be linked with all sorts of human vicissitudes and options such as those connected with the course of capitalism? Does he experience that theological life laid hold of in history as a need for judging Calvinism by its fruits? What might its value be in the interpretation of Scripture, once one realizes that this interpretation gives structure to the lives of many human beings in precisely that form?

Strange as it may seem, none of those questions interests Max Weber: "We are here concerned not with the *evaluation*, but the historical significance of the dogma."[28] Even if this particular religious belief were the cause of an atomic war, in other words, Weber would still not be interested in evaluating it. He would simply be interested in considering its historical significance, its bare results. He expresses the same basic intention a bit more precisely elsewhere in the same book: "In such a study, it may at once be definitely stated, no attempt is made to evaluate the ideas of the Reformation in any sense, whether it concerns their *social* or their *religious* worth."[29]

If we can still hear the echo of Marx's passionate voice, we will find it relatively difficult to believe in Weber's impartiality when we read some of his statements. He notes, for example: "The emphasis on the ascetic importance of a fixed calling provided an ethical justification of the modern specialized *division of labor*. In a similar way the providential interpretation of profit-making justified the activities of the businessman."[30] Why? Because "it gave him the comforting assurance that the unequal distribution of the goods of this world was a special dispensation of Divine Providence, which in these differences, as in particular grace, pursued secret ends unknown to men. Calvin himself had made the much-quoted statement that only when the people, i.e. the mass of laborers and craftsmen, were poor did they remain obedient to God."[31]

This description of the ethical attitudes deriving from religious ideas, the unequivocal irony in Weber's tone and the use of certain terms that echo Marx, would seem to suggest a clearcut partiality, a value judgment, on the author's part. We find the same thing in another similar description: "This consciousness of divine grace of the elect and holy was accompanied by an attitude toward the sin of one's neighbour, not of sympathetic understanding based on consciousness of one's own weakness, but of *hatred* and *contempt* for him as an enemy of God bearing the signs of eternal damnation."[32] To any unprejudiced listener, the attitudes thus described would seem ignoble and inhuman. Yet in Weber's eyes such a description does not constitute a negative judgment on the theological ideas that lend support to those attitudes.

To go even further, Weber is quite capable of "impartially" using descriptive phrases such as "extreme inhumanity." In a central passage of the book, he writes:

> In its extreme inhumanity this doctrine must above all have had one consequence for the life of a generation which surrendered to its magnificent consistency. That was a feeling of unprecedented inner loneliness of the single individual. In what was for the man of the age of the Reformation the most important thing in life, his eternal salvation, he was forced to follow his path alone to meet a destiny which had been decreed for him from eternity. No one could help him.[33]

Not even when he uses such qualifying phrases and descriptions as these does Weber admit that he is making a value judgment on Calvinism. And he insists on his impartiality explicitly. One might well wonder whether it is not even more inhuman to perceive and comprehend that whole network of implications without judging it than to have created it in the first place in the belief that it was the only thing that fully and logically dovetailed with the fonts of divine revelation.

At two points Weber does allow himself to challenge the soundness and solidity of Calvin's interpretation of the Bible. But they are only passing observations; they do not represent an evaluational theological commitment. Just before the section cited in the last note, Weber writes this: "The Father in heaven of the New Testament, so human and understanding, who rejoices over the repentance of a sinner as a woman over the lost piece of silver she has found, *is gone*. His place has been taken by a transcendental being, beyond the reach of human understanding."[34] A little later he writes: "It was thus in the last analysis the peculiar, fundamentally ascetic, character of Calvinism itself which made it *select and assimilate those elements of Old Testament religion which suited it best*."[35]

At first glance such judgments might seem to indicate that Weber is making his first moves from the third to the fourth stage of the hermeneutic circle: in other words, that he is moving towards a new and enriched interpretation of the biblical sources. But that is not the case. Weber is not interested in finding a more authentic and richer theology to liberate people from the anxiety and loneliness which, among other things, are part of the influence of Calvinist theology on their society. For the sake of extending the range of knowledge as far as possible, Weber simply wants to make comparisons between different religious ideas insofar as they exert influence on different economic attitudes. There is no personal commitment involved.

Karl Mannheim, another disciple of Marx, can help to explain this attitude for us. The reader will recall that Mannheim posits an "act of will" on the part of the thinker as a necessary precondition for authentic sociological interpretation. But later on, after he has demonstrated the need for an ideological analysis of all the ideas and molds of a culture, Mannheim seems to forget his point of departure regarding the "act of will." For he concludes with this remark: "That which within a given group is accepted as absolute appears to the outsider conditioned by the group situation and recognized as *partial*. . . . This type of knowledge presupposes *a more detached perspective*."[36] That is precisely the case with Weber.

Right now I think I have made it sufficiently clear to the reader what the last systematic obstacle for any theology committed to human liberation is. It is a certain type of academicism which posits ideological neutrality as the ultimate criterion; which levels down and relativizes all claims to absoluteness and all evaluations of some ideas over others. This is the theological equivalent of another great ideological adversary of liberation: the so-called quest for the *death of ideologies* or their suicide on the altars of scientific and scholarly impartiality.[37]

FOURTH SAMPLE ATTEMPT:
CONE AND BLACK THEOLOGY OF LIBERATION

Let us move on to a fourth example. This time the hermeneutic circle will be completed. Remember that this fact in itself is not a sufficient proof of the truth of the theology in question. The hermeneutic circle itself merely proves that a theology is alive, that it is connected up with the vital fountainhead of historical reality. Without the latter source, the other font of divine revelation would remain dry, not because of anything wrong with it but because of our own opaqueness.

The fourth example is provided by James Cone in his book entitled *A Black Theology of Liberation*. Though the language of the book might seem to be a bit demagogic and shocking—all depending on the color of your skin and your thinking perhaps—Cone's book is a much more serious theological effort than many people might think at first glance. In any case it affords us a chance to see and examine all four points in our hermeneutic circle.

Cone's interpretation begins with personal experience and an act of will on the part of the investigator, as Mannheim posited. Now it is obvious that any "act of will" in the limited range of human possibilities comes down to taking a stand for some individual or community over against other individuals and communities. There is no help for it. Every hermeneutic entails conscious or unconscious partisanship. It is partisan in its viewpoint even when it believes itself to be neutral and tries to act that way.

What is noteworthy and important here is the fact that partiality is not in itself inimical to universality. The possibility of achieving a higher degree of universality through an interpretation of facts does not depend on some sort of impossible *horizontal* partiality, so to speak. It depends on making a good choice insofar as our commitment and our partial point of view is concerned. For the universality in mind here has to do with getting down to the deeper human roots that explain attitudes which are truly universal in their value and influence.

Right from the start of Cone's book, a consciously accepted partiality shows up as a positive and decisive element. For him theology is

a rational study of the being of God in the world in light of the existential situation of an oppressed community, relating the forces of liberation to the essence of the gospel, which is Jesus Christ. This means that *its sole reason for existence* is to put into ordered speech the meaning of God's activity in the world, *so that the community of the oppressed will recognize that their inner thrust for liberation is not only consistent with the gospel but is the gospel of Jesus Christ.*[38]

Thus Cone, not worrying about causing scandal to academic theology, goes on to establish the usefulness of a particular historical community as the criterion for any subsequent theological investigation: "Black Theology will not spend too much time trying to answer the critics *because it is accountable only to the black community.*"[39] The universality that is renounced on the horizontal level is recovered in spades on a deeper level of the human condition—that is, where it is revealed to us in an oppressed community that is still in need of liberation. In the process of liberation, the one and only truth is the truth of liberation itself as defined by the oppressed in their struggle: "The revolutionary situation forces Black Theology to shun all abstract principles dealing with what is the 'right' and 'wrong' course of action. There is only one principle which guides the thinking and action of Black Theology: an unqualified commitment to the black community as that community seeks to define its existence in the light of God's liberating work in the world."[40]

Before moving on to the second stage of the hermeneutic circle, a few comments on this point of departure are very much in order. In seminaries and universities we are used to the idea of considering theology as an academic discipline, as a degree program in the liberal arts. The historical fact is that once upon a time theologizing was a very different sort of activity, a dangerous one in fact. It certainly was not a "liberal art" for men like the prophets and Jesus. They died before their time because of their theologizing, because of their specific way of interpreting the word of God and its implications for the liberation of the oppressed.

Perhaps the reader may now understand more readily why only academic theologians can talk about the "death of God." In the concrete struggle for liberation, the danger is not the death of God but the death of the theologian, God's interpreter. The theologian may well die in the very name of God, who draws a sharp dividing line between the two opposing positions with regard to liberation.

Faced with these two alternatives (that is, theology as an academic profession versus theology as a revolutionary activity), I must confess that I can understand those who refuse to do theology or to have anything to do with it, because they feel it has no meaning or value for the liberation process, much better than I can understand those who practice it as an academic discipline in the security of some chamber immune to the risks of the liberation struggle. We are fortunate that our God takes a stand in history, and our interpretation of God's word must follow the same path. Cone is quite right when he refers to theology as a "passionate language."[41]

Arriving at the second stage in our circle, we must find a theory of some general nature which will enable us to unmask the reality of oppression in general, and specifically its repercussions in theology. For oppression usually does not reveal itself in barefaced fashion; it hides and hallows itself behind ideologies that obscure what is really happening in concrete human reality.

One cannot say that Cone is Marxist in his analysis, for he explicitly diverges from Marx on occasion. For example, he states that the basis of exploitation is not an economic difference which forms different social classes but rather the racial difference which is rooted far more deeply in human psychology. At the same time, however, Cone's divergence here is not as alien to historical materialism as it might seem at first glance. Rather it complements or corrects Marx, pointing up a factor which has been, and continues to be, important in the division of labor. What Mannheim says in a general way might be applied to Cone here. The fact is that many of the elements which Marx used in his ideological analysis of the exploitation of the proletariat have become general features of Western culture—more specifically, of the general methodology of the sociology of knowledge. This means that they can and often are used independently of any Marxist or even socialist commitment.

Cone is certainly aware of ideological mechanisms and takes them into account in his theologizing. For example, he writes:

> This does not mean that Black Theology rejects white theology entirely. Unfortunately, this cannot be done, since oppression always means that the communication skills of an oppressed community are determined to a large degree by the oppressors. That is precisely the meaning of oppres-

sion! Since black theologians are trained in white seminaries and white thinkers make decisions about the structure and scope of theology, it is not possible for black religionists to separate themselves *immediately* from white thought.[42]

At the same time, however, Cone does not forget that theology is only *one* of the forms of the total superstructure that go to make up the state. He notes:

> Unfortunately, American white theology has not been involved in the struggle for black liberation. It has been basically a theology of the white oppressor, *giving religious sanction* to the genocide of Indians and the enslavement of black people. From the very beginning to the present day, American white theological thought has been "patriotic," either by defining the theological task *independently of black suffering* (the liberal northern approach) or by defining Christianity as compatible with white racism (the conservative southern approach). In both cases theology becomes *a servant of the state*, and that can only mean death to black people.[43]

The fine edge of Cone's ideological analysis shows up in the fact that he manages to espy the most potent weapon of the adversary in this ideological conflict. That weapon is an ideology claiming to be *color-blind*. In other words, the oppressor constructs an ideological edifice in which the *cause* of the oppressed people's suffering is not even mentioned, much less studied. In this way law, philosophy, and religion join with the mechanism of oppression and become its witting or unwitting accomplices: "That is why American theology discusses sin in the abstract, debating it in relation to *universal man*. In white theology, sin is *a theoretical idea and not a concrete reality*."[44] In other words, "there is no place in Black Theology for a colorless God in a society *where people suffer precisely because of their color*."[45]

Cone therefore calls for a more concrete and realistic sensitivity so that this sort of rationalization will be wiped out in a society where color is a decisive factor:

> When blackness is equated with freedom as a symbol both of oppression and of the possibility of man, white people feel left out of things. "What about the oppression of whites?" they ask. "Is it not true that the enslaver also enslaves himself, which makes him a member of the community of the oppressed?" There is a danger inherent in these questions. If white intellectuals, religionists, and assorted liberals can convince themselves that the white condition is *analogous* to the black condition, then there is no reason to respond to the demands of the black community. "After all, we are all oppressed," they say, *rationalizing* with a single stroke the whole white way of life.[46]

The more a humanism purports to be universal and spiritual, the more danger there is that it will leave concrete liberation aside. Why? Because then the real cause of oppression fades from the mind. As Cone puts it:

> White theologians. . .would probably concede that the concept of libera-tion is essential to the biblical view of God. But it is still impossible for them to translate the biblical emphasis on liberation to the black-white struggle today. Invariably they quibble on this issue, moving from side to side, *always pointing out the dangers of extremism on both sides. . . .* They really cannot make a decision, because it has been made already for them. The way in which scholars would analyze God and black people was decided when black slaves were brought to this land, while church-men sang "Jesus, Lover of My Soul."[47]

That final note of ironic spiritualism verifies what we said above: both univer-sality and spirituality are ideological mechanisms of theology.

It should be evident that Cone arrives at the third stage of the hermeneutic circle with a new experience of theology and with an act of will to place it in the service of the black community. Thus the new direction to be taken by scrip-tural interpretation will be dictated by the uncovering of the mechanisms of ideology and by the will to root them out of theology.

In doing the latter, the important thing is not so much not to accept the accustomed answers of theology but rather not to shoulder the accustomed questions of theology. As Cone puts it:

> It is clear, therefore, that the most important decisions in theology are made at this juncture. The sources and norm are presuppositions that determine *which questions are to be asked*, as well as the answers that are given. Believing that the biblical Christ is the sole criterion for theology, Barth not only asks questions about man that arise from a study of Christology, but he also derives his answers from the man Jesus. Tillich, on the other hand, deals with questions that arise from the cultural situation of man, and endeavors to shape his answers according to that situation. Both approaches are conditioned by their theological perspec-tives. Because a perspective refers to *the whole of a man's being in the context of a community*, the sources and norm of Black Theology *must be consistent with the perspective of the black community.*[48]

Put another way: "Black theologians must work in such a way as to destroy the corruptive influence of white thought by building theology on the sources and norm that are appropriate to the black community."[49]

If we should ask Cone what he considers "appropriate to the black commu-nity," his initial response would be that an oppressed community needs a theology by which to become aware of itself as people "who are in search of new ways of talking about God which will enhance *their understanding of themselves.*"[50] If this particular task is to be properly undertaken by theology (rather than by education or politics, for example), then of course there must be a change in the notion of God and God's plans: "It is unthinkable that the oppressors could identify with oppressed existence and thus say something relevant about God's liberation of the oppressed. In order to be Christian theology, white theology must cease being white theology and become Black Theology by denying whiteness as a proper form of human existence and affirming blackness as *God's intention for humanity*."[51]

From the theological standpoint it is worth noting that Cone, with only one exception, makes these decisive options regarding the pathway that theology is to take before he comes to treat the sources and norm of an authentic theology specifically. At first glance it might seem that theology is being determined by alien criteria. But since theology is part of the superstructure, the ground must be broken by first rooting up the ideological traps. Hence ideological criteria are logically *prior*, but in no way *alien* to theology.

When Cone begins to list the fonts of theology, he begins by listing the experience, the history, and the culture of black people rather than Scripture. He fully realizes that this will scandalize academic theology, which has a long tradition of proceeding quite differently. But he is not alone in such an approach, and he can cite Tillich in his favor: "I am not unaware of the danger that in this way [the method of relating theology to culture] the substance of the Christian message may be lost. Nevertheless, this danger must be risked, and once one has realized this, one must proceed in this direction. Dangers are not a reason for avoiding a serious demand."[52]

Cone goes on to say:

> Though Tillich was not speaking of the black situation, his words are applicable to it. To be sure, as Barth pointed out, God's Word is alien to man and thus comes to him as a "bolt from the blue," but one must be careful about which man one is speaking of. For the oppressors, the dehumanizers, the analysis is correct. However, when we speak of God's revelation to the oppressed, then analysis is incorrect. His revelation comes to us in and through the cultural situation of the oppressed. His Word is our word; his existence, our existence.[53]

On the other hand, if Scripture stands as the unique and unbalanced criterion for theology, then one cannot avoid *literalism* and the consequent ideological justification of oppression. As Cone puts it:

> Literalism always means the removal of doubt in religion, and thus enables the believer to justify all kinds of political oppression in the name of God and country. During slavery black people were encouraged to be obedient slaves because it was the will of God. After all, Paul did say "slaves, obey your master"; and because of the "curse of Ham," blacks have been condemned to be inferior to whites. Even today the same kind of literalism is being used by white scholars to encourage black people to

be nonviolent, as if nonviolence were the only possible expression of Christian love. It is surprising that it never dawns on these white religionists that oppressors are in no moral position to dictate what a Christian response is. Jesus' exhortations "turn the other cheek" and "go the second mile" are no evidence that black people should let white people beat the hell out of them. We cannot use Jesus' behavior in the first century as a literal guide for our actions in the twentieth century. . . . Scripture . . . is not a guide which makes our decisions for us.[54]

To avoid the danger signaled by Tillich as well as the danger of literalism, one need only erect a theology on a twofold base or source:

Black people have heard enough about God. What they want to know is what God has to say about the black condition. Or, more importantly, what is he doing about it? What is his relevance in the struggle against the forces of evil which seek to destroy black being? These are the questions which must shape the character of the norm of Black Theology. On the other hand, Black Theology must not overlook the biblical revelation. This means that Black Theology should not devise a norm which ignores the encounter of the black community with the revelation of God. Whatever it says about liberation must be said in the light of the black community's experience of Jesus Christ.[55]

In short, "the norm of Black Theology must take seriously two realities, actually two aspects of a single reality: the liberation of black people and the revelation of Jesus Christ."[56]

With this new experience of theological reality, this act of will and its directional impulse, Cone arrives at the fourth stage of the hermeneutic circle: that is, the new interpretation of Scripture based on new and decisive questions. His hermeneutic orientation might be summed up in these words:

If I read the New Testament correctly, the resurrection of Christ means that he is also present today in the midst of all societies effecting his liberation of the oppressed. He is not confined to the first century, and thus our talk of him in the past is important only insofar as it leads us to an *encounter* with him *now*. As a black theologian, I want to know what God's revelation means right now as the black community participates in the struggle for liberation.[57]

It must be stressed once again that the simultaneous presence of past and present in biblical interpretation is an essential hermeneutic principle. The value of this orientation for achieving a richer interpretation of Scripture lies in the fact that one thereby rediscovers a pedagogical principle that presides over the whole process of divine revelation. The fact is that God shows up in a different light when God's people find themselves in different historical situations. That does not simply mean that we must take pains to re-create each specific historical context in the past. For if God is continuously revealed in a different light, then the truth about God must be different also. The Israelites moving out of Egypt and heading for the promised land received the revelation of God's wrath towards their enemies. That particular revelation has little or nothing to do with the image of God which the gospel message conveys when it urges people to ''turn the other cheek,'' or when Paul urges slaves to obey their masters.

When all is said and done, what is one to say about God today to people who are in a situation akin to that of the ancient Israelites? That the latter and later image wipes out the earlier one? Cone gives his answer: "Black Theology then asks not whether love is an essential element of the Christian interpretation of God, but whether the love of God itself can be properly understood without focusing equally on the biblical view of God's righteousness. Is it possible to understand what God's love means for the oppressed without making *wrath* an essential ingredient of that love?"[58] Somewhat further on he says: "The wrath of God is the love of God in regard to the forces against his liberation of the oppressed."[59]

It may well be difficult for us to appreciate the total novelty and freshness of this principle which is introduced into theological interpretation by Cone. For the fact is that from the viewpoint of orthodoxy one of those images of God must necessarily be false at a given moment. Either the old or the new image has to be false at a given point if God is to continue being *universal,* according to the orthodox viewpoint. Cone's logic forces him to reject this search for universality which seems to be the key to the orthodox interpretation of the Bible. He writes: "Some readers will object to the absence of the 'universal note' in the foregoing assertions, asking, "How can you reconcile the lack of universalism regarding human nature with a universal God?' The first reply is to deny that there is a 'universal God' in the normal understanding of the concept."[60]

What is Cone trying to say here? Unless I am mistaken, he is asserting that orthodoxy possesses no ultimate criterion in itself because being orthodox does not mean possessing the final truth. We only arrive at the latter by orthopraxis. It is the latter that is the ultimate criterion of the former, both in theology and in biblical interpretation. The truth is truth only when it serves as the basis for truly human attitudes. "Doers of the truth" is the formula used by divine revelation to stress the priority of orthopraxis over orthodoxy when it comes to truth and salvation.

Needless to say, there are many hermeneutic dangers in this approach to conceiving and carrying out biblical interpretation, just as there were in the previous stage. But just because it entails dangers one cannot rule out a particular theological method which is consistent.

Speaking of dangers, for example, one can readily appreciate the fact that the community which Jesus counseled to turn the other cheek could not very well represent the Israelite community that was physically enslaved in Egypt or

Babylon. So one should not be too quick to generalize Jesus' advice as if it had been given to humanity for any and all ages, thereby correcting the Old Testament which was also the revelation of God. As it turns out, however, one of the things revealed by God to the exiles in Babylon was the redemptive value of suffering as personified in the Suffering Servant of Yahweh. One might well ask Cone himself why that message to a physically enslaved people is not God's revelation to the Black community of the present day. For Cone claims that it is not: "The black prophet is a rebel with a cause, the cause of over twenty-five million American blacks and all oppressed men everywhere. It is God's cause because he has chosen the blacks as his own. And he has chosen them *not for redemptive suffering but for freedom. Black people are not elected to be Yahweh's suffering people.*" [61]

I certainly hope that they are not so chosen, even as I cherish the same hope for my country and my continent. But then what about Jesus himself? He, too, was chosen for freedom and, at the same time, for redemptive suffering. I fully agree with Cone when he says that we cannot accept such decisions about our "election" when they are imposed on us by our oppressors. But if we remain faithful to the Bible, what key enables us to decide which is our real election?[62]

Leaving that issue aside here, I hope that it is quite clear that the Bible is not the discourse of a universal God to a universal humankind. Partiality is justified because we must find, and designate as the word of God, that *part* of divine revelation which *today,* in the light of our concrete historical situation, is most useful for the liberation to which God summons us. Other passages of that same divine revelation will help us tomorrow to complete and correct our present course towards freedom. God will keep coming back to speak to us from the very same Bible.

Hence I have no intention here of disputing Cone's interpretation of the Scriptures. Sometimes I am in agreement with him, sometimes I am not. Be that as it may, I think that his theological efforts afford us a fine example of the hermeneutic circle.

If we understand and appreciate this circle, then we also will understand and appreciate something that is very important for Latin American theology of liberation. When it is accused of partiality, it can calmly reply that it is partial because it is faithful to Christian tradition rather than to Greek thought. It can also say that those who attack it are even more partisan, though they may not realize it, and tend to muzzle the word of God by trying to make one particular portion of Scripture the word of God not only for certain particular moments and situations but also for all situations and all moments.

NOTES

1. "Interpretation based on faith adds nothing to reality; it simply explicates an element that is overlooked or confused by other interpretations. Thus where there are no signs of mystery in secular life, one would have to say that Christianity and any other

religious interpretation would never be anything more than *a superstructure and an ideology.* But that is not the case if one can show that such signs do exist in secular life itself. . . . The only thing that a religious or faith-based interpretation can do is to explicate what is already there in life. . . . The designation 'ideology' cannot be applied to an interpretation which spotlights some aspect of reality itself. For that is simply an explication that gives a name to something that was already there before" (in *La respuesta de los teólogos,* Span. trans., in collaboration with K. Rahner, Congar, Schoonenberg, Metz, and Daniélou [Buenos Aires: Carlos Lohlé, 1970], pp. 60–61).

2. Karl Mannheim, *Ideology and Utopia* (New York: Harcourt, Brace, Jovanovich, Harvest Book, 1936).

3. Harvey Cox, *The Secular City,* rev. ed. (New York: Macmillan, 1966), p. 60.

4. Ibid., p. 70.

5. Ibid., pp. 68–69.

6. Ibid., p. 95.

7. Ibid., p. 172.

8. Ibid., p. 194. Cox states, "The Girl symbolizes the values and aspirations of a consumer society" (ibid., p. 171).

9. "This also applies to the realm of theology. The choice of a point of departure is determined and regulated by norms which themselves are based on the theology which should really be the continuation of the first beginning. But in that case there can be no question of a point of departure without prejudice. What is held to be an unprejudiced point of departure turns out to be an 'arbitrary' leap into a certain stream of thought and belief. Sometimes it happens that a person slowly comes to the realization that the stream he has jumped into leads nowhere. Then this experience makes it clear to him that he must get out of this stream; arriving once again at the banks of the stream he must choose a new point of departure and risk another leap. . . . Any choice of a point of departure in science, philosophy and theology is an a priori choice of a certain view of the world or life. . . . From the very beginning the choice proves that a person has chosen *even before the choice was made"* (W. H. van de Pol, *The End of Conventional Christianity,* Eng. trans. [New York: Newman Press, 1967], p. 191).

10. On the influence of Marxist thought on the creation of a theology of liberation in Latin America, see especially the next two chapters of the present work. It must be admitted, however, that there are problems connected with applying the label "Marxist" to a line of thought or a source of influence. First of all, those who identify themselves with Marx and his thinking have a thousand different ways of conceiving and interpreting "Marxist" thought. Aside from that fact, the point is that the great thinkers of history do not replace each other; rather, they complement and enrich each other. Philosophic thought would never be the same after Aristotle as it was before him. In that sense all Westerners who philosophize now are Aristotelians. After Marx, our way of conceiving and posing the problems of society will never be the same again. Whether everything Marx said is accepted or not, and in whatever way one may conceive his "essential" thinking, there can be no doubt that present-day social thought will be "Marxist" to some extent: that is, profoundly indebted to Marx. In that sense Latin American theology is certainly Marxist. I know my remark will be taken out of context, but one cannot go on trying to forestall every partisan or stupid misunderstanding forever.

11. Karl Marx, *Manifesto of the Communist Party,* Great Books of the Western World, 50 (Chicago: Encyclopaedia Britannica, 1952), p. 419.

12. Ibid., pp. 419–20.

13. Ibid., p. 423.

14. Ibid., p. 428.

15. Karl Marx, *A Contribution to the Critique of Political Economy* (Chicago: Charles H. Kerr and Co., 1913), pp. 11–12.

16. *Karl Marx: Selected Writings in Sociology and Social Philosophy,* newly translated and edited by T. B. Bottomore (London: Watts, 1956; New York: McGraw-Hill, 1964), p. 75.

17. Ibid., p. 54.

18. Ibid., pp. 64–65.

19. *Capital I,* in *Selected Writings,* p. 64.

20. *Critique of Hegel's Philosophy of Right,* in *Selected Writings,* p. 26.

21. Ibid., p. 27.

22. The need for a *third* and *fourth* stage in our hermeneutic circle stems from the fact, established at the very start, that we are dealing here with a hermeneutic for *Christian theology.* The fact is that hermeneutics is always necessary vis-à-vis a *tradition,* and in practice it is impossible to have any systematic thought or specific, coherent vision of reality without interpreting that reality. So the first two points of the hermeneutic circle are necessary and adequate to ensure that any tradition whatever may give rise to a richer and more creative line of thought as new situations and problems arise in history. Now tradition is often conveyed in and through specialized methodologies, so that we are led to talk about *theological* tradition, *philosophical* tradition, *sociopolitical* tradition, and so forth. In such specific instances, the one who is tackling the tradition in that concrete form must probe into the *specific* realm involved and concretize his commitment and his overall suspicion there. Only then can there appear a new and richer hermeneutics and subsequently a new and richer reality. Now theology, unlike philosophy, does not derive its interpretation of existence from itself but rather from certain written sources. So the hermeneutic circle requires it to propose a new interpretation for those sources if something profound is to change, in line with the basic commitment from which the hermeneutic circle started. One might then ask: Why does the circle have to go specifically through the Bible rather than other existing theological traditions? For that question, see note 55 below.

23. As is well known, from 1890 on Engels had to speak out against a purely "materialistic" or "econometric" version of *historical materialism.* He did so whenever the opportunity arose. This is what he has to say in a letter to Bloch (September 21–22, 1890): "According to the materialistic conception of history, the determining element in history is *ultimately* the production and reproduction in real life. More than this neither Marx nor I have ever asserted. If therefore somebody twists this into the statement that the economic element is the *only* determining one, he transforms it into a meaningless, abstract and absurd phrase. The economic situation is the basis, but the various elements of the superstructure—political forms of the class struggle and its consequences, constitutions established by the victorious class after a successful battle, etc., forms of law, and then even the reflexes of all these actual struggles in the brains of the combatants (political, legal, philosophical theories, *religious ideas and their further development into systems of dogma*)—also exercise their influence upon the course of the historical struggle and *in many cases preponderate in determining their form"* (Marx and Engels, *Selected Correspondence: 1846–1895* [New York: International Publishers, 1942], Letter 213, p. 475). See also Engels's letters to K. Schmidt (August 5, and October 27, 1890), and his letter to N. F. Danielson (October 17, 1893).

If one does not accept the "relative independence" of the superstructure, then it becomes difficult to explain many examples gathered by Marx himself and noted in his works. One will find it hard to explain (e.g.) the contrast which Marx points up in *Capital I* between the "unchangeableness of Asiatic societies" and the "never-ceasing changes in dynasty" (Great Books of the Western World 50, [Chicago: Encyclopaedia Britannica, 1952], p. 175). A mechanistic materialism might be able to explain the unchanging societal economy, but it certainly could not explain the countless fluctuations and torments of the superstructure.

24. Max Weber, *The Protestant Ethic and the Spirit of Capitalism* (New York: Charles Scribner's Sons, 1958), p. 91.

25. Ibid., p. 97.

26. Ibid., p. 232. This psychological tieup is explored even more fully from a psychoanalytic viewpoint by Erich Fromm in chap. 3 of *Escape From Freedom* (New York: Holt, Rinehart, and Winston, 1941).

27. Translator's Foreword to Weber, *The Protestant Ethic,* p. 7.

28. Weber, *The Protestant Ethic,* p. 101.

29. Ibid., p. 90.

30. Ibid., p. 163.

31. Ibid., p. 177.

32. Ibid., p. 122.

33. Ibid., p. 104.

34. Ibid., p. 103.

35. Ibid., p. 123.

36. Mannheim, *Ideology and Utopia,* p. 282.

37. As is well known by now, liberation theology arose as a reaction against the developmentalist theories and models formulated by the United States for Latin America in the decade of the sixties. The developmentalist model was characterized by the fact that it covered over and tried to hide the critical and decisive relationship of dependence versus liberation. Underlying this approach was the vaunted notion that the economic process, without undergoing any substantial modification, could turn the "underdeveloped" countries into modern, prosperous societies once it reached the "takeoff point." From there on it would accelerate cumulatively and come to resemble more and more the process in developed countries. To bolster this ideology, the point was often stressed that this modernization process meant that people would have to accept the "death of ideologies" brought about by a scientific and *neutral* technology common to any and every social model. On this point see chap. 2 of Gustavo Gutiérrez, *A Theology of Liberation* (Maryknoll, N.Y.: Orbis Books, 1973).

38. James H. Cone, *A Black Theology of Liberation* (Philadelphia: Lippincott, 1970), p. 17. See also Second Revised Edition, Maryknoll, N.Y.: Orbis Books, 1986 (Ed.).

39. Ibid., p. 33.

40. Ibid.

41. Ibid., p. 45.

42. Ibid., p. 117.

43. Ibid., p. 22.

44. Ibid., p. 191.

45. Ibid., p. 120.

46. Ibid., p. 184.

47. Ibid., pp. 122–23.

48. Ibid., pp. 52–53.

49. Ibid., p. 53.
50. Ibid., p. 40.
51. Ibid., pp. 32–33.
52. Ibid., p. 62.
53. Ibid.
54. Ibid., p. 68.
55. Ibid., p. 77. In the interdenominational faculties of the United States, and particularly among certain Protestant denominations, I have found that this last stage of the hermeneutic circle, which is hardly ever debated by Latin American theologians, is often questioned. Americans question the necessity of returning to the sources or fonts of *Christian* revelation. They pose such questions as: Why not construct another religious theory closer to our own problems? Or why not have recourse to other "revelations" such as that of Buddhism, for example? Since we find a strong *ideological* influence exerted on and by the Christian tradition, why need we return hermeneutically to its source? Why should we imagine that God has been revealed only in the Judeo-Christian tradition? Cone, for example, cannot ignore the fact that many blacks in the United States chose to move on to the Muslim tradition after making the hermeneutic turn that he himself made. They chose that course over the possibility of returning with new questions to a source which they felt to be irremediably lost for black people. The women's liberation movement has reached a similar conclusion, deciding to rule out any return to a "revelation" that is totally dominated by the male element. Now it is certainly true that one need not inevitably move from the third stage of the hermeneutic circle to the fourth stage we present here. One can certainly move on to a new theology or a different tradition of "revelation." What seems odd to me is that any such new theology would continue to call itself "Christian," as they often do. The designation seems to make sense in such a case only as an indication of the point of departure.
56. Ibid., pp. 79–80.
57. Ibid., p. 64.
58. Ibid., p. 130.
59. Ibid., p. 133.
60. Ibid., p. 156.
61. Ibid., p. 108.
62. On this point see chap. 4, "Ideologies and Faith," in *The Liberation of Theology* (Ed.).

7

Rubem Alves

From Paradise to the Desert: Autobiographical Musings

*Rubem Alves's views have changed considerably in recent years. This auto-
biographical sketch, "From Paradise to the Desert: Autobiographical Mus-
ings," is taken from Rosino Gibellini, ed.,* Frontiers of Theology in Latin
America *(Maryknoll, N.Y.: Orbis Books, 1979), pp. 284–303.*

Neither in the paradise of Genesis nor the holy city of the Apocalypse are
there any temples. In paradise religion is not yet necessary, and in the holy city it
is no longer necessary. Religion is the memory of a lost unity and the nostalgia
for a future reconciliation. Under the surface layers of happiness and peace
which it proclaims, religion always presupposes an I unreconciled with its
destiny.

The oldest memories of my own religious nostalgia go back to my early
childhood. I was eleven years old. It was not a matter of a precocious theological vocation. It was rather a precocious experience of fear. That was the first
time that I personally experienced what is known as anxiety.

Up to that time I had lived in a small town. Everything in it had been friendly
and familiar to me: the streets, the trees, the streams, the people. The "other"
people who were "relevant" for me were my mother, my father, my brothers
and sisters, and my friends; and I looked on them with calmness and respect.
They were part of my universe. I scarcely was aware of myself as such, because
I and my world were fused into one single whole. Waking up in the morning,

going to school, playing outside, and going to bed at night were part of a liturgy that was picked up again every day and that celebrated a world that made sense.

Suddenly, without realizing it, I was driven out of paradise. They transferred me to a big city. My "relevant others" were dissolved in the incomprehensible complexity of city life. They remained "others" but they were no longer "relevant." They were no longer the emotional center of my world, from which I drew my sense of identity and the meaning of my future. They were not to blame for what had happened to me because they, too, were lost.

For the first time I experienced the uneasiness of being different. I became self-conscious. My accent revealed who I was: a country bumpkin. My school-mates would not pardon me for that. How cruel children can be! I found myself alone, without friends, without knowing what to do. I was different and ridiculous. I did not possess the human resources needed to sustain myself in that abysmal solitude. Sociologists call that situation anomie. How much suffering is buried in that little word! Primitive cosmogonies always talk about a primordial conflict between the dry land and the sea. Dry land is the place where human beings can walk with security. The waters of the sea symbolize the horrendous possibilities that menace human beings unceasingly. Chaos and the void ever threaten to engulf the world of human beings. My dry land had been invaded by those waters, my universe had been engulfed by their waves.

But human consciousness cannot survive indefinitely in a state of anomie. Inevitably we must resolve the problem of loneliness and impotence in a hostile world, and consciousness makes use of a trick to solve the problem. By means of a magic trick it tries to make the real unreal, organizing its perception of reality as if its own desires and aspirations were the ultimate reality. Its own desires and aspirations are ontologized and reified. Thanks to the magic power, the "omnipotence" of thought, human beings weave together a verbal world out of the depths of their impotence and the heights of their passion. It is a verbal world that affirms and confirms their own values. The new world constructed in this fashion becomes their "vicarious gratification," their new world of happiness that compensates for the frustration and suffering encountered in the real world. And frequently, though not always, this "vicarious gratification" is religion.

That was the route I unwittingly followed. I became religious. After all, it did not matter that the world mocked us. True religion is above and beyond all that. Even if our "relevant others" are reduced to impotence and insignificance, there is a Relevant Other who knows and loves us and who has infinite power at its disposal. I do not mean to reduce religion to this type of experience at all, but neither can I conceal what really happened to me.

I became a fundamentalist, a pious fundamentalist. Fundamentalism is an attitude which attributes a definitive character to one's own beliefs. The really important feature is not *what* the fundamentalists say but *how* they say it. Fundamentalists are characterized by a dogmatic and authoritarian attitude with respect to their own system of thought and by an attitude of intolerance (the Inquisition) toward every "heretic" or "revisionist."

You can have revolutionary fundamentalists, be they devotees of Marxism, women's liberation, or black power. You can have scholarly and scientific fundamentalists, especially when they forget that they are working with models, as Kuhn points out,[1] or with simple opinions, as Popper suggests.[2] You can have counterculture fundamentalists who absolutize their own personal experiences. And you can even have liberal fundamentalists. The fundamentalist is a person full of self, a person incapable of the slightest *humor* where self is concerned, a person whom Kolakowski characterizes as "the priest" as opposed to "the clown."

The important feature in fundamentalism is not the ideas that are affirmed but the spirit in which they are affirmed. You cannot just shift the bottles around on the shelves. If the shelves stay exactly as they were, then the system itself remains the same. To put it a bit more abstractly: It is the *structure* that defines the fundamentalist mentality, not the elements that go to make up its content.

Fundamentalism may well be the great temptation facing us. As the serpent tells Adam: "You shall be like God, knowing good and evil." And do we not all long to trade in our opinions for images of reality, our doubts for certainties, our provisional status for eternity, our distress and incompleteness for peace and self-fulfillment? The fundamentalist solution frees us from our painful encounter with a reality that ever remains incomplete, changing, upsetting, and distressing.

Convert to fundamentalism—the type doesn't matter. You will find yourself liberated from the endless process of building up and then tearing down only to begin again. Fundamentalists are those who have already finished the job. Nietzsche rightly described them as the enemy of the future because the fundamentalists *already* know who and what is good. That is very useful and functional from the emotional standpoint. From that standpoint religion provides us with certainty and security. And when one has discovered a religion of that sort, the logical next step is to become an apostle of one's truth. So it was that I entered the seminary.

But language is unpredictable, and remember that it is language that sustains our world and the structure of our personality. Language is a tool, as it were. It is created, used, and preserved so that it may adequately serve us for the solution of our existential problem. But suppose now that this basic problem, this emotional matrix around which we have structured our existence, suddenly alters. The old language suddenly becomes superfluous and no longer has any function. The function of my fundamentalist language had been to resolve the anomie that arose out of my loneliness. Meanwhile in the seminary I had found a group of companions like myself who shared the very same problems; the scripts of our biographies were very much alike. We became friends and formed a community, and in sharing our problems we found a solution. The anomie was overcome, along with the fundamentalist language. That language was no longer needed.

Wittgenstein once observed that language has a magic power.[3] Linguistic structures tend to situate us in an enchanted realm where we can see the world only in the way that language itself allows. So when we "forget" some language, we somehow begin to see the world in a completely different way. We experience *astonishment* at suddenly seeing things that were always there but that we had not noticed before. We cannot help but ask ourselves: Why am I incapable of seeing so many things? How could I have failed to notice so many features of reality that were right before my eyes?

So it was that I discovered the social roots of our religion—and also its neurotic origins. Its negation of the world, its absolutization of eternity, its rejection of liberty, its discomfort in the face of human, sensuous reality, and its rejection of all that was provisional: Didn't all these things represent a conspiracy against life?

Our perspective on reality changes according to the standpoint from which we examine it. My new vision of our space, our time, and our existence revealed a Bible that had been hidden from my eyes up to that point. What a surprise it was to discover that the human beings in the Bible felt at home in the world! From beginning to end the Bible celebrates life and its goodness. It is good to be alive, to be flesh and blood, to exist in the world. Suddenly the Calvinist obsession with the glory of God seemed to me to be profoundly inhuman and antibiblical. Isn't God's only concern the happiness of human beings? Isn't that the very epitome of God's will? Isn't God a humanist, in the sense that humanity is the one and only object of God's love?

Bonhoeffer became our friend. We read him passionately:

It is only when one loves life and the world so much that without them everything would be gone, that one can believe in the resurrection and a new world. . . . To long for the transcendent when you are in your wife's arms is, to put it mildly, a lack of taste, and it is certainly not what God expects of us. We ought to find God and love him in the blessings he sends us. If he pleases to grant us some overwhelming earthly bliss, we ought not to try and be more religious that God himself. . . . It is not with the next world that we are concerned, but with this world as created and preserved and set subject to laws and atoned for and made new. What is above the world is, in the Gospel, intended to exist *for* this world.[4]

Salvation *from* the world, that touchstone dogma of Brazilian Protestantism—was it not in direct opposition to the Bible itself? Personal salvation cannot take place to the detriment of the world because humanity and the world belong to each other. It is first and foremost in our struggle for the redemption of the world that we achieve our personal totality. Thus saviors of souls were transformed into rebuilders of earth. One thing seemed certain to us: the church would have to free itself from the spell of fundamentalist language that had kept it prisoner. Once this was realized the church would take the lead in the battle to transform the world, or so we hoped.

In our minds the reform of the church and the redemption of the world were one single task. We left the seminary with the assurance that we had settled that question. Wasn't our idea intoxicating? Who could help but fall under its spell?

But reality made a mockery of our naive aspirations. We were not ready for the reality of institutional life. To the ears of ecclesiastical officials our new reading of the gospel sounded like apostasy. Their experience had been different. They could not comprehend or love what had been felt so immediately by us. We were accused of being heretics, pointed out as people with dangerous political ideas, and rejected as apostates because we committed the sin of accepting Catholics as our brothers and sisters. We were forced into exile: "Love it or leave it, but do not try to transform the church."

Two things became clear. The first thing was that the institutional church was not the church we loved. Reading the prophets, we found that Hosea had the same experience. God's exclamation, "You are not my people," became the name of one of his children. The church for which we yearned, the community of liberty and love, was not to be found in the confines of the ecclesial organization. We would have to give up the ideal of reforming it. You cannot sew patches of new material on old cloth. You cannot pour new wine into old bottles. It is impossible. More to the point, it is stupid.

But how is one to survive in solitude, far from any community? If values are not shared, they tend to be forgotten. To the extent that values are not hard facts, they are absent entities. Not yet born, they persist as a possibility, a promise, a hope. Their presence in the present depends on a language proclaiming their realization. Hence our disillusionment with the ecclesiastical organization did not mean that we had given up hope of finding a community. On the contrary, we began to look for it in places where we had never looked before. New questions confronted us: "Was it possible that today the church was dispersed, hidden, unrecognized in the world?" Was it not possible that those who are truly living in expectation of the kingdom did not know its name?

To our surprise we found more signs of the Spirit outside the restricted bounds of our ecclesial communities than inside. A new type of ecumenism emerged, completely different from the institutionalized ecumenism that is found on the upper levels of ecclesiastical hierarchies and that is based on agreements over doctrine or ecclesiastical discipline. We discovered a new unity on a different front, where people were preoccupied with human beings and the renovation of the world. Indeed it seems to me that the more the church closes in on itself, even if its intent is to find some lost unity, the more it sinks down into its own contradictions. On the other hand when it gives itself up totally to the cause of redemption in a concrete, experiential way, it then discovers something that it had not even been looking for: its own unity.

The second thing that seemed clear was a byproduct of the first. The patronizing guardians of God, those who allege to hold some monopoly on the divine, use God's name in a way that bears strong resemblances to the Inquisition. "God" becomes an ideological weapon designed to preserve the power structure, justify the status quo, and assassinate dissidents. Thus the word

"God" suddenly ceased to make any sense. Or, to put it better, it was stripped of meaning in its institutional and traditional theological context. God's name was no longer the symbol of liberty and love. For many this meant that God was dead. They suddenly found themselves faced with the task of reconstructing the world. Out of ecclesiastical frustration was born a secular humanism. Theology was traded in for sociology, the church for the world, God for human beings.

Others, however, did not take that path. From their hopes and frustrations, from their reading of the Bible and the daily newspaper, there arose a new way of talking about God and a new way of envisioning the community of faith. This new approach was given the name "liberation theology." Essentially it comes down to a dialectical hermeneutics in which people read the Bible from the standpoint of the hopes and anxieties of the present, and read the present from the standpoint of the hopes and anxieties of which the Bible speaks.

Quite logically, then, an act of faith is present in this procedure. With Paul it assumes that "all creation groans and is in agony even until now," awaiting "the revelation of the sons of God." The pangs of childbirth entail both tears and smiles. They point to an emerging reality. The Spirit has impregnated creation. Its womb filled with new life, creation waits and anxiously hopes for the advent of the new, even as we, groaning inwardly, look for the same thing (see Rom. 8:22–23).

The theology of liberation cannot rest content with remaining indifferent to life and the world. Isn't the gospel message an account of the good news of the incarnation? Doesn't Christ's life bear witness to God's solidarity with human beings? There is no question of reducing faith to sociology. The primary assertion is that transcendence is concretely revealed both in the groaning cries for liberty and in the struggle against everything that oppresses people.

Many years have now gone by. Our age-old hopes have not been fulfilled. We live amid the ruins of our religious expectations. One form of captivity was abolished only to be replaced by another. Now, in trying to find meaning in our biographies, we find that we have been steadily beating a retreat. Our backs are to the wall, and there is no escape. The exodus of which we dreamed earlier has miscarried. Instead we now find ourselves in a situation of exile and captivity.

Let me explain. We were born in a world illuminated by transcendental certitudes and absolute values. Our hopes were indestructible. Our world was a universe that drew meaningfulness from a vision of the heavenly Jerusalem. God was in heaven, all would go well on earth.

But our gods are dead. Or, if not dead, they are hushed and still. They were sent into exile, even as we were. In their place came our heroes, and politics was transformed into religion. With the help of politics, all that had been mere expectant groaning would find concrete fulfillment in reality.

But now even our heroes are dead. We were not able to carry out the task we proposed to ourselves. The universe was invaded by chaos. What else could we do but beat a retreat once more? Lacking gods and heroes, we still had our day-to-day values. It is almost incredible to find how our horizons have narrowed. In the beginning, with religion, our horizon stretched to the very boundaries of time and space. With politics it became a bit more restricted; we were bounded within the confines of history. Now our universe is confined to the narrow walls of our own house and the brief span of our own life. Lacking gods and heroes, we still have a wife or husband, children, friends, our work, music, and the contemplation of nature.

I was told that after the 1968 student uprising in France there was a great increase in vocations to the agrarian way of life. That is very interesting. At least farming is an activity where we can be fairly certain that we won't reap thorns if we plant grapes. If we cannot control history, we resign ourselves to a more restricted world. But even this retreat is condemned to failure. We cannot preserve rural values in a technocratic world. Once upon a time peasants could resolve the problem of anomie that arose when they moved to the big city by going back to their original world. Today, however, the problem is no longer a spatial one. Something has happened to our space. It has been engulfed by the new time that bureaucratic and technological society has created. We cannot win out over anomie by going back to our lost paradise because it no longer exists. Chaos has invaded every sector of our civilization.

One day we saw our gods die. The next day we embraced heroes, only to see them die. Then we were restricted to our domestic confines. Now we suddenly discover that unless we ourselves succeed in generating new gods, we will be left with no alternative except to go mad. Even Nietzsche, who proclaimed the death of God, pointed out that a universe in which God is dead is dark and cold.

Biography and history go together. As Marx saw so well: "Man is not abstract being squatting outside the world. Man is *the world of man,* the state, society."[5] Even if we mark off our own space with the signposts of private property, even if we refuse to look at the world that is assaulting us, even if we cherish the illusion that we are living our own individual lives, the fact remains that our personal destiny is rooted deeply in the destiny of civilizations. In one way or another, our biography is always a symptom of the conditions prevailing in our world. That is the reason behind the discovery we all frequently make. Despite the fact that we live in different places, posts, and political contexts, our biographies stongly resemble slight variations of one and the same script. They have the same structure. They go through the same sequence of hopes and frustrations.

It is this personal history that drives me into theological research. I have lost my points of reference. I find no concrete signs to give me hope. What we find in our present historical situation allows us no trace of optimism. But I know very well that we cannot live without hope. It is hope that gives us what Prescott Lecky describes as "self-consistency."[6] Psychotherapy has discovered that objectively there is no hope for those who subjectively do not possess hope.[7] Hope is a *wager* . We bet on the possibility of our values being fulfilled.

And it is this wager that gives us the emotional energy to live through feelings of frustration and impotence. And so I myself feel caught painfully between the anthropological necessity of hope on the one hand and its historical impossibility on the other. I do not know how to associate my biography with history, the personal with the structural, the existential with the material. I do not have at my disposal any paradigm that will enable me to reconstruct my universe.

That is the problem which lies at the roots of my theology. Theology is a science for people who have lost the pristine unity of paradise or who have not yet found it. It is a search for points of reference, for new horizons that will enable us to find meaning amid the chaos that engulfs us. It is an attempt to piece back together the shattered fragments of a whole that has been destroyed. At its origin lies the problem of hope, the plausibility of the human values we cherish in a world that conspires against them.

Thus theology and biography go together. Religion, noted Feuerbach, is "the solemn unveiling of a man's hidden treasures, the revelation of his intimate thoughts, the open confession of his love-secrets."[8] Religion is the proclamation of the axiological priority of the heart over the raw facts of reality. It is a refusal to be gobbled up and digested by the surrounding world, an appeal to a vision, a passion, a love. When the heart constructs some utopia, is it not translating into words a world that just might be divine? Does it not embody a nostalgia for the kingdom? When I evince a passionate desire for peace and justice despite the fact that I do not see any concrete possibility for them in this world, am I not—even though I may claim to be an atheist—saying in my heart something like the following: "How wonderful it would be if there were a God to confirm my values. Though I cannot come to believe in such a God, how I wish such a God did exist"? When, in the midst of misery and oppression, I feel overwhelmed with sentiments too deep to be expressed, may I not be unwittingly praying?

We must recognize and acknowledge the human origins of religion. Even if it were possible for some religion to exist that did not arise out of our existential situation, how could I comprehend it? How could it be the object of my love? We must agree with Nietzsche: "The belly of being does not speak to humans at all, except as a human."[9] If that remark sounds a bit too human to pious ears, those people would do well to reread a bit of Luther. Human beings can assume a religious atttude only toward something that they sense to be a value, something that has to do with life and death. It is completely wrong to say that religion is mere anthropology. We would be closer to the mark if we said that anthropology is religion. As Feuerbach puts it: " If the plants had eyes, taste, and judgment, each plant would declare its own flower the most beautiful." Hence "the Absolute to man is his own nature."[10]

Theology is our effort to bring together the petals of our flower that is continuously torn apart by a world that does not love flowers. It is "the sigh of the oppressed creature" (Marx) who is incapable of resurrecting its dead flower yet dares to hope that its seeds will germinate once the winter is over. Theology is the expression of that unconscious and unending project that is the very heart of human beings: the creation of a world with human meaningfulness.

Norman O. Brown remarks: "It is the human ego that carries the search for a world to love."[11] The ego, in other words, does not remain closed up in itself. It yearns to flow out over nature and fecundate it with its seed. The human ego seeks to humanize nature, to impregnate it with the future, to transform the physical universe into an *ordo amoris* (Max Scheler). What is coarse and lifeless and incapable of feeling must become an extension of the human body, an instrument for human hands and an expression of the human heart:

> Human existence is, *ab initio,* an outgoing externalization. As man externalizes himself, he constructs the world *into* which he externalizes himself. In the process of externalization, he projects his own meanings into reality. Symbolic universes, which proclaim that *all* reality is humanly meaningful and call upon the *entire* cosmos to signify the validity of human existence, constitute the farthest reaches of this projection.[12]

This is the origin, function, and meaning of theology. I appeal to the words of an antitheologian, Nietzsche, to express what lies behind the folly of theology: "Let the future and the farthest be for you the cause of your today."[13] Theology is contemplation of today in the light of the future. It looks facts in the face in order to effect their abolition and fulfillment *(Aufhebung).* It dissolves objectivity magically in the name of a utopian order that becomes one's prospect and final destination.

Here the reader might well interpose an objection: "If that is the case, if theology is a projection of human desires, then it has no objective validity. It is nothing more than an evasion, an illusion, a vicarious gratification invented to evade the harsh facts of reality." To clear up that problem we must for a moment drop the line of thought we have been pursuing and start over from a different perspective.

Our way of thinking is conditioned by a whole set of unconscious presuppositions[14] that we accept as our point of departure in the process of knowing. They are the "silent adjustments" of which Wittgenstein speaks,[15] the "God-terms" noted by Philip Rieff.[16] These silent adjustments are our eyes, as it were. We see *through* them but we do not see *them.* They fashion our reality, but we do not advert to the fact that they themselves have been fashioned too. All together, they constitute a kind of collective unconscious underlying our mental processes. They are unconscious and we do not see them; that is why in most cases they are inaccessible to our criticism and exert such strange "magical" power over us. They make it impossible for us to contemplate the world in any way different from the way we have programed it.

Our ability to see reality and the faculties used by us are conditioned by a whole set of "silent adjustments" that have been codified by science. First of all, we assume that knowing is duplicating. Underlying the scientific ideal of objectivity we find the assumption that knowledge is nothing more nor less than a simple copy or reflection of what is given. In this respect academic Western sociology does not differ one whit from what is called Marxist science. I recall Engels's observation: "Modern Socialism is nothing but the reflex, in thought, of this conflict in fact."[17] Whether we admit it or not, we are empiricists; we assume that thought must be a copy of the datum in reality. Consequently we also assume that propositions have meaning only when they can be verified through a confrontation with the data of experience.

The second dogma of our collective unconscious derives logically from the first. If knowing is duplicating, then people are considered normal to the extent that their mental processes do not contradict the rules of the "copying" process. It is worth noting that Freud sees neurotics as people who attribute "excessive value to their own desires" in their behavior. In other words, behavior that takes values as its point of reference is regarded as unhealthy. Freud puts it very succinctly: "One thing only do I know for certain and that is that man's judgments of value follow directly his wishes for happiness—that, accordingly, they are an attempt to support his illusions with arguments."[18] The conclusion is inescapable: To the scientific ideal of objectivity there corresponds, on the epistemological level, a psychosocial understanding of normality in terms of adaptation.

This unconscious metaphysics of ours further maintains that historical and social processes are independent of human beings. The essence of Marxist science, notes Lukács, is the realization that the forces that really move history are completely independent of any psychic awareness that human beings might have of them.[19] Even Marx himself remarked that what the proletariat imagined directly was completely irrelevant. The important thing is what *really* is and what that obliges us to do.[20]

What are the cause and explanations for human behavior? The intentions and aspirations of human beings, perhaps? Definitely not. The content of consciousness is a secondary phenomenon. It is an effect, not a cause, of social processes. It is the social structure that explains consciousness, not vice versa.

Academic sociology in the West accepts the same axiom. Social structures are independent and autonomous; hence they are self-explanatory. As Peter Blau puts it: "Once firmly organized, an organization tends to assume an identity of its own which makes it independent of the people who have founded it or of those who constitute its membership."[21] What Althusser says of Marxist science can be applied here too. To know the human world, the scholarly scientist must put humanity itself in parenthesis. Concrete human beings contribute nothing to our knowledge and comprehension of the institutions to which they belong: "Strictly in respect to theory . . . one can and must speak openly of Marx's *theoretical anti-humanism,* and see in this *theoretical anti-humanism* the absolute (negative) precondition of the (postive) knowledge of the human world itself and of its practical transformation."[22]

This presupposition is not peculiar to just the social sciences. Psychological behaviorism, especially that influenced by B. F. Skinner, also takes it for its point of departure. Human behavior is to be understood as a simple response to stimuli. Human action, is, in reality, re-action. As behaviorism sees the matter, the whole complex of stimuli perform the same function that social structures perform in the view of the social sciences. In the last analysis, human beings are not *factors* at all. They do not make history. Their activity does not flow from their freedom but from the complex web of concrete determinisms surrounding them.

The last axiom I should like to consider here is implicit in the third just mentioned. The imagination does not make history. Freud's fight against the neurotic is the same fight Marx waged against the utopian socialist. Both the neurotic and the utopian refuse to accept the verdict of reality. They act as if their values were in a position to alter the inevitable course of objective reality. They think that imagination is capable of creating new conditions. But since imagination represents a refusal to accept and duplicate what is given and implies a magical transformation of the objective world (Sartre),[23] it must be abandoned as false consciousness and a form of illness.

It is this last axiom that is of most interest to us here. After all, what is religion but a form of imagination? Religion is imagination and, by the same token, imagination always has a religious function. It is obvious that religion does not seek to describe what is given in experience. As Feuerbach observed: "Religion is the dream of the human mind. . . . We only see things in the entrancing splendor of imagination and caprice, instead of in the simple daylight of reality and necessity."[24] According to the logic of the scientific mentality, then, religion along with imagination must be classified as a form of illness or false consciousness.

Thus when we reject religion as *mere* imagination, we are unconsciously accepting the hidden metaphysics that governs the scientific mentality. We are assuming that knowledge is duplication and that normality is adaptation. Consciousness is taken to be like a camera that takes photographs of the world. And since religion does not take photographs, since it transfigures the data according to the logic of the heart, we reject it as meaningless.

But the world as a concrete way of existing is not the objective world of scientific abstraction. As Dewey put it: "Empirically, things are poignant, tragic, beautiful, humorous, settled, disturbed, comfortable, annoying, barren, harsh, consoling, splendid, fearful. . . . "[25] Our experience of the world is primarily emotional. To this the objective scientist might reply: "True, but that is because we are *not yet* used to true, pure, and disinterested knowledge." That is wrong. Things are that way because human beings, in their relationship with their surroundings, are always faced with the imperative of survival. It is precisely because they wish to live that they never perceive their milieu as neutral. Their surroundings promise life and death, pleasure and pain. Hence anyone really enmeshed in the struggle for survival is forced to perceive the world in emotional terms. It is the immediate and emotion-laden experience, which in most instances is not and cannot be verbalized, that determines our way of existing in the world. This emotional matrix constitutes the structure of the world in which we live.

What I am saying here is that consciousness is not pure. The mind does not exist as an entity independent of matter, as Cartesian philosophy would have it. It is not pure, free reason existing beyond interference from the vital and emotional components of the subject, as Kant believed. Consciousness is a function of the body. It exists to help the body solve the problem of its survival. And since survival is always the ultimate human value, even when one commits suicide, consciousness is structured around an emotional matrix. As Nietzsche put it, the body is our "Great Reason." What we call "reason" is really a little reason, a tool and plaything of our Great Reason.

If the core of consciousness is emotion and value, then consciousness is radically religious. As we have already noted, it is not a mechanism for duplicating an order that is given empirically. Piaget tells us that consciousness is not a copy but an organization of the real.[26] And since the real is devoid of human significance, it becomes a human world only after we give it structure by attuning it to our own needs and values. In other words, what we call reality is the construction of the religious matrix of consciousness. As Emile Durkheim has pointed out, religion is the origin and foundation of the categories of reason.[27]

The reason we tend to downgrade religion as mere imagination is that we are caught in the snares of our collective unconscious. We are inclined to know things solely through the logic of the subject-object relationship, or what Martin Buber calls the "I-it" relationship.[28] What does the scientific criterion of verification mean except that every sign stands for some object? But life exists prior to any such artificial fragmentation, since life is relationship. An organism and its milieu must be immersed in a process of dialectical relationships if life is to manifest itself. Once that process terminates, life is overcome by death. Insofar as religious thinking has to do with life rather than with dead abstraction, its point of reference is the set of relationships that precede the dichotomy between subject and object.

It is precisely for that reason that religion makes use of symbols rather than signs. The function of a symbol is to represent a living relationship. Relationships are not perceived; they are not objects. First and foremost they make up the milieu in which life exists.

One of the great contributions of psychoanalysis was the discovery that dreams have meaning. The apparent absurdity of dreams is a veiled way of revealing some truth. The problem is that their meaning lies hidden. If we try to decipher them with the logic of the subject-object relationship, then we will end up with absurdities. Why? Because in dreams serpents are not serpents, rivers are not rivers, and mountains are not mountains. They are symbols, revealing and hiding at the same time. If we think that in dreams we are dealing with *signs* that point to certain objects, if we forget that we are dealing with *symbols* that express relationships, then the meaning of dreams will remain forever hidden from our understanding.

But what is religion except the dream of whole groups of human beings? Religion is for society what the dream is for the individual. If that is true, then we are making a great mistake if we classify it as a form of false consciousness. *Religion reveals the logic of the heart, the dynamism of the "pleasure principle," insofar as it struggles to transform a nonhuman chaos around it into "ordo armoris" (an order of love).*

At this point the reader might rightly make a complaint: "You are offering an apology for religion. But even suppose we accept it. You still have not offered us any convincing reason why we should dedicate ourselves to theology. You have not made it clear why we should go beyond the fantastic variety of religious experiences that arise naturally even today in order to immerse ourselves in things that happened long ago in biblical times."

You would be perfectly right, but let me try to explain myself. You know that all of us are neurotics to a greater or lesser degree. We are not free. We live our daily lives under the power of an infinite number of "evil spirits" that our past has bequeathed to us. Our personal histories, which have molded us, are fraught with frustrations, aggressive feelings, sado-masochistic tendencies, guilt-feelings, and fears. It makes no difference that we struggle against them with all our strength. We are defeated day after day. So long as we remain within the boundaries of our own biographies, we simply shuffle and reshuffle our gods and our evil spirits between us. We may indeed live through different emotional experiences, but the actors of our script remain the same. In desperation we realize that there is no substantive change.

The great discovery of Luther in going through his own personal conflicts was the realization that there is no hope for us if we try to solve our contradictions without going outside ourselves. You know that we become a person only to the extent that the Other rises before us. We are what we are by virtue of the "relevant others" with whom we speak. The I takes shape to the extent that it responds to a Thou. If we remain imprisoned within our selves, at the mercy of an anonymous "self" (Heidegger's *Das Man*[29]), then our only possible way out is to find a new set of "relevant others."

That is theology as I understand it. It is an effort to overcome biography through history, to expand the circle of "relevant others" with whom we are in contact in order to overcome the straitened boundaries in which our life has imprisoned us. Evaluating my own personal experience, I came to see that I scarcely engage in any serious discourse with the people who are in a strictly spatial relationship with me. Our talk ranges from the functional-bureaucratic realm to the other extreme of polite banalities and habitual remarks. My serious conversations, the ones which are a matter of life and death, have almost exclusively been with absent people who are no longer alive: Jeremiah, Jesus, Luther, Nietzsche, Kierkegaard, Berdyaev, and Buber—not to mention such artists as Bach, Scarlatti, Mozart, and Vivaldi. So it is true for theology too: First and foremost theology has to do with the "relevant others" whom we include in our dialogue concerning the problem of our day-to-day life.

What is involved is not an article to publish or a book to write. They are secondary byproducts of the ultimate question: how to survive as a human being in a cold world that has sent our values into exile. It is not a neutral problem that can be broached objectively or dispassionately. What is at stake is my destiny, and so infinite passion is demanded of those who take part in the dialogue. "Doing theology" is making a decision about the battles that ought to be fought. In that sense I find myself fighting those battles all the time. Even if I do not use theological jargon or religious symbols, I am always caught up in religion and theology.

In any case there is more to be said here. If you want to play a certain game you must know the rules. Discussion and debate is a game. If we do not agree on the implicit rules, there will never be any communication. We can still talk, but at the end we will be exactly where we were when we started. The boundaries and structures of our personality will remain unchanged. So before we begin the discussion called "theology," we must realize who and what it is that establishes the rules of the game. We can decide to be in charge of the game. Indeed that is what happens in most cases. It is *my* experience that is absolute. What matters is what I *think*. I am the very navel of the world. My own ego becomes the ultimate criterion for understanding the whole world. Insofar as I take that tack, I affirm that reality must be subjected to the criteria of my own personal experience.

The problem is that all our ingenuity and optimism about ourselves, and even all our mental gymnastics, will not save us. If we adopt our own neurotic ego as the criterion for understanding ourselves, we cannot possibly get away from the snares of our own neurosis. The point I am trying to make here is somewhat in line with the wise gospel remark: "He who would save his life must lose it." Luther noted that the human being, in its inmost depths, is a *cor incurvatum in se ipsum,* "a heart curved in upon itself." We start off from our personal experiences, we absolutize them, and then we try every which way to get a new vision of reality. We do discover some new facet and then we exclaim: "I see, I see. I have seen the face of God." And we do not notice that we have seen nothing more than our own fears, frustrations, fantasies, good intentions, and naiveté: that is, the gods and devils that populate our own unconscious. Our hope of salvation is nothing more than our condition of damnation. We are not saved; we are simply bedazzled by our own illusions.

That is the reason why I myself, in trying to find new horizons, identify myself emotionally with the experience of "captivity": "By the streams of Babylon we sat and wept when we remembered Zion" (Ps. 137:1). Captivity is characterized by the sorrowful juxtaposition of yearnings for freedom and a conscious awareness of impotence. Only dreamers and visionaries feel impotent. Those who do not have dreams and visions drown in a settled world. They adapt to it, become functional, and are content.

That is one of the reasons why I have serious suspicions about psychoanalysis. It alleges and seeks to solve the problem of neurosis not by transforming the objective pole of experience but by altering the subjective pole and making it adapt to established reality. But adaptation always implies passive acceptance of a world that has not been redeemed.

To feel oneself a captive, on the other hand, is to refuse to accept the world as it is. It is a sad and painful refusal, however, because it is not accompanied by the optimism of those who feel strong enough to complete the transformation demanded by consciousness. Captives are condemned to sadness, and the sadness is not transformed into desperation or accommodation if, in the midst of captivity, one glimpses a hope of liberty. But this hope of liberty is not fashioned by our own strength. We are impotent. To hope for liberation in captivity is to hope for the impossible: the unexpected. In the old idiom of religion it is to have trust in a God who summons things that do not exist into existence and makes the barren fruitful.

But why choose this particular way of seeing things rather than another way? I don't know. In the last analysis it is a matter of love, of hope. But that is true for all the dimensions of our life. Even in science, as Kuhn has pointed out, there can be no advance without the risk of faith and a vision of hope.[30] Perhaps our choice is mistaken, but we have no alternative except to make some choice. Even not choosing is making a choice.

We are condemned to gods and demons. We are condemned to religion. It is even possible that we may be ashamed of this and that we will cloak our values and dreams in the respectable dress of science. Of one thing I am certain: Life is not accompanied by inescapable certitudes but by visions, risks, and passions. As Nietzsche put it: "Whoever had to create also had his prophetic dreams and astral signs—and had faith in faith."[31]

NOTES

1. Thomas S. Kuhn, *The Structure of Scientific Revolutions* (Chicago: University of Chicago Press, 1962).

2. "We do not know: we can only guess. And our guesses are guided by the unscientific, the metaphysical . . . faith in laws" *(The Logic of Scientific Discovery* [New York: Harper & Row, 1968]), p. 278.

3. Ludwig Wittgenstein, *The Blue and Brown Books* (New York: Harper & Row, 1958), p. 27.

4. Dietrich Bonhoeffer, *Letters and Papers from Prison* (New York: Macmillan Paperback, 1962), pp. 103, 113, 168.

5. Marx-Engels, *On Religion* (New York: Schocken Books, 1964), p. 41.

6. Prescott Lecky, *Self-Consistency: A Theory of Personality* (New York: Double-day, 1961).

7. Ezra Stotland, *The Psychology of Hope* (San Francisco: Jessy-Bass, 1969).

8. L. Feuerbach, *The Essence of Christianity* (New York: Harper Torchbooks, 1957), p. 13.

9. F. Nietzsche, *Thus Spoke Zarathustra,* in *The Portable Nietzsche* (New York: Viking Press, 1968), p. 144.

10. Feuerbach, *Essence of Christianity,* pp. 5 and 8.

11. Norman O. Brown, *Life Against Death* (Middletown, Conn: Wesleyan University Press, 1959), p. 46.

12. P. Berger and T. Luckmann, *The Social Construction of Reality* (New York: Doubleday, 1966), p. 96.

13. *Portable Nietzsche,* p. 174.

14. A. Gouldner, *The Coming Crisis of Western Sociology* (New York: Basic Books, 1970), p. 29.

15. L. Wittgenstein, *Tractatus Logico-Philosophicus* (London: Routledge & Kegan Paul, 1922), section 4.002.

16. Philip Rieff, *The Mind of the Moralist* (New York: Doubleday, 1961), p. 35.

17. F. Engels, *Socialism: Utopian and Scientific* (New York: Scribner's, 1892), pp. 47–48.

18. S. Freud, *Civilization and Its Discontents* (New York: Norton, 1962), p. 92.

19. G. Lukács, *History and Class Consciousness* (Cambridge: M.I.T. Press, 1971).

20. Ibid.

21. A. Gouldner, *Coming Crisis,* p. 51, citing Blau, "The Study of Formal Organization, " in T. Parsons, ed., *American Sociology* (New York: Basic Books, 1968), p. 54.

22. L. Althusser, *For Marx* (New York: Vintage Books, 1970), p. 229.

23. J. P. Sartre, *The Psychology of Imagination* (New York: Washington Square Press, 1968), p. 159.

24. Feuerbach, *Essence of Christianity,* p. xxxix.

25. John Dewey, *Experience and Nature* (Chicago: Open Court, 1925), p. 96.

26. "Le vrai n'est pas copie, il est alors une organization du réel" (*Biologie et connaissance* [Paris: Gallimard, 1967], p. 414).

27. "We have established the fact that the fundamental categories of thought, and consequently of science, are of religious origin" (Emile Durkheim, *The Elementary Forms of Religious Life* [New York: The Free Press, 1969], p. 466.

28. Martin Buber, *I and Thou* (Edinburgh: T. & T. Clark, 1955).

29. Martin Heidegger, *Being and Time* (New York: Harper & Row, 1962), pp. 167–68.

30. See Kuhn, *Structure of Scientific Revolutions.*

31. *Portable Nietzsche,* p. 232.

8

Leonardo Boff

Jesus, a Person of Extraordinary Good Sense, Creative Imagination, and Originality

Leonardo Boff has sought to develop an adequate Christology for Latin America. This selection, "Jesus, a Person of Extraordinary Good Sense, Creative Imagination, and Originality," is taken from Jesus Christ Liberator *(Maryknoll, N.Y.: Orbis Books, 1978), pp. 80–99. The book was originally published in Brazil in 1972.*

Before giving divine titles to Jesus, the Gospels permit us to speak of him in a very human way. With him, as the New Testament tells us, "appeared the goodness and humanitarian love of God." He does not paint the world as better or worse than it is. Nor does he immediately moralize. With extraordinary good sense, he faces up to reality; he possesses a capacity to see in perspective and place all things in their proper place. Allied to this good sense was the capacity to see human beings as greater and richer than their concrete and cultural surroundings. In him, that which is most divine in humanity and that which is most human in God was revealed.

The message of Jesus is of a radical and total liberation of the human condition from all its alienating elements. He already presents himself as a new man, as of a new creation reconciled with itself and with God. His words and attitudes reveal someone liberated from the complications that people and a history of sin created. He sees clearly the more complex and the simple realities and immediately goes to the essential in things. He knows how to speak of them, briefly, concisely, and with precision. He showed an extraordinary good sense that surprised all about him. Perhaps this fact gave origin to Christology, that is, an attempt on the part of faith to decipher the origin of the originality of Jesus and to answer the question: But who really are you, Jesus of Nazareth?

JESUS, A PERSON OF EXTRAORDINARY GOOD SENSE AND SOUND REASON

To have good sense is the natural endowment of people that are truly great. We say that people have good sense when they immediately discover the core of things, when they have the right word and the necessary comportment for each situation. Good sense is related to concrete knowledge of life; it is knowing how to distinguish the essential from the secondary, the capacity to see things in perspective and place them in their proper place. Good sense is always situated opposite exaggeration. For this reason, the lunatic and the genius, who resemble one another in many ways, are fundamentally distinguished on this point. The genius is one who has radicalized good sense. The lunatic is one who has radicalized an exaggeration.

Jesus, as he is presented by gospel witnesses, gave evidence of being a genius of good sense. A freshness without analogies pervades all that he does and says. God, human beings, society, and nature are immediately present to him. He does not theologize. Nor does he appeal to superior moral principles. Nor does he lose himself in a minute and heartless casuistry. But his words bite into the concrete world until it is forced to make a decision before God. His determinations are incisive and direct: "Be reconciled with your brother" (Matt. 5:24b). "Offer the wicked man no resistance. On the contrary, if anyone hits you on the right cheek, offer him the other as well" (Matt. 5:39). "Love your enemies, and pray for those who persecute you" (Matt. 5:44). "When you give alms, your left hand must not know what your right hand is doing" (Matt. 6:3).

Jesus Is Prophet and Master: But He Is Different

Jesus' style recalls the great prophets. Certainly he emerges as a great *prophet* (Mark 8:28; Matt. 21:11, 46). Nevertheless he is not like the prophets of the Old Testament, who needed a divine call and legitimation on the part of God. Jesus does not claim any vision of celestial mysteries to which he alone has access. Nor does he pretend to communicate hidden incomprehensible truths. He speaks, preaches, discusses, and gathers disciples around him like any *rabbi* of his day. And nevertheless the difference between the rabbis and Jesus is as the heaven is to the earth. A rabbi is an interpreter of the Sacred Scriptures: a rabbi discerns in them the will of God.

Jesus' doctrine is never a mere explanation of the sacred texts. He also discerns the will of God outside of the Scriptures: in creation, history, and the concrete situation. He accepts people into his company that a rabbi would very clearly reject: sinners, tax officials, children, and women. He draws his doctrine from the common experiences that all live and can verify. His listeners understand immediately. The only presuppositions demanded of them are good sense and sound reason. For example, all know that a city built on a hilltop cannot be hidden (Matt. 5:14); that each day has enough trouble of its own (Matt. 6:34); that we ought never to swear, not even by our own head since we cannot turn a single hair white or black (Matt. 5:36); that we cannot add one single cubit to our span of life (Matt. 6:27); that the human person is worth much more than the birds in the sky (Matt. 6:26); that the sabbath was made for humanity, not humanity for the sabbath (Mark 2:27).

Jesus Does Not Want to Say Something New Merely for Effect and Whatever the Cost

Jesus never appeals to a higher authority, one coming from outside, to reinforce his own authority and doctrine. The things he says possess an internal evidence. He is not interested in saying something esoteric and incomprehensible, something new at any cost. He says rational things that people can understand and live. On close inspection, we see that Christ did not come to bring a new morality, different from the one people already had. He brings to light that which people always knew or ought to have known but because of their alienation were unable to see, comprehend, and formulate.

Consider as an example the golden rule of charity (Matt. 7:12; Luke 6:31): "Always treat others as you would like them to treat you."[1] Thales of Miletus (600 B.C.) relates that on being asked to state the highest rule of good living he answered: "Do not do the evil you find in others."[2] In Pittacus (580 B.C.) we find a similar formula: "Do not yourself do whatsoever you dislike in others." Isocrates (400 B.C.) states the same truth in a positive formula: "Treat others as you would wish them to treat you." Confucius (551–470 B.C.), when asked by a disciple if a norm existed that one could follow throughout one's life, said: "Love of the neighbor. Whatsoever you do not desire for yourself, do not do unto others." In the national epic poem of India, the *Mahabharata* (between 400 B.C. and A.D. 400), one finds the following truth: "Learn the highest point of the law and when you have learnt it, think on it: Whatsoever you hate, do not do unto others." In the Old Testament one reads: "Do to no one what you would not want done to you" (Tob. 4:15). At the time of King Herod, a pagan appeared before the celebrated Rabbi Hillel, teacher of St. Paul, and said to him: "I will accept Judaism on condition you tell me all the law while I am standing on one foot." To which Hillel answered: "Do not do unto others whatsoever you do not wish them to do unto you. The law consists in this. All the rest is commentary. Go and learn!"

Jesus never read Thales of Miletus, or Pittacus, much less Confucius and the *Mahabharata*. Jesus stated his formulation in the positive form that infinitely surpasses the negative, because it puts no limit to one's openness to, and preoccupation for, the suffering and joy of others. He thus joins the long line of great sages who preoccupied themselves with *humanitas.* "The epiphany of the humanity of God is culminated when Jesus professed the golden rule of human charity."³ Jesus does not wish to say something new, merely for effect and whatever the cost, but something as old as humankind; not something original, but something that is valid for all; not astonishing things, but things people can comprehend on their own if they have clear vision and a little good sense. St. Augustine had good reason for thinking: "The substance of that which today is called Christianity was already known to ancient peoples, nor was it absent from the beginnings of the human race to the time when Christ came in the flesh. Since that time, the true religion that already existed began to call itself the Christian religion."⁴

Jesus Wants Us to Understand:
He Appeals to Sound Reason

Other examples taken from the many possible will give us evidence of Jesus' good sense and the appeal he makes to sound reason: He commands that we love our enemies. Why? Because all, friends and enemies, are children of the same God who causes the sun to rise on the wicked as well as the good, and the rain to fall on the honest and dishonest alike (Matt. 5:45). He commands that we do good to all without distinction. Why? Because if we do good to those who do good to us, what thanks can we expect? For even sinners do that much (Luke 6:33). He forbids men to have more than one woman. Why? Because monogamy existed at the beginning of creation. God created one couple, Adam and Eve (Mark 10:6). It is no good simply to say: Do not kill, or do not commit adultery. Anger and covetous looks are already sinful. Why? What use is it to combat the consequences if first one does not heal the cause (Matt. 5:22, 28). Human beings were not made for the sabbath, but the sabbath for human beings. Why? If an animal fell down a hole on the sabbath day, would one not go and take it out? A person is far more important than an animal (Matt. 12:11–12).

We ought to have faith in the providence of God. Why? Because God looks after the lilies in the field, birds in the sky, and every hair on our heads. "You are worth more than hundreds of sparrows" (Matt. 10:31). "If, then, you who are evil know how to give your children what is good, how much more will your Father in heaven give good things to those who ask him" (Matt. 7:11). The law says that it is a sin to walk with sinners, because they will make one unclean. Christ is not worried on this score. He uses sound reason and argues: "It is not the healthy who need the doctor, but the sick. I did not come to call the virtuous, but sinners" (Mark 2:17). It is not what enters a person that makes one unclean, but what comes out. Why? "Whatever goes into a man from outside cannot make him unclean, because it does not go into his heart but through his stomach and passes out into the sewer. . . . It is what comes out of a man that makes him unclean. For it is from within, from men's hearts, that evil intentions emerge: fornication, theft, etc." (Mark 7:18–22). This use of sound reason by Jesus is still theologically very relevant for us today because it shows us that Christ wants us to understand things. He did not demand a blind submission to the law.[5]

Jesus Does Not Paint the World
Better or Worse Than It Is

Jesus' look at the world is penetrating and without preconceptions; he goes immediately to the core of the problem. His parables show that he knows the whole reality of life, good and bad. He does not paint the world better or worse than it is. Nor does he immediately moralize. His first position with regard to the world is not one of censure but of comprehension. Nature is not celebrated as numinous, as in Teilhard de Chardin and even St. Francis of Assisi. Rather nature is seen in its created naturalness. He speaks of the sun and rain (Matt. 5:45), of storm clouds and the south wind (Luke 12:54–55), of lightning that strikes in the east and flashes far into the west (Matt. 24:27), of birds that neither sow nor reap nor gather into barns (Matt. 6:26), of the beauty of the flowers growing in the fields and the grass that is there today and thrown into the furnace tomorrow (Matt. 6:30), of the sprouting of the leaves of fig trees as a precursor of summer (Mark 13:28), of the harvest (Mark 4:3ff., 26ff.; Matt. 13:24ff.), of moths and woodworms (Matt. 6:19), of dogs that lick sores (Luke 16:21), of vultures that eat corpses (Matt. 24:28). He speaks of thorns and thistles; he knows the gestures of the sower (Luke 12:16–21); he refers to the farm that produces (Luke 16:21); and he knows how to construct a house (Matt. 7:24–27).

He knows how a woman makes bread (Matt. 13:33); with the care of a pastor he goes in search of the lost sheep (Luke 15ff.). He knows how peasants work (Mark 4:3), rest, and sleep (Mark 4:26ff.). He knows how the master demands an account of his employees (Matt. 25:14ff.) and how they can be whipped (Luke 12:47–48). He knows that the unemployed sit in the square waiting for work (Matt. 20:1ff.); that children want to play at marriage in the public square but their companions are unwilling to dance; that they want to play at a burial service but the others do not wish to lament (Matt. 11:16–18). He knows the joy of a mother when a child is born (John 16:21) and that the powerful of the earth enslave others (Matt. 20:25). He knows what the obedience of soldiers is like (Matt. 8:9).

Jesus uses strong examples. He takes life as it really is. He knows how to draw a lesson from the steward of a company who steals and is smart (Luke 16:1–12). He refers with naturalness to the king who goes to war (Luke 14:31–33). He knows the jealousy that people experience between themselves (Luke 15:28), and he compares himself to a robber (Mark 3:27). There is a parable that is considered authentically of Jesus and transmitted in the apocryphal Gospel of St. Thomas that shows clearly the strong and real sensitivity of

Christ: "The kingdom of the Father is like a man who wished to kill an important lord. When at home, he took out his sword and pierced the wall. He wanted to know if his hand was sufficiently strong. Afterwards, he killed the important lord."[6] With this he wanted to teach that when God begins some project he always concludes it, just as this assassin.

All this clearly shows that Jesus is a person of extraordinary good sense. Whence did he derive this? To answer this question is to do Christology. We will return again to this theme.

All That Is Authentically Human Is Seen in Jesus: Anger and Joy, Goodness and Toughness, Friendship, Sorrow, and Temptation

The gospel stories tell us of the absolute normality of Jesus' life. He is a person of profound sentiments. He knows natural affection for the children he embraces (Matt. 9:36); he lays his hands on them and blesses them (Mark 10:13–16). He is impressed by the generosity of the rich young man: "Jesus looked steadily at him and loved him" (Mark 10:31). He rejoices over the faith of a pagan (Luke 7:9) and the wisdom of a scribe (Mark 12:34). He is surprised at the incredulity of his compatriots from Nazareth (Mark 6:6). On seeing the funeral of a widow's only son, he was moved and "felt sorry for her"; he approached and consoled her, saying: "Do not cry" (Luke 7:13). He took pity on the hungry people because they lost their way like sheep without a shepherd (Mark 6:34). If he is angered by the lack of faith in people (Mark 9:18), he is so happy with the good will of simple people that he says a prayer of thanks to God (Matt. 11:25–26). He feels the ingratitude of the nine blind men that were cured (Luke 7:44–46), and he irately reproaches the cities of Chorazin and Bethsaida and Capernaum because they have not done penance (Matt. 11:20–24). He is grieved by the blindness of the Pharisees, and "he looked angrily around at them" (Mark 3:5).

Jesus employs physical violence against those who profane the temple (John 2:15–17). He complains of the disciples because they too do not understand (Mark 7:18). He gives vent to this against Philip and says to him, "Have you been with me all this time, Philip, and you still do not know me" (John 14:19). He also gives vent to his anger toward the Pharisees "with a sigh that came straight from the heart" (Mark 8:12): "Why does this generation demand a sign?" (Mark 8:12). He is agitated by the revengeful spirit of the apostles (Luke 9:55) and with Peter's insinuations: "Go behind me Satan" (Mark 8:33). But he rejoices with them on their return from a mission. He concerns himself to see that they want for nothing: " 'When I sent you out without purse or haversack or sandals, were you short for anything?' 'No,' they said" (Luke 22:35). When with them, he does not want them to call him master but friend (Luke 12:4–7; John 15:13–15). All that is his is also theirs (John 17:22). Friendship is a characteristic theme with Jesus because to be a friend to someone is a form of love.[7] And he loved all even to extremes.

The parables demonstrate how well Jesus knew the phenomenon of friendship: one gets together with friends to celebrate (Luke 15:6, 9, 29) and have banquets (Luke 14:12–14); one runs to a friend even though it may be inopportune (Luke 11:5–8); there are inconstant friends who betray others (Luke 21:16); friendship can exist even between two rogues like Pilate and Herod (Luke 23:12). Jesus' comportment with the apostles, his miracles, his action at the wedding in Cana, the multiplication of the loaves—all reveal his friendship. His relationship with Lazarus is one of friendship. "Lord, the man you love is ill. . . ." "Lazarus our friend is resting, I am going to wake him," said Jesus (John 11:11). When Jesus weeps at the death of his friend they all comment: "See how much he loved him" (John 11:37). He felt at home in Bethany with Martha and Mary (Matt. 21:17) and liked to return there (Luke 11:38, 42; John 11:17).

For many men friendship with women is tabu. This was even more so at the time of Christ. A woman could not appear in public with her husband, much less with a traveling preacher like Jesus. And nevertheless we know of Jesus' friendship with some women who followed him and fed him and his disciples (Luke 8:3). We know the names of a few: Mary Magdalene; Joanna, the wife of Chuza, a functionary of Herod; Susanna; and others. There is a woman beside the cross. It is they who will bury him and go to cry for the dead Lord at the sepulcher (Mark 16:1–4). It is also women who see the resurrected Jesus. He breaks a social tabu by allowing a woman of ill repute to anoint him (Mark 14:3–9; Luke 7:37ff.), and he converses with a woman heretic (John 4:7ff.).

Aristotle used to say that friendship could not be possible between divinity and human beings because of the differences in nature. The philosopher could not have imagined the emergence of God in warm, receptive human flesh. All that is authentically human appears in Jesus: anger and joy, goodness and toughness, friendship and indignation. He possesses all the human dimensions of vigor, vitality, and spontaneity. He partook of all our feelings and the common conditionings of human life such as hunger (Matt. 4:2; Mark 11:12), thirst (John 4:7; 19:28), tiredness (John 4:6; Mark 4:37ff.), cold and heat, an insecure life without a roof (Luke 9:58; cf. John 11:53–54; 12:36), tears (Luke 19:41; John 11:35), sorrow and fear (Matt. 26:37), and strong temptations (Matt. 4:1–11; Luke 4:1–13; Heb. 4:15; 5:2, 7–10). His psyche can plunge to the depths of desperation: "My soul is sorrowful to the point of death" (Matt. 26:38); he lived through the terror and anguish of a violent death (Luke 22:44). For this reason the good shepherd of souls that wrote the Epistle to the Hebrews commented that Jesus is capable of "feeling our weaknesses with us, because we have one who has been tempted in every way that we are, though he is without sin" (Heb. 4:15).

JESUS, A PERSON OF EXTRAORDINARY CREATIVE IMAGINATION

It may seem strange to speak of the creative imagination of Jesus.[8] The church and theologians are not accustomed to express themselves in this manner. Nevertheless, we ought to say that, as the New Testament itself shows us, there are many ways of speaking about Jesus. Is it not possible that for us this category "imagination" may reveal the originality and mystery of Christ? Many understand little about imagination and think that it is synonymous with dreams, a day-dreamer's flight from reality, a passing illusion. In truth, however, imagination signifies something much more profound. Imagination is a form of liberty. It is born in confrontation with reality and established order; it emerges from nonconformity in the face of completed and established situations; it is the capacity to see human beings as greater and richer than the cultural and concrete environment that surrounds them; it is having the courage to think and say something new and to take hitherto untread paths that are full of meaning for human beings. We can say that imagination, understood in this manner, was one of the fundamental qualities of Jesus. Perhaps in the whole of human history there has not been a single person who had a richer imagination than Jesus.

Jesus, a Person Who Has the Courage to Say: I

We have already seen that Jesus does not accept without question the Judaic traditions, laws, sacred rites, and established order of his day. At the beginning of his Gospel, Mark says that Christ taught "a new doctrine" (Mark 1:27). He does not repeat what the Old Testament taught. Consequently he had the courage to rise up and say: "You have heard what was said by our fathers"— and here he was thinking of the law, Moses, and the prophets—"I however say to you." He is a person who boldly proclaims "I" without guaranteeing himself by other authorities from outside himself.

The new tidings he preaches are not completely unknown to humankind. Rather, his message is what good sense commands and what had been lost by the religious, moral, and cultural complications created by the people. Christ came to discover the good tidings of what is most ancient and original in the human person made to the image and likeness of God. He does not concern himself with order (which is often order in disorder) but allows creative imagination to reign. In so doing he disconcerts established people who now ask themselves: Who is he? Is he not the carpenter, son of Mary? (Mark 6:3a; Matt. 13:53–58; Luke 4:16–30; John 6:42).

He walks among forbidden people and accepts doubtful persons in his company, such as two or three guerillas (Simon, the Canaanite, Judas Iscariot, Peter bar Jonah);[9] he gives a complete turnabout to the social and religious framework, saying that the last shall be first (Mark 10:31), the humble shall be masters (Matt. 5:5), and tax officials and prostitutes will find it easier to enter the kingdom of heaven than the pious scribes and Pharisees (Matt. 21:23). He does not discriminate against anyone, neither heretics nor schismatic Samaritans (Luke 10:29–37; John 4:4–42) nor people of ill repute like the prostitute (Luke 7:36–40) nor the marginalized (sick, leprous, and poor)[10] nor the rich whose houses he frequents even while saying to them: "Alas for you who are rich: you are having your consolation now" (Luke 6:24). Nor does he refuse the invitations of his indefatigable opposition, the Pharisees, though seven times he takes the liberty of saying to them: "Alas for you, scribes and Pharisees, you hypocrites and blind guides" (Matt. 23:13–39).

Jesus Never Used the Word "Obedience"

The established order is relativized and human beings liberated from the tentacles that have kept them prisoners. The preaching and demands of Christ do not presuppose an established order. Rather, on the contrary, he frustrates it because of his creative imagination and spontaneity. Insofar as we can judge, the word "obedience" (and its derivatives), while occurring eighty-seven times in the New Testament, was never used by Christ.[11] We do not mean to say by this that Jesus made no harsh demands. Obedience for him is not a question of fulfilling orders, but a firm decision in favor of what God demands within a concrete situation. The will of God is not always manifested in the law. Normally it reveals itself in the concrete situation where conscience is caught unawares by a proposal that demands a response.

The great difficulty encountered by Jesus in his disputes with theologians and masters of his time consisted in precisely this: We cannot resolve the question concerning what God wants from us by merely having recourse to the Scriptures. We must consult the signs of the times and the unforeseen in a situation (cf. Luke 12:54–57). This is a clear appeal to spontaneity, liberty, and the use of our creative imagination. Obedience is a question of having our eyes open to the situation; it consists in deciding for and risking ourselves in the adventure of responding to God who speaks here and now. The Sermon on the Mount, which is not a law, is addressed to everyone, inviting us to have extremely clear consciences and an unlimited capacity for understanding people, sympathizing with them, being tuned into them, and loving them with all their limitations and realizations.

Jesus Does Not Have Prefabricated Notions

Jesus himself is the best example of this way of life, as is summarized in a phrase of the Gospel of John: "Whoever comes to me, I shall not turn him away" (John 6:37). He receives everybody: the sinners with whom he eats (Luke 15:2; Matt. 9:10–11) and the little ones (Mark 10:13–16); he pays attention to the crippled woman (Luke 13:10–17), the anonymous blind man by the wayside (Mark 10:46–52), the woman who is ashamed of her bleeding (Mark 5:21–34). He receives the well-known theologian at night (John 3:1ff.). He did not even have time to eat (Mark 3:20; 6:31) and goes into a deep sleep because of fatigue (Mark 4:38). His speech can be harsh when inveighing against those who do things for appearance' sake (Matt. 3:7; 23:1–39; John 9:44), but it can also be full of comprehension and forgiveness (John 8:10–11).

In his way of speaking and acting, in his treatment of various social strata, he never sees people according to prefabricated notions. He respects all persons in their own originality: the Pharisees as Pharisees, the scribes as scribes, the sinners as sinners, the sick as sick. His reaction is always surprising: he has the right word and corresponding gesture for every person. John properly says: "He never needed evidence about any man, he could tell what a man had in him" (John 2:25). Though no one had told him, he knew of the sin of the paralytic (Mark 2:5), of the state of Jairus's daughter (Mark 5:39), of the woman who suffered from a hemorrhage (Mark 5:29ff.), of the man possessed by a demon (Mark 1:23ff.; 5:1ff.), of the intimate thoughts of his opponents (Mark 2:8; 3:5). He is surely a charismatic figure without analogy in history.[12] He demonstrates impressive superiority.[13] He unmasks trick questions (cf. Mark 12:14ff.) and gives surprising answers. He can make his adversaries speak, but he can also silence them (Matt. 22:34). The Gospels often refer to the fact that Christ was silent himself. Listening to the people and feeling their problems is also one of the ways of loving them.

Was Jesus a Liberal?

Some years ago one of the greatest exegetes of the day asked this question and answered:

> Jesus . . . was a "liberal." No qualification whatsoever of this statement is possible, even though churches and devout people should declare it blasphemous. He was a "liberal," because in the name of God and in the power of the Holy Spirit he interpreted and appraised Moses, the Scriptures, and dogmatics from the point of view of love, and thereby allowed devout people to remain human and even reasonable.[14]

To see how true this is, we need only remember the following episode that marvelously puts into relief the liberty and open-mindedness of Jesus: "Master, we saw a man who is not one of us casting out devils in your name, and because he was not one of us we tried to stop him." But Jesus said, "You must not stop him: No one who works a miracle in my name is likely to speak evil of me. Anyone who is not against us is for us" (Mark 9:38–40; Luke 9:49–50).

Christ differs from many of his sectarian disciples throughout history. Jesus came to be and to live Christ and not to preach Christ or announce himself.[15] Because of this he feels his mission realized wherever he sees people that follow him and—even though there be no explicit reference to his name—do what he wanted and proclaimed. What he wanted is clear: the happiness of human beings that can be found only if we open ourselves to others and to the Great Other (God) (cf. Luke 10:25–37; Mark 12:28–31; Matt. 22:34–40). There is a sin that is radically mortal: the sin against the humanitarian spirit. According to the parable concerning anonymous Christians in Matthew 25:31–46, the eternal Judge will not ask people about the canons of dogma, nor whether they made any explicit reference to the mystery of Christ while they lived. He will ask if we have done anything to help those in need. Here all is decided. "Lord, when did we see you hungry or thirsty, a stranger or naked, sick or in prison, and did not come to your help?" He will answer them: "I tell you solemnly, insofar as you neglected to do this to one of the least of these, you neglected to do it to me" (Matt. 25:44–45). The sacrament of compassion is absolutely necessary for salvation. Those who deny this deny the cause of Christ, even when they always have Christ on their lips and officially confess themselves for him.[16]

Imagination postulates creativity, spontaneity, and liberty. It is precisely this that Christ demands when he proposes an ideal like the Sermon on the Mount. Here, one can no longer speak of laws, but of love that surpasses all laws. Christ's invitation: "You must therefore be perfect just as your heavenly Father is perfect" (Matt. 5:48) knocked down all possible barriers to religious imagination, whether they had been raised by religions or by cultures or by existential situations.

THE ORIGINALITY OF JESUS

When speaking of the originality of Jesus we ought first to clear up an equivocation. Original does not refer to someone who says entirely pure and new things. Nor is original synonymous with strange. "Original" comes from "origin." Those who are near the origin and root of things and by their lives, words, and works bring others to the origin and root of their own selves can be properly called original, not because they discover new things, but because they speak of things with absolute immediacy and superiority. All that they say and do is translucent, crystal clear, and evident. People perceive this immediately. All those in contact with Jesus encountered themselves and that which is best in them. All are led to discover their own root. Confrontation with this source generates a crisis: one is constrained to make a decision and either convert or install oneself in that which is derived, secondary, and part of the current situation.

Good sense consists in grasping the original nature of human beings, which we all live and know but find difficult to formulate and translate into images. Christ knew how to verbalize this original core of human nature in a genial manner, as we saw above. Consequently he can resolve conflicts and put an "and" where most put an "or." The author of the Letter to the Ephesians tells us the truth: Christ broke down the walls that separated Gentiles from Jews and "has made the two into one" (Eph. 2:24, 15).[17] He broke down all barriers, sacred and profane, of conventions and legalism, of divisions between peoples and sexes, of people with God, because now all have access to God and can say "Abba, Father" (Eph. 3:18; cf. Gal. 4:6; Rom. 8:15). All are sisters and brothers and children of the same God. Therefore the originality of Jesus consists in being able to grasp the profundity of the human person, which is a concern of all peoples without exception. Thus, he does not found yet another new school nor elaborate a new ritual of prayer nor prescribe a supermorality. But he arrives at a dimension and marks a horizon that obliges all reality to be revolutionized, to be renewed, and to be converted.

Why is it that Christ is so original, superior, and exalted? The Christology of yesterday and today emerges from this question. Before giving divine titles to Jesus the Gospels themselves permit us to speak very humanly about him. Faith tells us that in him "appeared the goodness and humanitarian love of God" (Tim. 3:4). How do we discover this? Is it not perhaps in his extraordinary good sense, in his singularly creative imagination, and in his unequaled originality?

CONCLUSION: THE THEOLOGICAL RELEVANCE OF THE COMPORTMENT OF JESUS

Interest in the attitudes and comportment of the historical Jesus begins with the presupposition that in him is revealed that which is most divine in persons and most human in God. Therefore, what emerged and was expressed in Jesus ought to emerge and be expressed also in his followers:[18] complete openness to God and others; indiscriminate love without limits; a critical spirit in confronting the current social and religious situation because the situation does not incarnate the will of God in a pure and straightforward manner; a critical spirit that cultivates creative imagination, which in the name of love and the liberty of the children of God challenges cultural structures; and giving primacy to persons over things, which belong to and exist for persons. Christians ought to be free and liberated persons. We do not mean by this that they may be lawless anarchists. Christians understand the law in a different way. As St. Paul says "we are no longer living by law" (Rom. 6:15) but living by "the law of Christ" (1 Cor. 9:21) that permits us—"being totally free" (1 Cor. 9:19)—to live with those who are subjects of the law or again with those who have no law so as to win both (1 Cor. 9:19). The law is relativized and put at the *service* of love. "When Christ freed us, he meant us to remain free. . . . Do not submit again to the yoke of slavery" (Gal. 5:1).

We see all this realized in exemplary fashion by Jesus of Nazareth with a spontaneity that is not paralleled, and never will be, in the history of religions. He detheologizes religion, making people search for the will of God not only in holy books but principally in daily life; he demythologizes religious language, using the expressions of our common experiences; he deritualizes piety, insisting that one is always before God and not only when one goes to the temple to pray; he emancipates the message of God from its connection to one religious community and directs it to all people of good will (cf. Mark 9:30–40; John 10:16); and, finally, he secularizes the means of salvation, making the sacrament of the "other" a determining element for entry into the kingdom of God.

Nevertheless he did not come to make our life more comfortable. Rather, the contrary is true. In the words of Dostoevski's Grand Inquisitor:

Instead of dominating conscience, you came to make it even more profound; instead of encircling human liberty, you came to make its horizon even wider. . . . Your desire was to liberate people for love. Free, they ought to follow You, feel themselves attracted to You and as Your prisoners. Instead of obeying the harsh laws of the past, people ought to begin as of now to decide in Your presence what is good and what is bad, having Your example before their eyes.

To attempt to live such a lifestyle is to follow Christ with the richness that this term—to follow and imitate Christ—has for the New Testament. It means liberation and the experience of a new redeemed and reconciled life. But it can also include, as in the case of Christ, persecution and death.

In conclusion, how beautifully resound the profound words of Dostoevski on returning from the house of the dead, his prison of forced labor in Siberia:

At times God sends me moments of peace; on these occasions, I love and feel that I am loved; it was in one such moment that I composed for myself a credo in which all is clear and sacred. This credo is very simple. This is it: I believe that there is nothing on earth more beautiful, more profound, more appealing, more virile, or more perfect than Christ; and I say to myself, with jealous love, that greater than he does not and cannot exist. More than this: should anyone prove to me that Christ is beyond the range of truth, and that all this is not to be found in him, I would prefer to retain Christ than to retain the truth.[19]

NOTES

1. E. Stauffer, *Die Botschaft Jesu; Damals und Heute* (Bern-Munich: Francke, 1959), pp. 55–56; L. J. Philippidis, *Die goldene Regel, religionsgeschichtlich unter-sucht,* 1929; J. Jeremias, "Goldene Regel," in *Die Religion in Geschichte und Gegenwart,* 1958, pp. 1688ff.

2. H. Diels, *Die Fragmente der Vorsokratiker, griechisch und deutsch,* 6 vols. (Berlin: Weidmann, 1951).

3. Stauffer, *Die Botschaft Jesu,* p. 59.

4. St. Augustine, "Retractationum," in J. P. Migne, *Patrologiae Latinae* (Paris: Garnier Frères, 1877), 32:602–3.

5. Cf. E. Käsemann, *Der Ruf der Freiheit* (Tübingen, 1968), p. 43; Eng. trans., *Jesus Means Freedom* (Philadelphia: Fortress Press, 1970).

6. C.-H. Hunzinger, "Unbekannte Gleichnisse Jesu aus dem Thomasevangelium," in *Judentum, Urchristentum, Kirche,* Fest. J. Jeremias, ed. W. Eltester (Berlin: Töpelmann, 1960), pp. 209–20, esp. pp. 211–12.

7. Cf. E. Bouet-Dufeil and Jean-Marie Dufeil, "L'amitié dans l'Evangile," *La Vie Spirituelle* (June–July 1968): 642–60; C. Jean-Nesmy, "Les amitiés du Christ," *La Vie Spirituelle* (June 1964): 673–86.

8. Cf. D. Sölle, *Phantasie und Gehorsam* (Stuttgart: Kreuz, 1968), pp. 56–71; M.

Meschler, *Zum Charakterbild Jesus* (Freiburg, 1916), pp. 95–104.

9. See L. Boff, "Foi Cristo um Revolucionário?", *Revista Eclesiástica Brasileira* 31 (1971): 97–118.

10. Cf. J. Jeremias, "Zöllner und Sünder," *Zeitschrift für die Neutestamentliche Wissenschaft* 30 (1931): 293–300, esp. p. 300.

11. Luke 17:6 does not have a moral context; moreover it represents an editorial revision of Mark 11:23; cf. Matt. 21:23. Matthew's other text (Matt. 18:17) is evidently a theological elaboration of the primitive church. Also Luke 10:20 does not have a moral context. However, see R. Deichgraber, "Gehorsen und Gehorchen in der Verkundigung Jesum," *Zeitschrift für die Neutestamentliche Wissenschaft* 52 (1961): 119–22.

12. Cf. R. Otto, *Reich Gottes und Menschensohn* (Munich: Beck, 1934), pp. 277–83; Eng. trans., *The Kingdom of God and the Son of Man* (Boston: Starr King Press, 1957).

13. G. Bornkamm, *Die Frage nach dem historischen Jesus* (Göttingen: Vandenhoeck and Ruprecht, 1962); H. Braun, *Jesus. Der Mann aus Nazareth und seine Zeit* (Stüttgart: Kreuz, 1969), pp. 73ff.; W. Gründmann, *Die Geschichte Jesu Christi* (Berlin: Evangelische Verlagsanstalt, 1961), pp. 261–70; J. R. Geiselmann, *Jesus der Christus* (Munich: Kösel, 1965), 1:218–21.

14. E. Käsemann, "War Jesus liberal?", in *Der Ruf der Freiheit,* pp. 28–58, esp. p. 42.

15. Cf. H. E. Brunner, *Dogmatik* (Zurich: Zwingli, 1950), 2:263ff.; Eng. trans., *Dogmatics* (Philadelphia: Westminster Press, 1950); W. Pannenberg, *Grundzüge der Christologie* (Gütersloh: G. Mohn, 1966), p. 42; Eng. trans., *Jesus, God and Man* (Philadelphia: Westminster Press, 1968).

16. Cf. R. Schnackenburg, "Mitmenschlichkeit im Horizont des Neuen Testments," in *Die Zeit Jesus,* Fest. for H. Schlier, ed. G. Bornkamm and K. Rahner (Freiburg/ Basel/Vienna, 1970), pp. 70–93, esp. pp. 84–86.

17. J. Gnilka, in *Die Zeit Jesus,* ibid., pp. 190–207.

18. Cf. F. Gogarten, *Jesus Christus, Wende der Welt* (Tübingen: Mohr, 1966), pp. 32–39; G. Ebeling, "Die Frage nach dem historischen Jesus und das Problem der Christologie," in *Wort und Glaube* (Tübingen: Mohr, 1960), pp. 300–318, esp. p. 308–11.

19. *Correspondence* I, Calmann-Levy (Paris, 1961), p. 157, writing to Baronesa von Wizine.

9

Hugo Assmann

The Christian Contribution to Liberation in Latin America

Hugo Assmann spells out the distinctive role the church must play in allying itself with the liberation struggle. "The Christian Contribution to Liberation in Latin America" is taken from Theology for a Nomad Church *(Maryknoll, N.Y.: Orbis Books, 1976), pp. 129–45. The book was originally published in Spain in 1973.*

Perhaps the first important contribution Christians can make to the process of liberation is not to add to the process of diluting the revolutionary implications that circumstances have dictated it should contain.

I do not propose to deal with the Christian contribution in a universal or idealist fashion; what is of concern is not what this contribution *should* be, but what it *is* and *can be* in the present circumstances. I shall concentrate on real events and possible events, not on what we might like to see happening ideally.

WHAT IS MEANT BY THE PROCESS OF LIBERATION

Once more, I have to begin with a reminder that commitment to the process of liberation in Latin America means starting from a particular analysis of our situation as oppressed peoples, that opting for a particular social analysis is not a neutral step. It involves the necessary choice of an ethical and political stance; there is no such thing as an uninvolved social science, and to pretend that there is is itself to adopt a reactionary ideological position. This fact has already become central to discussions of methodology on the level of the social sciences. There is probably no more obvious example of a committed science anywhere today than sociology in Latin America, which has taken the decisive step of making "dependence" the central theme of its investigations into the real situation in Latin America. This situation of dependence is the basic starting-point for the process of liberation. On the theological level an analysis of dependence has produced the language of the theology of liberation. That is not a natural development from postconciliar church reform, but a decisive break with the earlier language of development and all that it signified on the sociological, political, and other levels.

Talking of liberation implies taking a new analytical stance with regard to the situation of our countries, a basically new conception of the phenomenon of underdevelopment, and, consequently, a new point of departure from which to map out the political and economic ways out of this situation. The conclusions drawn are inevitably revolutionary, and the language of liberation is the language that articulates them. This relates it directly to the new analysis of underdevelopment. It springs *pari passu* from the accumulated frustrations produced by "development" models and expresses our rejection of them.

The theory of dependence springs from the crisis of the theory of development. Rather than complementing it, it represents its total rejection, seeing underdevelopment not as a backward state preceding developed capitalism, but as a direct consequence of it, a special and engineered form of development: dependent capitalism. The fact that dependence has been a situation constant throughout our history, and productive of it, means that it can become a scientific category to explain our history: underdevelopment as a form of dependence.

Dependence is not simply an "external factor" affecting international relations; it is a situation that has moulded the internal structures of our countries. Dependence can be seen as part of the worldwide framework of imperialism, but it has a reality of its own. One has not only to broaden one's concept of imperialism, but to reformulate it in some essential aspects.

The process of liberation comes to mean the new revolutionary direction the countries of Latin America must take if they are to find a real way out of their situation as dependents. The newness of this direction consists in its total break with the ways sought through development in its various guises, including those masquerading as "Third World roads" (state capitalism, revolutionary nationalism, and so on).

The option for a way "of liberation" has not yet been taken in the strategic and tactical details of how the struggle for liberation is to be carried out, such as, for example, whether one way can be taking power through the electoral process in order to radicalize the power structure later, as happened in Allende's Chile; or what the first steps in economic liberation have to be. The abstract option has to be translated into action according to the circumstances. There can be no real commitment to liberate one's country on the general level alone. Liberation, if it is to be an effective revolutionary way to the ending of dependence, has to include the working out of a strategy (which must involve choosing a particular political approach) and of the tactical steps for carrying out this strategy in the light of the most urgent needs.

In terms of political activity, this means not evading commitment on the burning struggle and tactical questions implicit in defining what one means by "party," "proletariat," "vanguard," "methods of action," and so on. Nevertheless, to talk in general terms of the process of liberation, provided that one takes account of the minimal elements implied by the antidevelopment option, in itself involves elements of social analysis and political approach, which enables us to establish basic demarcation lines between the differing viewpoints of Christians and the rest of the population. Of course we have to beware of a vague commitment to liberation that shies away from involvement in the practical result.

THE CHRISTIAN APPROACH TO LIBERATION

The major factor to be taken into account in the Latin American situation is the growing, clear, and definite choice that avant-garde Christian groups are making in favor of commitment to liberation, on the basis of the sociological analysis already referred to and in full consciousness of the necessary implications. The situation in each country varies.

Perhaps one of the most significant new aspects is the growing severity with which committed Christian groups are approaching the task of liberation. For them, general statements and proclamations are not enough; those who require a definite connection between ideological and political thinking on liberating action, and reflection on faith as the historical embodiment of love, are far from unthinking activists. They remember too well past frustrations in this field, such as the rapid evaporation of the euphoria that followed the Second Vatican Council and the Medellín Conference, and the subsequent withdrawals into ecclesiastical reform.

The Churches on a World Scale

The ecclesiastical hierarchies of the various Christian denominations and the ecclesiastical bodies responsible for social questions (the Justice and Peace Commission and its equivalent on the World Council of Churches, various national institutes, and so on) have not yet assimilated the more prickly implications of the process of liberation, and show no signs of doing so in the immediate future.

Nevertheless, there have been some signs of progress in Christian social doctrine, even in offical documents such as papal encyclicals and the declarations of the Beirut and Uppsala conferences, and in some more or less symbolic acts, such as the financing of liberation movements in Africa by the World Council of Churches, which have begun to show world opinion a swing on the part of the churches towards a revolutionary position. This impression is of course a significant break with the conservative image that the churches have presented up until now, and Christianity as a whole is viewed even by Marxists as a source of energy behind the process of changing the world.

Yet despite these auguries, the churches of the affluent societies are structurally incapable of becoming even more or less open "support areas" in the struggle for liberation in Latin America, except in the most general terms of drawing attention to international injustices, abandoning their naively anticommunist stance, tolerating the progress made by certain Christian action groups, and so on. All these phenomena are signs of a certain loosening of the earlier rigid attitude toward explicit revolutionary ideals. Basically, however, the churches of the affluent world remain inward-looking, concerned in a bureaucratic way with internal ecclesiastical affairs—with a "social action" sector as it were tacked on to the main body. In theological terms one can ask whether they are actually remaining true to their own doctrine on the nature of the church, which is to be an organ of service to humankind. The church cannot find its raison d'être in itself, in the internal workings of its structures, because its vocation is one of radical service to the world. Without discounting the importance of the ecclesial aspect, with its center in worship and the proclamation of the word, it would seem that what the churches themselves proclaim as their missionary nature should imply a far more decided shift to a stress on the "world" pole of their activities.

"Political nonintervention" is still one of the most explicitly cultivated characteristics of the churches of the developed world. It is exported to the Third World. The classic ideological and pseudo-theological grounds for this attitude—the church's special mission, the autonomy of the temporal sphere, and so forth—constantly reappear under new guises, with new theological pretexts—secularization theology, for one. These churches still do not seem to have grasped the political significance of their so-called nonpolitical stance. Even where there are some signs of a theoretical change of heart, their superstructure of ethics, doctrine, and legalism lags a long way behind taking any practical steps to put it into effect.

The progressive elements in exegesis and theology in the affluent world, with a few exceptions, concentrate on matters of only peripheral relevance to really major world problems. It would, as I have said, be virtually impossible to get an international theological congress to agree on a concept like "underdevelopment as a form of dependence." The sometimes aggressive manner in which Latin American theologians now reject even the progressive contributions of the developed world is quite understandable. Without disparaging the undoubted contribution that European and North American theology has made to the development of thinking in other areas, it cannot as a whole be described as a theology sensitive to the urgent demands of history or as one that has contributed to sensitizing the process of history. In many cases it has demonstrated a cynical insensitivity to the plight of the thirty million who die of starvation and malnutrition each year, as well as to the clamor for liberation arising from the oppressed.

As far as world opinion is concerned, the chief spokespersons for Christianity are still the Christians of the developed world. They are "the Christian world." "Baptized" Latin America is the exception in the Third World. This is perhaps a major sociological factor in the special vocation of the church in Latin America, and one that will lead to a growing alienation from the Christians of the developed world if they continue on their present course. Geography is coming to be an essential ingredient of Christian witness.

The Churches of Latin America: Official and Popular

If dependence is the situation that decides the condition of our countries, not as some simple external factor but as the historical determinant of the internal components of our present reality, then this interpretative key is also basic to our understanding of the situation of Latin American Christianity. It is a dependent Christianity. That is a simplification, but it should be borne in mind to avoid falling into inconsistencies and euphoric expectations of rapid and radical change in the structures of Latin American Christianity, particularly at the level of ecclesiastical hierarchies and the baptized masses. Although there are signs of initial breaks in certain aspects of this dependence, the mechanics of dependence remain powerful at infrastructural and superstructural levels.

Not only is no explicit change in the present direction of commitment to the process of liberation discernible at either the hierarchical or mass level, but there is no sign of such a thing happening in the near future. It cannot therefore be relied upon as a possibility in any strategy of liberation. What is evident is a general, verbal drawing near to the theme of liberation, evident even in documents emanating from official sources. But that cannot be taken as implying even a theoretical understanding of the historical implications of the process of liberation, let alone any effective commitment that will result in action. On these levels, in other words, one cannot say there is a definite rejection of development models and a clear new historical consciousness opposed to the status quo.

Nevertheless, the churches in Latin America are changing, at the official level, and even overall, by comparison with those of the developed world. The language may still be vague, but it is different, and so are the priorities. A language of vague denouncement of injustice, that would be totally impotent in other circumstances, may still have some power in Latin America; in the same way, small groups can wield an influence out of proportion to their numbers. Prophetic minorities often come to exert a surprising influence at the level of decision-making, particularly when they meet and issue declarations.

The churches in Latin America today often seem to be leapfrogging over each other in their desire to make verbal advances. This creates the ambiguous phenomenon of a sort of *kenosis* leading to inevitable rethinking but at the same time to a new set of reference points from which those who are determined to go forward can start. Perhaps the greatest novelty, and the one of most political significance, is the impression of decided advance made on public opinion, which has so frightened some governments. The right is more and more coming to the conclusion that it cannot count on the support of the church, whereas the left is beginning to regard it as a potential ally.

It may be no exaggeration to say that this impression—and it is still more impression than reality—of a broadening of the base of support for liberation on the part of the churches, is in fact becoming a real beachhead, acting as a sort of self-fulfilling prophecy. The Medellín documents are perhaps the clearest example of this process in action: issued with the highest official credentials, they in fact propose measures beyond the capabilities of the bishops; the bishops therefore cannot adopt them, but they become a rallying-point for the avant-garde, which in turn prods the consciences of the hierar-chies and those Christians who have not yet made up their minds, who therefore begin to give at least verbal support. The impression is then created of an at least half-formed alliance between the official and avant-garde church.

But there are still structural blockages, brought about by an ethics and a theology conditioned by a "middle-class" background (ideologically the churches were formed by the upper and middle strata of society) and by strong outside pressures brought to bear by the churches of the affluent world, whose domination is no less real, though more subtle and respectful in form. Some examples: the continued attempt to disavow prophetic groups operating out-side official channels; the doctrine of unity at any price; the inability to face conflicts in society openly and name them; verbal insistence on the force of charity conceived without its historical dimension; or on the universal validity of some vague social teaching of the church, without subjecting it to analysis in terms of locally valid strategy and tactics; and finally, since the process of shifting the option towards the historical process and its demands is still far from complete, a continual temptation to slide back into internal ecclesiastical concentration on purely pastoral reforms.

The greatest differences between Christians, therefore, are no longer those between preconciliar traditionalists and postconciliar progressives (who are equally preoccupied almost exclusively with internal pastoral reforms and tend to be politically inactive). The real discrepancy is between those who, fed on North Atlantic progressive theology, are concerned with internal church re-form and those who are motivated and committed by the prior challenges of the process of liberation. This discrepancy is taking on the dimensions of an abyss.

Christians Committed to Liberation

Who are they? On the basic strategical and tactical level, there are groups of all sorts, the best-known being those formed basically by priests and pastors and "ministerial communities" from the different churches. In the "Christian" socio-cultural subsoil of Latin American society, their impact has been the greatest. The polarizing power of Camilo Torres's action should be seen in this context. Typical groups are: Priests of the Third World, in Argentina;

Golconda, in Colombia; the Young Church, in Chile. In Bolivia, one group, Church and Society in Latin America (ISAL), has had a really astonishing impact. Its composition is original too: its constitution was drawn up by Protestants, but its membership is more than 90 percent Catholic; it has an unusually large secular membership, many of them confessed Marxists. For many, including priests and nuns, ISAL-Bolivia has become almost a new church. This is not the place to examine its complexity and possible ambiguities of motivation; suffice to say that its political stance has placed it in the van of the struggle for liberation.

It should not be forgotten that if Christian participation in the struggle for liberation is now a "major event"—just as the theology of liberation is seen to be above all a critical reflection on the actions of those who participate in this major event—this is due primarily to the growing lay presence in the front ranks of the struggle. This is not the place for a detailed account of the methods used by each group in working out the tactics they will employ in their commitment; what is important is the tremendous impression made by the growing number of Christians active in movements of the new left, in direct action groups, such as the Tupamaros and others, and national liberation fronts. One example was the case of Teoponte, in Bolivia, where (as I have described in a book withdrawn from circulation by the Bolivian police in 1971 and republished in Caracas in 1972) the Christian participation in the guerrilla activity was a decisive factor in its outcome.

The distinctive elements that characterize the growing Christian option for the struggle for liberation would seem to be the following:

1. The increasingly conscious acceptance of the sociological implications of a new concept of development, in the terms I have described earlier. The adoption of the language of liberation among Christian groups is closely connected with an appreciation of the mounting frustrations arising from the concept of development.

2. Their antidevelopment stance is what commits them in the first instance to the concept of liberation. This has weighty consequences; firstly, because the churches at world level cannot keep up at this point, and, secondly, because the political implications are quite definite in the context of different countries. In Bolivia, for example, it involved the rejection of the option offered by "revolutionary nationalism" and opposition both to the vagueness of the government of the day as well as to the imperialist charter proposed by the MNR (National Revolutionary Movement).

3. On the political level, these groups see the need to express their views by unequivocal commitment. Their reflection on faith as the historical process of liberation has to operate on the level of strategy and tactics, as well as on that of ideas.

4. Theologically, they effectively embody a shift of the basic reference point of their faith, which is no longer a body of doctrine or a form of worship (both of which remain important, but in a complementary role), but the territory occupied by the historical process of liberation. This evidently entails a fresh

look at their manner of belonging to the church and a revision of the central tenets of traditional theology. What emerges very clearly is that the prophetic element of Christianity—prophecy as word and action—acquires a greater importance for them than the institutional element.

5. In general they realize that the traditional contributions of Christian social teaching—which has been discussed with growing freedom in Latin America in recent years—are wholly inadequate for acting on the more radical implications of faith as the practice of liberation. As a result, until a viable Christian body of thought can be elaborated, they inevitably turn to the analytical techniques of Marxism, often without taking account of the possible overall consequences.

6. For many, the step beyond the euphoria of being "revolutionaries in theory," imposed by involvement in real action, has brought a full realization of the ambiguity, originality, and isolation of their position seen in the context of worldwide Christianity. This brings a fresh seriousness to both their political and theological reflection and their actions.

7. An increasingly significant element is the realization that their commitment to liberation means introducing the class struggle into the church itself. They know they are not *with* other Christians, but rather *in open conflict with* the majority of them. But they also know there is no escaping this minority opposition role, because they have to range themselves on the side of the exploited. Hence the theme of conflict in history and in present-day reality has become so central to the theology of revolution. They find themselves obliged to denounce the ideology of a false unity-without-conflict in the church, which is a major point of difference between them and others in viewing the whole historical existence of the church. They can no longer accept that eucharistic conditions can automatically obtain in a church that includes oppressors and oppressed. An element of tension and conflict is introduced at the center of the life of faith. Its practical implications can easily be imagined.

THE CHRISTIAN CONTRIBUTION

Breaching the Superstructure

There is a serious limitation to the Christian contribution to liberation which has been a source of frustration to many committed Christians. It need not be so in the Latin American context.

If one analyzes the impact made to date by the presence of Christians in liberation movements, the area in which they have been most effective is that of the superstructure represented by traditional bourgeois values, in which they have opened a major breach. In that sense, Christian revolutionary action has already been most effective; for the traditional concept of the ideal Christian above all as a person of "peace," pacifically stationed within the existing order, quietly collaborating with the rules of the game of the status quo, has virtually become a thing of the past.

But is that the first objective of the revolutionary process? In Marxist terms, obviously not: the structural changes brought about by the process of liberation should be primarily on the level of the infrastructure—economic, social, and political—but always at the grass-roots level. Christian revolutionary aims are evidently in the same direction, but has their influence been appropriate so far?

It all depends on how one views historical effectiveness. There is a short term and a long term. Those who look only for the short term have to discount many actions as ineffective—guerrilla activity in Latin America to date would probably be the prime example. But if we take a longer view of the revolutionary process, the opposite might be true: it is a long process with many different steps to be taken, and apparent failures often come to be seen as having made a tremendously significant contribution to later successes.

Furthermore, strictly orthodox Marxism often seems incapable of appreciating the features peculiar to the Latin American situation. I do not want to undertake a cultural analysis here, as it would be inadequate unless integrated with the results of a structural dialectical analysis. It is essential to understand the "relative autonomy" of the elements that make up the superstructure of our society, because this is where many of the obstacles to change are to be found. If obstacles could be removed at that level, a significant contribution would be made to the revolutionary process. The obstacles to change at the superstructural level, particularly those represented by petit-bourgeois values and the tendency to acquiesce in the passivity of the populace, undoubtedly owe much to pseudo-Christian traditions and values both in origin and maintenance. In this context, it is worth recalling what Engels wrote to Josef Bloch on the subject of false interpretation of Marx and himself by those who believed that Marxism had to concentrate exclusively on the proletariat:

> According to the materialist view of history, the factor that determines history in the final instance is the production and reproduction of real life. Neither Marx nor I have ever said more than that. The economic situation is the base, but various elements of the superstructure that rise from it (the political forms of the class struggle and its consequences, the constitutions that the victorious class draws up once the battle is won, and juridical forms. . .) also exert their influence on the course of historical events and determine their shape—in some cases, more than any other factor.

From the Christian point of view, the fact that liberation in Latin America involves important changes in the superstructure has an added significance in regard to a basic point of faith: we are born of the gift of the Lord; we are created, as persons, from outside. That may sound vague, but it has very definite implications, directly related to our faith in revelation. One does not appear as a spontaneous product of structures, even though these are the necessary conditioning material of his or her "birth" as a new person. If the formative context of material structures is not joined by the loving process of call and response, the result is a simple product of the environment and not the new person. Hence the much-used Christian term "witness" still retains its full meaning at the heart of the liberation process. Nor should it be forgotten that the new revolutionary ethic that was Che Guevara's constant dream was based on this concept—a concept that makes use of most specific channels for the efficacy of love in its transformation of history.

If, however, the Christian contribution to the revolution has so far been most effective in removing obstacles at the superstructural level, that does mean that Christians cannot yet claim to be the "revolutionary vanguard" pure and simple, because they are in fact acting as auxiliaries to the vanguard and no more. They must accept this as their position. While this is conducive to humility, it should not lead them to belittle their own efforts, but to deepen their effective commitment still further. The Christian guerrillas of Teoponte were radical to the end in their actions, but their chief effect was to breach the superstructure of that Bolivia characterized by traditions and native religions—with its superficial "Christian" overlay—and tremendously retarded by elements of "religiosity" in the superstructure of its society.

Revolution in the Infrastructure

Those who take the plunge of a real option for the process of liberation have to recognize, on the basis of their sociological analysis, that changes in the infrastructure of our countries must be at the root of any true revolution. But what genuine Christian contribution can be made to this process?

First of all, Christians have to be open in declaring their revolutionary objectives. An open challenge to imperialism, from within and without, is not merely a revolutionary slogan, but the basis on which the changes to come have to be made on the infrastructural level. Not only can there be no revolution without revolutionary theory—just as, conversely, there can be no revolutionary theory without action, because the theory has to be a theory of action—but there can be no true revolutionary theory without working out a historical project. Revolutionary theory is more than the simple tactical elaboration of a method of fighting; it is that, but more too: it has to include plans for the objectives of liberation in the form of a historical project. This can be a long business. In the Latin American context, the political situation and the urgency of the struggle have tended to lead left-wing groups to reduce to a minimum their statement of a clear historical project. Here Christians have a real contribution to make, and not merely on the level of repeating fragmentary political platforms for immediate political consumption. There is in fact already a growing Christian presence among the true theorists of the aims and methods of the process of liberation.

The question of who forms the revolutionary vanguard is intimately linked to that of the infrastructural changes needed. The oppressed and the exploited, those who have a vital interest in the outcome of revolution, become the revolutionary vanguard when the revolution is really made for them and by them. Those who are directly concerned in the changes to come are really called to form the van of the revolution in the true sense of the term. This again is a manysided question, and one which Christians have tended to approach with a certain lack of historical realism, dreaming of a revolution inspired by pure love, while the Marxists recognize that it will be carried out by those who have a direct interest in its success. Historically incarnate love is in no sense removed from interests, provided "interests" is not understood in the bourgeois, individualist sense. The clear definition and realization of the interests of the oppressed is the historical embodiment of love. Christians will more easily become authentic revolutionaries the more they identify their way of life with that of the exploited. This evidently should not be taken as meaning that those Christians of middle-class extraction, who are disinterestedly fighting for the interests of those who stand to benefit from the revolution, and against their own interests, cannot be true revolutionaries. Their kenotic or self-emptying presence can even have a humanizing influence on the revolutionary process, but this must not be idealized as an act of idyllic, abstract, and petit-bourgeois love.

The process of liberation aims at being an anti-imperialist (and on the national level, antioligarchic) and at the same time an antitechnocratic revolution. The latter aspect is clear from its antidevelopment stance. The double perspective distinguishes it from earlier revolutionary models. If the liberation we are seeking aims not only at an adequate supply of goods for all, but at active human participation at all levels, it opens up a whole range of questions and problems, all of which coincide with the deepest Christian concerns for the welfare of humankind.

How Effective?

Our final consideration is the vexed question of a "specifically Christian" contribution to liberation. I believe this has usually been presented in a false, pretentious, and triumphalist manner which assumes that Christians must know more than nonbelievers about the true human character of liberation. But instead of worrying about their "specific contribution," surely what Christians in growing numbers ought to do is to make a real contribution to the process as they find it. Constantly to insist on the original dynamism of the social teaching of the churches, and blithely to pass over the terrible sociological fact of the massive reactionary presence of "Christianity" in practice, merely transforms what is best in Christianity—its effective possiblity of being a real humanizing influence—into trivial ideology.

In the present sociological situation of world-scale Christianity as well as in Latin America, neither the structures of the church nor the theology in vogue offer any natural resources for a specifically Christian contribution to liberation. Nowhere is there evident, even on the theoretical level, a Christian understanding of humanity so incarnate in our historical reality that it alone can provide the definite imperatives for a more complete work of humanization.

But this does not exhaust the question of the "specific" contribution Christians can make. That is still a valid question and one that is vital to those of us who believe in embodying the love that springs from the sources of our faith. But we have to learn humility again; we do not know it all so well. Nor are we the only ones concerned with the truly loving dimension of the problem of living together as human beings. The general direction in which we have to look for a specifically Christian contribution seems clear enough: it is in what is specifically and fully human, in the line of fidelity to all that is involved materially in loving one's neighbour. But theoretical insistence is not enough: we have an overall vision of the purpose of humanity to urge us to action. A truly historical reading of the Bible, particularly of the message of Christ, leads to a whole series of radical questions to which Marxism has not paid sufficient attention, of which perhaps the most significant is the Christian affirmation of victory over death, that final alienation to which Marxism can find no satisfactory answer.

Tackling this infidelity to history, the aspect that emerges as most significant is not the belief in "something after death" (which can easily become selfish), but this: the God who raised Jesus from the dead is not a God of the dead but also of the living. Since life is God's "medium," God also wants it to be humanity's sphere above all else. Once this is understood in a historical and transhistorical sense, in terms of a Christian eschatology whose questions about ultimate meaning can only be grasped through historical and immediate questions, we come to the marrow of the loving mystery of what it means to risk one's life for one's fellow human beings. Marxism asks all revolutionaries to be prepared to do this, but I do not believe it can really answer the question of the human sense of laying down one's life for others—so deeply relevant to revolutionary practice. I do not believe Marxism has really tried to see the importance of the problem.

I believe that the Christian formula "love = death-life," kept on a historical and existential plane, can become the key to the series of radical conundrums that impose themselves daily on those who live entirely for others. Perhaps this is the best way to understand the specifically Christian contribution to liberation.

CONCLUSION

In conclusion I must stress the urgent need of specific action in Christian witness. It must reflect a commitment made in specific circumstances and having a specific outcome. Reflection on the challenges our faith presents us with in history is a precious necessity. But there is no sense in discussing these matters in the abstract unless discussion leads to the one thing that counts: our effective commitment to the liberation of the oppressed.

10

Jon Sobrino

Thesis for a Historical Christology

Like Leonardo Boff, Jon Sobrino focuses on the need to develop an adequate Christology for Latin America. This selection is taken from Christology at the Crossroads *(Maryknoll, N.Y.: Orbis Books, 1978), pp. 346–81. The book was originally published in 1976.*

---

1. PRESUPPOSITIONS FOR CHRISTOLOGY

1.1. Theology in general and Christology in particular deal with themes that sum up the full, all-embracing meaning of existence and history. This comprehensive meaning derives from the very realities under study: God, Christ, liberation, and the sinfulness of the world. These themes recapitulate the option of faith and express the total meaning of life and history. If these themes were viewed as incomplete and partial, then our Christological study would not be Christian. It would be motivated by some other set of reasons: for example, apologetic intent, intellectual curiosity, political concerns, or mere sympathy for the figure of Jesus.

1.2. From such a standpoint, then, the theme "Christ" is a limit-theme, a reality around which all human limit-realities revolve: transcendence, liberation, love, truth, justice, the sinfulness of the world, and the meaning of history. If they are limit-realities, however, then Christology cannot intuit them in themselves, and the same applies to the figure of Jesus himself, who Christianizes them. Our affirmations about them cannot be isolated from the path and process that leads us toward knowledge of them. Our statements about such realities draw life and breath from historical experience itself, and only to that extent do they have a meaningfulness that can be formulated. This leads us to conclude that the real approach of theology is none other than the path of faith itself. No Christology can or does explain the reality of Christ from outside. Theology in general and Christology in particular have a maieutic task to perform. They must help us to draw out those viewpoints that enable us to do a better job of explaining how the faith is to be lived in real life. They must also help us to frame those questions, at least on the theoretical level, that will enable us better to comprehend Christ as the limit-reality that provides the total meaning of life and history and that will also help us to interpret our historical experience as a Christian experience. This will involve both criticizing historical experience on the one hand and marking out its Christian channels on the other.

1.3. We are looking for those viewpoints that will enable us to study Christology as something that offers the total meaning of life and history. I would propose the following points to help us in that search:

a. Wittingly or unwittingly every Christology is elaborated within the context of a specific situation. The need for a "new" Christology is felt in a "new" situation where people clearly feel the meaninglessness of the existing situation and glimpse the direction in which a new meaningfulness might be found. The interaction between Christology and a new concrete situation can take place on various interrelated levels: on the intratheological level, as a reaction to the unsatisfactory nature of some particular Christology (scholastic Christology, for example); on the philosophical level, as a critical or positive reaction to new philosophical currents (such as existentialism, evolutionism, personalism, and Marxism); on the cultural level, as a critical or positive reaction to the cultural milieu (which may be sacral or secularized); and on the level of concrete reality itself, where one may face such structured situations as that of the Third World, the consumer society, or the socialist state.

Christology must take cognizance of what sort of situation it finds itself in and on what level it is situated. In passing we might note here one fact that can be verified historically. When the level of discussion has merely been theological, philosophical, or cultural, Christology has preferred to focus on the resurrected Christ as the symbolic expression of an explanatory and comprehensive vision of reality, but when the level of discussion has been that of concrete reality itself, Christology has naturally tended to focus on the figure of the historical Jesus.

The fact that Christology must be innovative in a new situation does not derive solely from the feelings of dissatisfaction to which an outmoded Christology gives rise. It derives from the very object of Christological study: Christ. If Christ could fail to be of novel interest in a novel situation, if he could not be experienced and lived in new and different ways, then he would not be Christ. Thus the reformulation of Christology in a new situation is nothing else but an expression of faith in the universal significance of Christ.

b. Broad segments of humanity today live with a deep yearning for liberation. This movement for liberation found expression as far back as the Enlightenment, which specifically saw it as human liberation vis-à-vis theology. The movement has had two structurally distinct phases. One phase concentrated on the liberation of reason from dogmatic faith (Kant). The other phase championed the liberation of the whole person from a religious outlook that supported or at least permitted social, economic, and political alienation (Marx). We might sum up the two phases as a general yearning for reasonableness and for transforming praxis.

Today no Christology can sidestep the challenge posed by the Enlightenment. If it does not respond to that challenge, no Christology is credible or relevant. But every Christology must take cognizance of the underlying interest that motivates it. Is it trying to show that the truth of Christ can be justified before the bar of reason or is it trying to show that it can be justified before the demands and yearnings for a transforming praxis? The two standpoints are not mutually exclusive, of course, but the emphasis given to one or the other will shift the thrust and direction of a given Christology. History indicates that European Christology has been more interested in demonstrating the truth of Christ before the bar of reason, though more recent political Christologies do move in a somewhat different direction. By contrast Christological reflection in Latin America seeks to respond to the second phase of the Enlightenment noted above. It seeks to show how the truth of Christ is capable of transforming a sinful world into the kingdom of God.

c. From all that has been said so far, one can readily see the importance of a given hermeneutics for Christology. Specifically one can see its importance for the biblical texts in which the figure of Jesus is presented. Hermeneutics does not simply presume to settle the question as to the truth of statements about Christ. It also entails the task of figuring out a way to make them comprehensible and operational, to turn the tradition about Christ into something that continues to be alive and relevant here and now. The kind of hermeneutics used in Christology must do justice to two realities. First, it must do justice to the real situation today so that Christ will really be *comprehensible.* Second, it must do justice to the history of Jesus himself so that the now comprehensible Christ is not simply a wraith conjured up by present-day Christians. To put it another way, we must try to see what viewpoint is demanded by the gospel texts themselves if the figure of Christ is to be comprehended as such rather than as just another figure in past history. We must investigate to find out whether the gospel texts present themselves as merely to be comprehended by the mind or as words to be realized in practice as well.

d. If the very nature of Christology is to offer some complete, all-embracing meaning of total reality, it cannot ignore the element of discontinuity and rupture to be found in that totality. Total meaningfulness and fulfillment does not exist in history, nor is it possible in the strict sense. Hence all serious thinking and all Christology arises in the presence of some ultimate quandary. The problem is to pinpoint the specific quandary that will make Christological thinking truly fruitful.

On the theological level we find two basic approaches used to specify and resolve the quandary in Christological terms. One approach sees Jesus as the solution to the problem of reconciling God with all that is positive in reality (e.g., nature, history, and human subjectivity); this is the approach of natural theology. The other approach sees Jesus as the embodiment of, and the unexpected solution to, the problem of reconciling God with what is negative in life and reality (e.g., sin, injustice, oppression, and death); this is the approach of theodicy. Every Christology operates on one of these two implicit presuppositions. It either assumes that Christ will prove to be the positive affirmation of humanity insofar as he fulfills all our natural potential, or else it assumes that Christ will affirm humanity by criticizing the natural person and thus helping to generate the new person. Either supposition will have an impact on the resultant conception of Christ and the emphasis given. While one brand of Christology will focus on the risen Christ as the paradigm of human fulfillment, the other will focus on the crucified Jesus as the incarnate criticism of the natural person. In short, the dominant underlying presupposition will profoundly affect the way a given Christology views the relationship between Jesus' cross and resurrection, two basic data about Jesus that no Christology can ignore.

e. Finally, every given Christology must focus consciously on its own role within theology as a whole. Does it see Christology as the Christian concentration of all theology or merely as just another chapter in theology—though admittedly an important chapter? To put it concretely, it must ask itself whether or not its conception of God, sin, liberation, and transcendence are derived from Jesus and are hence Christological, or whether they are viewed as realities already known logically from some other source quite independent of Jesus' appearance in history. How radically rooted in Christ are all the realities considered by theology? Is Jesus merely a privileged example and embodiment of things that can be learned quite independently of him?

The notion of Christological concentration has another aspect that should be clarified right at the start. Even if we acknowledge the radicality of the revelation of Christ, we must go on to ask what this revelation is assumed to be. Do we picture it as a revelation of the ultimate essence of God or as a revelation of the Son? In other words, is Christ the sacrament of God or the way to God? Depending on which alternative we choose, we will get a different Christological hermeneutics and a different overall view of revelation. One view will tend to be more epiphanic, stressing that "God" was revealed in Christ. The other view will be more operational, stressing that Jesus reveals not so much the mystery of God as something to be *known cognitively* but rather the way to God that now can and should be traveled by humanity. So we will get two different Christologies. One will logically tend to be more praxis-oriented while the other will tend to be more contemplative, though of course there is no complete disjunction between them.

2. THE STARTING POINT OF CHRISTOLOGY

2.1. Granting that Christology has the task of spelling out the all-embracing meaningfulness of the Christ-reality, we must acknowledge that it is not easy to find some a priori starting point that will shed light on all the features of that reality. However, we certainly must be fully aware of the starting point that we do choose for it represents a hermeneutic principle that will illuminate and also condition all our reflection on Christ. The value of spelling out our starting point is that it puts us on guard against the possible limitations it imposes on us. If we do not spell it out, we may think that we are getting at the full and total reality of Christ when in fact we may be disregarding basic features of it (see 2.4).

2.2. When we talk about our starting point, we must keep in mind both the subjective and the objective aspect. The subjective starting point of Christology is faith as a lived experience, as I noted above. The next problem—which we shall consider further on—is how we are to live the faith so that the figure of Jesus as the Christ may be unveiled to us through that experience.

2.3. Looking for an objective starting point means looking for that aspect of the total and totalizing reality of Christ that will better enable us to find access to the total Christ. Here I propose the historical Jesus as our starting point. By that I mean the person, proclamation, activity, attitudes, and death by crucifixion of Jesus of Nazareth insofar as all of this can be gathered from the New Testament texts—with due respect for all the precautions imposed by critical exegesis. This particular starting point contrasts sharply with any Christological approach that *begins* its reflection with the already glorified Christ. Put in positive terms, our approach here asserts that both for reflection and life it is the historical Jesus who is the key providing access to the total Christ.

There are several reasons for adopting this particular point of departure. First, as we noted at the start, the total Christ is a limit-reality in this world and can be comprehended only in connection with Jesus' actual course toward fulfillment as the Christ. Second, Jesus himself demands this, insisting that the fundamental contact with him comes through following his historical life: that is, through real praxis of faith motivated by hope and love. This same demand holds primacy for any understanding of the total Christ. It takes priority over any "intentional" sort of contact with Christ: for example, prayer, worship, and orthodoxy. Christian discipleship, however, can be understood only on the basis of the historical Jesus and his life. Third, a look at history makes it clear that things go wrong when faith focuses one-sidedly on the risen, fulfilled Christ and forgets the historical Jesus. It then tends to be turned into a "religion" in the pejorative sense of the term, working against the life of faith and downgrading all that is really and typically Christian.

2.4. Besides the positive reasons adduced above, the deficiencies evident in other starting points justify using the historical Jesus as the proper point of departure. The dogmatic formula of Chalcedon disregards the concrete features of Jesus and his God. When a biblical Christology is based solely on the titles applied to Christ, it tends to view Jesus in terms of concepts already known: for example, Messiah, Son of Man, Lord, Logos, and so forth. Instead it really should point out that the proper meaning of those terms can be gleaned only through the figure of Jesus himself. The resurrection of Jesus certainly is the culmination of Christology, but it calls for a hermeneutics if it is to be understood (see thesis 8). Such a hermeneutics is feasible only through a consideration of the history of Jesus. The kerygma about Christ, the proclamation of his cross and resurrection, does place humanity in a crisis. But emphasis on the kerygma has tended to individualize its thrust rather than "personalize" it as it claims to do, thereby ignoring the public aspects of its activity in history. Finally, an approach motivated by soteriological interests tends to disfigure Jesus also insofar as it manipulates him and reduces him to an example of what is of deep interest to humanity in any historical situation.

2.5. There is an important epistemological implication in the fact that we make the historical Jesus the starting point of Christology. It is Jesus himself, in his own historical life, who raises the whole question of his own person. We are forced into a very different position. Instead of asking questions, we ourselves are now called into question by Jesus. Thus it is the historical Jesus who brings Christology into crisis, effecting the epistemological break that is necessary if Christology is not to be simply the outcome of the natural person's inertial wishes and projections.

2.6. It can be historically verified that the various interpretations of liberation theology in Latin America seem to agree on one point: If a Christology disregards the historical Jesus, it turns into an abstract Christology that is historically alienating and open to manipulation. What typifies Jesus as a historical reality is the fact that he is situated and personally involved in a situation that displays structural similarities to that of present-day Latin America. At least we can detect a similar yearning for liberation and a similar situation of deep-rooted sinfulness. It is the historical Jesus who brings out clearly and unmistakably the need for achieving liberation, the meaning of liberation, and the way to attain it.

3. JESUS AND THE KINGDOM OF GOD

3.1. History means activity, change, evolution. A Christology centered around the historical Jesus must follow the characteristic features and events of Jesus' life in chronological order if it is to evaluate them properly as historical realities. The most certain historical datum is that Jesus began his activity by proclaiming the coming of God's kingdom: "After John's arrest, Jesus appeared in Galilee proclaiming the good news of God: 'This is the time of fulfillment. The reign of God is at hand! Reform your lives and believe in the gospel!' " (Mark 1:14).

3.2. To understand the figure of the historical Jesus and his relationship with the kingdom of God, we must differentiate two structurally distinct stages in his life: the period before the Galilean crisis and the period after it (see thesis 5). Here we find a rupture that will affect not only his outer attitude but also the very depths of his person and his conception of God and the kingdom. In this section we shall focus on the characteristics of the first stage, never forgetting that a profound change in Jesus would take place later on.

3.3. We can sum up the characteristic features of Jesus' early proclamation of the kingdom by saying that it was eschatological in character and that it was embodied both in words and in deeds.

The Eschatological Character of the Kingdom

3.4. Toward the end of the last century exegetes discovered that Jesus' preaching was eschatological and also that Jesus preached about the kingdom of God rather than the church.

a. The importance of this discovery lay in the fact that it seriously questioned the figure of Jesus presented by liberal theology or pietistic thought. That figure seemed to embody the ideal of bourgeois society and its value-system. Harnack's book *The Essence of Christianity* may be taken as representative of the liberal view. As one writer puts it, it was "the highest expression and perfect manifestation of the age of bourgeois idealism, an age which was inspired by an optimistic faith in the human mind and in progress in history, and believed it could unite God and the world, religion and culture, faith and intellect, divine righteousness and earthly authority, throne and altar in a natural and almost unbroken harmony, and which therefore looked forward with confidence to the future."[1] Jesus was the one who embodied and fulfilled the yearnings of the bourgeoisie, but he did not criticize those yearnings or call them into question.

The discovery of Jesus' eschatological character was made in the same German-speaking bourgeois milieu. A. Schweitzer and J. Weiss played an important role in this process. In preaching the coming of God's kingdom Jesus brings people into serious crisis. Things cannot go on as before because the end is now at hand. A basic and important step forward was thereby taken by Christology, for it became evident that the authentic historical figure of Jesus had to be looked at in true perspective.

b. The eschatological crisis brought on by Jesus has been viewed in two ways by theology. One views it in temporal terms: the chronological end of history is now imminent. The other view interprets it in anthropological terms: the ultimate reality of humanity and history is now at hand. The common feature in both interpretations is the fact that Jesus offers us the possibility of attaining our true identity by facing up to a crisis and undergoing a conversion. Only in that way can the kingdom come about. The whole process may be viewed in different terms. Bultmann interprets it in existential terms. Pannenberg interprets it in terms of faith and trust. Moltmann interprets it in terms of praxis, insofar as Jesus offers us the possibility of some ultimate and definitive way of behaving. Boff interprets it in terms of liberation, insofar as the proclamation of the kingdom triggers partial but functional ideologies of liberation.

c. A whole series of important systematic conclusions flows from the basic fact that Jesus' preaching of the kingdom was eschatological in character. First, eschatology means crisis. The approaching kingdom is a judgment even though it is approaching as a grace. Second, eschatology has a temporal aspect. The present situation is not the ultimate possibility for us. The future is not simply an extrapolation based on the present; it is an as yet unrealized utopia. Third, eschatology poses the problem of God all over again, but from a different slant. God is now to be viewed in terms of the future rather than in terms of past origins and primeval genesis. The way to approach God is no longer described as some sort of contemplative possession of God; it is through hope, and we must now see whether that hope should be merely passive or active as well. Fourth, eschatology presents the old tensions basic to classical theology in a new light. Where classical theology had talked about God versus creature, nature versus grace, and faith versus works, we must now talk about the church versus the kingdom of God, injustice versus liberation, the old person versus the new person, and the gratuitous entry of the kingdom versus active effort on its behalf.

The "Words" of Jesus

3.5. To begin with, Jesus expresses his teaching in the terminology of earlier Jewish tradition. Strictly speaking, he did not *say* anything that was totally new. He did not claim to be an innovator insofar as religious ideas were concerned. Instead he was a reformer who radicalized the best traditions of his people. And like any really good reformer, he created something new in the process of seeking out the essence of the old.

We find various Old Testament traditions at work in Jesus' preaching about God, and two stand out in particular. One is the sapiential tradition, which stresses God's goodness, providence, and patience on the one hand and people's corresponding response of trust and patience on the other. The other is the prophetic-apocalyptic tradition, which stresses God's renewing love, judgment, and the renovation of reality on the one hand and the corresponding inner crisis produced in people as the means of their own renewal.

Formally speaking, we can say that the latter line of tradition is the more important in the preaching of Jesus. It is the one that molds his preaching into its typical and distinctive shape. Jesus' preaching about God is always framed in the context of his proclamation about the "kingdom of God." Implied in that expression is a transformation of all reality—personal, social, even cosmic—through which the reality of God will be revealed in a definitive way. The essential reality of God is inseparably bound up with the operative reality of the reign of God.

3.6. From his preaching about God we can deduce certain important things about the figure of Jesus. First, Jesus did not preach about himself. His whole preaching is relational in character. The center of Jesus' person is not in himself but in something distinct from himself. Second, Jesus did not simply preach about "God" either. He preached about the "kingdom of God." The correlate of Jesus' person is not God but the "reign of God."

Jesus' view of God, then, is taken from the Old Testament. God does not simply "exist." God exists insofar as God "acts," insofar as God "reigns" in the world. God's revelation is not simply epiphanic, designed to disclose his essence; it is historical, designed to create a wholly new situation. To put it succinctly we can say that in Jesus' view God "is" or "exists" insofar as God creates community and human solidarity. In principle, then, access to God necessarily calls for some sort of historical mediation. There is no access to God except insofar as there is access to the kingdom. To put it another way, our filiation vis-à-vis God is necessarily mediated through solidarity among human beings. Without the solidarity, the filiation is wholly and purely idealistic. Solidarity is not just an ethical consequence deriving from a God already constituted and known; it is the very way in which God really is revealed as the Parent of humankind; it is the way in which God is revealed as God. In Jesus' eyes, a God who does not create solidarity simply is not God at all.

A third important conclusion about Jesus can be derived from his preaching about God. Jesus preached the good news that God was drawing near in grace and liberative love. Precisely because that was the content of his preaching, Jesus' proclamation could not stop with mere words. A word of love simply must be incarnated in a historical gesture or act. Jesus did not seek to propound a doctrine about the abstract truth of God. He sought to call attention to a reality, namely, God's liberative love for human beings. Hence Jesus' message had to be historicized in acts of love and liberation signifying the gradual fulfillment of the kingdom.

The "Actions" of Jesus

3.7. The first thing to be stressed here is that Jesus' actions are concrete. They are signs of a reality greater than concrete history, but signs displayed within history. They are actions within a situation characterized by two features: an expectant longing for liberation on the one hand and an objectively sinful situation on the other. It is this situation that rules out any merely idealistic expression of love on Jesus' part, that demands that his love be expressed in concrete acts that take the situation itself into account. Jesus does not perform abstract gestures of reconciliation; he performs concrete acts of reconciliation in a situation characterized by oppression. His basic positive gesture is to draw near to people and situations where there is no reconciliation, to break down the hard and fast barriers that society, religion, and politics had erected, and thus to show in a concrete historical way that God does indeed draw nigh to those whom nobody else will approach. This is the typological import of Jesus' approach to sinners, publicans, prostitutes, lepers, cultically impure people, Samaritans, and so forth. His word of hope has to be fleshed out historically in an act of hope.

Among the actions that Jesus performed in the first phase of his public life, his miracles merit special consideration. The marvelous and unwonted nature of these prodigies is not their typifying feature insofar as the New Testament is concerned. That is why it does not use the Greek word *teras* to describe them.

Instead it uses such words as *ergon* ("work"), *semeion* ("sign"), and *dynamis* ("power"). This gives us a clue to the authentic Christological import of Jesus' miracles. The important point is that they are signs of God's presence, which is concretely experienced as liberation from some type of oppression. They are active deeds of power performed by Jesus, symbolizing his mastery over the negative power operative in the world—personified in the devil.

This leads us to consider the relationship between Jesus and power. In the first stage of his public life it is concretely embodied in his use of miracles. Jesus utilizes power, placing all that is his in the service of the kingdom: his idea of God and the kingdom, his time and energy, the power of his preaching and of his miracles. At this point, then, Jesus does not ignore power nor underestimate the value of power; rather he simply places it in the service of the kingdom when he uses it.

The second phase of his public life will raise serious questions about such use of power. Is that enough to usher people into the kingdom of God? Is an all-conquering power enough to communicate the message that God is love in a concrete situation where sin and injustice triumph over love and justice? Is it possible that the power of love must somehow be broken by evil so that evil can be conquered from within? Jesus' attitude toward power and its use does not change in the sense that he gives up the power with which he was invested as a human being. What happens instead is that the sin-ridden concrete situation strips Jesus of his power, and so Jesus learns something new about the use of power. He knows that the power he exercised in the first phase of his public ministry is very real and ought to be used. But it must become secondary to another sort of power in the second phase of his public life: that is, the power of truth and of the sacrifice of one's life for others out of love.

3.8. To sum up the first phase of Jesus' public ministry, we may say that the figure of Jesus must be seen against the backdrop of God's kingdom. Jesus begins his ministry with an orthodox view of God and the kingdom that is prior to his own person. Following the logic of the kingdom, he puts all his energy and activity in its service. This basic relationship of Jesus to the kingdom will encounter a serious crisis in the second phase of his ministry, and there will be a real switch in the process of understanding both. Instead of moving from an understanding of the kingdom to an understanding of the figure of Jesus, concrete understanding and realization of the kingdom will have to be based on the concrete journey of Jesus himself (see thesis 5).

4. FAITH AND DISCIPLESHIP
BASED ON THE HISTORICAL JESUS

4.1. One of the demands posed by the historical Jesus is conversion, which finds expression amid a tension that cannot be resolved intellectually. On the one hand Jesus proclaims that the kingdom is drawing nigh as a grace, that it is the work of God; on the other hand Jesus demands radical conversion. Confronted with Jesus' eschatological proclamation, we cannot continue to live on the inertial routine of our past life.

4.2. To appreciate the nature of Jesus' demand, we must consider his conception of God and of God's kingdom. We must also realize that it is a "situated" demand, which is to say that it will be expressed in different ways according to the particular situation in which Jesus proclaims his message. Here the main dividing line which characterizes Jesus' concrete situation is that between oppressors and oppressed. The demand for conversion will have different concrete mediations, depending on different concrete contexts and circumstances. Putting the basic demand in schematic terms, we can say that Jesus calls for radical trust in God and discipleship in the service of the kingdom.

4.3. In the first phase of Jesus' ministry, both faith and discipleship derive their motivation from the notion of God and God's kingdom, not directly from the concrete person of Jesus himself.

a. Jesus proclaims a God who is approaching in grace, and he calls for complete and total trust in that God. This proclamation is personified in the Gospels by those people who have lost all hope and all possibilities of a future because of social, religious, political, and economic ostracism. Jesus demands that those people believe in a God who is greater than the one presented by the orthodox belief of the standing order. He asks them not to consider their personal situation of ostracism and alienation as the ultimate possibility of their life because in fact it is not the ultimate possibility of God. Even sin against the law does not constitute a barrier for the God who is approaching in grace; hence it should not bar them from hope.

b. In systematic terms this means that we are to accept this greater God, this God who cannot be captured in images, this coming God who opens up a future for us. In concrete terms it is a God of love, who draws near to proffer grace and re-create the poor person rather than to reward people according to their works. Faith in this God, then, must be translated into radical trust in God. This demand of Jesus applies to every human being, though in his own history it seems to be directed mainly to those who have least cause for hopefulness.

c. Since Jesus proclaims the kingdom of God rather than simply God, he also proposes another kind of demand. He asks for active service on behalf of the kingdom, dedicated effort like that which he himself is expending. He selects and sends out disciples to exercise power over unclean spirits, to heal the sick, and to preach the good news. This demand may be considered the summons to discipleship as opposed to the other demand for hope in the coming God. As yet, however, it is not a demand to follow Jesus himself in the strict sense; it is rather a demand to proclaim the good news of the kingdom of God, and it was not a wholly new idea to Jesus' listeners and followers.

4.4. In the second phase of Jesus' ministry we see a change in his demands for faith and discipleship even as his own view of himself and his mission changed. Whereas the demands he made in the first phase of his public life could be deduced more or less logically from the notion of God's kingdom, the demands made in the second phase of his public life must be viewed more strictly in the light of Jesus' own concrete person and destiny.

a. The faith required now is no longer simply confidence in God; it involves one's acceptance of Jesus with all his scandalousness. Jesus seems to be a failure and there is no sight of God's kingdom. The hope and confidence he proclaimed earlier must now become a hoping against hope. Trust in God is now put to the test because Jesus, the one who triggered that trust in the first place, proves to be a failure. Radical hope in God must now encompass not only one's own desperate personal situation but also the scandal of Jesus' failure.

b. The same shift can be seen in the notion of discipleship. It is no longer service to the kingdom that flows from a logic prior to Jesus. Discipleship now means following the concrete person of Jesus in a situation where it is not at all obvious that Jesus himself has very much to do with the coming of the kingdom as people had envisioned it before. Discipleship is no longer the following of some Messiah viewed in older orthodox terms. Now it is the following of Jesus on his journey to the cross, with all the demands that made the journey both possible and inevitable (see thesis 6).

4.5. If we wish to view Christian living as an obligation imposed by the historical Jesus, we must take account of both factors mentioned earlier. While the Gospels seem to make a typological distinction between two kinds of people, both the obligation of faith in God and of discipleship must be brought together in the life of the Christian individual. Both factors, faith and practice, are indispensable and interrelated.

It is also important that we take note of the change in Jesus' demands when he moved from the first phase of his public life to the second. If Christian living is viewed as a journey toward God, then the first phase seems to presume that God is somehow already known at the start while the second phase centers wholly on Jesus himself. In the first phase Jesus might be one more possible road to a God already known. In the second phase Jesus is the one and only way to a God not yet really known.

5. THE CONSCIOUSNESS OF JESUS

5.1. One way of coming to know the reality of Jesus is to become familiar with his consciousness. Traditional theology began from the dogmatic supposition that Jesus had to be explicitly aware of his divine sonship. It alluded to certain passages in the New Testament to back up this supposition, focusing particularly on Johannine theology. Since Jesus explicitly said certain things about himself, he must have known exactly who he was from the start; all we have to do, then, is to read what he said about himself. When modern exegesis ruled out that approach, attempts were made to discern the explicit consciousness of Jesus on the basis of the Christological titles that he himself used or permitted others to apply to him. Modern exegesis has posed serious obstacles to that approach also. In my opinion the way to solve this whole problem is not to consider the *absolute* consciousness of Jesus (what Jesus explicitly thought about himself) but to focus on his *relational* consciousness. In other words, we should try to deduce what Jesus thought from his attitude toward God and the kingdom of God.

Jesus' Consciousness vis-à-vis the Kingdom

5.2. It seems quite apparent that Jesus had a distinctive personal conscious-ness vis-à-vis the kingdom of God, though it might not be wholly accurate to describe it precisely as a messianic consciousness. Various facts support this contention. Jesus performs certain signs indicating the imminent approach of the kingdom: exorcisms, the forgiving of sins, meals with publicans, and so forth. He comes forward with an interpretation of the law that is even more original than that of Moses. Unlike the earlier prophets, he does not justify his actions by saying that he is acting in the name of Yahweh; instead he speaks and acts on his own authority. He seems to claim that his own person is functionally decisive insofar as salvation is concerned, and he poses a strict and unheard-of demand that people must follow him personally.

All these facts point indirectly to Jesus' distinctive consciousness vis-à-vis the kingdom. He realizes that the arrival of the kingdom has its privileged moments and its own proper timeliness (Greek *kairos*), and he is convinced that he himself has a decisive role to play insofar as the "right moment" is con-cerned.

Jesus' Consciousness vis-à-vis God

5.3. In the Gospels we find that Jesus has an explicit awareness of God and his own relationship to God. This awareness differentiates Jesus from all other human beings, though one cannot deduce from it that Jesus knew himself to be the "eternal Son" of God. This consciousness of sonship is expressed in relational rather than absolute terms. His felt relationship to God finds expres-sion in two characteristic traits: confident trust in God and obedience to his mission. Trust in God comes out in Jesus' prayer, which expresses both his theological poverty and his theological richness as well as his awareness of sonship. It also finds expression in his fidelity to his mission right to the cross. So we might make this general statement about the psychology of Jesus: Jesus becomes conscious of his distinctive relationship to God through the concrete mediation of his life and the external difficulties he must face.

5.4. This relational view of Jesus' consciousness can cause surprise and give rise to misunderstandings because we have been used to using a concept of person and of perfection that goes back to Greek philosophy. In that view perfection is basically knowledge, so personal perfection and fulfillment means full possession of self through knowledge. If Jesus was perfect, then he had to know that he really was the "eternal Son" of God.

Such a view, however, is grounded on a wholly gratuitous supposition. It does not really correspond with the biblical conception of person or with many current conceptions, though that in itself would not be decisive. The biblical conception of person is quite different. It was further elaborated in discussions about the Trinity, and Hegel formulated it in more modern terms. Basically it says that the essence of being a "person" is surrendering oneself to another and finding fulfillment precisely in that other. To know who Jesus really was, then, we do not have to know exactly what Jesus thought about himself. Instead we should find out how and to whom he dedicated himself as a person.

Crisis and Growth in Jesus' Consciousness

5.5. Consciousness is a subordinate feature of the human person. Its development does not take place in some idealistic realm. It takes place in and through some concrete situation that is outside consciousness itself and that is fraught with conflict. The repercussions of such conflicts are abundantly evident in the life of Jesus, and from them we can understand the real growth and development of his awareness. Jesus "had to become like his brothers in every way" (Heb. 2:17) except in knowing sin (2 Cor. 5:21). He "learned obedience" (Heb. 5:8), and it is through the learning process that he became a human being and God's Son. Basically the development of his consciousness involved his overcoming of negative influences, and it can be described in terms of the shift that took place between the first and second phase of his public life.

a. The Galilean crisis, which is noted by all the evangelists, marked a sharp break in Jesus' consciousness, specifically with reference to his conception of the kingdom of God. His preaching mission, as he had conceived it, was a failure by any external measure. Now it is no longer simply a matter of dedicating all his energy and activity to the kingdom. Now he must actually surrender all the ideas he had held about God as well as his own person. After the Galilean crisis Jesus moves toward an unknown future over which he has no control. That crisis is what makes it possible for Jesus to radicalize and concretize his relationship to God in trust and obedience.

b. The same thing is spelled out programmatically in Jesus' temptations, though the gospel accounts situate them at the start of his public life for theological reasons. The temptations have to do with Jesus himself, with what is most basic to his person and his mission. That is why they are placed alongside the account of Jesus' baptism, for Christian theological reflection saw his baptism as Jesus' decision to accept his mission from God. Temptation is the general atmosphere in which Jesus grows and develops, as is the case with every human being. It is not a matter of choosing between good and evil but of choosing between two very different ways of conceiving and carrying out his mission, of using power, of picturing God, and of rendering the kingdom present to people.

On the historical level Jesus' basic temptation is depicted in his agony in the garden of Gethsemane. Jesus overcomes that temptation by bowing to God's will and surrendering wholly to it. It is in that way that Jesus' person, and more indirectly his consciousness, is fashioned and developed.

c. It is, then, through crisis and temptation that Jesus' person is fashioned concretely. Accepting that view, we can see the positive role of Jesus' *ignorance* and *mistakes,* both of which are mentioned in the gospel accounts. It is important to note that Jesus' ignorance is not just in matters of detail; it has to do with something fundamental for him. Jesus does not know when the day of Yahweh will come nor does he know what the future course of his mission will be. He did not envision a "church," though a church could arise as a possible continuation of Jesus' work.

Greek philosophy would regard Jesus' ignorance as an imperfection. In reality it is supremely positive. It makes it possible for Jesus' dedication to God to be concrete and real rather than merely idealistic and abstract. Paradoxical as it may seem, it helps to perfect Jesus' dedication and surrender to God because it allows God to remain God. Jesus comes to know God precisely in not knowing the day of Yahweh, for he thereby allows God to be the ineffable mystery and the absolute future.

5.6. Jesus' consciousness was fully human, so we are perfectly justified in talking about the faith *of* Jesus. Here we must understand faith in the biblical sense of the term. Instead of picturing it as basically a cognitive act, we must see it as loyal surrender of self to God. Thus Jesus was the first to live faith in all its fullness and originality, as the Epistle to the Hebrews makes clear.

But Jesus' faith was a historical one. It underwent growth and development because it was immersed in history. After the Galilean crisis Jesus did not think about God and the kingdom in exactly the same way, nor did he act in the same way. His view of trust in God and obedience to God was also greatly altered. This movement in Jesus' consciousness, in his faith in God, was viewed as heretical by orthodox Jewish belief. In reality, however, it was the movement that faith must undergo if it is to be concrete, historical, and real. In that sense we can say that Jesus underwent a "conversion." It is not that he had to get beyond some personal sin. It is that he had to get beyond the inertia of a particular way of thinking and acting that was good in itself but was too bound up with his own notion of God and the kingdom. By undergoing a "conversion" in his way of thinking and acting, his sonship would attain fulfillment and perfection.

6. THE EXTERNAL CONFLICTS OF JESUS

6.1. The crisis in Jesus' consciousness was mediated through his external conflicts. It was embodied in his opposition to those who wielded religious, economic, and political power. The import of this feature of opposition and conflict cannot be brought out fully if we simply look at isolated incidents in Jesus' biography. We must consider the following points: *(a)* Jesus took on a nature that was not only human but also historical. It was "situated" in a concrete context. He became human through finding himself in a given situation and reacting to it. *(b)* A structurally important feature of that situation was the real sinfulness existing in it. It did not simply exist alongside Jesus' work but reacted sharply against that work. *(c)* The conflict surrounding Jesus paved a course leading to the cross, to the death of the Son. From the final episode we can see how deep-rooted the conflict was. *(d)* This course taken by Jesus is simultaneously a test of God's authentic divinity. Two questions stand out: Does the true essence of God find expression in the de facto situation of religion? Is the power of God truly mediated through the de facto situation and use of political power?

6.2. Jesus was condemned for *blasphemy,* not for heresy. Thus his conception of God was not only different from, but radically opposed to, that held by the established religion of the standing order.

a. Jesus unmasked people's domination of others in the name of religion, people's manipulation of the mystery of God through merely human traditions, and the religious hypocrisy that used the mystery of God to avoid the obligations of justice. In that sense the religious leaders were correct in realizing that Jesus was preaching a God opposed to their own.

b. Jesus' religious revolution had to do both with his conception of God and with his conception of the place and means that provided access to God. First of all he preached a God who was drawing nigh in grace, thereby breaking all connections with the works stipulated by the law. Religious people could not feel secure against God simply because they performed certain works. Rather than offering "things" to God, they must offer up their own persons and security as well. Second, Jesus also desacralized the locale that provided access to God. The privileged locus of access to God was not cultic worship, scholarly knowledge, or even prayer. It was service to the lowly and oppressed. Insofar as the oppressed are totally "other" to those who approach them, they serve to mediate the total otherness of God and show how we can gain access to God, namely, through a liberative praxis.

c. Thus Jesus' conflict with the representatives of religion is a deeply rooted one, and he is condemned to death as a result of it. A direct consequence of Jesus' conception of God, the cross poses the whole problem of the true essence of the deity and leaves open the question of who God is and what the meaning of history is. Faced with the cross, we must ask who God is exactly: the God of Jesus or the God of religion? Is Jesus' God an illusion, or—even though the established religion killed the Son—the real God?

6.3. Jesus was actually executed as a *political rebel,* not as a blasphemer. His conception of God necessarily entailed his proclamation of God's coming kingdom, and this could not help but bring him into conflict with those in political power. If the kingdom of God entails human reconciliation, then Jesus could not help but unmask a situation that did not correspond with that vision.

a. Jesus calls attention to the coexistence of oppressors and oppressed, insisting that such a situation is the result of human free will rather than something willed or even permitted by God. Denouncing the situation in the prophetic manner, Jesus says there is poverty because the rich will not share their wealth, ignorance because the learned have stolen away the keys to knowledge, and oppression because the Pharisees have imposed intolerable burdens on people and because the rulers are acting despotically.

The strongest anathemas voiced by Jesus are collective, aimed against groups. They point up an unjust situation that is the collective fruit of egotism on the part of many individuals. They also point up hypocrisy, suggesting that this oppressive use of power is justified by appealing to God and claiming that it is a legitimate mediation of God and God's power.

b. The political death of Jesus makes sense in that Jesus had a different conception of God as power. He shared the conviction of the Zealots that God's kingdom had to be established and hence he bore certain similarities to them, but his conception of God was very different from theirs. God is not simply power, as most people were inclined to think. God is love, and God is manifested in the dialectics of an impotent love. Moreover, God's approach is an act of grace rather than a result of some law as the Zealots maintained. Even harsher is Jesus' implicit attack on the Roman Empire. The emperor is not God. Jesus desacralizes that kind of power and its claim to be the absolute mediation of God. The *pax romana* is not the kingdom of God. The political organization of Rome might dazzle the world with its power, but it was oppressive; hence there was nothing sacred or divine about it.

c. The issue at stake here was the essential nature of power insofar as it mediates God. That was the deepest underlying question in Jesus' own eyes. He certainly used all the power he had, displaying it in his persuasiveness, his lucid ideas, and his miracles. But gradually he came to realize that the revelation of God as love can only come about when power is subordinated to the law of service in a sinful world. Thus power is transformed into a love willing to accept suffering and defeat at the hands of the world's sinfulness.

d. In Jesus' eyes God's ultimate historical word is love, whereas the ultimate historical word of power in the human world is oppression. Jesus' journey to the cross is a trial dealing with the authentic nature of power. In the penultimate stages love must be fleshed out in schemas and structures that effectively render service to human beings, and so it has need of real power. But the ultimate stage and the last word is simply love. Jesus makes it clear that without love power in history turns into oppression.

e. Jesus does not advocate a love that is depoliticized, dehistoricized, and destructuralized. He advocates a political love, a love that is situated in history and that has visible repercussions for human beings. Rather than simply advocating the complete abolition of the Zealot spirit, he proposes an alternative to Zealotism. Historically speaking, Jesus acted out of love and was for all human beings. But he was for them in different ways. Out of love for the poor, he took his stand *with* them; out of love for the rich, he took his stand *against* them. In both cases, however, he was interested in something more than retributive justice. He wanted renewal and re-creation.

7. THE DEATH OF JESUS

7.1. One thing differentiates Jesus' death from that of other religious and political martyrs: Jesus died in complete rupture with his own cause. At his death he felt completely abandoned by the God whose nearness he had felt and proclaimed. The typifying features of his death can be glimpsed when one considers his message about the approaching kingdom, his cry on the cross, and his abandonment by God.

7.2. The distinctive character of Jesus' death does not lie in his biographical finale but in the new questions about God and the new revelation about God that arise from it.

a. The cross radicalizes the transcendence of God, which was already recognized by the Old Testament. It does this in two ways especially. First, the Old Testament prohibition about making images of God is radicalized. There is no image of God on the cross. Second, the cross radicalizes the Old Testament view of God coming in power at the end of history to re-create everything. On the cross there is no hint of divine power as natural humanity might understand it.

b. The cross rules out any access to God by way of natural theology. Natural theology assumes that we can gain direct access to God on the basis of the positive elements in creation: for instance, nature, history, and human subjectivity. The cross challenges such an assumption. Not only does it show up the inadequacy of all human knowledge about God insofar as the actual reality of God is concerned; it also points up the contradiction faced by all human knowledge about God when people actually attempt to think about God. Natural humanity did not and could not have imagined that suffering rather than power might be a mode of being for God. To know God from the standpoint of the cross is to abide with God in God's passion.

c. The cross poses the problem of God, not in terms of theology (discourse about God), but in terms of theodicy (the justification of God). On the cross theodicy is historicized. The Son is not crucified by some natural evil that embodies the creaturely limitations of nature or humanity. He is crucified by a historicized evil, that is, the free will of human beings. What justification is there for a God who allows the sinfulness of the world to kill the Son (and hence other human beings as well)?

7.3. On the positive side the cross presents a basic affirmation about God. It says that on the cross God is crucified. God suffers the death of the Son and assumes all the sorrow and pain of history. This ultimate solidarity with humanity reveals God as a God of love in a real and credible way rather than in an idealistic way. From the ultimate depths of history's negative side, this God of love thereby opens up the possibility of hope and a future.

7.4. The crucified God, the powerless God on the cross of Jesus, draws the dividing line between Christian faith and every other type of religion. Christian faith lies beyond conventional theism and conventional atheism. But it is quite obvious that it has not been easy for Christians to maintain the scandal of the cross. From the time of God's revelation in Jesus' resurrection there has been a tendency to view the cross as a passing transitional stage leading to the definitive reality in which God is seen as sheer power and Jesus is viewed solely as the exalted one.

a. In the New Testament itself Jesus' death is toned down and stripped of its scandalous aspect: that is, his abandonment by God. Mark's account, the most original one, is modified by Luke and John. Luke depicts Jesus dying as a confident martyr and John depicts him dying in majestic control of the situation.

b. The title "Servant of Yahweh" fades from the scene relatively quickly. That particular Christology is probably due to Peter himself, who personally had to suffer the scandal of a suffering Messiah. It soon takes a second place to other titles that have more to do with Jesus' glorification than with the cross.

c. Gradually the scandal of the cross was reduced to little more than a cognitive mystery. Jesus died in accordance with some mysterious divine plan that can be discovered in the Scriptures: when we interpret the Scriptures correctly, we will find no reason to be scandalized by the cross.

d. Another way to eliminate the scandal of the cross is to focus solely and exclusively on the cross's salvific value. By focusing all consideration on this positive redemptive value of the cross, people could forget the scandalous fact that the cross affected God. The model explanations used to bring out the salvific value of the cross also tended to assume an a priori knowledge of what salvation is (the forgiveness of sin) and who God is.

7.5. It has been equally difficult to maintain the scandal of the cross in the history of the church and its theology. By way of example, we may cite the following instances:

a. Even many of the early fathers of the church took no serious note of Jesus' abandonment by God on the cross. Some fathers explained it allegorically, saying that it was really sinners who were abandoned by God on the cross. Others claimed that Jesus was complaining that the Logos was going to abandon his body in the tomb in the short interval between his death and resurrection.

b. The classic and extremely influential theory of vicarious satisfaction presupposes knowledge of who God is, what sin is, and what salvation is. The cross of Jesus does not call those a priori concepts into question at all, and hence it is completely emasculated. It is fitted into a neat theological scheme when in fact it shatters every such scheme.

c. The repeatable nature of the Mass as a sacrifice has posed a great danger to the cross. There has been a real danger that the Mass might reduce the real, historical cross of Jesus to nothing more than a cultic, ritualized cross. In that case the cross would simply make it possible for Christian faith to become just another religion with a sacrificial worship of its own.

d. There has been a tendency to isolate the cross from the historical course that led Jesus to it by virtue of his conflicts with those who held political and religious power. In this way the cross has been turned into nothing more than a paradigm of the suffering to which all human beings are subject insofar as they are limited beings. This has given rise to a mystique of suffering rather than to a mystique of following Jesus, whose historical career led to the historical cross.

7.6. In the last analysis the metaphysical and epistemological roots of this emasculation are to be found in the conceptual armory of Greek thought in which the mystery of God and Jesus was formulated right from the beginning.

a. The cross implies suffering, and hence change. A Hellenized theology could not conceive of suffering as a divine mode of being for that very reason. It saw God as apathetic toward history, and so God's love could not be formulated in historical terms that would be credible to suffering human beings who carry on the passion in history.

b. Greek philosophy never pondered death in itself. Death was either the end of life or the transition to another higher state of existence. In no way could death as such serve as the mediation of God.

c. Greek epistemology was based on the principle of analogy: we come to know something through its resemblance to something already known. If the deity is pictured in terms of power or intelligence or wisdom, then one can hardly recognize God on the cross of Jesus because it displays no trace of power or wisdom. The principle of dialectical knowledge, of coming to know things through their seeming contrary, was not developed by Greek philosophy. That is in marked contrast to the gospel scene of the last judgment, where it turns out that the Son was concealed in the oppressed and needy and persecuted. Greek epistemology could not take account of the surprise needed to recognize God on the cross.

d. Greek epistemology saw admiring wonder as the motive force behind human knowledge. It did not envision suffering as a source of knowledge, and hence it did not see that suffering embodied the required solidarity and the authentic kind of analogy for encountering God on the cross. Moreover, admiring wonder can stop at contemplation while suffering cannot. The former approach to knowledge lacks the feature of praxis, which is required if one is to comprehend the cross.

8. THE RESURRECTION OF JESUS

8.1. With the resurrection we come to the culminating point of any historical Christology, even though the resurrection of its very nature points toward some final, ultimate, and hence transcendent fulfillment of history. Three aspects of the resurrection must be considered. They are intimately connected with each other, but their interrelationship presents peculiar problems because the resurrection is an eschatological happening and hence has a distinctive relationship of its own with what is historical. The three aspects to be considered are the historical aspect (what really happened), the theological aspect (what exactly is the significance of the resurrection-event), and the hermeneutic aspect (how is it possible to comprehend the event and its meaning).

The Historical Aspect of the Resurrection

8.2. In the New Testament we do not find any canonical tradition that narrates the event of Jesus' resurrection itself. The gospel narrative recounts two types of traditions that deal with it, one dealing with the apparitions of the risen Jesus and the other with the empty tomb. In asking about the historicity of Jesus' resurrection, we are asking first and foremost about the historicity of those two kinds of tradition.

8.3. The historicity of the "empty tomb" tradition is a moot question. It does not appear in the oldest narratives about the resurrection, and this suggests that it might have arisen in the interests of apologetics. It is equally improbable, however, that people would have proclaimed the resurrection of Jesus in Jerusalem if his corpse could have been easily located. This has led some to suggest that Jesus may have been buried in a common grave so that his corpse could not be easily identified in any case. Critically studied, however, the New Testament data do not provide any real foundation for this hypothesis—though the data do not rule it out either. Two points are important and noteworthy:

a. In the New Testament itself faith in the risen Jesus does not depend on the existence (or nonexistence) of the empty tomb, but on the concrete experience of Jesus' apparitions.

b. Centering the whole discussion around the empty tomb may prejudice one's conception of Jesus' resurrection, leading one incorrectly to envision it as the revivification of a corpse. This view is certainly not shared by the New Testament.

8.4. The traditions dealing with apparitions of the risen Jesus are far more important and decisive. The oldest of these traditions, perhaps going back to A.D. 35 or 40, is the one found in 1 Corinthians 15:3–5, 7. Those which talk about Jesus' appearances to the women and the disciples offer more difficulties, contradicting each other on various points such as place of appearance, chronology of events, and the nature of Jesus' new corporeal state. Did Jesus appear in Jerusalem or Galilee? Did the ascension take place on the day of his resurrection or forty days later? Was his resurrected body a solid corporeal mass or a spiritual entity?

Many of these discrepancies can be explained in terms of the theological, apologetic, or kerygmatic motives of the final redactors and the situation in their respective communities. Yet we also do find certain literary schemes shared by both traditions dealing with Jesus' apparitions (to the women and to his disciples). This might indicate the existence of very old traditions that were literally historical but that were then filled out with divergent details.

8.5. All we can deduce so far, then, is the existence of certain *traditions* that are very ancient, at least insofar as their nucleus is concerned. This would point toward their historicity. The next question is whether the *events* narrated in these traditions are historical.

Concretely the problem comes down to the historicity of people's experience of Jesus' appearance. There can be no historical doubt that the disciples had some sort of privileged experience. It is evident not just because they say so but because we can verify the impact it had on their lives and their behavior. The cross was the end of their faith in Jesus, yet shortly afterwards they are preaching about Jesus and are willing to give up their lives for this faith. What took place between those two very different historical situations? The disciples themselves said that they had seen the crucified one "alive." Can that assertion be verified as historical in principle or not? That is a question we shall consider when we get to the hermeneutic aspect below. Here we want to consider the origin of the disciples' new-found faith.

We can pose this issue in terms of an alternative: Either their novel experience can be explained by some natural mechanism or else it was caused by the "presence of the risen one" that made itself known. In the last analysis choosing between these two possibilities is not a matter of historical science at all, because prejudices of all sorts are at work here even more so than they are on many questions. If people do not accept the possibility of resurrection, then they will attempt to prove that the apparitions were hallucinations. If people do allow for that possibility and accept the credibility of the narratives, then they will point out that the atmosphere was scarcely conducive to hallucinations. The disciples could hardly have been disposed in that direction after what had happened on the cross, and Jesus' appearance at different times and places hardly fits the general pattern of collective hallucinations.

8.6. Though it is an extremely difficult task, historical exegesis can show that certain things are historical: that is, that the disciples did in fact have faith in Jesus after Easter even though the cross had shattered their earlier faith in him; that they tied their new faith to appearances of the risen Jesus (not to the empty tomb); and that the nucleus of those traditions gives indications of being authentic. Thus countless presuppositions underlie any effort to find out in what sense Jesus' resurrection is historical and how it can be understood as such. Those presuppositions must be considered under the hermeneutic aspect of the resurrection.

The Theological Aspect of the Resurrection

8.7. The first thing that the resurrection affirms is something very similar to the Old Testament's efforts to define God in historical terms rather than in terms of abstract characteristics. It is a new historical credo that asserts that the new definition of God is the one who has raised Jesus from the dead and who brings into being things that have not yet existed. God is defined as a liberative power that has also become a historicized love after the cross of Jesus. God not only raised Jesus from the dead but also handed him over out of love for human beings.

8.8. The resurrection of Jesus says something also about humanity and history. God's action in Jesus has been a salvific action of pardon and revitalization rather than of retribution. Humanity has been offered a new kind of life based on hope and love. Because Jesus rose from the dead as the "firstborn of many brothers and sisters," we are now pointed toward our own fulfillment and the revitalization of history. Because the resurrection also confirms the life of Jesus himself, we are now offered the possibility of living a particular way of life in the footsteps of Jesus. We can and should live as new, risen human beings here and now in history.

8.9. Finally, the resurrection says something about Jesus himself. If God did resurrect Jesus, then Jesus stands in a distinctive relationship to God. The various Christologies of the New Testament attempt to determine the nature of that relationship, and we can now try to give a brief overview of the basic stages through which that reflection went.

a. If God did raise Jesus from the dead, then he also gave confirmation to Jesus' concrete way of living, to his preaching, his deeds, and his death on the cross. In the early stages, however, there was not too much reflection on Jesus' cross for its own sake.

b. With his resurrection from the dead Jesus came so close to the awaited Messiah, the figure who was to come, that people more and more come to the notion that the Messiah was none other than Jesus himself. Thus Jesus' distinctive relationship to God came to be expressed in terms of people's expectation of the parousia.

c. If Jesus was raised from the dead and then exalted by God, then obviously God was manifested in a definitive way in Jesus. Here we have the fundamental step forward. Rather than adhering to the model of the Messiah in trying to understand Jesus' relationship to God, Christians now glimpsed the possibility of exploring that relationship further. This they did, and they ended up professing that Jesus was the eternal Son of God.

d. Alongside this process of universalizing the significance of Jesus there arose the possibility that Jesus could and should be preached to every human being. We now get a movement toward the Gentiles and toward a view of the new community (the "church") as something new and different rather than as the mere continuation or extension of the people of Israel.

8.10. Christian reflection on Jesus' oneness with God took place basically on two levels. On one level it explored the various honorific titles of Jesus. On the other level it sought to develop a theological interpretation of the major events in his life. The earliest reflection began exploring Jesus' special relationship of oneness with God in terms of the parousia yet to come or Jesus' exaltation in the present. It then went on to consider his oneness with God on the basis of Jesus' earthly life, gradually pushing that oneness further and further back toward the very beginning: transfiguration, baptism, virginal conception, pre-existence with God.

The various honorific titles express Jesus' oneness with God in terms of theological models already known. As we have said, some focus more on his earthly work ("Prophet," "Servant of Yahweh," "High Priest") while others stress his transcendent character ("Logos," "Lord," Son of God," "God"). The first set of titles faded out rather quickly, and preference was given to those titles that were grounded on a priori theological models and that related Jesus more directly to God ("Lord," "Messiah," "Son").

It is important to note the twofold movement involved in the New Testament's attempt to attribute titles to Jesus. On the one hand it attempts to spell out the special importance of Jesus' person by giving him titles whose meaning was already familiar to biblical or Hellenic theology. On the other hand the novelty of Jesus is brought out by stressing that the meaning of those titles can be known only through Jesus himself.

The utilization of those titles was simply a way to help people understand the import and relevance of Jesus' person within the context of a specific culture and theology. There is no reason why such titles need be the exclusive prerogative of one particular culture, even that of the New Testament writers. Thus today Jesus could quite rightly be called "the liberator," so long as we remember that it is through Jesus that we learn what liberation really is and how it is to be achieved.

8.11. The New Testament normally does not talk about the absolute divinity of Jesus. It discusses it in terms of Jesus' relation to God. Jesus' divinity is relational, and this point is expressed in various terms. In personal terms Jesus is the Son. In functional terms Jesus is the one who holds lordship. In temporal terms Jesus will hand the kingdom over to God at the end of time. Thus the divinity of Jesus is depicted in relational terms rather than in terms of his own absolute nature.

The Hermeneutic Problem

8.12. Because Jesus' resurrection is an eschatological happening, it is not readily and immediately comprehensible as such. We must look for some standpoint or hermeneutics that will do justice to all the pertinent aspects. First of all, we must do justice to the fact of the resurrection itself as it is understood by the New Testament; otherwise we will simply be talking about some symbol of utopia rather than about the resurrection of *Jesus* specifically. Second, we must be able to make the resurrection comprehensible today; otherwise it will not be an eschatological event of universal significance.

It is not easy to find such a hermeneutical standpoint, and in the end it will depend on a person's most basic personal options. Here I want to propose one possible hermeneutics that has three characteristics and which, in my opinion, does do justice to both the New Testament texts and the present-day situation.

8.13. First, the expression "resurrection of the dead" is a utopian formulation that derives from the Old Testament and later Judaism rather than from the Hellenic world. The Greek formulation focused on the "immortality of the soul." The biblical formulation suggests the total transformation of the person and history. Thus the first hermeneutic condition for understanding the resurrection of Jesus is a hope in such a transformation, a hope that overcomes all the negative elements of the world. It is a hope *against* death and injustice (the biblical model) rather than simply a hope *above and beyond* death and injustice (the Greek model).

8.14. Second, grasping the meaning of the resurrection presupposes that we grasp history as a promise and are conscious of a mission to be performed. The disciples were aware that they were not simply spectators of an event, that they were witnesses who necessarily had to give testimony on behalf of what had happened. Thus the resurrection is comprehensible only insofar as one is conscious of building up history and trusts in the promise.

8.15. Third and finally, in the New Testament the appearances of the risen Jesus go hand in hand with a vocation, with a summons to a mission. The disciples realize that something new has entered the world with Jesus' resurrection. Hence his resurrection initiates a praxis that can be described as service to both the work of proclaiming the risen Jesus and to the content of the promise that his resurrection embodies for the world. Like Jesus, they must serve the cause of establishing a new creation. This means that the meaning of Jesus' resurrection cannot be grasped unless one engages in active service for the transformation of an unredeemed world.

8.16. Understanding the resurrection of Jesus today, then, presupposes several things. One must have a radical hope in the future. One must possess a historical consciousness that sees history both as promise and as mission. And one must engage in a specific praxis that is nothing else but discipleship—the following of Jesus. The last condition seems to be the most necessary because it is praxis inspired by love that concretizes Christian hope as a hoping against hope, and because love is the only thing that opens history up. Like knowing God, knowing the resurrection of Jesus is not a one-time event, something given once and for all. Our horizon of understanding must be constantly fashioned anew. Our hope and praxis of love must be kept alive and operational at every moment. Only in that way can Jesus' resurrection be grasped not only as something that happened to him alone but as the resurrection of the "firstborn" and a promise that history will find fulfillment.

NOTES

1. Heinz Zahrnt, *The Question of God* (New York: Harcourt, Brace and World, 1969), p. 15.

11

José Miranda

Christianity Is Communism

José Miranda believes that there is a direct correlation between Christianity and communism. "Christianity Is Communism" is taken from Miranda's Communism in the Bible *(Maryknoll, N. Y.: Orbis Books, 1982), pp. 1–20. The book was originally published in Spanish in 1981.*

For a Christian to say he or she is anti-Marxist is understandable. There are numerous varieties of Marxism, and it is possible that our Christian is referring to one of the many materialistic philosophies which style themselves Marxist without having much at all to do with Marx.

For a Christian to claim to be not only anti-Marxist but anti-Marx as well, it is probably owing to not having read all of Marx, and the repugnance is a symptom of simple ignorance. But when all is said and done I do not really care. I am under no obligation to defend Marx.

But for a Christian to claim to be anticommunist is quite a different matter and without doubt constitutes the greatest scandal of our century. It is not a good thing to weigh a book down with cries and shouts, but someone finally has to voice the most obvious and important truths, which no one mentions as if everyone knew them.

The notion of communism is in the New Testament, right down to the letter—and so well put that in the twenty centuries since it was written no one has come up with a better definition of communism than Luke in Acts 2:44–45 and 4:32–35. In fact, the definition Marx borrowed from Louis Blanc, "From each one according to his capacities, to each one according to his needs," is inspired by, if not directly copied from, Luke's formulation eighteen centuries earlier. There is no clearer demonstration of the brainwashing to which the establishment keeps us subjected than the officially promulgated conception of Christianity as anticommunist.

At this moment two-thirds of Latin America writhes under the yoke of atrocious anticommunist dictatorships. Nearly all the rest of Latin America suffers from a most ill-concealed anticommunist repression. The international politics of nearly all the countries of the world, and their consequent criminal armament ideology, rallies to this contradictory watchword: "Defend Christian civilization from communism!" At such a moment there are no words adequate to this other cry: But what if, in the history of the West, it is Christianity that *started* communism? What if, from the first century to the nineteenth, groups of Christians were never lacking who, in spite of repression by the established powers and by the church, vigorously advocated communism, Bible in hand! What manner of insanity has swooped down on the Western world that it combats the Christian project par excellence as if it were its greatest enemy?

INTENTIONAL MISUNDERSTANDINGS

Ultimately the Marxists have been doing us a favor by propagating the idea of communism in our absence—our culpable absence. But to identify communism with Marxism implies a crass ignorance of history. It is far from certain that the establishment is struggling against atheistic materialism, as the powerful tell themselves in order to tranquilize their consciences. The repressive struggle of theirs dates from much earlier. It existed for many centuries when no communist was a materialist and no communist was an atheist; it existed when materialism and atheism did not even exist. Marxism is a mere episode in the history of the communist project. The pope and the other powerful ones are not fighting atheism, but us, who are Christians, who believe in God and Jesus, and who only want to see the gospel become reality.

Surely there are different interpretations of the gospel, and the purpose of this book is to air them. But then the powerful are attacking an interpretation of the Bible different from their own. This onslaught of theirs is nothing but the continuation of what they were carrying on all through the Middle Ages and the first three centuries of the modern era. The denunciation of materialism is a mere pretext for anticommunist persecution. If these persons did not have this pretext they would invent another—as in fact they did throughout the Middle Ages, with different pretexts in the sixteenth century, and still others in the seventeenth and eighteenth centuries. If materialism were the reason for the anticommunist persecution, how do you explain the fact that they persecuted communism long before materialism existed? No, what they persecute and repress is communism as such. But the communist project is explicitly defended in the Bible as proper to and characteristic of Christianity. It was invented neither by the Marxists nor by the medieval or modern Christian groups!

When the official doctrinal propaganda asserts that the communist idea is inseparable from materialist ideologies, it is denying facts as evident and as impossible to conceal as daylight. In primitive Christianity, and for eighteen centuries after, the communist idea existed without materialism of any kind. And even today, what logical relationship can be pointed out between "having everything in common" (Acts 2:44) and denying the existence or efficacy of the Spirit? The truth is precisely the reverse: communism cannot be actualized unless we recognize the infinite respect due God in each of our neighbors, including those who are economically unproductive by weakness or age or natural gifts. The failure of Russian communism is the evidence. (What you now have in the Soviet Union is state capitalism.)

Then why does official Christianity make war on an idea that is expressly sponsored in the fonts of Christianity, and which, logically, can only be brought to realization on the basis of authentic Christianity? The denial of the existence of the Spirit is far more inseparable from each one's selfishly seeking his or her own proper advantage and gain, as capitalism teaches us to do. The thesis that communism cannot be separated from materialism is one of those monstrous Hitler-style falsehoods that are proclaimed with all the greater aplomb the more false they are. Examined objectively, it is the diametrical inversion of the real facts.

Another deliberate misunderstanding is the allegation that we Christian communists are only being fashionable, or adapting to progressive currents, or zealously keeping up to date. In the name of my Latin American brothers and sisters I here formally declare that we are shameless conservatives. We are looking for the literal gospel. We detest that opportunist principle according to which Christianity ought constantly to adapt and accommodate to changing circumstances. As if Christianity had no content of its own to proclaim and actualize! We reject the feebleminded notion that Christianity must be Roman in Roman imperial times, feudal in the Middle Ages, absolutist during the monarchy, liberal for the French Revolution, and so on. We leave such flexibility to a church which, for many centuries now, has considered it of no importance to verify objectively what it is that Christ wanted to bring about in the world. It is those who repress us who are being "fashionable"—those who are anticommunist by adaptation to the Trilateral Commission and the Chase Manhattan Bank. We, on the contrary, believe that Jesus Christ came to save the world, not to adapt to the world. And they say we are the ones who run after the current fashion? We who accept no other criterion than the one formulated in the first century in the fonts of Christianity?

They can likewise lay aside the notion that, while not actually denying the existence of Spirit, we care more for the material than for the spiritual. But in the first place, the final criterion established and left us by Jesus as the *only one* is, "I was hungry and you gave me to eat; I was thirsty and you gave me to drink, was a stranger and you took me in, was stripped naked and you clothed me; sick and you visited me, imprisoned and you came to see me" (Matt. 25:35–36). If this is preoccupying oneself more with the material than with the spiritual, then the self-styled official spiritualism ought to stop beating about the bush and direct its accusations against Jesus himself. Here we see all over again that the confrontation is between two interpretations of the Bible, not between Christians and atheists. And the difference is that we take the message of Jesus literally and without gloss.

But in the second place, is unrestricted fidelity to Jesus Christ to be reproached as preoccupation with the material? How are we going to give food to all who are hungry if we leave the means of production in private hands, which *necessarily* destine these means to the augmentation of capital and not to the satisfaction of the needs of the population? Do the official theologians really think they can maintain that there is more spirituality in the escapist selfishness of people who tranquilize themselves by saying, "There have always been people who starved to death, we are not divine providence," than in the decision of the people who want to be faithful to Jesus by undertaking all possible means to give food to the hungry, knowing that they are exposing themselves to repression, prison, and torture? Is there less spirituality in ruining one's future and social prestige by taking Jesus seriously than in adapting to the sweet enchantment of a bourgeoisie singing "I am dedicated to spiritual things"?

Furthermore, they can lay aside the notion that, while not actually denying the existence of God, we care more about human beings than about God. We have dedicated our lives to Jesus. Don't these theologians think Jesus is God? And this is where the antirevolutionary onslaught smites the essential point, the very essence of biblical revelation. Let it be clearly understood: the one thing the Christian revolutionaries advocate and defend is the adoration of the true God, in contrast with the adoration of idols, which for many centuries now has been inculcated by a theology radically ignorant of the Bible. This is not a theme that can simply be listed as item number so-and-so in a list of objections. It is not even just a theme. It is the one single motive of our rebellion, and the one single content of our theology. We have never pretended to do more than *theo*-logy, in the strict and literal sense of the word.

The God of the Bible is not knowable directly. The idols are. And the mental idols are more important than the material ones. There are those who believe that the only thing they have to do is put the word "God" in their minds to be directed toward the true God. But this is what the Bible fights to the death. The god of these adorers is a concept within their minds. With this intramental act they fail to transcend their own subjectivity, their own psychism, their own *I*. Either the true God is transcendent or the true God does not exist. The otherness constituted by the oppressed neighbor, who calls on our aid seeking justice, bursts our solipsism asunder. This is the only way we transcend ourselves. The God of the Bible is knowable only in otherness, in the call for help of the poor, the orphan, the widow, the stranger. Our revolutionary message has this objective only: that all people may come to know the one true God, and knowing God be saved. Those who accuse us of preferring the human to the divine are not only committing calumny; they are above all committing ignorance—supine ignorance of the Bible itself.

Last, they can abandon the notion that we care more for the transformation of structures than for the transformation of persons, that we care more for the social than for the personal. The contrary is the truth. Our revolution is directed toward the creation of the new human being. But unlike the attackers, we seek to posit the necessary means for the formation of this new human being. And the indispensable means is a new social structure. Is it not perfectly obvious that an existing social system has more efficacy for education or miseducation than the exhortations of classroom or temple? How far can you get with the idea that a person should not place his or her heart in money and material things (the central idea of the Sermon on the Mount) if the existing social system inculcates just the contrary under pain of blows and death? Perhaps an insignificant minority can heroically resist the peremptory mandates of such a system. But Christianity cares about all human beings. It cannot content itself with saving a tiny minority. The majority cannot even assign a sense of realism to the Christian message of solidarity with neighbor, when the social structure imposes upon it, under pain of annihilation, the task of seeking its proper interest and letting the chips fall where they may, without preoccupying itself with other people. Structural change will be a mere means for personal change—but a means so obviously necessary that those who fail to give it first priority demonstrate by that very fact that their vaunted desire to transform persons is just empty rhetoric.

To return to where we began, the five establishment pretexts for their unscrupulous crusade against communism are mere diversionary maneuvers: identifying communism with materialism and atheism, accusing us of chasing mode and fashion, imputing to us a lack of spirituality, alleging we care more for human beings than for God, and attributing to us a greater preoccupation with structures than with persons. It is time to drop all these side issues and concentrate on the fundamental fact: the Bible teaches communism.

ORIGINAL CHISTIANITY

All the believers together had everything in common; they sold their possessions and their goods, and distributed among all in accordance with each one's need [Acts 2:44-45].

The heart of the multitude of believers was one and their soul was one, and not a single one said anything of what he had was his, but all things were in common. . . . There was no poor person among them, since whoever possessed fields or houses sold them, bore the proceeds of the sale and placed them at the feet of the apostles; and a distribution was made to each one in accordance with his need [Acts 4:32, 34-35].

Luke's normative intention stands out. There is no question of a special lifestyle that could be considered peculiar to some Christians in contrast with the general mass of Christians. His insistence on the universality of communism from a literary point of view is even a little affected—*pántes hoi pisteúsantes* (2:44), all the believers, all who had believed in Jesus Christ, all Christians; *oudè heîs* (4:32), not a single one said anything was his; *hósoi ktétores* (4:34), whoever possessed fields or houses, whoever had anything. If they wanted to be Christians the condition was communism.

The anticommunist commentators allege that this is Luke's personal point of view and that the other New Testament writers fail to corroborate it. The argument is invalid because none of the other writers describes the life of original Christianity, and hence there is no document upon which one could base an attempt to give Luke the lie. But let us suppose (not concede) that some other New Testament author were to differ with Luke; how would this justify the persecution (styling itself "Christian") of a social project that is explicitly and repeatedly promoted by one of the principal authors of the New Testament?

We shall see that the hypothesis is false, for Jesus himself was a communist. But let us place ourselves hypothetically in the worst possible position: that only Luke teaches communism. With what right, indeed with what elemental logic, is it thereupon asserted that communism is incompatible with Christianity? Does not the very fact that they make this assertion demonstrate that the anticommunists who call themselves Christians are alienated and are merely claiming Christianity when in reality they are being moved by an anti-Christian motivation of which they are unaware? If at least the Lucan part of the New Testament teaches communism, how is it possible to maintain that communism is at odds with Christianity?

Let us suppose (not concede) that there are parts of the New Testament which lend footing to the projection of social systems different from Luke's. Well and good. That some Christians today may prefer these other parts of the Bible to Luke's is their affair. But with what right do they deny the name Christian to what the Lucan part of the Bible teaches emphatically and repeatedly? The origin of the communist idea in the history of the West is the New Testament, not Jamblichus or Plato. The banner the communist groups and movements marched under—from the first century through the Middle Ages all the way to Wilhelm Weitling (1808–1871), in whose procommunist organization Marx and Engels were active in their youth[1]—was the New Testament, not *The Republic* or the *Vita Pythagorae*. The ruthless repression of the communists in the name of Christianity for the last seventeen centuries is a farce and the most grotesque falsification that can be imagined.

A second anticommunist allegation against the texts we have cited from Luke is: the communism of the first Christians failed. It is flabbergasting that sermons, documents of the magisterium, books, and bourgeois public opinion should brook the notion that this is an argument. The Sermon on the Mount failed too, but this does not deprive it of its normative character. In the clear intention of the original report, communism is obligatory for Christians. This is not modified, not in the slightest, by the fact of a failure of the original communist intent. What should concern us is to find out why it broke down and bring communism to realization without committing whatever error caused the first Christians to break down. This would be the only logical conclusion if our objectors had the flimsiest desire to be guided by the Bible. But what our objectors have done is make an antecedent and rigid decision to disagree with the Bible, and to this purpose they bring forward every pretext, even if it tramples upon the most elemental logic.

To cite that initial failure is pure pretext. It is as if we told ourselves we were eliminating the Ten Commandments because they failed in history. The establishment theologians confound the normative with the factual—and they confound them deliberately, in order to be able to disagree with any biblical teaching for which they have no taste. This is anti-Christianity, disguised as "Christian civilization" for the purpose of rejecting the gospel.

According to Marx[2] the cause of the failure was that the first Christians neglected the political struggle. We shall speak of the political order in another chapter. Personally I think that a communist island in an economic sea characterized by the exploitation of some persons by others cannot be maintained, and that this is why the first Christian communism failed. That is, as we have said above, the surrounding, involving social system has far more power than exhortations have. The communism of the first Christians failed because the first Christians were very few. But today we Christians are the majority in the West and the principal force in the world.

There is a third charge made against the communism of the first Christians. But the reader has already perceived that this whole cascade of objections, one replacing another as each turns out absurd, is only a series of emotional symptoms proceeding from the objectants' instinctive repugnance to the message of the Bible. The third objection runs as follows: the communism of the first Christians was optional as can be seen from Peter's words to Ananias, "Was it not still yours if you kept it, and once you sold it was it not yours to dispose of?" (Acts 5:4). One would love to know what cohesion there is among these objections. First they were saying that Luke is lying; then that he is not lying, but that the project collapsed; and finally, not only is he not lying, but his report is so reliable that they are going to use Acts 5:4 to beat communism. It is plain to see that the so-called objections are just irrational reactions, the spasms of an uncontrollable visceral revulsion.

Still, let us examine the convulsion as if it were an objection. It is astonishing that there was ever considered to be any validity in this third charge. Let us take, hypothetically, the worst possible position. Let us suppose (falsely, as we shall see) that, according to Luke, communism was *optional*. I answer: but you combat it as if it were *evil*! According to yourselves, the Bible (merely) *recommends* it; so you *prohibit* it!

"Optional" ought to mean that we Christians may opt for it. Nevertheless you persecute, as seditious, criminal, and anti-Christian, whoever opts for communism. I have never seen anything more distracted and demented. To forbid communism they bend all their efforts to prove the Bible recommends it.

But the hypothesis is false. According to Luke, what is optional is not communism, but Christianity. Peter does not tell Ananias that he could have come into the Christian community without renouncing the private ownership of his goods. Nor could he say such a thing after it was explicitly emphasized that of the Christians "*not a single one* said anything was his" (Acts 4:32). Ananias lied to the Holy Spirit by pretending to become a Christian *via* a simulated renunciation.

The objection belongs to the type of reader who thinks a work can be understood without understanding the thought of the author. Luke would have to have been a very slow-witted writer if he claimed to assert, in the Ananias episode (Acts 5:1-11), the optional character of communism, when four verses earlier (4:34) he had insisted that "*whoever* possessed fields or houses sold them," and so on, and two verses above that, "and *not a single one* said anything was his" (4:32), and still earlier, "*all the faithful together* had everything in common" (2:44). This is the Luke who had placed these words on the lips of Jesus: "*Every one* of you who does not renounce all he has cannot be my disciple" (Luke 14:33); and now the rightists would have it that according to Luke one can be a disciple of Christ without renouncing all one has. What they ought to be doing is rejecting Luke as a jabbering cheat. But to assert that according to Luke one can be a Christian without renouncing private property is an insolent rejection of the documentation which all of us have right before our eyes.

Let it be well noted that the last verse cited is concerned with the simple fact of being disciples of Christ and not of some "special vocation" or other. See the beginning of the pericope: "Many crowds accompanied him, and he, turning, said to them: . . ." (Luke 14:25). He is not addressing the Twelve, but the crowd. It is a simple matter of the conditions for being a Christian, exactly as in the texts we cited from Acts. What is optional is to be a Christian, to be a disciple of Christ. Those who wrest the Ananias episode from its context are trying to read it as if it had no author, as if no one had written it. As Hinkelammert has said, this episode means: pain of death for whoever betrays communism, Christianty's indispensable condition.

But the most curious and paradoxical thing about the objection we have just been considering is that it supposes that *our* communism is not optional, or that the communism of Marx is not optional. With supreme fury it attacks a nonexistent enemy. Never have we thought that communism can be realized except by free decision of the workers, rural people, and unemployed, who together form the immense majority of the population. And Marx thought the same.

It must be taken into account that a system is a system. Let it not be thought that we in capitalism are outside all systems, although this is the absurdity which, at bottom, the objection assumes. It is impossible that, within one and the same country, the criteria for the destination of its resources be the satisfaction of the needs of the population, and at the same time be to make profit for capital. Either the system is capitalist or the system is communist. Those who wish that communism be optional for the capitalists are preventing it from being an option for the vast majority of the population. So where does that leave us? They wanted it to be optional, did they not?

It is preposterous to suppose that the proletariat are in capitalism by free decision—or that capitalism is a kind of point zero, the "natural" situation imposed on no one, and that only if you want to move from this point does the dilemma arise of doing so either by free option or by a constraint that violates your freedom.

The *real* dilemma is this one: either practically the whole population imposes communism upon an insignificant minority or a handful of persons imposes capitalism on practically the whole population. Those who love freedom must choose between *these* alternatives. There is no third way. In one country there cannot be more than one system, precisely because it is a system. The illusory "mixed economy" is capitalism; the state firms have to obey the rules of capitalism and become the pawn of the private firms.

Where would the capitalists get the human resources to run their factories if the workers of the country were to opt for a communist system? Let us suppose that a communist revolution leaves the capitalists in freedom of option. To whom will they sell their products if the population wishes to have nothing to do with capitalist production? The theoreticians who seek freedom of option even for the insignificant minority are closing their eyes to the fact that this freedom of option cannot exist without eliminating freedom of option for the vast majority. Here it can be seen how much they really love freedom. They want the freedom to deprive everyone else of freedom.

It is what the objectants *suppose* that is most false in all of this—that the proletariat are in capitalism by free decision. But in order to have freedom there must be a knowledge of the alternatives. If all ideological sources, including the church, television, and films, characterize the communist idea as satanic, criminal, and anti-Christian, what freedom of option do the proletariat have?

THE KINGDOM IS ON EARTH

Now let us investigate whether the first Christians invented their communism or based it upon the teachings of Jesus and the whole biblical tradition. In other words, our task is to extend our vision beyond the book called *The Acts of the Apostles*. And here we begin to specify the moral and obligatory reason for communism. But as we are going to base our discussion primarily upon three authentic logia of Jesus concerning the kingdom of God, and inasmuch as the supposition that the kingdom is in the other world has prevented so many from understanding these statements, we must prefix an explanation—of paramount importance of itself, but, from the viewpoint of the logical thread of this book, having the character of a prenote.

To begin, let us compare Matthew 13:11 ("To you has been given to know the mysteries of the kingdom of the Heavens") on the one hand with Mark 4:11 ("To you has been given the mystery of the kingdom of God") and Luke 8:10 ("To you has been given to know the mysteries of the kingdom of God") on the other.

Also, compare Matthew 3:2 ("The kingdom of the Heavens has come") on one hand with Mark 1:15 ("The kingdom of God has come") and Luke 10:9 ("The kingdom of God has come to you") on the other.

This is a sample. We could lengthen the list of comparisons between the text of Matthew and the texts of Mark and Luke. Scholars agree that Matthew systematically substitutes "kingdom of the heavens" for the original "kingdom of God" and have inquired into the reason for this systematic editorial modification.

They also agree on the answer. This is important to emphasize. All the exegetes who broach the subject, be they conservatives or liberals, those of an other-worldly penchant or those of an earthly penchant, explain the editorial phenomenon by the late Judaic custom of avoiding all explicit use of the name "God." People said "the heavens," or even "the Name," instead of saying "God." It was believed that this constituted obedience to the commandment of the decalogue forbidding taking the name of God in vain. Today this respect seems excessive to us, and even Christ did not observe it. But the literary fact cannot be denied. It is superabundantly documented in the rabbinical writings of the first century B.C. and the first century of the Christian era. Even today in our Western languages there are vestiges, as when we say "Heaven help us" when what we really mean is "God help us."

And so there is no question of Matthew's placing the kingdom in the other world. He simply uses the habitual circumlocution of late Judaism to avoid as much as possible mentioning the name of God. The editor we call Matthew (who is surely not the apostle) either introduced this circumlocution himself or found it in the writings he utilized in redacting his Gospel. And where there is special motive, the motive warrants the exception.

As to where the kingdom is to be realized, Matthew has no doubts. In the parable of the weeds (Matt. 13:24–30, 36–43), which is a parable about the kingdom, he says expressly that "the field is the world" (v. 38), and at the end of the story he does not say that the kingdom will be transferred to some other place but that "the Son of Man will send his angels, who will remove from his kingdom all scandals and all workers of iniquity" (v. 41), and that then "the just will shine like the sun in the kingdom of their Father" (v. 43).

And so for Matthew too, just as for all the other known sacred authors, in the Old Testament as in the New, the kingdom is on earth. Now, the Matthean expression "the kingdom of the heavens" was the only one serving the escapist theologians as pretext for maintaining that the kingdom was to be realized in the other world. Not even texts about glory or entering into glory provided them any support, for the Psalms explicitly teach, "Salvation surrounds those who fear him, so that the glory will dwell in our land" (Ps. 85:10).

Of course the Matthean circumlocution "of the heavens" was only a pretext.

If they had not been blinded by the scorn their escapist theology holds for our world, they could have seen where the kingdom is right from the Psalter. For instance, Psalm 74, wholly dedicated to "Yahweh my king from olden time" (v. 12), whose rule consists in saving "the poor and the needy" (v. 21), ends by begging Yahweh to attack all oppressors (vv. 22–23), since Yahweh must "make salvation real in the midst of the earth" (v. 12). And Psalm 10 proclaims, looking into the future, "Yahweh is king eternally and for ever, the gentiles have been swept from their land" (v. 16). They could have found the same thing throughout chapter 32 of Isaiah, in Psalm 146, and in hundreds of other Old Testament texts.

But there is no demonstration of this blindness to equal the fact that the theologians are not even impressed by the prayer which Christ taught us and which they pray every day—"Thy kingdom come" (Matt. 6:10; Luke 11:2). He does not say, "Take us to your kingdom," but "your kingdom come." Where is it to come if not to the earth, which is where we are when we say "come"? That the escapists do not read the Psalter carefully is a frequent fault of theirs, though it ought not to be; but that they pay no attention even to the Lord's Prayer is really the height of blindness.

Furthermore, not just a part of the content but *the* content of the "good news" Jesus proclaimed, that is, the content of the gospel in the strict sense, is that "the kingdom has come" (Mark 1:15 and parallels). Where can it have come if not to earth? Besides, Jesus says "the kingdom of God has come to you" (Luke 11:20; Matt. 12:28); the only possible meaning is that it has come to the earth on which those to whom Jesus says "has come to you" are standing. Accordingly, to maintain that the kingdom is in the other world is equivalent to denying the very content of the gospel. And to say in escapist desperation that the kingdom is "partly in this world and partly in the other" is to launch a thesis totally without support in Jesus' teaching.

Even the Book of Revelation, which talks of nothing but the heavenly Jerusalem, finally tells us: "And I saw the holy city, the new Jerusalem, coming down from heaven from God" (Rev. 21:2); "and I was shown the holy city, Jerusalem, descending from the sky, from God" (Rev. 21:10). The kingdom is made ready in heaven, or resides temporarily in heaven, but its final destination is earth. Hence the visionary says he "saw it coming down," since it is on earth that it is to be established. He had already told us, "And he made them to be a kingdom, and priests for our God, and they will reign over all the earth" (Rev. 5:10), and at the end of the book he adds, "And they shall reign for ever and ever" (Rev. 22:5). If he expressly says that the kingdom or reign will be over the earth, it becomes idle to inquire where the new Jerusalem descends to as it "comes down from heaven."

Our reference to the Book of Revelation in this context is important, since in 2:7 this book mentions the word "paradise." And this, erroneously, has been seen as the ace in the hole for the escapists. First, though, let us note once more that the kingdom of God is on earth, as is demonstrated by the texts we have cited, and that on this point there is not the least wavering on the part of the sacred authors. Hence what paradise might be, or being with Christ, or Abraham's bosom, or the heavenly treasure, is a question we could well leave aside, because what matters to us is the definitive kingdom, which constitutes the central content of the message of Jesus. The escapists can have paradise. But the passages cited from Revelation give the same key as the most competent researchers (Strack-Billerweck and Joachim Jeremias) have found in the copious Judaic documentation.

> Without using the term paradise, in Revelation the garden of God appears as a summation of the glory and of the fullness: Revelation describes the final Jerusalem as paradise when it speaks of the trees of life and the water of life (22:1; cf. 22:14, 19), the destruction of the serpent of old (20:2; cf. 20:10), the elimination of suffering, of need, and of death (21:4). The place of residence of the definitive paradise is, according to 21:2, 10, the Jerusalem of the renewed earth.[3]

Paradise is Jerusalem, provisionally heavenly, which will at last descend from heaven and be installed on our earth for ever and ever. According to the Bible, situations outside our world are transitory and temporary, whether they are known as paradise, or the bosom of Abraham, or heavenly treasure, or being with Christ, or third heaven. As the New Testament employs the terminology of contemporary Judaism, and as the latter offers abundant documentation, scholars have not entertained the least doubt in the matter.

For example the Lucan parable of the rich man and Lazarus (Luke 16:19–31) typically places the rich man in *hádes* (v. 23), which is the technical name for the place of torment after the death of the unjust, in contrast with *géenna*, the definitive place of torment after the final judgment.[4] "Abraham's bosom" (Luke 16:22), used in conjunction and contrast with *hádes*, is equally provisional, until such time as the kingdom is realized, including the resurrection of the dead.

In like fashion, Matthew 5:12 does not say, You shall receive much recompense in the heavens, but "Your recompense is great in heaven," which is the place where it is provisorily kept. Theodor Zahn comments: "After the beatitudes of Matthew 5:3–10, it is obvious that the reward (mentioned in 5:12) will be given to the disciples only in the kingdom which is to be established on earth".[5] And indeed there cannot be the shadow of a doubt in this respect, as Matthew has just said of the generous that "they shall inherit the earth" (5:5). The idea in Matthew 5:12 is the same as in Acts 10:4: "Your prayers and your alms have arisen as a reminder before the presence of God." This same idea is found in Tobit 12:12–15.

Likewise the conversation of the crucified Christ with the good thief demonstrates precisely the contrary of what escapist theology would like it to. "When you come to your kingdom" is in deliberate contrast with "This very day . . . in paradise" (Luke 23:42–43). Jesus does not deny that it is only later that he will come into his kingdom—but he wishes to have the good thief in his company right from today. Evidently, paradise, as in all the literature of that time, is a provisional place, pending the arrival of the moment in which the Messiah comes to his kingdom—which is surely on the earth, since the good thief is on the earth when he says "when you come."

Well and good, but it is not to be thought that an interpretation of the Bible is a conceptual construct, which each scholar invents according to his or her mentality, and which is presented alongside other interpretations for the public to choose the one it finds most suitable. To speak of a kingdom of God in the other world is not only to found a new religion without any relationship with the teaching of Christ (for none of the texts wielded by escapist theology mentions the kingdom); it is to assert exactly the contrary of what Christ teaches: "The kingdom has come to you," and "Your kingdom come." The fact that tradition has taught for centuries that the kingdom is in the other world only demonstrates that that tradition betrayed Jesus and founded another religion completely different.

This concludes the explanation of our third point. It was a necessary prenote for what is about to follow. But consider the importance it has in itself: the conservatives' resistance to the elimination of private property in the kingdom of God depends on where you situate the kingdom. This is truly prodigious inconsistency. If the kingdom is in heaven, they accept the texts abolishing private property in the kingdom. If the kingdom is on earth, they deny that these same texts abolish private property. Evidently, they cannot maintain that private property persists in heaven. But according to Jesus, what they think is in heaven is really on earth. To doubt this they have to deny the Lord's Prayer and the central and single content of the good news, of the gospel. We leave it to the reader to judge how they can conscientiously switch interpretations of the very same texts, depending on whether the texts are about heaven or earth.

A CLASSLESS SOCIETY

Now that we have proposed our explanation concerning the kingdom, let us resume the thread of our argumentation in this chapter. The teachings of Christ upon which the first Christians were able to base their establishment of communism are, among others, Mark 10:25, Luke 6:20, 24, Matthew 6:24 (= Luke 16:13), and Luke 16:19-31. The first three refer to the kingdom, hence the above disgression was necessary.

Of course, the first Christians were also influenced by Jesus' example and personal conduct. For Jesus, whether the conservatives like it or not, *was in fact a communist*—as can be seen in John 12:6, 13:29, and Luke 8:1-3. Judas "carried the purse," so they had everything in common and each received according to his need.

The doctrinal betrayal of later centuries, as we have seen, has sought to interpret this communism as a "way of perfection," not to be identified with the simple fact of being a Christian. But such an interpretation is dashed to smithereens when it impinges on the fact that Jesus made the renunciation of property a condition for simply "entering into the kingdom" (cf. Mark 10:21, 25). There is no room for a third way, when the dilemma is to enter into the kingdom or not to enter into the kingdom.

Besides, hypothetically, if being communist is more perfect than simply being Christian, I should like to know why they forbid it—why they teach that what according to Jesus is more perfect is evil. It is easy to see that the famous "way of perfection" is a mere escape route invented when the church became rich and began to constitute an essential part of the establishment. If it is decreed that communism is more perfect, the logical conclusion would have been to betake oneself to promote its realization in the world. Instead the conclusion has been to devote oneself to combating it, and to persecute to the death whoever promoted it. It is difficult to imagine anything that would demonstrate more clearly that the "way of perfection" doctrine is just an escape route, just a doctrinal subterfuge.

It was not only Jesus' example that taught communism to the first Christians; it was his word as well. Scientific exegesis recognizes that Mark 10:17–31, about the rich young man, is more reliable than its Matthean (Matt. 19:16–30) or Lucan (Luke 18:18–30) transcriptions, which make obvious editorial changes. A simple comparison shows that Matthew and Luke had the text of Mark before them. And yet this is precisely where one can feel the difficulties and conflicts faced by the first missionaries when they wanted to proclaim to the world this authentic logion of Jesus: "It is easier for a camel to pass through the eye of a needle than for a rich person to enter the kingdom of God" (Mark 10:25). Since Jesus had already said, "The kingdom of God has arrived" (Mark 1:15), the question is who can and who cannot form part of the kingdom which Jesus Christ is founding on earth. And what Jesus says is: the rich cannot.

In order to sidestep the conflict, but without betraying the words of Christ, the first missionaries added: "For men it is impossible, but not for God; since to God everything is possible" (Mark 10:27). They meant that by an act of God it is possible for a rich person to enter the kingdom—*by ceasing to be rich, of course*, since otherwise they *would* have been betraying the authentic logion of Jesus (Mark 10:25). Any minimizing interpretation of Mark 10:27 is incompatible with Mark 10:25, and incompatible with the declaration at the source of the pericope "Go, sell everything you have and give it to the poor" (Mark 10:21). If they come to us now and say that to enter into the kingdom a rich person need neither go nor sell everything he has nor give it to the poor, this is no longer interpretation but bold out-and-out tergiversation.

Verses 21 and 25 could have been invented neither by the missionaries nor by the communities nor by the editor Mark, since these verses raise insuperble difficulties for the proclamation of the gospel. They are the authentic words of Jesus. Everything else in the pericope is open to question.

Recall that the question is simply that of "entering the kingdom," and that, as we saw in section 3 above, the kingdom is on earth. Jesus goes about recruiting people for the kingdom and says straight out: the rich cannot be part of it. People generally forget that "rich" and "poor" are correlative terms. We say that someone is rich in contrast with the rest of the population, or with a majority of the population, which is not. As we shall see at the beginning of our next chapter, Jesus is not against wealth in the absolute sense of the word, but in the relative sense, in the meaning of social contrast. When he says "Happy the poor, for yours is the kingdom of God" (Luke 6:20) and adds "Woe to you the rich, because you have received your comfort" (Luke 6:24), he is saying exactly the same thing as in Mark 10:25: the rich cannot enter the kingdom. Only the poor can. (In passing, let us observe that this demonstrates that, as the vast majority of exegetes maintain, Luke 6:20 is the original version and Matthew 5:3 the later, since Luke 6:20 says the same as Mark 10:25, whose authenticity no one denies.) Now, what this teaching is saying, in concurrence with Mark 10:25 and Luke 6:20, 24, is that in the kingdom there cannot be social differences—that the kingdom, whether or not it pleases the conservatives, is a classless society.

The anticommunist reaction has to abominate this, of course. But it is worth repeating that they themselves, in their eschatological conceptions, admit that according to the Bible there are no social differences in the kingdom. The only thing they are missing is the place, since if the kingdom is on earth they indignantly reject social equality. This is why we introduced our digression in section 3 above. What they admit for heaven is, according to the gospel, on earth.

Marx did not invent the classless society. Except for the formulation, the idea is unequivocally in the most authentic and least disputed logia (Mary 10:21, 25) of Jesus Christ. [6]

NOTES

1. Karl Marx and Friedrich Engels, *Marx-Engels Werke* (Berlin: Dietz, 1955–1973), 17:485.
2. Ibid., 18:160.
3. Joachim Jeremias, *Theologisches Wörterbuch zum neuen Testament* (Stuttgart: Kohlhammer, 1933–1978), 5:767.
4. This same terminology is used in Testamentum Abrahae 20. A and in Esd. 7:85, 93. See Hermann Strack and Paul Billerbeck, *Kommentar zum neuen Testament aus Talmud und Midrash* (Muncih: C.H. Beck, 1922–63), 2:228 and 4:1040.
5. Theodor Zahn, *Das Evangelium des Mattäus,* 3rd ed. (Leipzig: A. Deichert, 1910), p. 197.
6. The Matthean version of Mark 10:21 is recognizably later: "If you wish to be perfect, go and sell what you have," etc. (Matt. 19:21). Here there is question of a perfection which is indispensable for entry into the kingdom (cf. Matt. 19:24), clearly superior to the morality of the Jews (cf. Matt. 19:18–20), but not excluding any particular group of Christians, inasmuch as it is impossible to imagine a third alternative between entering the kingdom and not entering the kingdom. The same thing appears with the only other occurrence of the adjective "perfect" (Matt. 5:48).
As the Catholic exegete Rudolf Schnackenburg recognizes, "perfection is demanded

of *all*" (*Lexikon für Theologie und Kirche* [Freiburg: Herder, 1957–1968], 3:1246—emphasis his). Catholic J. Blinzler, as well, says: "The requirement of perfection is for all" (ibid., 10:864). The alternative is not to enter the kingdom: "If your justice were to be no greater than that of the scribes and Pharisees, you would not enter the kingdom of the Heavens" (Matt. 5:20). And the contrast in Matt. 5:46–48 is not with Christians of lesser perfection, but with "publicans" (v. 46) and "pagans" (v. 47). What is not demanded of all Christians is celibacy (cf. Matt. 19:10–12)—here there is a contrast between "not all have room for this word" on the one hand, and "but those to whom it has been given" on the other. It is the passage about eunuchs. There is no indication that one alternative is more perfect than the other. As Schnackenburg well says, "Jesus is only making an observation: 'There are those who. . . .' Doubtless his preaching of the kingdom had fired up some of his followers in such a way that they felt called to a virginal or celibate life" (ibid., 3:1245).

12

Segundo Galilea

Jesus and the Liberation of His People

Segundo Galilea believes that if we can understand how Jesus related to the people of his day, we can have a better appreciation of our responsibilities as Christians today. "Jesus and the Liberation of His People" is taken from Following Jesus *(Maryknoll, N.Y.: Orbis Books, 1981), pp. 97–109. The essay was first published in Chile in 1974.*

THE SPIRIT OF THE LORD HAS BEEN GIVEN TO ME;
FOR HE HAS ANOINTED ME.
HE HAS SENT ME TO BRING THE GOOD NEWS TO THE POOR,
TO PROCLAIM LIBERTY TO THE CAPTIVES
AND TO THE BLIND NEW SIGHT,
TO SET THE DOWNTRODDEN FREE,
TO PROCLAIM THE LORD'S YEAR OF FAVOR [Luke 4:18–19].

Many Christians today are committed to the integral liberation of their brothers and sisters, particularly of the "little ones," those who suffer all kinds of injustice and other kinds of sin which characterize Latin American society. In many instances these Christians are in no condition to assume a militancy that is in itself political. In other cases this militancy is either not advisable or it is functionally—not doctrinally—incompatible with another mission. This is the case of the hierarchy of the church and in general of those dedicated to the official pastoral ministry.

176

For these and for many other Christians there remain the demands—if they are truly to follow Christ and his gospel—of liberating the "little ones" from all types of injustice and sin. They realize that they must influence society in favor of the poor through their apostolic mission; that as Christians their action should have a sociopolitical dimension; and that in this, as in other aspects of the apostolate, Christ and the gospel are their model.

However, many of them seem to find themselves today at an impasse. They appear lost in the maze of a sociopolitical pastoral approach and do not find their inspiration and orientation in the gospel. That is to say, they do not see Jesus as a model in this field. In other aspects of life, Jesus and his gospel orient them with words and deeds. In the attitude of Christ in regard to the social and political problems of his time they find a vacuum or a complete abstention that leaves them in the dark. Or they would like to see in Jesus a definite option regarding the demands of the social liberation of the Jewish people and against the Roman system, in the style of a militant, a revolutionary, a contemporary political prophet. And in this field, Jesus' life does not seem to give them any message that can be imitated. From all this arise two temptations: that of a purely "religious" apostolate with no reference to social change, or that of replacing Christ with other persons apparently more committed to the historic liberation of the oppressed.

THE PROBLEM OF A "POLITICAL CHRISTOLOGY"

It seems to me that this is a real problem in Latin America, and its cause is the absence of a Christology that responds to this uneasiness, a Christology with social and political dimensions. The Christology that many of those Christians received did not prepare them for a sociopolitical reading of the life of Christ and the gospel. To grasp the liberating and temporal dimension of the words and deeds of Jesus, it is necessary to integrate this Christological dimension. A Christology thus conceived and which, of course, does not forget all the other dimensions of Christ's message is going to be the foundation of everything else: of the problems having to do with the relations among the church, society, and politics and among pastoral activity, politics, and liberation; of questions proper to a spirituality of liberation; of a political theology and of a theology of liberation.

The lack of a correct reading of the gospel leads to deformed views of Jesus' stand on the sociopolitical situation of Israel. This is not the place to go into detail on this situation, which is well known. The Jewish people, subjugated by the Roman authorities, was looking for its political and economic liberation from the oppression of Caesar's representatives and from various taxes. In the time of Jesus there were politico-religious movements for this purpose. The idea of authority as something *sacred* and of theocratic states united in these movements the political and the religious orders to a point of confusing them in the work of oppositon to the Roman power. Of these factions, the ones particularly important for us are the Herodians, who allied with the Roman authority and who took advantage of the system. These would correspond to our present-day Latin American oligarchies. Then there were the Essenes, a sect of deep and intense religious life and organization who kept themselves free from temporal and political matters. Their attitude is similar to the Christian sects of today who steer clear of the sociopolitical dimensions of the faith.

The most significant group for our present discussion was the Zealots. Very nationalistic, the Zealots actively sought independence through subversion. Religious, they were involved in the battles for liberation of Israel with messianic zeal. They awaited the Messiah as the political leader who would free them from the Romans. Their influence was great, and the background of many of Jesus' disciples, and probably some of the Apostles, was Zealot: "Do you want us to command that fire come down from heaven to consume them?" (Luke 9:54). They would correspond to the present-day Latin American revolutionary movements.

We must situate the mission of Jesus with regard to this reality and this historical process. The absence of the political dimension of Christology tends to divorce Jesus from the problems of his day socially: disincarnate, a preacher of a message of salvation for people and of a kingdom that has nothing to do with this world. The concrete historical and sociopolitical situations are a backdrop for and an occasion of Jesus' purely religious activity, but they are not intrinsically bound up with it. The events and the people in the passion, for example, would be like actors prepared beforehand by God so that the redemption could be carried out. This perspective sees a strong influence of the Essenes on Christ.

Moreover, this Christology gives birth to a vision of the church and its mission with no reference to society and with no political dimension. It encloses the pastoral ministry in this type of mission, and any apparent breaking out of this enclosure is judged as an undue intrusion by the official representatives of the church ("The priests are getting involved in politics. . .").

Reacting against this ahistorical Christology and seeking in the life of Christ an inspirational model for the tasks of sociopolitical liberation, others have seen in Jesus' mission in Israel the work of a revolutionary messiah, who, besides giving a religious message, put into motion a form of political subversion. They consider him if not a Zealot, at least someone closely connected to the Zealots. This is how they would explain, in the last analysis, that the motives for his being taken prisoner were of a political nature (wanting to be equal to Caesar, making himself king of the Jews, endangering the stability of society: "If we allow him to continue this way, everyone will believe in him and the Romans will come and destroy our holy place and our people" [John 11:48]). This is the Christology of the revolutionary Christ, the model of the struggle for the temporal liberation of the oppressed. This leads to an ecclesiology in which the church and its hierarchical ministers would be called upon to act in a partisan manner, in the strict political sense, using power and social influence to change society. In the name of pastoral action the official church forms a temporal pressure group and the ministers assume sociopolitical leadership.

This Christology likewise does not correspond to the deeds and to the true nature of Jesus' messiahship. Things are not quite so simple and Christ's position toward the society of his time and toward the liberation of his people was much more profound than what appears at first sight. It is significant that Jesus has been linked to both the Zealots and the Essenes, and that today it can be shown, without a doubt, that he did not participate in either of these movements.[1]

To situate authentically the mission of Christ in relation to the political situation of his time, we need to apply to this question the mystery of the incarnation. To speak of a redemptive-historical incarnation of the Son of God is not just to affirm that God became human at a determined and identifiable time and place. It is to affirm that Jesus also came to participate in some way in the historical, religious, social, and political movements of his time and that these movements influenced and conditioned his activity.

Specifically, if we do not want to fall into a sort of disguised monophysitism, we must accept the fact that Jesus was a Jew, subject to the conflicts and aspirations prevalent in the Palestine of his day. Subject to the Romans like the rest of the Jews, he shared their desires for liberation, subject to the pressures of the social, political, and religious movements that we mentioned earlier. His attitudes and his preaching touched on the political questions of his day, and he could hardly avoid coming into conflict with both the pharisaic religious powers and the civil authorities (John 11:47ff.). In this sense it becomes clear that his trial before the Sanhedrin and before Pilate took the historical form of a political trial: "We caught this man perverting our nation, and forbidding us to give tribute to Caesar, and saying that he himself is Christ, the King. . . . He stirs up the people" (Luke 23:2, 5). "Anyone who makes himself a king sets himself against Caesar" (John 19:12). Even the way of his death had a political nuance. It is well known that the cross was a torture reserved especially for subversives.

Moreover, in the messiahship of Jesus there is no seeking for anything temporal or political, and he himself avoided being taken as a social leader. This is so clear in all Christological tradition that it is unnecessary to enlarge upon it. His message contains no program or strategy of political liberation. Jesus was fundamentally a religious leader who announced the kingdom of God as a religious, pastoral message. Not by his stance before the established authority (John 18:33–37; Luke 20:20–25, etc.), or in the content of his preaching (the eschatological kingdom of God and the message of the Beatitudes), or in the orientation he gave to his disciples did there appear anything comparable to a political messiah or a social leader.

But still he was thought of by many people, including the disciples and apostles, as a political, temporal messiah to the point that one of the chief preoccupations of Jesus was to dispel this false impression (Matt. 16:22ff.; John 6:15; Matt. 20:22ff.; Acts 1:6, etc.).

We should look for the answer not only in the Jews' fervent expectation of a messiah who would be a political liberator. Above all we should seek it in the very nature of Christ's message. In announcing the kingdom of God and the reconciliation of human beings with God through the redemption of all sin, Jesus reveals the destiny and the demands for conversion of people and societies. The kingdom of God as a promise that even now is present among us (Mark 1:14–15) implants in society values that will allow for the criticism of all forms of social and structural sin, including all forms of exploitation and domination. Thus, the preaching of the kingdom is not properly speaking a political discourse, but it can give rise to authentic liberation movements among human beings: insofar as it makes them conscious of various sinful situations and insofar as it inspires them to transform society because of a gospel of the kingdom in which they have believed.

In this sense, the religio-pastoral message of Jesus gave rise to a dynamic of social changes for his time and for all time to come. The sociopolitical order is a dimension of the very proclamation of the Christian faith, which is contemplation, commitment, and a personal and social criticism of all that would separate us from the kingdom. In this very precise sense the action of Christ—and the action of the church—is involved with the political order, insofar as they are called upon to bring about changes in the political systems.

Therefore, the religious messiahship of Jesus was susceptible to confusion. Developing in a society oppressed in many ways, it could not but appear as critical of a system both religiously and civilly totalitarian, thus unleashing hopes of a temporal liberator. This same Christological danger is also ecclesiological in that the church, whose pastoral activity has the same characteristics, can be attracted toward political power and a purely temporal liberation. This, evidently, is a constant temptation of pastoral activity.

THE TEMPTATION OF POWER AND "POLITICAL ACTION"

This temptation raises complex issues for the hierarchy of the church and for those who participate in the church's pastoral activity. Because of the close solidarity that exists between true religious messiahship and temporal messiahship, this was the fundamental temptation of the public life of Jesus. We have already spoken of the highly politicized situation of Israel and expectations of liberation from the Roman rule. We have spoken of how the people and Jesus' followers to the very end desired him to be a temporal savior of Israel and their king. In this sense the death of Christ was a collective frustration.

The temptation to be a political messiah assailed Jesus not only externally but internally as well. His messianic consciousness was constantly besieged, as is clearly shown in the triple temptation on the mountain after his forty days in the desert (Matt. 4:1–11). To change stones into bread simply to satisfy hunger; to cast himself down from the pinnacle of the temple to demonstrate his divine power; to gain possession of all the kingdoms of the world and their glory in exchange for the acceptance of Satan's power—these are all forms of one single temptation: that of renouncing the power of the word and of evangelical means of action in order to give himself to ways of temporal and political pressure. This demon was constantly confronting the mission of Jesus (Matt. 16:23; John 6:15) and caused a crisis in the agony in the garden the night of the passion (Matt. 26:39ff.). The temptation of Jesus in Gethsemane is of this same kind; the chalice that he had to accept was that of redeeming and freeing people through the poverty and the destruction of the cross and not through any spectacular success of a political messiahship.

It ought not to surprise us then that the temptation to power and to political action is prevalent also among the ministers of the church in their pastoral activity. They are activities that dovetail in many aspects, and there is no greater temptation than that of substitution. (Just as angelism and the lack of temporal commitment is the temptation of the contemplative, Machiavellism is that of the Christian revolutionary.)

The ever-present risk of politicizing the evangelical mission of the church and the abuses that are always—even today—made of this mission ought not to cause a contrary reaction. Just as Christ did not avoid the painful consequences and the conflicts with the system brought about by the proclamation of the gospel, pastoral activity should never lose its sociopolitical challenge, which is part of its very essence. The apostolate, bearer of an eschatological-incarnational message, follows the laws of Christology. In Christology, in the sense that we have explained, it finds its true liberating significance in the path of Christ, who liberates completely, including from temporal oppression—although through nonpolitical mediations. And so Jesus remains truly the way and the model of all Christian commitment to liberation, the prophetic figure in the liberation of his people and of *the little ones* throughout history. "The Spirit has sent me to bring the Good News to the poor, . . . to set at liberty those who are oppressed. . ." (Luke 4:18).

THE MESSAGE OF JESUS AS LIBERATOR OF ISRAEL

The liberating temporal consequences of Jesus' message in the society of his time were due to the fact that it sowed in the Roman system the lasting seeds of liberty and community.

To proclaim the one, true God as the Lord of all puts an end to any idolatry. It relativizes people and values that in that society took the absolute place of God: in the first place, the emperor and his authority, cornerstone of the cohesion and of the mythical power of the empire. It destroys the ideological basis of its totalitarianism. Along with this, it gives each person a sense of dignity and equality before the political authority, firmly establishing the ultimate basis of participation and solidarity. Even beyond this, Jesus does away with the concept of theocracy and of a theocratic state—whether Christian or secular—the foundation of absolute and oppressive systems. "Render to Caesar the things that are Caesar's and to God the things that are God's"

(Matt. 22:21). With this phrase Jesus desacralizes political power, striking out at the same time against Jewish theocracy and against Roman totalitarianism.

These are struck down at their very foundations, not through a maneuver of political strategy, but through the proclamation of the truth about God and humanity, a truth that is prophetic, that unmasks injustices, that makes us free (John 8:32). Socially and politically, this undercuts evil, both in the short and the long term. More than the ambitions of the Zealots and more than any revolutionary plan or action, Jesus destroys the very bases of the imperial system.

In the second place, the message of Jesus is a liberating one because he summoned the poor to form his kingdom in a privileged way. He even proclaimed that one had to become poor in spirit in order to enter the kingdom (Matt. 5:3; Luke 6:20; 16:19ff.; 18:18ff., etc.).

In the cultural context of his time, this could not help but have deep sociopolitical repercussions. Practically speaking, it set into motion and gave a certain mystique and social power to a group hitherto neglected and without social significance. It introduced into the empire and into the aristocratic society that this group had given rise to a new power, conscious of its own dignity, independent of the system and of the established authorities, and desirous of establishing justice. This new force would be decisive in the weakening and collapse of the empire. This call to the *little ones* to establish the kingdom will be at the root of all authentic liberation movements.

In the third place, Jesus proclaims his kingdom as universal, fulfilling the prophecies. He breaks through the limits of Jewish nationalism and of a salvation exclusively for them (Matt. 21:43ff.; 24:14). He thus overcomes the tribalism of the Pharisees and the Zealots, sending forth his disciples on a universal mission that carries them to the heart of the empire as well as beyond its borders. This dynamism not only eroded the traditional Jewish religious, nationalistic, and sectarian system. It made its influence felt also in all strata of the imperial society and of all future totalitarian societies.

In short, in proclaiming the condition of the new human being in the Sermon on the Mount and in the Beatitudes, Jesus created a new prophetic consciousness in his disciples. He renewed their vocation to equality and community, demanding of them values that were diametrically opposed to those promoted by the dominant social system. To the extent that the values proposed by the Beatitudes penetrate the hearts of people and of society, they will condemn any sociopolitical structure incompatible with those ideals.

Without putting forth a model for a better society, of a concrete program of liberation, Jesus creates a movement of liberation and solidarity that we find at the origin of many later social changes.

It is for this reason that the religious messiahship of Jesus and his predominantly eschatological mission could not avoid being accused of *being involved in politics* and of his being a *wordly messiahship*. This temptation of ambiguity remains even today, having been transferred to the mission of the church. Without being a politician and without wishing to assume any temporal leadership, Jesus is an authentic liberator in the deepest sense of the word, even including the social consequences. And he is a dangerous liberator, more dangerous for the oppressing powers—political and religious—than the revolutionary politicians, the Zealots, and others. Whatever might be the exegetical judgment regarding the historical fact, the confrontation of Jesus with Barabbas the day of the crucifixion is very significant in this respect (Matt. 27:15ff.). The message the gospel gives us, from the point of view of our present discussion, is sufficiently clear. Barabbas was an *important prisoner*. Given the antecedents and the political context of Israel, today many agree that he was a revolutionary, a subversive, a Zealot. They had to choose between the freeing of Jesus or a political revolutionary. And the leaders preferred to set Barabbas free. For the *system* Jesus is more dangerous than a revolutionary and his message is more subversive than a political proclamation.

A reading of the life of Christ that takes into account the political context in which it developed makes it evident, then, that it is the inspiration and model for all those Christians committed to liberation through prophetic, rather than political, means. The sociopolitical dimension of Christology is undeniable, as are the temporal consequences of the kingdom that Christ announced. It is very important today to take into account this dimension of Jesus in a theology as well as in a spirituality of liberation. It is equally obvious that this sociopolitical dimension of Christology does not exhaust either the mission or the message of Jesus. The Lord also announced personal conversion, the forgiveness of sins, reconciliation with God, the cross, the kingdom, the future life, and so forth. What we mean is that if we do not deepen our understanding of the *political* dimensions of the messiahship of Jesus, many Christians, in their temporal commitments, will find themselves in great difficulties with their faith, believers in a Christ who has no meaning for the liberation in history of the *little ones*.

NOTES

1. See, e.g., Martin Hengel's statement: "The interpretation, again popular, of Jesus as a political-social revolutionary connected with the Zealots is based on a one-sided interpretation that does violence to the sources" (*Evangelische Kommentare* [1969]).

13

J. B. Libânio

Prayer

J. B. Libânio insists that prayer and politics must go hand in hand. "Prayer" is taken from his Spiritual Discernment and Politics *(Maryknoll, N.Y.: Orbis Books, 1982), pp. 26–30. The work was originally published in Brazil in 1977.*

Discernment is a function of grace. It is not something that can be gained by effort but is a free gift of God's grace. Thus it is impossible for an act of spiritual discernment to take place outside a climate of faith, hope, and charity. The theological virtues create the necessary spiritual environment. The tradition of the church has persistently emphasized the fundamental importance of prayer in maintaining the theological climate, the native soil, of discernment. Hence the importance of understanding how prayer is related to the three theological virtues that constitute the spiritual climate of discernment.

We are not just studying the tactics for a sociopolitical operation. We are looking for concrete mediations to bring about the kingdom of God, which is the fruit of God's gift and of our activity, of divine grace and of human decision. Prayer performs an important role here.

PRAYER AS CLARIFICATION OF FAITH

Faith is above all an adherence, a commitment of one's life, to the person of Jesus Christ, the revealer of God. Faith brings us in contact with Christ himself through the mediation of the great tradition of the church that extends from apostolic times to our own era.

Faith is a dimension that encompasses our whole life. It embraces our way of thinking, of forming opinions and desires, of viewing things. It is an atmosphere that both penetrates us and enfolds us. On the other hand, because it is an encompassing reality, it is constantly threatened by distortions. Spurious elements, deriving from collective and individual sin, penetrate this horizon of faith and mingle with it. Thus it may happen that the expressions of our faith take on a number of theologically uncritical elements. We find difficulty in isolating or eliminating them, because their infiltration takes place so subtly, almost imperceptibly. We are bombarded by the communications media and by swarms of suggestions, insinuations, and value judgments often presented to us in a religious guise that obscures their anti-evangelical character. Our vision of faith is deformed, with a consequent distortion of our Christian interpretation of reality.

And there is more. Faith, as a view of the totality of our existence and a radical commitment, can become attenuated in everyday life. The vision grows dimmer. Commitment grows lax. Here is where prayer is fundamental to faith. It purifies it. It brings our way of seeing the world, human beings, and history more into line with the gospel, purifying it of astigmatic foreign elements. It redimensions commitment. It extends our faith to our lesser acts, so that no recess of our heart and our life is left in the dark. Thus discernment has a greater chance of being clairvoyant. Faith set on fire by prayer puts us in a position to have a more Christian vision of reality, a necessary condition for making a coherent choice on the basis of our faith.

Prayer intensifies the light of faith. It helps us to perceive the religious and salvific meaning of the doctrinal teachings of the church. "Being in tune with the church," which is so basic to discernment, ceases to be juridical dogmaticism and instead fosters the increasing interiorization of the various truths of the faith, truths whose real meaning is recovered thanks to prayer. Prayer permits us to savor within us the truths of the faith. To be sure, these truths of the faith are for many of us a challenge to our intelligence rather than an invitation to live the mystery of God. It is the task of prayer to correct this intellectualism and to show that faith, above all, is life, commitment, experiencing the mystery of God. It also removes the risk of rationalism and "illuminism," which can so easily infiltrate the process of discernment.

Finally, as faith is constantly threatened by these extraneous elements, it finds in prayer an occasion for taking inventory and for purification. Only a faith continually purfied by prayer can guarantee us spiritual discernment unthreatened by delusion.

PRAYER AS STIMULATION OF HOPE

When we interpret a given reality, with the key of faith, we look for a meaning that transcends our own petty perceptions. Faith beckons onward to a universality. Hope enters the picture as that which makes our history concrete, involving us personally in the vision of reality interpreted through faith. Whereas faith speaks to everyone in every age, hope has something to say to us here and now. It is essential to us in that it rescues us from any foreign element that faith might be harboring. Hope brings us into history-in-the-making and informs us that all of this is for us and that our role in it is precisely what faith reveals to us.

In its role of incorporating us into historical reality, hope is transformed into a motivation, a propellant force of history and of our own life. It negates the arrogance of overpowering reason. It works against our tendency to absolutize ourselves and our ambitions. It negates any claim of the present and of the transitory to be definitive. Ideology tends to absolutize a partial view of reality. Hope, as the proclamation of a new future, of an unforeseen and unmanipulable newness, exercises a critical function. In its eschatological aspect, hope is a relativization of human ambitions. If ideology seeks to freeze the historical process in its present structures, hope, with its knowledge of human beings and their potentialities for achievements, proclaims the future of the world and of history as an aspiration to the plenary dominion of nature, the plenary socialization of humankind, in total harmony with the interests of all. It points to a utopia, which has still not taken place in history but which demands realizaton and undergoes its transformation under the impetus of hope. Hope, in the proper sense of the word, has as its scope the inviolability of a given situation; it trusts in the promises of God and not in the calculated predictions of our human designs.

Hope in particular is the motive power of history, giving meaning to human aspirations for fellowship, justice, and solidarity. From within its genuine eschatological structure of "now" and "not yet," hope affirms the presence of the kingdom of God among us. It affirms the absolute character of God's intervention in history. It affirms the definitive victory of the grace of Christ in the sacraments, in the word, in the acts of the church, and in the signs of charity. It affirms the final victory of Jesus Christ over death and sin, as manifested in our lives. It affirms that God, in Jesus Christ, has already spoken a decisive, irrevocable word concerning the world and history. And the effectiveness of that word fashions history each day in our task of liberation.

Hope sharpens our vision to see the gratuitous nature of God's gift, as opposed to any commercialistic or meritorious view of grace. It negates a capitalistic, accumulative notion of grace. It brings us into the world of liberality, of free, unpretentious relationships with our brothers and sisters.

This spiritual orientation engendered by hope is a must for discernment. But we are still perverse, tempted to live in quite another way. We are assaulted by innumerable arguments and data that prompt us to skepticism, doubt, and despair. The ascendancy of the rational, the programmed, and the structural over the free, the creative, the unforeseen, the original, and the spontaneous is more a source of discouragement than a reason for optimism. Widespread insecurity and fear confront us on all sides. We see the bankruptcy of great visionary dreams. Humanism, slowly and laboriously elaborated by Western civilization, shows signs of necrosis. There are many respected commentators who tell us that we live in a world without much hope, precisely because the scope of properly human outreach is being curtailed.

It is within this historical context of a threat to hope that prayer becomes a twofold necessity. It eliminates those extraneous elements that are rooted in the deceptiveness and arrogance of the human heart. And it activates our perception of those future dimensions that are already present in the mystery of Christ. In a word, prayer kindles hope in us, hope that is sustained by an unobscured discernment in a world threatened by skepticism, fear, and insecurity.

PRAYER AS PURIFICATION OF CHARITY

Spiritual discernment can occur only in charity, love. Charity is quite sufficient of itself. If we were to live charity in all its purity and clairvoyance, we would need neither discernment nor prayer. Our life would be the best of prayers and a sustained act of discernment:

> Love is patient; love is kind and envies no one. Love is never boastful, nor conceited, nor rude; never selfish, nor quick to take offense. Love keeps no score of wrongs; does not gloat over other men's sins, but delights in the truth. There is nothing love cannot face; there is no limit to its faith, its hope, its endurance [1 Cor. 13:4-7].

Our charity, however, inasmuch as it is mediated, is impure. Our love is ambiguous, divided, marked by inconsistencies, infected at the root by sin and inordinate desire. Egotism is endemic. It is like a worm, always present within the fruit, threatening to destroy it altogether. And this is how we are. What guarantees discernment is the purity of our charity. Hence the importance of prayer.

Prayer purifies charity. It kindles the love of God—the purifying force par excellence—in the human heart. It awakens the conscience. It illuminates the turnings and twistings of hypocrisy and sheds light on the darkened labyrinths of our selfishness. It gives us strength to overcome the sin that clings to us. It makes us a part of its own triumph. It sets us free from our closed circle, opening us up to the purifying factor of the presence of the other, especially the architectonic Other, God.

Charity has a missionary dimension. By its acting and being it proclaims a word that calls into question, that unsettles, as opposed to the anonymity that conforms to the given situation. Charity, as a liberating praxis, is the source of discernment. And prayer, in turn, is its life's breath. Charity, in its weakness, gives up easily. Prayer sustains it.

SUMMARY

The prerequisites for discernment relate to an on-going effort and ascesis. They have nothing to do with static elements, as the term may seem to imply.

They are basic attitudes, over which we must maintain a constant vigilance and discipline. Purification, generosity, prayer: three recommendations for our spiritual conduct. And discernment will take place as we so conduct ourselves. As we proceed, there is always something new to overcome.

Here we confront the gospel teaching on vigilance. This is not the same thing as expectation of the imminence of the *parousia*. The scope of a historical evangelical vigilance will lie far beyond this. Today, vigilance is becoming very important in terms of emotional and ideological involvements, kept on edge on such a wide scale by an enormous propaganda machine. Only an attitude of constant spiritual discipline, of an aroused critical consciousness, can preserve our prerequisites for discernment. In this setting, prayer occupies a privileged place as we prolong our moments of reflection in the light of revelation and as we reinforce our voluntary decision on behalf of generous commitment. Prayer encompasses the two preceding elements: it is purification, and it is an incentive for generosity. It also guarantees that we will walk within the context of faith and spirituality, allaying suspicions of excessive politicization.

14

Elsa Tamez

Good News for the Poor

Elsa Tamez maintains that a preferential option for the poor represents the basic mandate of biblical faith. "Good News for the Poor" is taken from her Bible of the Oppressed *(Maryknoll, N.Y.: Orbis Books, 1982), pp. 66–74. The following selection was originally published in Spanish in 1978.*

I BRING YOU GOOD NEWS
OF A GREAT JOY WHICH WILL COME
TO ALL THE PEOPLE [LUKE 2:10].

In the first century A.D. the ordinary people of Palestine found themselves in extremely difficult circumstances. Like all Jews they had to pay heavy taxes to the Roman Empire; in addition, they suffered greatly from the inflation that was prevalent from Egypt to Syria. In the cities there was growing unemployment, and slavery was on the increase. For these reasons, slaves and farm workers abandoned their places and formed robber bands to prey on the caravans of traders and pilgrims.[1]

Meanwhile, there was another social class that did not suffer from this situation but, on the contrary, possessed economic and political power in Palestine and profited from inflation. These were the people who formed the council of elders (generally men from the noble and powerful families), the chief priests, the great landowners, the rich merchants, and others who exercised some political and ideological control (the scribes, Pharisees, Sadducees). This class collaborated with the Roman Empire and acted in ways hostile to the masses of the people. Its members were the open enemies of the Zealots, a guerrilla group that wanted to take power and drive out the Romans.[2]

It was in this historical context that the good news came.

In Latin America there are also great masses of people who live in extremely difficult circumstances. Inflation is a very serious problem in almost all the countries of this part of the Third World, and it is evident that its effects bear most heavily on the masses, that is, the poor.

Other serious problems the poor have to face are unemployment, lack of housing, malnutrition, extreme indigence, exploitation.

On the other hand, there is a group that is small by comparison with the population as a whole, but that nonetheless has great economic and political power. Some in this group exploit the proletariat in order to accumulate capital; others derive great profit by becoming partners in foreign companies or by enabling the latter to operate freely in Latin America.

The ruling class, as in first-century Palestine, collaborates in the expansion of the wealthy nations. Latin American countries governed by the military receive weapons from abroad in order to put down the discontented masses. In some Latin American countries governments favor the entrance of the multinational corporations on the pretext that this will foster industrial development.

At the international level, the economies of the Latin American countries are dependent on foreign nations and are structured according to the interests of the wealthy nations of the world. As everyone knows, these nations see Latin America as a source of raw material and cheap labor.

In such a situation the poor feel oppressed; they are hard put to breathe and stay alive. Extreme poverty and exploitation are killing them. They are forced to rise up and fight for the life of the masses.

At this moment in history good news is urgently needed.

THE GOOD NEWS

The good news takes a very concrete form. The central message is this: the situation cannot continue as it is; impoverishment and exploitation are not God's will; but now there is hope, resurrection, life, change. The reign of God, which is the reign of justice, is at hand.

We have often been told that the message contained in the good news is that Christ came into the world to save us or free us from sin. But sin is identified with those actions that society considers immoral: drug taking, adultery, excessive drinking, and so on. Thus the gospel of life is reduced to a simple behavioral change.

But the good news cannot be so reduced. After all, any non-Christian religion can propose that kind of moral teaching, which amounts to nothing but a set of patches designed to cover over the great sin that lies underneath: oppression at the national and international, the individual and collective levels.

The message of the good news is of the liberation of human beings from everything and everyone that keeps them enslaved. That is why the good news brings joy and hope.

Mary, the humble mother of Jesus, sang this song when she visited her cousin Elizabeth:

> My soul magnifies the Lord,
> and my spirit rejoices in God my Savior,
> for he has regarded the low estate of his handmaiden. . . .
> He has shown strength with his arm,
> he has scattered the proud in the imagination of their hearts,
> he has put down the mighty from their thrones,
> and exalted those of low degree;
> he has filled the hungry with good things,
> and the rich he has sent empty away . . . [Luke 1:46–53].

Mary is here speaking not of individuals undergoing moral change but of the restructuring of the order in which there are rich and poor, mighty and lowly (vv. 52–53).

The priest Zechariah likewise saw the good news as the fulfillment of the promise of liberation:

> Blessed be the Lord God of Israel,
> for he has visited and redeemed his people,
> and has raised up a horn of salvation for us. . . ,
> as he spoke by the mouth of his holy prophets from of old,
> that *we should be saved from our enemies,*
> *and from the hand of all who hate us* [Luke 1:68–71].

The news is therefore good news to the people; it is a reason for joy and gladness, since it gives the hope of a total change. In Luke 2:10 a messenger of the Lord tells the shepherds: "I bring you good news of a great joy which will come to all the people."

The good news is evidently not so good for some people. King Herod was deeply concerned when he was told that the king of the Jews had been born. We are told that because he feared to lose his throne he ordered the killing of all children in Bethlehem who were less than two years old (Matt. 2:16).

The shepherds, on the other hand, rejoiced when they heard the news. The shepherds were men who lived in the fields and took turns watching over their flocks at night (Luke 2:10). They enjoyed little respect because they were part of the masses. When they received the good news, they were glad; they listened to it and shared it with others.

The good news that speaks of the liberation of the oppressed cannot be pleasing to the oppressors, who want to go on exploiting the poor. But the good news is indeed good to those who want to change and to see a more just society.

For the most part, those who want to live in a society in which justice and peace reign are those who suffer hunger, oppression, poverty. For this reason the good news is directed especially to the poor. Jesus himself said so when he read from the Book of Isaiah:

> The Spirit of the Lord is upon me,
> because he has anointed me
> to *preach good news to the poor.*
> He has sent me to proclaim release to the captives
> and recovering of sight to the blind,
> to set at liberty those who are oppressed,
> to proclaim the acceptable year of the Lord [Luke 4:18–19].

Then he added: "Today this scripture has been fulfilled in your hearing" (Luke 4:21).

THE POOR

Knowing, then, that the good news is addressed especially to the poor, let us reflect on who the poor are and why they are poor.

For many centuries now the biblical passages on the poor have been spiritualized and distorted. Poverty is regarded as a virtue, as an abstract quality that can be attributed to rich and poor alike. As a result, a rich person can be understood to be poor "in spirit," and a poor person rich "in spirit."

The Beatitudes that Jesus addressed to the poor have been read as referring to something spiritual. In this distorted view, the "poor in spirit" may be: (1) those who have accepted (material) poverty voluntarily and without protest; (2) those who, though rich, are not proud but rather act humbly before God and their fellows (neither the riches nor the way they have been acquired are an *obstacle* to acting humbly); and (3) those who are restless spirits and lack any element of the mystical in their religious outlook.

And yet, when Jesus reads the promise now fulfilled in him: "He anointed me to preach good news to the poor," he is referring to all those who lack the basic necessities of life. When he says: "Blessed are you poor" (Luke 6:20), he is referring to material poverty. The poor in spirit are the "poor of Yahweh," that is, they are the poor and oppressed who acknowledge their poverty, and who stand before God as poor people. In other words, they are not the kind of poor people who think, and try to live, as members of the bourgeoisie.

To sum up: the poor in the Bible are the helpless, the indigent, the hungry, the oppressed, the needy, the humiliated. And it is not nature that has put them in this situation; they have been unjustly impoverished and despoiled by the powerful.

In the Old Testament there are a number of Hebrew words that are often translated as "poor."[3] These are:

1. *'ani* in its most fully developed use describes a situation of inferiority in relation to another. Concretely the *'ani* is one who is dependent. When used in combination with *dal* it describes an economic relationship. The contrary of the *'ani* is the oppressor or user of violence. God is protector of the *'anim* because they are people who have been impoverished through injustice;

2. *dal* is used in two senses: it may refer either to physical weakness or to a lowly, insignificant position in society;

3. *'ebion* often refers to those who are very poor and in a wretched state. Originally it meant someone who asks for alms, a beggar;

4. *rash* is the poor or needy person; its antithesis is the rich person. The social and economic meaning is the prominent one;

5. *misken* means "dependent," a social inferior.

I have listed these Hebrew words with their connotations in order to show that according to almost all of them the poor are individuals who are inferior to the rich or the powerful. Their situation is not the result of chance but is due to the action of oppressors. This point is brought out in many passages of the Bible: "They sell the righteous for silver, and the needy for a pair of shoes— they that trample the head of the poor into the dust of the earth, and turn aside the way of the afflicted" (Amos 2:6–7); "The people of the land [or: the landowners] have practiced extortion and committed robbery; they have oppressed the poor and needy, and have extorted from the sojourner without redress" (Ezek. 22:29).

There is evidently no need to reread the entire Bible in order to discover that poor persons are those who do not have the wherewithal to live because their means have been snatched away.

The authorities, for their part, frequently prove to be on the side of injustice. They close their eyes to the sinful activities of the powerful, and their role is, in fact, to maintain this order of things. Isaiah denounces them: "Your princes are rebels and companions of thieves. . . . They do not defend the fatherless, the widow's cause does not come to them" (Isa. 1:23).

Orphans and widows were listed among the poor and helpless, because they had no one to defend them and no means of subsistence.

The accumulation of wealth is incompatible with Christianity, since any accumulation of possessions is at the cost of the very poor. The denunciation pronounced by Jeremiah is very clear: "Woe to him who builds his house by unrighteousness, and his upper rooms by injustice; who makes his neighbor serve him for nothing, and does not give him his wages" (Jer. 22:13).

The New Testament also launches a strong attack on those who heap up possessions:

Come now, you rich, weep and howl for the miseries that are coming upon you. Your riches [i.e., hoards] have rotted and your garments are moth-eaten. Your gold and silver have rusted, and their rust will be evidence against you and you will eat your flesh like fire. You have laid up treasure for the last days. Behold, the wages of the laborers who mowed your fields, which you kept back by fraud, cry out; and the cries of the harvesters have reached the ears of the Lord of hosts. You have lived on the earth in luxury and in pleasure; you have fattened your hearts in a day of slaughter. You have condemned, you have killed the righteous man; he does not resist you [James 5:1–6].

At this point we are in a position to infer two points about the poor as seen by the Bible. First, poverty is regarded as something decidedly negative; it is "a scandalous condition" and the manifestation of "a degrading human condition."[4] Secondly, this situation of poverty is not the result of some historical inevitability nor is it "just the way things are"; it is the result of the unjust actions of oppressors.[5]

BLESSED ARE THE POOR

God, of course, is not indifferent toward situations of injustice. God takes sides and comes on the scene as one who favors the poor, those who make up the masses of the people. The Bible makes perfectly clear this divine predilection and option for the poor.

The poor alone are worthy to take part in the kingdom of God. Unless the rich break with their way of life, they cannot enter this kingdom. Zacchaeus, who was a chief tax collector and a very rich man, had to give half of his goods to the poor and pay a fourfold recompense to those he had exploited. We see a quite different response in the case of the rich young man whom Christ calls: he has the opportunity to share in the kingdom of God, but since he cannot detach himself from his possessions and give them to the poor, there is no place for him in the kingdom. With reason does Christ say: "Truly, I say to you, it will be hard for a rich man to enter the kingdom of heaven. Again I tell you, it is easier for a camel to go through the eye of a needle than for a rich man to enter the kingdom of God" (Matt. 19:23–24).

In chapter 6 of Luke's Gospel we find contrasting but parallel statements that are part of Jesus' teachings to his followers:

> Blessed are you poor, for yours is the kingdom of God [v. 20].
>> But woe to you that are rich, for you have received your consolation [v. 24].

> Blessed are you, that hunger now, for you shall be satisfied [v. 21].
>> Woe to you that are full now, for you shall hunger [v. 25].

> Blessed are you that weep now, for you shall laugh [v. 21].
>> Woe to you that laugh now, for you shall mourn and weep [v. 25].

The reason the Bible opposes the rich is not because they are rich, but because they have acquired their riches at the expense of their neighbors (James 5:1–6).

Chapter 5 of Matthew's Gospel contains further beatitudes for the poor:

> Blessed are the poor in spirit, for theirs is the kingdom of
>   heaven.
> Blessed are those who mourn, for they shall be comforted.
> Blessed are the meek, for they shall inherit the earth.
> Blessed are those who hunger and thirst for righteousness, for
>   they shall be satisfied.
> Blessed are the merciful, for they shall obtain mercy.
> Blessed are the pure in heart, for they shall see God.
> Blessed are the peacemakers, for they shall be called sons of
>   God.
> Blessed are those who are persecuted for righteousness' sake, for
>   theirs is the kingdom of heaven [Matt. 5:3–10].

God identifies with the poor to such an extent that their rights become the rights of God: "he who oppresses a poor man insults his Maker, but he who is kind to the needy honors him" (Prov. 14:31); "he who mocks the poor insults his Maker; he who is glad at calamity will not go unpunished" (Prov. 17:5).

It is clear that these many passages of the Bible in favor of the poor are in serious danger of being subjected to another kind of spiritualization: that of calling upon the poor to be satisfied with their state, not of poverty as such, but of privilege in God's sight. This would be disastrous because then even the rich would feel tempted to experience certain wants in order that they too might be God's favorites. Then the situation of injustice that God condemns would be alleviated in the eyes of the world.

We must keep in mind, therefore, that poverty is an unworthy state that must be changed. I repeat: poverty is not a virtue but an evil that reflects the socioeconomic conditions of inequality in which people live. Poverty is a challenge to God the Creator; because of the insufferable conditions under which the poor live, God is obliged to fight at their side.

In Latin America the poor are blessed, but the reason is not that they have resigned themselves to poverty but, on the contrary, that they cry out and struggle and have their mouths shut for them on the grounds that "they are rebels and have recourse to violence." They are blessed, but not because they voluntarily seek to be poor, for it is the mode of production forced upon Latin America that leads them to penury. They are blessed, but not because they have scorned riches; on the contrary, it is they themselves who have been scorned by those who monopolize the world's riches.

The poor in Latin America are blessed because the reign of God is at hand and because the eschatological promise of justice is drawing ever nearer to fulfillment and, with it, the end of poverty.

NOTES

1. Fernando Belo, *Uma leitura política do evangelho* (Lisbon: Multinova, 1974), p. 43; Eng. trans., *A Materialistic Reading of the Gospel of Mark* (Maryknoll, N.Y.: Orbis Books, 1981).

2. Ibid., pp. 37 and 44.

3. Julio de Santa Ana, *Good News to the Poor: The Challenge of the Poor in the History of the Church* (Maryknoll, N.Y.: Orbis Books, 1979), p. 10, n. 1.

4. Gustavo Gutiérrez, *A Theology of Liberation: History, Politics and Salvation* (Maryknoll, N.Y.: Orbis Books, 1973), pp. 291–92.

5. Ibid., pp. 292–93.

PART 2

AFRICA

15

John Mbiti

The Encounter of Christian Faith and African Religion

John Mbiti believes it is very important that Africans recover their own distinctive religious heritage. "The Encounter of Christian Faith and African Religion" is reprinted with permission from The Christian Century *97 (August 27–Sept. 3, 1980), pp. 817–20.*

The editor of *The Christian Century* has given me an undeserved privilege in asking me to contribute some reflections on "How My Mind Has Changed" in the course of the past decade. I wish to apply "change of mind" here to mean theological growth, and not necessarily a rejection of or turn-around from ideas that I may have held ten years ago. Indeed, ten years ago I had no significant theological position. I was like a snail shyly peeping out of its house after a heavy thunderstorm.

" . . . IN AFRICA, GOD IS NOT DEAD"

I completed my doctoral studies at the University of Cambridge in 1963, the year that *Honest to God,* by J. A. T. Robinson, came out. That book was followed by a flurry of literature on the so-called death of God theology (if "theology" it was, for I would call it "atheology"). Following a period of parish work in England, I went to teach at Makerere University, Uganda, where I remained for ten years until 1974. One read *Honest to God* and a variety of other works in an effort to understand the hot debate then raging in

Europe and America. Some peoples tried to involve Africa in the debate. But to the disappointment of those theological exporters, this fish was not attracted by the bait. A prominent European New Testament professor visited Makerere University and interviewed me on what I thought about the "death of God" discussion. I simply and honestly answered him that "for us in Africa, God is not dead." That finished the interview. On returning home, the learned professor wrote an article using my brief answer as his title.

At Makerere University I taught New Testament, African religion, and other courses. Since I myself had never heard any lectures on African religion, I set out to do research on the subject in order to teach the course adequately. The first and most intriguing topic that immediately engaged my attention was the thinking of African peoples about God. So I read on and on, and conducted field research to learn more and more. My findings were used in teaching, but eventually I put them together in a book, *Concepts of God in Africa,* published by the British publisher SPCK (1970). The book comprised ideas that I had gathered from three hundred African peoples ("tribes"—a term that today is sometimes used in derogatory ways). The previous year I had published *African Religion and Philosophy* (Doubleday, 1969).

Some individuals have criticized these books—and no book is perfect. But whatever the shortcomings of these and my other publications, the materials that went into these two have raised extremely important issues for me that have continued to engage my reflection. At many points I see intriguing parallels between the biblical record and African religiosity. In particular, the concepts about God provide one area of great commonality. There are also other parallels in social, political, and cultural areas, just as there are some significant differences. In one case the thinking and experience of the people produced a written record of God's dealings with the Jewish people in particular. In the other case no such written record exists. But God's dealings with the African people are recorded, nevertheless, in living form—oral communication, rituals, symbols, ceremonies, community faith. "For us in Africa, God is not dead"—and that applies whether or not there is a written record of God's relations with and concern for people.

A GOD ALREADY KNOWN

Since the Bible tells me that God is the creator of all things, his activities in the world must clearly go beyond what is recorded in the Bible. He must have been active among African peoples as he was among the Jewish people. Did he then reveal himself *only* in the line of Abraham, Isaac, Jacob, Moses, Samuel and other personalities of the Bible? Didn't our Lord let it be clearly known that "before Abraham was I am" (John 8:58)? Then was he not there in other times and in such places as Mount Fuji and Mount Kenya, as well as Mount Sinai? The decisive word here is "only." The more I peeped into African religious insights about God, the more I felt utterly unable to use the word "only" in this case. In its place there emerged the word "also." This was an extremely liberating word in my theological thinking. With it, one began to explore afresh the realm of God's revelation and other treasures of our faith. I find the traditional Western distinction between "special revelation" and "general revelation" to be inadequate and unfreeing. This is not a biblical distinction. If they are two wavelengths, they make sense only when they move toward a convergence. When this happens, then a passage such as Hebrews 1:1-3 rolls down like mighty waters, full of exciting possibilities of theological reflection.

The God described in the Bible is none other than the God who is already known in the framework of our traditional African religiosity. The missionaries who introduced the gospel to Africa in the past two hundred years did not bring God to our continent. Instead, God brought *them*. They proclaimed the name of Jesus Christ. But they used the names of the God who was and is already known by African peoples—such as Mungu, Mulungu, Katonda, Ngai, Olodumare, Asis, Ruwa, Ruhanga, Jok, Modimo, Unkulunkulu, and thousands more. These were not empty names. They were names of one and the same God, the creator of the world, the father of our Lord Jesus Christ. One African theologian, Gabriel Setiloane, has even argued that the concept of God which the missionaries presented to the Sotho-Tswana peoples was a devaluation of the traditional currency of Modimo (God) among the Sotho-Tswana.

No doubt there still remain much research and reflection to be done in order to work out a consistent theological understanding of the issues entailed here. But the basic truth seems to be that God's revelation is not confined to the biblical record. One important task, then, is to see the nature, the method and the implications of God's revelation among African peoples, in the light of the biblical record of the same revelation.

Revelation is given not in a vacuum but within particular historical experiences and reflections. When we identify the God of the Bible as the same God who is known through African religion (whatever its limitations), we must also take it that God has had a historical relationship with African peoples. God is not insensitive to the history of peoples other than Israel. Their history has a theological meaning. My interpretation of Israel's history demands a new look at the history of African peoples, among whom this same God of Abraham, Isaac, and Jacob has indeed been at work. In this case, so-called salvation history must widen its outreach in order to embrace the horizons of other peoples' histories. I am not a historian, and I have not done careful thinking in this direction. But I feel that the issue of looking at African history in light of the biblical understanding of history is clearly called for.

A MASSIVE EXPANSION

My research into and teaching of African religion has led to another important area of development. In Kenya I grew up in home, school, and church milieus which held that the African religious and cultural background was demonic and anti-Christian. In this overpowering environment, one simply accepted this stand and looked at the world from its perspectives. Later, my theological studies in America and England did not challenge this position, since that was not a living issue for my professors and fellow students. But upon my return to work in Africa, and upon careful study of the religious background of our people, there emerged gradually the demand to examine this issue and to form my own judgment.

The statistical expansion of the Christian faith in Africa in this century is one of the considerations that led me back to the issue of its relation with African religion. In 1900 there were an estimated 9 million Christians (accounting for about 7 percent of the population of Africa). This number has since grown rapidly, to the point that in 1980 there were estimated to be 200 million Christians (or about 45 per cent of the population). This massive expansion within a short time is unprecedented in the history of Christianity. What factors are responsible for it?

We can list some obvious and often publicized factors. They include the work of missionaries (of whom there are about 40,000 today, without counting their family members); the work of African Christians in evangelism and pastoral care (their numbers are infinitely greater than those of overseas missionaries, and include men, women, and children, both lay and ordained); the role of Christian schools; the translation and distribution of the Bible (which is now available in full or in part in nearly 600 of Africa's 1,000 languages); and the ending of the colonial era during the decades 1960–1980. But I have discovered that there is also the fundamental factor of African religion, without which this phenomenal expansion of Christianity would not be a reality. Of course, behind all these factors is the Holy Spirit working through them.

There is not space here to argue the case for the role played by African religion in the establishment of the Christian faith in Africa. We have already noted that the overseas missionaries did not bring God to Africa. God was not a stranger to African peoples. Spiritual activities like prayer, thanksgiving, and the making of sacrifices were well-established facts of life for the existence and continuation of the community.

THE CHURCH IN THE AFRICAN SCENE

It is in this complex of religiosity that the preaching of the gospel makes sense; it is this preparedness that has undergirded the spreading of the gospel like wildfire among African societies which had hitherto followed and practiced traditional religion. Consequently, people are discovering that the biblical faith is not harmful to their religious sensibilities. This is, obviously, a general statement, one which needs detailed elaboration. But in practical terms, there is a Christian yes to African religiosity. It may be, and needs to be, a qualified and critical yes. But it is nevertheless a working yes and one that demands theological understanding. A close geographical correlation exists between the location of African religion and the rapid expansion of the Christian faith. This is not an empty coincidence. It is the southern two-thirds of Africa (including Madagascar) which we can rightly call Christian Africa, as the northern one-third is Muslim Africa.

This rapid spreading of the Christian faith where people have been predominantly followers of African religion provokes interesting questions. That which had been seen as the enemy of the gospel turns out (to me) to be indeed a very welcoming friend. African religion has equipped people to listen to the gospel, to discover meaningful passages in the Bible, and to avoid unhealthy religious conflict.

Theological development in Africa must inevitably grow within this religious setting. For this reason, some African theologians take African religiosity to be one of the sources of theological reflection (besides the Bible, Christian heritage, etc.). A conference of mainly African theologians, held in Ghana in December 1977, said in its final communiqué: "The God of history speaks to all peoples in particular ways. In Africa the traditional religions are a major source for the study of the African experience of God. The beliefs and practices of the traditional religions in Africa can enrich Christian theology and spirituality." These statements await further exploration by African theologians. Currently I am about to complete a book on this question of the encounter between the biblical faith and African religion.

The African church is composed largely of people who come out of the African religious background. Their culture, history, world views and spiritual aspirations cannot be taken away from them. These impinge upon their daily life and experience of the Christian faith. So the church which exists on the African scene bears the marks of its people's backgrounds. No viable theology can grow in Africa without addressing itself to the interreligious phenomenon at work there. I feel deeply the value of biblical studies in this exercise, and the contribution of biblical insights in this development.

THE QUEST FOR CHRISTIAN UNITY

I have concentrated these comments on the role of African background in my theological reflection. There are other areas of exploration in which I continue to be engaged. There is no room to describe them, and I can mention only two or three of them briefly. My doctoral studies in New Testament eschatology led me also to the field of Christology. I want to reflect and write on this topic, but somehow it makes me feel frightened. I want to make a pilgrimage into Christ. I want to walk with Jesus of Nazareth on the shores of Lake Galilee, on the hillsides of Judea, and through the gates of Jerusalem. I want to see his healing hand, to hear his word that exorcises evil spirits.

For six years I worked with the World Council of Churches in Geneva. That experience gave me a face-to-face encounter with the ecumenical movement and left a lasting mark on me. It sensitized my thinking in many areas, one of these being the quest for Christian unity. I have seen the quest more sharply. I cannot claim that I have witnessed much progress in that quest at the organizational level, but perhaps I had expected too much. The council made me aware, perhaps even frightfully so, of the problems of our world. The council's programs in response to these problems are impressive. They constitute an important channel of the church's prophetic witness today. The WCC's very existence as a council of churches is a living hope. But it has been a sorrowful disappointment to me to experience the fact that some individuals who exercise great power in the council are not angels: they sometimes practice the exact contrary of those values and goals to which the council is committed. Nevertheless, I am convinced that the World Council of Churches is a great witness of the Christian response to the prayer of our Lord that we may all be one. And this witness deserves one's support through service and prayer.

A TILTING FROM NORTH TO SOUTH

The concept of the church as the body of Christ in the whole world is another growing development for me. I have been greatly enriched by working at the Ecumenical Institute at Bossey, 1974–1980. It is here that I have discovered the church in Burma, in the Pacific islands, the house church in China, the basic Christian communities in Latin America, the struggling church in South Africa, plus countless other endeavors of Christians all over the world. I have met here the church not only in its geographical outreach but also in its historical roots—seeing, for example, the rich traditions of the Orthodox church, the universality of the Roman Catholic church (even though it is based in the Vatican), the reconciling positioning of the Anglican communion, the dynamic vitality of African independent churches, and so on. I have received much in a short period. It will keep me chewing for a long time, and it will most certainly feed my theological development.

I am very excited, for example, by the estimate that in 1987 there will be a statistical balance of Christian population between the north (Europe, Soviet Union, and America) and the south (Latin America, Africa, Asia, and Oceania). After that date there will be more Christians in the south than in the north. This statistical tilting of Christendom from the north to the south, after two thousand years, holds tremendous prospects and challenges. Its consequences for theological and ecclesiological developments are yet to be faced. They will certainly be overwhelming, and I feel very excited about them.

The theological horizon continues to expand. I am tantalized by the fact that my vision cannot cope with that horizon. But I am grateful for that one step I may be taking under the light of this vision. So, "Lord, help Thou my unbelief!" Amen.

16

Manas Buthelezi

Toward Indigenous Theology
in South Africa

Manas Buthelezi distinguishes between ethnographical and anthropological approaches to the rediscovery of the African religious tradition. "Toward Indigenous Theology in South Africa" is a paper taken from Sergio Torres and Virginia Fabella, eds., The Emergent Gospel *(Maryknoll, N.Y.: Orbis Books, 1978), pp. 56-75. The paper was delivered at the Ecumenical Dialogue of Third World Theologians held August 1976, in Dar es Salaam.*

ETHNOGRAPHICAL APPROACH

Missionaries' Quest for Indigenous Theology

The church, which is a creation of the gospel message addressed to the whole world, does not consequently lose its solidarity with the world. One word that perhaps sums up the salient features of this solidarity is "indigenous." The indigeneity of the church is the presupposition of its mission in the world.

The church as a "communion of saints" does not exist in airy abstraction isolated from the concrete affairs of people and has not become a semiangelic fellowship. The phenomenological aspect of the reality of this communion pertains to its faith and life. It listens to the word of God preached in words and phrases coined according to the rules of grammar, syntax, and diction. It enunciates the essence of its faith in theological categories informed by human

205

logic and epistemology. It sings praises to God in songs that are a product of human poetical imagination and musical composition. It expresses the genius of its discipleship in, with and under the given cultural and social structures.

In the milieu of churches in Africa and Asia, the focus has been on the urgency of indigenous church structures and theology. This arose from the feeling that there is a "hermeneutical gap" between the existing functional Western moulds and methods of preaching and teaching the Christian faith, and the respective African and Asian traditional thought patterns.

John V. Taylor has summed up this problem as follows:

> Christ has been presented as the answer to the questions a white man would ask, the solution to the needs that Western man would feel, the Saviour of the world of the European worldview, the object of the adoration and prayer of historic Christendom. But if Christ were to appear as the answer to the questions that Africans are asking, what would he look like? If he came into the world of African cosmology to redeem Man as Africans understand him, would he be recognizable to the rest of the Church Universal? And if Africa offered him the praises and petitions of her total, uninhibited humanity would they be acceptable?[1]

One of the basic presuppositions has been that of thinking that the phenomenon of the "hermeneutical gap" of current Christianity in Africa arises from epistemological factors. In the last century Duff Macdonald illustrated this with rather a touch of humor.

> One cause of error is that we mix up what the African tells us with our own ideas, which are European. As a consequence of this, we put questions to him that he cannot understand. Many of our questions strike the African exactly as a question like the following would strike a European, "If seventy miles of the sea were burned, who would be the losers, the Insurance Companies? or the Harbour Administration? or——?" If an African put this question to a European, the European would laugh at him; but if the European put it to an African, the latter would be more polite, and would think that the European was very ingenious in finding out a supposition that would have never occurred to himself.[2]

Along the same vein, Junod attached much importance to the study of the "African soul" as well as of its fears and longings. He is of the opinion that, in failing to study African institutions and customs, missionaries betray their Master. In another context, he gave the missionaries an edge over the secular representatives of Western civilization on the basis of the opportunity they have to understand the "African soul." He maintained that nobody will have a lasting influence on the Bantu people without understanding that the greatest thing in them is their soul.[3]

John V. Taylor, to whom we have already referred, has sympathetically argued the case for the validity of the categories of thought found in the African worldview. He has illustrated his case from his concrete experiences in Africa. One of the presuppositions of his case is that the African worldview, which is at the same time inherent in and independent of the traditional religion, "stands in the world as a living faith, whether in the residual paganism of millions, or in the tacit assumptions of very many African Christians, or the neo-African culture of the intellectual leaders."[4] Taylor feels that the African insights can enrich and supplement the heritage of the universal church.

In his discussion of "indigenous theology," Bengt Sundkler sees the possibilities for a "Christian theology in Africa" in the usage of certain traditional insights. He writes:

Theology, in essence, is to understand the fact of Christ; theology in Africa has to interpret this Christ in terms that are relevant and essential to African existence. Here the background in the myths of African religion is important, for it provides certain broad patterns of which theology in Africa must take account.[5]

African theologians must use as their point of departure the "fundamental facts" in terms of which the African interprets existence, according to Sundkler. To demonstrate his case, Sundkler refers to what he calls "the two foci of the theological encounter in Africa," namely, the concept of the "beginning" and the notions of the "community of the living and the dead." Like Taylor, Sundkler's presupposition is that there is a store of traditional ideas that should be used as a frame of conceptual reference for African theology. He sums it up as follows:

Traditional African thinking was mythical. It was bound up with the Beginning of Things, with Creation and the Primeval Age; the Myths of the Origin of the First Man and Mankind are fundamental to this conception of life and the world. They constitute an "original revelation," which is re-enacted in annually recurrent festivals, in a rhythm which forms the cosmic framework of space and time. The myths span the whole of existence, from heaven to the hut and the heart of the individual; in fact, from cosmos to clan. Macrocosm and microcosm are tuned to each other and are included in an all-embracing order.[6]

Writing from another angle, in his work on Bantu philosophy, Placide Tempels also presupposes what he calls "the presence of a corpus of logically coordinated intellectual concepts, a 'Lore.' "[7] He therefore refutes the assumption of those who are of the opinion that "primitive people possess no system of thought."[8] He writes, "To declare *a priori* that primitive peoples have no ontology and that they are completely lacking in logic, is simply to turn one's back on reality.[9] The presence of this corpus of traditional intellectual concepts is a vital phenomenon not only among the un-Westernized Africans but also among the "évolués" and the "déracinés."

> Need we, then, be surprised that beneath the veneer of "civilization" the "Negro" remains always ready to break through? We are astonished to find one who has spent years among whites readapt himself easily by the end of a few months to the community life of his place of origin and soon become reabsorbed in it. He has no need to readjust himself because the roots of his thought are unchanged. Nothing and nobody made him conscious of any inadequacy in his philosophy.[10]

At the same time, Tempels feels that the Bantu are not capable of articulating that which is latent in them by way of formulating a philosophical treatise which is complete with an adequate vocabulary. Hence "it is our job," says Tempels, "to proceed to such systematic development. It is we who will be able to tell them, in precise terms, what their inmost concept of being is. They will recognize themselves in our words and will acquiesce, saying, 'You understand us, you now know us completely, you "know" in the way we "know." [11]

One of the elements in this approach to the quest for indigenous theology in Africa is the belief that, by analyzing and characterizing cultural factors with regard to their historical development in the African church milieu, it becomes possible by means of the "sifting" medium of the gospel to root out "un-Christian" practices and "baptize" those that are consonant with the gospel. Furthermore, by discovering those cultural factors and understanding them in the light of the totality of their respective worldview, it is possible to arrive at a hermeneutical principle by means of which one can translate the "Christian gospel" into a form congenial to the "African mind."

Since this theological method uses as a point of departure elements of the traditional African "worldview," which, from the literary point of view, exists as an ethnographical reconstruction, we shall refer to it as an "ethnographical approach."[12]

Kroeber, in defining ethnography, has remarked that "by usage rather than definition, ethnography deals with the cultures of the non-literate peoples." Unlike history, which deals with written documents, ethnography "does not find its documents; it makes them, by direct experience of living or by interview, question, and record. It aims to grasp and portray sociocultural conditions: merely summarized at first, and often moralized."[13]

Shortcomings of the Approach

Over a long time heated discussions on "indigenous theology" have left some with a feeling that the whole thing is virtually an occupational pet-project of missionaries who have suddenly become aware of the fact that they have to change the content of their leadership role during the passing of the "missionary era" if they are to have a place in the postcolonial dispensation at all. It is against this background that one has to understand Taylor's pointed remark: "Yet in all this a warning light flickers from the fact that the enthusiasts are mainly non-Africans. This can partly be explained by the conservatism of African clergy. The real reason is that the white 'indigenizers' are too superficial, and Africans know it."[14]

In one of the letters written to the editor of *Isithunywa,* a church periodical, E. Sibisi queries, as a matter of principle, what he reckons to be the unwarranted leading role played by missionaries in making suggestions about the specific ingredients of an "indigenized church." The case in point is an attempt to popularize traditional tunes in liturgical music. Sibisi says: "In my opinion it is a waste of money and time that Africans should be taught the traditional Zulu way of singing, and that, of all people, the ones who have to teach that kind of singing should be foreigners. Furthermore, why should the matter of singing according to traditional chants not be initiated spontaneously by Africans themselves, rather than be imposed upon us."[15]

There is, of course, a strong possibility that the objection of Sibisi may be countered by means of an equally valid argument, namely, that it is salutary for a church, especially during our ecumenical era, to open itself toward theological insight and suggestions from outside. Should the facilities and experiences of the European churches not be regarded as an ecumenical asset for the African churches, which on the whole do not have such facilities and wealth of centuries-old experience? Does indigenization mean self-sufficiency and programmed isolationism? We know, of course, that ecumenical ties may be a good catalyst in the struggle of African churches to be themselves. It was under the impulse of this spirit that, in one of the sectional reports during the All-Africa Lutheran Conference, it was recommended

> that the churches [in Africa] avail themselves of the existing programs of the various Lutheran World Federation commissions and that we encourage exchange programs involving experts in the fields of stewardship, education, parish life, etc., and that we further recommend that assistance, including adequate materials, be given in the conducting of courses of training with experts coming from the African churches, Lutheran World Federation, and other national and international organizations such as the National Christian Councils, the World Council of Christian Education and Sunday Schools, etc.[16]

These considerations, sound as they are, cannot be used to disprove Sibisi's basic theses. They are parallel, rather than incompatible with the thrust of Sibisi's argument. It is very easy to confuse the question of "indigenous theology" with that of salutary exchange programs among churches. The confusion occurs as soon as people think of indigenization in programmatic terms. If indigenization is thus conceived, it becomes a mechanical program in which objectively identifiable motifs of the African worldview are used to indigenize an already existing church which is unindigenized. In other words, we have before us two known objective entities: our task of indigenization simply consists in relating them. It is like a jig-saw puzzle in which you have, on the one hand, the design, and on the other the pieces that have to be fitted together in such a way that they image the design.

When we talk about the problem of indigenous theology in Africa, are we really dealing with such self-evident tangibles on the basis of which we can introduce indigenization in the church as a crash program? If questions like the handing over of church leadership to indigenous personnel seem to tempt us to think that it is possible to program "indigenization" in Africa, it is because these are external matters of administration and outward organization which make sense only when they are studied against the background of colonialism and European imperialism. But, if, by indigenization, we have in mind theology as a reflection on the Christian faith, we are then dealing with an internal matter of African genius that defies programming. We shall return to this point later. We should only mention for the present that, when we talk about indigenous theology in Africa, the temerity to have on hand the self-evident objective ingredients for its creation may lead to disappointing results. Sibisi has called our attention to this fact. In his letter, he asks: "By the way, is there still a past to which it is said we must return? Where is it? Who still live according to its precepts?"

Even though Sibisi does not spell it out himself, there is more in these questions than first appears on the surface. One may, for instance, jump to the conclusion that Sibisi does not do justice to empirical facts. To be sure, it is possible to demonstrate empirically that there are many Africans who still live according to the precepts of that "past." Taylor may be proved right at this point. Yet we feel that Sibisi's questions have an import which is worth taking seriously.

There is a difference between psychologically "living in the past" in order to compensate for the virtually existential emptiness of the present, thereby trying to mitigate the conscious awareness of the horror of its oppressive destitution, and "living in the past" because it is able to offer—as it did in the past—something substantial within the framework of the concrete realities of the present. Who can blame those who have the feeling that the missionaries, with their right hands, are diverting our attention to our glorious past so that we may not see what their left hands, as well as those of their fellow whites, are doing in the dehumanization of our lives in the present? Who can blame a person who sees no wisdom in "writing theological poetry" about a past era while our human dignity is being systematically taken from our lives every day in the present?

There is danger that the "African past" may be romanticized and conceived in isolation from the realities of the present. Yet this "past" seen as a worldview is nothing more than a historical abstraction of "what once was." Rightly or wrongly, one cannot help but sense something panicky about the mood which has set the tenor and tempo of the current concerns about "indigenous theology." The context of Sibisi's critical observation is a case in point.

The missionary seems to be having a guilty conscience. Looming above the horizon of the sunset of the missionary era is the horrifying specter of the question that history seems to be posing to the missionary: How can a church which fidgets under trappings and paraphernalia of a past colonial era survive in a postcolonial and revolutionary Africa? This question does not rise merely as a presentiment that is without concrete roots. If we think of the current spate of the Africanization of political, social, and economic life in many states in Africa, one cannot help wondering whether Christianity will not in the course of the process be dismissed as an irrelevant life proposition. Statements have been made to the effect that Christianity is merely a spiritual arm of European imperialism in Africa. Can the "arm"hope to outlive the "body" of imperialism? This is a nagging question whether or not we believe that Christianity was a battalion in the force of imperialism.

There is a sense in which one can say that when the missionaries seem to be presumptuous in suggesting "indigenous theology" to the African, they are, strictly speaking, looking for a solution to problems that stem from their own psychological "hang-ups." The missionaries have therefore to play a leading role in the formulation of indigenous theology in order to make sure that it solves their own problems as well. The suggestion here is that when the Africans seem to be encouraged to produce indigenous theology, they are just being used—as they have always been—to solve the psychological problems of the missionaries.

Hoekendijk has observed that the breakdown of Christendom as a solid, well integrated cultural complex dominated by the church in Europe has, among other factors, stimulated a romantic urge among many missionaries to go to Africa and Asia in order to rebuild and relive the life of the "good old days" of Christian Europe. In his words: "These are some of the undisclosed motives. In fact, the word 'evangelize' often means a biblical camouflage of what should rightly be called the reconquest of ecclesiastical influence. Hence this undue respect for statistics and this insatiable hunger for ever more areas of life."[17]

Furthermore when the missionaries came back to Europe on furlough, they were shocked by some of the radical theological accents that grew out of the new secularist Europe. Their theological "home base" from which they had drawn spiritual resources as they faced heathen "beliefs and superstitions" had all of a sudden been undermined by proponents of "liberal theology." The missionaries suddenly discovered that they were culturally and spiritually strangers in their own home. It is no wonder that the old traditional African rural culture seemed to fit the pattern of their dream about good old Europe. While they realized they could do nothing to stem the tide of cultural developments in Europe—especially if their training qualified them only to serve as missionaries abroad—they could realize emotional and spiritual compensation in Africa where their intellectual and theological expertise was, relatively speaking, not yet challenged. The task of the formation of African indigenous theology would then provide a convenient setting for the realization of the romantic ideal. The missionaries passionately wanted to "marry" Africa after Europe had proved "unfaithful in her love." African indigenous theology would be the theme of the new "love poetry" which would, it was hoped, prove itself more superior and satisfying than the new "adulterous love poetry" of new Europe.[18] So much for the metaphor.

The point is that it is not necessarily bad if missionaries seek cultural and theological shelter in Africa, but that it is bad if they at the same time dictate what kind of a shelter we should make for them. The case in point is an overemphasis on the old traditional world as the point of departure in the evolution of indigenous theology.

Without actually saying it, the implicit suggestion they seem to be making is that the old traditional insights represent more what is truly African than the insights of the modern Africans. The "true African" is the one who is described in the books of the ethnographers rather than the one whom we see in Johannesburg, Durban, and Cape Town trying to make ends meet in the framework of Influx-Control legislation. Just as modern Europe is a conglomerate of cultural and spiritual aberrations, the modern African is a cultural caricature of the "true African" who is the African of the "good old days."

The difficulty with an ethnographically reconstructed African worldview is not so much that it is necessarily inaccurate and not true to the original, as that this reconstruction as such can be readily regarded as a valid postulate for African theology. It is too presumptuous to claim to know how much of their past the Africans will allow to shape their future, once they are given the chance to participate in the wholeness of life that the contemporary world offers.

Second, allowance should be made for the fact that, even if Europe had not impinged upon Africa, Africa could still have undergone a metamorphosis on its own under the impulse of the changing needs of its people. Such internal changes could obviously not leave the worldview unaffected. It is, of course, understandable if people speak of the African past as having been something static, especially if one remembers that, for many centuries, African history has been nothing but an extension of European history, the history of its discovery and settlement by European peoples. Hence, the concept of progress in Africa has been identical with that of the Europeanization of Africa. Before Europe came to Africa, Africa was standing still! In acculturation studies, very often the aborigines emerge from the process as bottom-level members of the society and culture of the one who makes the study. One of the intriguing things becomes the mystery of their backwardness, that is, why in the first place they did not acquire on their own the level that the new culture regards as the norm of progressing peoples.

The essence of the weakness of the "ethnographical approach" is its tendency toward cultural objectivism. Too much focus is placed upon "the African worldview," as if it were an isolated and independent entity, of value in itself a part from African people as they exist today. What we miss is the person, the *causa efficiens* of the African worldview. The worldview takes precedence over its creator, the African person. That is why we remain incarnated within the orbits of a past African worldview and in the process miss present-day Africans and their existential situation.

ANTHROPOLOGICAL APPROACH

Essence of the Approach

The thesis here is that the point of departure for indigenous theology is not an ethnographically reconstructed worldview, but African people themselves. When we speak of an "anthropological" approach, we are thinking of the person, not as an object of study—the theme of anthropology as a discipline— but as God's creature who was entrusted with "dominion" over the rest of creation. We are thinking not of the "colonial person" who is the object of "dominion" by other people, a "black problem" to the white politicians, but a "postcolonial person" who has been liberated by Christ from all that dehumanizes.

We are thinking of persons not as "third person" entities: persons who are talked about and discussed and whose "minds" are analyzed and systematized, who become important simply because their problems provide fruitful material for specialists; we are rather thinking of the "first persons"—the Ego.

In his discussion about the selfhood of the church, D. T. Niles has used an illuminating illustration that sheds light on the statements we have made above:

> Thinking about the discovery of the self, my mind went back to my two boys when they were babies. They would say: "Baby wants ball," or I would say, "Does baby want milk?" Baby was the object that could be pointed out. On behalf of this object a request could be made. I would say, "Show baby," and my son would point to himself. Then suddenly, because it was sudden, Baby spoke and he said, "I want sweets," and my wife said, "You must eat your rice now." The self was the same but it had ceased to be an object to itself. It was no more the self to which relationships were established, rather it established its own relationships. "Baby" had become "I," "It" had become "You." Most of the churches founded by missionary societies found their self-hood in very much the same way. For many decades they were objects. They spoke about themselves and were spoken to in the third person. They were dots on a map of the mission field. Then suddenly church spoke to church. The forms of address became "I" and "You." The churches had become themselves.[19]

If we set out with the aim of defining the possibilities and postulates for indigenous theology in Africa, we must from the very onset be cognizant of the fact that we are dealing with a subject that belongs to the realm of human creativity. There is a sense in which we can speak of scientific theology as an art form and the theologian as an artist. This belongs to the aesthetic character of theology.

As soon as we predicate "indigenous" to theology, we imply that this particular theology is an artistic projection of the *causa efficiens* whom we know to be an indigene in relation to a particular milieu. Indigenous theology, therefore, means more than just a theology that treats as its object "indigenous" problems and issues, that is, *res indigenae.* The focus of current discussions and suggestions about indigenous theology seems to be on *res indigenae* like polygamy, *confessio Africana,* African liturgical forms, etc.

One is then left with the impression that the matter of the selection and the definition of the indigenous theological problems has been settled; all that remains is the emergence of someone who has the ingenuity of finding the solution to these already known problems; the assignment is cut and dried. The reason for this tendency is not hard to find. Currently the people most knowledgeable and articulate about the problem of indigenous theology in Africa are those who are either associated with missionary circles or have themselves personally experienced the problem of "missionary encounter" as missionaries. It is these problems of "missionary encounter" that are to be the subject matter of indigenous theology.

Therefore, what seems to be in the forefront of the task of indigenous theology is the discovery of the solution to these problems that could not be solved during the "missionary era." To pretend that these problems are not important in the practical life of the church would, of course, be unrealistic. Yet, at the same time, we have to recognize that there are problems which, as phenomena in any community, may be only symptoms of a real and basic problem. There may be "problems" which, in the final analysis, may turn out to be no problems at all: they may be a byproduct of a gross misunderstanding of the situation.

The virtually exclusive concern with *res indigenae* tends to locate the problems that indigenous theology has to resolve at the point of the conflict between two worldviews: the European and the African. The human factor recedes to the background, if recognized at all. It then becomes a problem of epistemological entites, of fixed impersonal data—things "out there," the body of categories for interpreting the universe. These categories are static entities which form something that can be located, studied, and defined—thanks to ethnography. Hence, Tempels can confidently say: "It is we [Europeans] who will be able to tell them [Africans], in precise terms, what their inmost concept of being is. They will recognize themselves in our words and will acquiesce saying, 'You understand us, you know us completely, you "know" in the way we "know." ' " This statement of Tempels reveals the element of truth involved in the statement that the missionaries who urge the production of "indigenous theology" are really seeking a solution to their own problems: the Africans are only a means to an end. At worst, the Africans have to bow to opinions and ideas of those whom they have been conditioned to associate with authority and enlightenment. At best, they have only to choose between alternatives that are offered to them. The consequence of this is that their minds have become channels, rather than fountains, of ideas.[20] Even when it comes to those things associated with the African "worldview," one gets the impression that these are in effect objective entities that lie outside the Africans. Some curious student can study these and then go back to the African and ask: "Is this not the way you think?" Then the African will courteously echo the expected answer: "You understand us: you know us completely. . . ."

This objectification and impersonalization of the "African mind" explains why it is then found necessary to teach the Africans to be interested in their *res indigenae*. By implication these *res indigenae* now exist outside their consciousness, and it has become necessary that someone must pedagogically familiarize the Africans with them and arouse their interest in them. If this is a logical absurdity, it at least points to a psychological reality.

Historical factors have caused the Africans to develop a masochistic complex, that is, the realization of personal fulfilment in unconscious self-hatred and the despising and loathing of everything with which their egos are identified in social and cultural life. The degree to which one is ready to go through this psychic mortification virtually becomes the criterion for ascertaining the level which one has reached in the course of the realization of the image of a "civilized and Christian person." The sublimated center of ego-existence becomes the outside human image of the missionary or Westerner. It is very easy to confuse this psychological inversion and depersonalization with conversion and sanctification. The social counterpart of this inversion has been the bourgeois sociocultural church life pattern around the mission station.[21]

It is our contention that the point of departure for the evolution of indigenous theology is not the manipulation of objectivized *res indigenae,* but the Africans' initiative in the context of their present existential situation. The first step is that the Africans should have both the material and spiritual means to be themselves. To be a person means to have power to be truly a person; it means power for liberation to be a person. Indigenous theology without freedom of thought is a contradiction in terms; freedom of thought without access to the material means of participating in the wholeness of life is like capacity without content.

No one can deny that, in principle, African churches do have the formal freedom to be themselves and to produce their own theology. The discussions about indigenous theology presuppose the existence of this freedom. Yet even apart from the fact that the principle had not yet been subjected to any rigorous test, there are obvious factors that seem to preclude its practical application.

Tshongwe has said that "when our seminaries can produce heretics, not through ignorance but conviction, then I would say the African is beginning to think." Let us pursue what is at stake in this statement.

Etymologically, the word "heresy" means an "act of choosing." Thus in classical antiquity it had a connotation of choosing to follow a distinctive *bios.* In Sextus Empiricus this meaning is expressed:

The word "believe" has different meanings: It means not to resist but simply to follow without any strong impulse or inclination, as the boy is said to believe this tutor; but sometimes it means to assent to a thing of *deliberate choice (hairesis)* and with a kind of sympathy due to strong desire.

As the above reference suggests, there was an inseparable relationship between the "act of choosing" and the "content" or "nature" of the thing chosen. Thus the "heresy" (choice) of a philosopher was always related to the "heresy" or "dogmata" of a particular "heresy" (school) of philosophy. It is interesting to note that Josephus refers to the Pharisees, Sadducees, and Essenes as philosophical partisans or *hairetistai*. The Christian concept of "heresy" issued from the new situation created by the historical introduction of the "Christian church." *Ekklesia* and *hairesis* become opposites (Galatians 5:20). Yet *hairesis* did not have the technical meaning it later acquired, especially at the time of the crystallization of ecclesiastical dogma. It is worthy of note that by implication 2 Peter 2:1 discriminates between salutary and destructive "heresies." Hence *hairesis* is qualified by *apoleias*.

As a matter of fact, historical ecclesiastical dogma has been a fruit of theological freedom, even though it has very often seen that freedom as a threat to it. Yet in essence—if you allow me some semantic indulgence—ecclesiastical dogma is nothing but a corporate "heresy" made from pre-existing sets of *theologoumena*.

Theology in Africa must reflect the throbbings of the life situation in which people find themselves. A theology of tranquility and dogmatic polish in times of restlessness due to people's alienation from the wholeness of contemporary life can only be the product of theological dishonesty. What we need is a theology of restlessness. By this we mean a theology that does not take itself seriously as the last word since it is the product of people who are indigenes of a world in process of formation. A theology that tries to find its point of departure by making "platonic" flights to an imagined past, where there was still an ordered system of ideas and indigenous concepts, may in fact be paying the heavy price of abandoning an important theological reality, namely, present-day people in creation under God.

To say that theology must get its cue for indigeneity from the existing human situation does not make the whole problem of indigenous theology any easier, especially when it comes to the question of freedom of thought. Alongside the clamor for indigenous theology, one also hears expressions like "our Christian heritage" and "the faith of our fathers." These expressions are used either in a broad ecumenical or narrow confessional sense. What seems to be self-evident in their usage is not only their meaning but also the implicit suggestion that the ecclesiastical kinship group which has that heritage has a commitment not only to keep the heritage alive, but also to pass it on intact to the next generations. Such a heritage may, for instance, be a historical creed and confession or a specific traditional system of theology.

Under the theme "The Faith of our Fathers" the Second All-Africa Lutheran Conference at Ansirabé made the following resolution, among others: "That the Lutheran confessions as expressed in the Book of Concord are still valid and relevant and the best doctrinal foundation for the Lutheran Church."[22]

At stake in this statement is more than just the old academic distinction between the fundamental and nonfundamental articles of faith, or the confession of faith and its theological elaboration. Regardless of whatever hermeneutical principle we may choose in making this distinction, it is immediately obvious that the Book of Concord, with regard to its content, represents more than just a statement of "first principles" or fundamentals of faith in its primordial forms. Rather, it represents a systematic theological tradition; a confluence of religious, cultural, social, and political ideas, as well as a type of a theoretical summary of the Greco-Roman tradition of the intellectual history of the church up to the sixteenth century.

Hence to speak of the "relevance" and "validity" of the Lutheran confessional corpus is more problematic than self-evident, especially as, at the same time, we have to express concern for the evolution of indigenous theology in Africa. It is one thing to speak of the Lutheran confessions as historical documents that have a historical value, but it is another thing to make a confessional resolution out of an attempt of promoting their present relevance and validity.

In the organization of indigenous churches in Africa, it has sometimes been necessary to merge several mission synods that have been working in the same geographical territory side by side. Some Lutheran synods have insisted on the recognition of the Book of Concord as expressing the doctrinal basis of the new church. It has to be remembered that in most, if not all, newly organized African churches the theologically sophisticated elite has been composed solely of missionaries. Therefore all the theological battles at the time of the merger discussions and the organization of the new church were merely a replay of the theological tensions and fights "back home" in Europe or America. The Africans had only to play the sorry part of purporting to grasp and feel what the whole theological hullabaloo was about. Very often they played their part remarkably well, to the great delight of their theological mentors.

Wherever it exists, confessional kinship solidarity that is worldwide is something salutary, not only because it has been a catalyst for the ecumenical movement, but also because it has helped positively in the growth of the so-called "younger churches" through the special attention they have received from their respective confessional kinship groups. Lutheran churches, in varying degrees, have been among the most insistent on the confessional basis of church fellowship. This is a multidimensional problem and we do not intend to take it up here. But we do want to raise the question whether, in the course of its emphasis on the doctrinal basis of Christian fellowship, Lutheranism, for instance, has not sacrificed the "human" for the "ideological."

In common parlance, "our Christian heritage" or "the faith of our fathers" includes a common holding of a definite attitude toward the question of human life and destiny. In the doctrinal or confessional contexts, this involves a mandatory historical understanding of the essential details of that which constitutes the characteristic outlook of the ecclesiastical kinship group, as an outward manifestation of its esprit de corps.

Ecumenical theology, in the sense of the catholic tradition of theology, is strictly speaking another name for the broad theological concepts that have survived as minimal points of agreement in the historical disputes among the theological schools of thought and have emerged from the Greco-Roman cultural background. It is these broad concepts that have served as a point of departure in the modern ecumenical dialogues, and they have been introduced to the churches in Africa and Asia as an unbroken traditional package from the European churches. We use the phrase "unbroken package" analogously to what Bonhoeffer means in his criticism of what he calls "positivist doctrine of revelation," when he says: " 'Like it or lump it': virgin birth, Trinity, or anything else; each is equally significant and a necessary part of the whole, which must simply be swallowed as a whole or not at all."[23]

If some aspects of the historical definitions of the Christian faith are already posing epistemological problems in the West, one begins to wonder whether African and European churches should not seek for another way of expressing kinship solidarity, rather than through the form of an uncritical profession of allegiance to a body of ideas about the faith. This should not be construed as a disparagement of the significance of doctrine in the life of the church. On the other hand, we want to raise the question whether the ideological basis of ecclesiastical kinship solidarity is adequate, even if it were not for its attendant epistemological problems. This leads us to the crucial point.

In our opinion, the category of the "human" has been neglected as a theological motif for understanding the expression of ecumenical solidarity in the interest of the ideological, namely, confessions and doctrines. Recent theological developments, as illustrated by the studies of the World Conference on Church and Society in Geneva in 1966, can only be welcomed with cautious optimism. The same is true of the theological accents of the Lutheran World Federation Assembly which met at Evian in 1970.

People in the "Third World" have learned that subscribing to certain confessions and doctrinal definitions is no guarantee that they are accepted on the basis of their integrity as human beings by those who happen to subscribe to the same doctrinal formulae. The confessional and doctrinal ecclesiastical umbrella has proved itself a poor shelter against the rain of racism. Very often solidarity on the basis of the profession of allegiance to the common "faith of our fathers" serves as a smokescreen for diverting attention from the patterns of socially and even ecclesiastically entrenched alienation on the human level. Yet genuine oneness in Christ manifests itself best on the level of "naked humanity," where the masks of "common faith" and "common confessions" as the basis of fellowship are very often removed.

The shift from the "ideological" to the "human" expressions of ecclesiastical kinship solidarity will serve as a freeing factor for indigenous theology. Considerations of a confessional esprit de corps will no longer be a haunting specter for theological freedom in Africa, since there will be another way of expressing this kinship solidarity.

In other words, this will leave African churches free to make their own theological options (heresies). Yet, at the same time, by focusing on the human, it will be possible for us to realize that material destitution, like ignorance, is no healthy atmosphere for the production of indigenous theology. In order to be an indigenous theologian, you must undergo rigorous educational discipline; in order to get education, you must have money, you must, as a human being, have access to the economic facilities of life; in short, you must have access to the wholeness of life.

The point I have been arguing here is in essence that the problem of indigenous theology in Africa primarily consists not so much in what the content of that theology must be (ethnographical approach) as in its *causa efficiens,* the Africans themselves (anthropological approach). The problem is not primarily that the Africans are finding it difficult to do theology or that they are failing to find the content for their theology—as suggested by the "ethnographical approach." It is simply that the life they find themselves in denies them the resources and tools for even making a beginning. We should pay more attention to the problem of and factors that account for the present lack of trained indigenous theologians than to the question of what the content of African theology should be. The latter will be the life-task of African theologians as soon as they exist. Let us give promising young people as much theological educational exposure and discipline as possible, and leave the rest to them.

In order to illustrate the "anthropological approach" we shall single out the case of "blackness" as one of the reference points in our method of theologizing.

Case Study of the Concept of Blackness

The years 1975 and 1976 have been characterized by the evolution of the phenomenon of black consciousness in South Africa. This in turn called for the need to relate the Christian faith to the experience of black people. This is what it means to be black in South Africa.

Blackness is an anthropological reality that embraces the totality of my daily existence: it daily determines where I live, with whom I can associate and share my daily experience of life. Life, as it were, unfolds itself to me daily within the limits and range of black situational possibilities. The word of God addresses me within the reality of the situation of my blackness. I can only go to black churches and the only pastor who normally can minister to me is a black like myself.

If I am a pastor, I can understand my ministry only within the context of a black flock. Christian fellowship and solidarity? Well, the only people with whom I can share daily the experience of Christ are black people like myself: only with these can I listen to the word and receive the sacraments.

This situation is neither a dream nor a mere fantasy: it is spiritual reality as it daily unfolds to me. Therefore I have to take this seriously and try to understand the redemption in Christ within the context of my black experience.

As far as the question of redemption is concerned, traditional Christian theology has not addressed itself to my situation. It has left me with the impression that my blackness is a negative rather than a positive quality. Liturgically, blackness is associated with death and mourning, while whiteness is a symbol of joy and victory. According to the author of the book of Revelation (3:5 and elsewhere), the victorious and resurrected saints are portrayed as dressed in white.

One can, of course, go on and on; but this should suffice to illustrate what I mean when I speak of theologically taking seriously the present situation of black people. For lack of a better term, I would label this method of theologizing "black theology." Therefore, for me, "black theology" is nothing but a methodological technique of theologizing. It is one case of what I called an "anthropological approach."

NOTES

1. J. V. Taylor, *The Primal Vision: Christian Presence and African Religion* (London: SCM Press, 1963), p. 16.

2. Duff MacDonald, *Africana, or the Heart of Heathen Africa* (London: Dawsons of Pall Mall, 1969; first published 1882), Vol. 1, p. 3.

3. See H. A. Junod, *The Life of a South African Tribe,* 2 vols. (New York: University Books, 1962; first edition, 1912). See for example vol. 2, pp. 361–64.

4. Taylor, *Primal Vision,* p. 21.

5. B.G.M. Sundkler, *The Christian Ministry in Africa* (London: SCM Press, 1962), p. 99.

6. Ibid., p. 100

7. P. Placide Tempels, *Bantu Philosophy,* p. 9. The English version is a 1959 rendition of the 1959 French version *(La philosophie Bantoe).* The original Dutch work was published in 1946 and translated into German in 1956.

8. Ibid., p. 10.

9. Ibid., p. 11.

10. Ibid., p. 12.

11. Ibid., p. 15.

12. Cf. B. Moore, ed., *BlackTheology: The South African Voice* (London: Hurst, 1973), pp. 43-46.

13. A. L. Kroeber, *An Anthropologist Looks at History* (Berkeley and Los Angeles: University of California Press, 1963), pp. 131–32.

14. Taylor, *Primal Vision,* p. 15.

15. Zulu language edition of the Monthly Parish Bulletin of the Evangelical Lutheran Church in South Africa, Southeastern Region, Durban, Lutheran Publishing House.

16. Third All-Africa Lutheran Church Conference, Addis Ababa, 1965.

17. Hans Hoekendijk, *Die Zukunft der Kirche und die Kirche der Zukunft* (Stuttgart: Kreuz-Verlag, 1964), p. 85.

18. See M. Buthelezi, "African Theology and Black Theology: A Search for Theological Method," in H. J. Becken, ed., *Relevant Theology for Africa,* Report on a Consultation of the Missiological Institute at Lutheran Theological College, Mapumulo, September 12–21, 1972 (Durban: Lutheran Publishing House, 1973), pp. 20f.

19. D. T. Niles, *Upon the Earth: The Mission of God and the Missionary Enterprise of the Churches* (New York: McGraw-Hill, 1962), pp. 140–41.

20. See Moore, *Black Theology: The South African Voice,* p. 119.

21. On masochism see also ibid.

22. "Der Glaube unserer Vater," Report of Section II of the Second AALC, 1960, published in J. Althausen, ed., *Christen Afrikas auf dem Wege zur Freiheit 1955–69* (Berlin: Union Verlag, 1971), pp. 74f.

23. D. Bonhoeffer, *Widerstand und Ergebung,* rev. ed. (Munich: Kaiser, 1970), p. 312; Eng. trans., *Letters and Papers From Prison,* enl. ed. (New York: Macmillan, 1971), p. 286.

17

Kofi Appiah-Kubi

Indigenous African Christian Churches: Signs of Authenticity

Kofi Appiah-Kubi sees in the development of indigenous African Christian churches an indication of the spiritual hunger of the African people. "Indigenous African Christian Churches: Signs of Authenticity" is taken from Kofi Appiah-Kubi and Sergio Torres, eds., African Theology En Route *(Maryknoll, N.Y.: Orbis Books, 1979), pp. 117–25. The paper was delivered in Accra, Ghana, December 1977 at the Pan-African Conference of Third World Theologians.*

One of the most prominent features of modern Africa has been the emergence of the so-called independent churches—which I prefer to call "indigenous African Christian churches." These are churches founded by Africans for Africans in our special African situations. They have all African membership as well as all African leadership. Some were founded by Africans in reaction to some feature of the Christianity of missionary societies; most were founded among those people who had known Christianity the longest.

The use of the term "independent" for these churches connotes a certain condescension. It suggests that there is some more important reference point outside these churches. Thus my preference for the term "indigenous African Christian churches."

REASONS FOR EMERGENCE

Reasons given for the emergence of these churches and their activities within the African societies are normally narrowed down to political, economic, and social deprivation and racial discrimination. However valid these may be in some cases, the present research among some of the indigenous churches in the Akan society in Ghana presents a different picture altogether.

On the basis of the data of the present research, I contend that spiritual hunger is the main cause of the emergence of the indigenous African Christian churches, not political, social, economic, and racial factors. In these churches, the religious needs of healing, divining, prophesying, and visioning are fulfilled by Christian means.

Spiritual experience is the pivot of most African religions. Healing, prophesying, and divining revolve around the supreme idea of spirit possession. In these churches the Akan Ghanaians seek a way of Christian expression, struggling for the selfhood of the church, and asking to be allowed to worship as Akan Christians. They do not want to be turned into Europeans before they can worship.

The most significant and unique aspect of these churches is that they seek to fulfill that which is lacking in the Euro-American missionary churches, that is, to provide forms of worship that satisfy both spiritually and emotionally and to enable Christianity to cover every area of human life and fulfill all human needs. These churches maintain that to satisfy Akan needs, Christianity should not only integrate all the good elements found in Akan culture, but find means also to unite Christianity and daily life in such a way that the first inspires the second.

In Akanland a revaluation is occurring, with emphasis on the traditional values, in an attempt to capture the capacity and the right to practice the full arc of Akan culture. There is desperate search for identity, an identity that has roots in tradition and reaches for a unity with which to face a pleasant and honorable future.

There is a conscious attempt on the part of the people to revive or perpetuate selected aspects of the Akan culture, which is considered more satisfying than Western patterns. By this noble and bold attempt these churches are meeting a need grossly ignored by the intellectualized Christianity of the missionary kind.

MAIN CHARACTERISTICS

For these indigenous African Christian churches Jesus Christ remains the supreme object of devotion. He is the Savior, the Baptizer in the Spirit, the Soon-Coming-King, and the Healer.

In contrast to a cold, frigid, professionally-aired Christianity that is mainly interested in form, these churches are free, emotional, and to some extent fanatical in their Christian worship. Several of the churches are charismatic, lay, egalitarian, and voluntaristic in contrast to the established, professional, hierarchical, prescribed religion of the missionary churches.

They view the divine as transcendent and immanent at the same time. The kingdom is to appear on earth—a new heaven and a new earth in this world. The belief is "this-worldly" rather than the "other-worldly." They think that salvation is for the elect; there is hope for the children of light and complete damnation for the children of darkness.

The majority of the churches are messianic. Salvation is brought about by a redeemer, who is the mediator between the human and the divine. The leadership tends to be charismatic and endowed with supernatural powers.

The members are said to be the channels through whom the supernatural gifts of the Holy Spirit may be transmitted to help others at their moments of greatest need. Some are endowed with the word of wisdom, others with knowledge, faith, the working of miracles, prophecy, the discerning of spirits, tongues and interpretation of tongues, or the gift of healing—indeed all nine charismatic gifts listed by Paul in 1 Corinthians.

The insistence of the churches that all the supernatural gifts are available even today in Ghana sets them apart from other Christians who chronologically restrict such charismatic gifts to the time of the apostles or the early Christians.

The indigenous African Christians believe their experiences to be part and parcel of the normal life for all Christians in all nations today. It is their greatest desire therefore to see all the supernatural gifts of the Holy Spirit renewed and properly functioning in the lives of contemporary Christians.

Every member is urged to become an evangelist to his or her neighbors and friends—a system of "priesthood of all believers." The believers are urged to enter the valley of human sin and suffering with the compassion of Jesus, bringing supernatural help to those who face problems without knowing that God loves them and desires to meet their needs.

The Bible is central to their religious and daily life. They have great love for reading the Bible, a love rarely found even in clergy or religious people of other churches. Members are quick to state that their religious practices are truly Christian, justifying themselves by the Bible. They read the Bible eagerly, souls hungry for the word of God, devouring and savoring every word. They read the Bible so assiduously that they have been nicknamed "the people with the dirty Bible."

For them the Bible is not just a historical record but a blueprint for life. They tend to be fundamentalists in this regard. To them the biblical message is simple, direct, and eminently personal. They are urged to listen carefully to the voice of God through the Spirit in prayer, which seems to say "God knows all your problems and will provide for your needs in due season." One does not understand this intellectually.

Unfortunately in Ghana as well as in other African countries, especially among the leaders and some sophisticated members of the established churches, these indigenous African Christian churches conjure up nothing more than images of emotionalism, fanaticism, religious mania, illiteracy, messianic postures, credulity, and panting after miracles. I am convinced that this public image no more reflects the true nature of these African churches than the Inquisition or the massacre of St. Bartholomew's Day reflects the essential quality of Catholicism.

REASONS FOR THEIR ATTRACTION

The teachings of the indigenous churches have attracted many adherents among the Akans, who believe that for any religion to be meaningful, it must be practical, dynamic, and problem-solving. Despite the negative criticism of the misinformed and uninformed, these churches are growing by leaps and bounds in numbers and strength.

While one major denomination after another reports seriously declining memberships and incomes, as well as declining overseas missionary staffs and supports in these days of moratorium, the indigenous African Christian churches are Africa's fastest growing body of Christian believers, indeed a third force in African Christianity beside Protestantism and Catholicism.

Thus serious researchers into activities of these churches and concerned leaders of the established churches ask: What attraction do these churches have to the general public who flock to their doors? What are the common denominators in these healing churches, and what are they really reacting against in the imported Western models? These are indeed crucial questions and require serious analysis.

Since it incorporates elements of the Christian religion, worship in these churches is quite familiar to converts from mission churches. At the same time, the African elements—particularly the supernatural powers of the prophets and the healing miracles that counteract the forces of evil, disease, and witchcraft—are sought by those unhappy and dissatisfied with the strictly Western nature of most of the mission churches.

Another important area of attraction is the emphasis these churches place on veneration of ancestors, who are said to be the custodians of law, morality, and ethical order of the Akans. The mission churches, while overlooking the Akan ancestors, urge their members to venerate St. George of England, St. Andrew of Scotland, or St. Christopher of the Vatican, who are very much removed from the converts' daily wants and anxieties.

In addition to the attractions of a religious nature, there are social attractions to these churches. Especially in the urban areas where anomie reigns supreme, the churches provide solace for the lonely. There is a fellowship in which individuals are encouraged to regard one another in a certain sense as siblings; hence the use of the terms "brother" and "sister" by members who are in no way related. The members are encouraged to behave as a family, to support and sympathize with one another. The churches stress traditional values such as respect for age and obligation toward family members. The members are also encouraged to marry from within their congregations.

The churches meet the strongly felt need for small groups of people supportive of the disadvantaged and the disappointed. In this respect the indigenous African churches are very important for the social and psychological life of the people since their congregations provide for their members small reference groups in relation to the wider society.

The churches help individual urban Akans to overcome the stresses and strains of urban and industrial life. Those who would be described as deviants and psychiatric cases in some societies are often accommodated by these churches and helped to become useful members of the society.

Alcoholics and drug and cigarette addicts are also helped to overcome their psychological incapacities. In fact, in Akan society it has become a joke among the youth that when one refuses to smoke or drink alcohol one is often asked: "Are you saved?"—meaning simply, "Are you a member of one of these indigenous African churches?"

To prevent their members from falling victims to the wild life at night clubs, the churches allow for full expression of emotional outburst through drumming, clapping, dancing, and spirit possession. The practice of comforting the despairing and the uncomforted is one of the hallmarks of the churches' attractions.

The churches offer spiritual and supernatural protection to members through the help of the prophets or the spiritual leaders. They attract people with needs in areas such as employment, promotion in business, education, marriage, and advancement in a political career.

Most of the people interviewed believe strongly that the churches offer the essential spiritual resources to help them achieve a satisfactory life's destiny, which is crucial to every Akan regardless of education or social standing. This includes wealth, children, and freedom from the fear of evil powers and witchcraft.

But the most important single reason people join the indigenous African Christian churches is *healing*. This came out quite clearly in the research. To the question: "Why did you join this particular church?" people invariably and quickly replied that they had been ill for a long time; they had tried all forms of treatment to no avail; they were directed to, for example, Prophet Prah, and, behold, they are fit as a fiddle: "Praise the Lord, Halleluja!"

In dealing with psychosomatic problems these churches are very successful through the powers, techniques, and willingness of the spiritually endowed leaders and members. They are also successful with chronic diseases considered incurable by Western technological medicine.

More often than not in the churches I visited the set pattern for recruitment was something like this: the original convert in a family or a village was cured of some incurable disease during a healing service or an annual convention. The convert in turn informed family members or fellow villagers by giving a testimony of what the Lord had done for him or her through the work of prophet so-and-so.

In the established churches, medical practice has become so specialized and secularized that the ordinary pastor has been radically excluded from service for the sick; thus healing and worship have become separate. In the indigenous African churches there is a reintegration of healing and worship. This corresponds with the Akan understanding, for religion in the Akan concept must be concerned with the health and fertility of human beings, animals, and land.

I was generally told that the prophets did not want to start their own churches but rather to use the gift of healing bestowed on them by the grace of God in already established Christian services. It was repeatedly reported, however, that after the patients had been healed they were mocked by the other members of their churches and so were often left without churches. This forced several of the prophets to form their own churches for their healed patients. This was the case of the Life and Salvation church, which was attached to Prophet Prah's Divine Healing and Miracle Ministry. Prophet Prah told me that he performed healing services in general churches and had no intention of founding his own church until the needs of his neglected, despised clients forced him to that action.

THE INDIGENIZATION OF WORSHIP

If the churches in Africa are to grow and develop, they must be allowed to take root in the soil of Africa where they have been planted. In this Africanization process the indigenous African churches have made a breakthrough and have a great deal to teach the missionary churches.

The indigenous African churches, through careful and concrete adaptation of certain cultural elements into their worship, have made Christianity real and meaningful to their African adherents. The following are a few of the areas where the indigenous African churches have adapted, and in some cases blended, the African culture with Christianity to root Christianity in the soil of Africa.

The Naming Ceremony

Among West African peoples the concept of corporate responsibility is very strong. This is especially manifest at birth, marriage, sickness, and death. The birth of a baby is the greatest blessing for the family, and to a large extent for the community as a whole. The Akans attach a special importance to the day on which the child is named. This day is generally the seventh or eighth day after birth. In fact, the new baby does not really belong to the family until the eighth day, when the child's continued existence would seem to indicate that it has really come to stay. The general assumption is that if by the seventh or eighth day the child still lives, then the ancestors, the gods, and the Supreme God have blessed the child for the family. At times it is simply said that the ghost-mother has relinquished the child into the world of the living.

Traditionally Akans name the child after the day of its birth. For example, a Friday-born male child is called Kofi, a Saturday-born male is called Kwame, and a Sunday-born male is called Kwasi. A Saturday-born female is called Amma, and a Sunday-born female is called Akosua.

The giving of the personal name has been adopted with small modifications by some indigenous African churches in Ghana and elsewhere on the continent. My present example is drawn from the practice of the Church of the

Messiah in Ghana. As in the traditional practice, among the members of the Church of the Messiah, the baby is taken to the temple on the eighth day. The father of the child presents about three names to the spiritual father (the priest) who, through meditation, selects the right name for the child.

The spiritual father then drops water three times into the child's mouth, saying, "The whole congregation will be a witness to your life, and when you say 'Yes' it is 'Yes' and 'No' must be 'No.' Let your Yes be Yes and your No, No." Taking salt, the spiritual father continues: "This day I give you salt, and according to the Bible you are the salt of the earth, but if the salt loses its taste, how shall its saltiness be restored? It is no longer good for anything except to be thrown out and trodden underfoot. Therefore from this day may your life be like the salt and may all trials and temptations which may be in your way be wiped away now and forever."

Finally, taking the honey (an alcoholic beverage is used in the traditional Akan custom), the spiritual father says: "This day I give you honey which is the witness of all humankind. May this honey wipe away all trials and temptations. Now Kofi Appiah-Kubi, we do not give you this name for you to be lazy, but rather that you should take up the cross of Christ and follow him in the wilderness, in the bush and in the villages. In the name of the Father, Son, and Holy Spirit, Amen."

Marriage

The indigenous African Christian churches recognize to a large extent the traditional system of African marriage. Instead of employing gold rings, wedding cakes, and other expensive articles used by the missionary churches, the Aladuras, for example, use eight different symbols. In place of the ring, they use the Bible. The couple grasp the Bible presented by the minister as the seal and sign of fidelity. Because of the hardiness and constant fruit-bearing of the banana plant with its large clusters of fruit, this plant is used to signify the profound hope of all African marriages—many children. The coconut is used to signify maturity or the secret blessing of God. Just as no one knows how the milk gets into the nut, so no one knows how the two are chosen by God for marriage. An orange is presented to symbolize a sound body and mind; bitter kola nuts symbolize long life and the wisdom and knowledge of God. Salt is given with the words "You are the salt of the earth; may you never lose your savor, but be a benefit to society." Honey is a sign of sweet marriage relationships with no bitterness, and finally a seven-branched candelabrum represents the prayer that the eyes of almighty God and the living Lord may ever be upon the couple.

Position of Women

It has hitherto been believed by many travelers, missionaries, and writers, and even by some uninformed or misinformed modern scholars that the

African woman is kept in a lowly state, that she is in fact little more than an animal, a property to be bought and sold, enjoying neither sympathy nor respect. This notion coincided with the patriarchal structure of the Western mission churches, with the result that ordination of women to the priesthood is non-existent in the mission churches.

The indigenous African churches have outstripped the missionary churches in this area. There are many women church leaders and prophetesses. In West Africa, for example, most of our traditional shrines have women priestesses (e.g., Nana Oparebea of the Akonodi shrine at Larte).

There are also some women founders of churches; for example, Alice Lanshina of Lumpa church in Zambia, Captain Abiodum of Cherabim and Seraphim, and Alice Tania of the Church of the Twelve Apostles in Ghana.

Music and Musical Instruments

The hymns and songs of most indigenous African Christian churches are often remarkably short and simple. They tend to be one-, two-, or three-line refrains. The contents embrace confessions, prayers, and praises, with constant refrains of "Amen," Halleluja," and "Praise God." Some of these hymns have been composed by the church members themselves; others are taken directly from the mission churches.

A few examples will suffice here:

> Jesus your grace abounds,
> Jesus your grace abounds,
> You have brought the wayward home.
>
> I patiently wait for my Lord.
> I have become like a new-born babe.
> I patiently wait for my Lord.
>
> Thank him, thank him,
> Thank your king,
> For he is good,
> and his mercy is bountiful.

Most of these hymns are sung with drum accompaniment, hand-clapping, and dancing. They are given also a typical African touch in rhythm, tempo, and style. Like most African music, they are sung as duets or trios, with several refrains and repetitions of particular lines.

The indigenous African churches have wholeheartedly accepted the use of locally made drums. The use of drums has been frowned upon by the missionary churches as pagan and therefore devilish. In fact, until recently no Christian could with impunity use any musical instrument in church except the piano and the organ, neither of which is built in Africa. Those who played the guitar were considered hooligans and unbelievers by members of the mission churches, and even today guitars are seldom allowed in churches of missionary origin. The indigenous African Christian churches use horns, rattles, and what may be called an African piano, in addition to drums and guitars of all sizes.

Sister Mary Aquina, in an article on the Rhodesian Zionists, remarks that the members of this church support their use of drumming and dancing with biblical quotations. In a sermon she heard, based on Psalms 149 and 150, the preacher said:

> We Zionists please God with our drumming. In Psalm 149, verses 3 and 4, we read: "Let them praise his name with dancing, making melody to him with timbrel [translated as drums] and lyre [translated as the African piano]. For the Lord takes pleasure in His people. . . . " Here we are told to use the drum and the African piano, because we are told both drum and African piano please God. The Bible is our witness that we please God with our drumming. But many do not understand what we are doing and they think that we are playing. Look also at Psalm 150. There we read: "Praise him with trumpet sound; praise him with timbrel and dance." This proves that we teach only what is written in the Book. The Bible is our teacher.

18

Lamin Sanneh

Reciprocal Influences: African Traditional Religions and Christianity

Lamin Sanneh underlines the tolerance of religious diversity and the inclusive view of human community that are prevalent themes in recently recovered African religions but are missing in "missionary" Christianity. This selection is taken from Lamin Sanneh, West African Christianity: The Religious Impact *(Maryknoll, N.Y.: Orbis Books, 1983), pp. 242–51.*

Several lines converge on the subject of the character of Christianity in Africa. The most significant of these is undoubtedly the contribution of traditional religions to a deepened sense of the religious potential of the message of the Bible. It is by that factor that we have to judge the African response to the church. It is a recurring theme in this book and deserves far greater attention than has been devoted to it. Merely to defend traditional religions against European missionary attack or criticism is not enough, and may, by diverting attention from the independent milieu of these religions and making them anticyclones whirling in a foreign element, be counterproductive. Such a defense, however well-intentioned, is nevertheless a byproduct of the strength of the missionary challenge and may not in fact be the form or substance of the response of traditional religions. Its value as a tool of conceptual analysis is thus restricted to the currency of the antiforeign cause it espouses.

The real questions we should ask relate to the phenomenon of the rich and diverse religious life that has flourished in African societies. For example, why did people draw a careful line between the world of the divinities and that of ordinary life? By what rule did a common substance or object, such as water or a piece of stone or wood, make the transition into a ritual symbol? Did the perception of a common object and its transformation into ritual subject become a factor in the use of mediation and intercession in African Christianity? Did the recognition of the plural world of the divinities contribute to the understanding of the universal doctrines of the Bible? Did the tradition of Christian renewal and reform, so prominent in African Christianity, occur in traditional religions under the category of dreams and visions? If so, did their widespread use in the churches owe more to such indigenous roots than to the Bible? Did the notion of religious hierarchy in traditional religions determine the way the church was assimilated in African societies? And so on. An underlying assumption in all these questions is the continuing vitality of African religions both as influences in the ordinary perception of Christians and as a force in the organizational aspects of Christianity. The issue is more than just of academic interest. It has implications for pastoral care and counseling, and for developing a meaningful theology for the church.

Another line concerns the *status* of Christianity in Africa. The phrase "African Christianity" or "African churches" has often acted as a cloak for the perpetuation of the idea of the inadmissibility of Africans as a legitimate part of the wider humanity, so that the history of Africa and its religious heritage is consigned into an area-study category, outside the mainstream of academic teaching and research. Regrettably, many educated Africans have capitulated to this piece of intellectual apartheid by the seductive device of fashionable arguments for African authenticity and uniqueness. Not only has this conceded the inferior position of Africa in the broader field of world Christianity, but it has allowed the history of the church in North Africa to be excluded from our concern, which is then promptly annexed as an exclusive province of the European church. Sometimes this intellectual apartheid has been extended to the Ethiopian Orthodox church, which is wrenched from the rest of Black Africa and made into a satellite of the Judeo-Christian center of gravity. Such academic categories are deeply divisive and distort profoundly the historical process of the unfolding story of Christianity from the time of the apostles. The espousal, in strident neonationalist terms, of the cause of a separate, ethnic African Christianity is one of the most damaging things to have occurred since the end of the European missionary era. The vital debate now is on how to rescue the subject of African Christianity from its exotic ghetto and at the same time compel the other parts of the Christian world to lower the barrier behind which they have cultivated a political and cultural ascendancy over the entire Christian heritage. This would rectify the over-concentration of intellectual resources in Western hands, and African Christianity would cease to be the preserve of so-called European experts. Such a reversal of the existing state of affairs would help to release the energies of the church for the service and witness of the one Lord it knows and claims.

A third factor is best described in terms of an irony. The usual conception of Christianity was to see it as bringing to Africa certain universal teachings about God which were lacking in traditional religions. In rallying to the defense of those religions, some African writers hastened to reply by latching on to the fact that since, for example, ideas of the Supreme Being were present before the arrival of the missionaries, African religions could be accorded the status of a *preludia fidei* in the Christian dispensation. In other words, the criticism of the missionaries was valid in itself, except that they had been forestalled in the case of African religions. And with that concession went the opportunity to understand those religions by the standard of their own true measure. And here is the irony, namely that missionary Christianity as the propounder of a universal God turned out to be an exclusive religion tied to an ethnocentric Western worldview, whereas traditional religions, criticized as restrictive tribal affairs, offered hope and reconciliation by their tolerance of religious diversity and by their inclusive view of human community. That makes them more in tune with biblical teaching than the politically divisive form of European Christianity. By recognizing this tolerant aspect of traditional religions we may be able to discover sources of strength which a missionary Christianity forfeited through its compromising subservience to colonial politics.

This would have far-reaching implications for an understanding of the mission of the church in Africa. The rather tarnished image of the church as an instrument of the imperial order, particularly in the formative years of colonialism between about 1890 and 1930, undoubtedly compromised its missionary task. African Christians, laboring under such inherited difficulties, often found themselves on the defensive, becoming easy prey to the popular criticism of Christianity as an alien religion. To break out from behind that psychological barrier has taken a long time. Without our realizing it, perhaps, the defensiveness has produced social barriers, with Christians inclined to enclose themselves for fear of exposure. Once a proper understanding of the religious basis of African Christian life has been acquired, it would be easier to separate it from the political role foisted on it by missionaries, and thus easier to remove defensive barriers. There is evidence that in many places Christianity has in fact moved into a more open phase.

To encourage this movement it is sufficient only to demonstrate the role of Africans as pioneers in the adaptation and assimilation of Christianity in their societies, with a corresponding scaling down of the role of Western missionaries in that process. The evidence for this is secure and needs no elaborate exegesis to establish it. The initiative passed out of the hands of the missionaries as historical transmitters and went instead to the countless Africans who presided over the reception and growth of the church. For example, in the early period in Freetown, it was clear from the start that the Nova Scotians were the key to the successful implantation of the church, with the Colonial Chaplaincy left floundering. With the emergence of recaptive Africans came the high-water mark of Christian activity, with a significant outburst of missionary initiative in Nigeria and elsewhere. In Ghana, similarly, the African contribution was decisive. This aspect of the spread of Christianity in Africa has been suitably dramatized in the phenomenon of Christian independency, but that it has existed as an important historical fact right from the beginning is without question. We may characterize it as the African factor in mission and make it a fitting successor to the previous classic definition of "the missionary factor" in African Christianity.

The question of African agency ties in with that of the status of African religions in Christianity. Those who adapted and promoted the faith in African communities remained themselves very close to sources of traditional religious vitality even if they had occasionally to make approving noises of condemnation to please the missionary who was often far removed from the scene of action. In African hands, then, Christianity spread along familiar religious channels, acquiring in the feedback a strong dose of local religious materials which the quarantined culture of the Western missionary had tried to filter out. It is not only inevitable that such an encounter should take place, but it is also immensely critical for the successful establishment of the faith. Seen in this light, the charge of "syncretism" so often invoked against the increasing importance of African leadership in the church loses its force. In a different sense, Christianity itself is one of the most syncretistic of religions, if by that we mean the amalgamation of ideals and realities, of principles and mundane practice, for it is a pre-eminent theological teaching that through the incarnation the transcendent and the terrestrial merged in human focus. The Christian poet describes it well:

> He laid his glory by,
> He wrapped him in our clay;
> Unmarked by human eye,
> The latent Godhead lay.

It is a logical consequence of this insight that in Africa such teachings should take local form, and that those who resisted them were out of contact with the overwhelming sense of the message they proclaimed. Thus religious compromise, if such indeed must be the price Africans must pay for embodying the faith, has a deeper affinity with the music of the Benedictus.

To reinterpret the decisive role of Africans as adaptors of the faith requires a corresponding adjustment to the position occupied by missionaries. Under the old categories, the missionaries were their own worst enemy, for by calling attention to their historical pre-eminence they minimized the roots of local assimilation whose irrepressible significance made the missionaries an easy target for attack. It is ironic that even in our own day when the African Christian idiom is an accepted part of the wider ecumenical discourse, some Western writers should still wish to insist on elevating the historical transmission of Christianity to a major status, completely overshadowing the African factor. Consequently the missionary contribution has suffered and continues to suffer: the missionary is cast in one of two roles, either as the whipping-boy of the nationalist or as the disembodied idol of the West. In both cases we are left with a caricature.

It is about time that we should once and for all move into a constructive stage and find a reappraisal that conforms to the complex historical situation, and one too that does not detract from the African factor. A way forward is to acknowledge that the missionary signified the stage of the historical transmission of Christianity, a stage which stimulated the more powerful wave of local response. Once whipped into action, this local wave acquired a force that rose from sources of traditional religious enterprise, sustaining the church in its intimate involvement in the life of the people. The discussion in the past has failed to recognize this. Instead the focus remained on what may be termed the missionary "hardware" of finance, bureaucratic machinery, political alliances, and the propaganda engine of Home Committees. When we tried to consider the missionary "software" through the men and women who passed through the Home Committees to arrive in Africa, we were hindered by the strong shadows cast over the field by the "hardware," with the consequence that a "tunnel" effect was superimposed on their role. Thus many writers, without even looking in detail at what happened on the ground, proceed to discuss missionaries in the light of what may be deduced from the "hardware." Thus is set up the abstract outline that reduces the missionary to a caricature. One line in an occasional dispatch about obtaining government support for a school project, for example, is enough to set the airwaves tingling with news of missionary collaboration with colonialism. A lifetime of dull, grinding service, by contrast, is ignored, either because it is a statistical "failure" in the view of the Home Committee or because its recognition by the nationalist would dilute popular rhetoric.

While it is true that the missionaries occupied a marginal position at the stage of the adaptation of Christianity, their contribution may often have been crucial. This would appear to have been true over the documentation of local languages, translations of the Scriptures, in the use of the vernacular in schools and as a vehicle of preaching and other forms of local religious activity. While Africans may have the advantage over the missionary in the appreciation of the deeper nuances of their own languages, the raw material and data upon which this advantage rests were provided by the missionary. From that relative advantage Africans have gone on to establish their unrivaled command of local resources, using as their model indigenous forms of religious life. The demand by the missionaries that Africans repudiate local religions and customary practices has to be understood against this background of the increasing marginalization of the missionary once the stage of adaptation has been reached. It should not be used in the manner of a "proof text," for the simple reason that its *prima facie* value is nil.

On another level too, the role of the missionary needs to be investigated for the light it may throw on the whole issue of indigenization. We would need to know more than pronouncements made from different ideological positions. It may often be the case that the missionary has stood in the way of indigeniza-tion, either deliberately or unwittingly. But it may happen that the missionaries facilitate indigenization, not only by their linguistic labors but by the attention they allow local Christians to pay to certain cultural themes, such as hymns and sacred songs in the local language, music, the decorative arts, and the writing down of local stories, myths, and folklore. Even the notion of looking to the past age of the church is capable of stimulating an enhanced apprehension of the African sacred past. Sometimes, indeed, it is this prior sense of the sacred past which attunes the African to the message of Christianity. But, for our purposes now, the order is not decisive. The fact that religious parallelism invests the two traditions with mutual significance suggests that the African religious model is not subservient to the external one of Christianity.

There is a theological way of representing all that we have been saying so far, and, without trying to be technical, we may thus present it briefly. A distinction is made between the *missio Dei* on the one hand and on the other the mission of the church. By *missio Dei* is meant the unceasing work of God in the great task of reconciliation and forgiveness and a maturing sense of God's love and fellowship. The mission of the church, by contrast, is the historical response to God's initiative and finds its most poignant expression in service, *diakonia*. But historical *diakonia* often falls far short of the *missio Dei,* and, what is equally important, other agents may be just as active in this *missio Dei* as are Chris-tians. By implication, God's initiative has anticipated and preceded the specific version of Christian mission, so that in Africa, the "good news" of divine love and reconciliation, for example, was long diffused in the local religious tradi-tions before the missionary came on the scene. It is this divine precedent which on the one hand authenticates the African religious experience and on the other validates the missionary vocation. Without it the African would rise to a materialist cosmology but no higher, while the missionary would represent his or her own cause. Furthermore, the historical fact that missionaries may have been allies of structures of privilege and power remains highly marginal from the point of view of the *missio Dei,* for it is evident that Africans proved more than adequate instruments in the extension of the church despite the obvious handicaps of powerlessness and material deprivation. From the perspective, then, of the *missio Dei,* the Western missionaries are merely heeding a call whose echo has long reverberated throughout the edifice of African religiosity. In the historical missionary vocation, the missionaries attempt to connect up with the ongoing task of the *missio Dei.* Theologically the historical mission is a venture of partnership with the *missio Dei,* even if in practice it may have been prosecuted by uncouth means. As a partnership it required the divine prece-dent to justify it and the African factor to make it efficacious.

The matter of indigenization becomes on this basis a logical extension of the reality of the *missio Dei.* Its logical opposite is the mission station tucked away on the hill-top above the village, resolutely setting its face against contagious contact with the people it aims to serve. It is easy enough to castigate this self-defeating practice of mission. But provided we keep our eyes on the *missio Dei* we should see that the divine initiative is actively and liberatingly at work among the outcasts in the villages below, that the Good Samaritan is encamped on the Jericho road of the villagers where God's purpose animates their spirit and fires their righteous indignation.

An important condition for recovering a true sense of the mission of the church is to recognize the African factor. Once this step is taken we shall see that mission is no longer a specialized department of the church into which so-called experts are drafted, but that it forms part and parcel of the church's life and witness. As such it elaborates the theme of discipleship and *diakonia* which constitutes the heart of the Christian life. It is therefore appropriate that the laity should play a significant part in mission, as they have done in Africa. It is a weakness of the church that it should excel in the professional training of priests and other members of the clergy on the one hand and on the other lag behind in a corresponding involvement of the laity in its normal life. The African experience of responsible flexibility in church life, so close in fact to the New Testament itself, should be set forward as a positive contribution to a Western church that is straitjacketed in lifeless forms and conventions. Only in movement may we keep pace with the living presence of the Lord who has called us.

One other matter that relates to indigenization is polygamy. Because it is an emotional issue, invested with high stakes by the patriot, it has been used as the touchstone of genuine indigenization. The discussion has been so over-concentrated that it has lost sight of the important contribution Christianity has made to the emancipation of women and their equal treatment before the law. The discussion has also played into the hands of those reared on the distorted myths of popular anthropology which asserts the superhuman sexual drive of the African, who is thus laid open to the puritanical disdain of the West. To attack the puritanical roots of this distortion does not advance the African cause one iota, for it leaves unchallenged the grounds on which polygamy is defended. There is nothing inherently African about the institution of plural marriages, nor can it be said to be a universal rule applied in all societies. We need also to avoid the danger of describing it in such a way that it is made to embody all the ideals of the African past. There was much abuse in the system, and its benefits were not always the unmitigated boon claimed. Its modern proponents, who are mostly men, risk alienating a whole community of women from the social and educational pressures which may tend towards a more just world. In any case it seems inconceivable that in such a vital area as marriage and family life the church should stand aside or else come into the picture only to make an opportunistic endorsement of an arrangement that panders to the male ego. To say that the rule of monogamy is unacceptable to the church in Africa on the grounds mainly that it is a Western-imported institution is to misunderstand both monogamy and the West's painful incon-sistency on the subject. There is a valid Christian understanding of the ques-tion, and to that discussion the church in Africa ought to contribute.

The whole area of interreligious encounter has been investigated in the

relevant chapters above. Although the value of African religions in this connection cannot be over-emphasized, we may leave them at this stage and
consider only how Christianity and Islam have been affected by the African
medium. It is part of received academic orthodoxy that when discussing these
two missionary religions in Africa, we should proceed to apply to them
standards derived from their Western and Middle Eastern incarnations. But
orthodoxy in this instance is in manifest error. Christianity in its European
transformation is a reconceptualization of the heritage of the apostles, and
Islam has been no less immune to the dynamic process of historical and cultural
experience. Yet in their African versions we have behaved as if these religions
have existed in sterilized form from their origin, still responding to the stimulus
of their immediate environment, and to that extent able to renounce the
African setting as contaminating. The theoretical invalidity of such assumptions is easy to demonstrate, but it would distract us from the main issue at
stake. The fact of the matter is that Africa has imposed its own character on the
two religions, subjecting them to its own historical experience and immersing
them in its cultural and religious traditions. Far from allowing Christianity or
Islam to siphon off those elements which constituted its own spiritual integrity,
Africa has dissolved much of what came to it and reconstituted the resultant
phenomenon as a reinforcement to pre-existing principles of the religious life.
Therefore, the most fundamental question that has faced the two missionary
religions in Africa is whether and how they can reciprocate with African
religions in a mutually recognizable idiom. They are not free to decide whether
or not they wish to be involved, nor indeed whether the contest is being staged
on propitious grounds, for the initiative lies with their African hosts. The
Arabic proverb which advises the guest to visit less frequently if he wishes to be
loved more greatly has an acute point to it. As permanent sojourners in the
African household, Christianity and Islam cannot any longer aspire to the
courtesies of the occasional visitor while wishing to retain the privileges of a
legal heir.

The effective transformation of these religions in Africa means that we
should apply African standards to their behavior, rather than continue to foster
them on transplanted soil. This historical and cultural transposition constitutes
a valid turning-point in the career of these religions. We ought to see them as
religious movements which spread over different terrains and which in the
African stage of their progress took on the strong hues of that tropical
interlude.

Such a step is being urged because it has numerous implications for Africa,
and for religion in general. The divisive measures we have adopted in summing
up Africa's potential continue to affect our methodology when we apply
divisive criteria to Africa's religious traditions as underdogs at the mercy of
outsiders. Often the motive is an apparently enlightened one, namely, that since
Christianity and Islam have a strong scriptural and intellectual tradition, we
show a progressive spirit if we concede their ascendancy over African religions.
Both the motive and the procedure share the grave flaw of received academic

orthodoxy. And with that recognition we have come much nearer to understanding the local and historical roots of religious adaptation. Such an African perspective is an invaluable asset to discussions of religious encounter and dialogue. It is also relevant to questions of identity and what constitutes the normative religious model. What is clear is that there exists a plurality of normative models and that we can restore them to their rightful place by viewing them in historical and comparative perspective. There is truly no one inherently superior model of representing the human enterprise. If Africa contributes nothing else to the large stock of religious ideas now within our grasp, this comparative dimension alone should secure it an honorable place in religious and academic counsels.

Of course, there is more to it than that. Our final point concerns the destiny of African Christianity. No one can miss the vitality of the religion in much of the continent. In spite of the strident forms of political nationalism that have followed the end of colonialism, the church in Africa has continued to play an active role in national affairs, sometimes paying a heavy price for refusing to bow to political pressure. If it were nothing more than the carbon-copy of the Western church, the African church would have merged with the political state and become a defender of the *status quo*. For in many parts of the West the church has been thoroughly neutralized, its prophetic sting drawn by the effective encirclement of institutional political privilege, with a fate no better than the church enjoys under communist domination in the East. This fate has not for the most part overtaken the churches in Africa, with the notable exception of South Africa. As long as support for the national cause is not exclusively identified with the cause of God, then the church is proportionately free to be the people of God. The alternative would be to make the national anthem the hymn of orthodox faith. Given this prophetic role of the church, it is indisputable that for much of Africa Christianity is embarked on the inexorable march of the people of God. It is salutary to recall that it was after St. Paul had established the church as the church of the *ethnoi,* the Greek word for Gentiles, that Christianity entered upon its universal course. Who can deny that a similar phenomenon may be about to unfold before our eyes as Christianity makes unprecedented progress in an ill-rated Africa?

19

Mercy Amba Oduyọye

The Value of African Religious Beliefs and Practices for Christian Theology

Mercy Amba Oduyọye emphasizes the need for Christianity to come to terms with African culture. "The Value of African Religious Beliefs and Practices for Christian Theology" is taken from Appiah-Kubi and Torres, eds., African Theology En Route, *pp. 109–16. The paper was given at the Pan-African Conference of Third World Theologians in December 1977.*

The "African" religious beliefs and practices referred to in this paper are specifically those of black Africa, that is Africa south of the Sahara, excluding the racist white minorities of the south and other immigrant groups. I am also excluding the beliefs and practices of Islam and nonindigenous religions like Hinduism and the Bahai faith. This is not to say that I am unaware of what Mbiti calls "contact religion." Most Africans, says Mbiti, do not see any contradiction in holding a mixture of beliefs and practices. Indeed it is this mixture that makes this paper possible.

Religious pluralism is found in Africa as elsewhere on the globe. The popular description of Africans as "notoriously" or "incurably" religious is belied by Africans who call themselves atheists or humanists. Secularization is a factor on the African scene. There are those who are to a greater or lesser degree Islamized or Christianized.

There is also a group that we may refer to as "traditionalists." Some of these are simply theorists, but there are masses of people in Africa who hold to the traditional religious beliefs and practices of their forebears to the exclusion of the missionary religions. Their religious customs blend with their social life and are at the base of all their institutions and festive celebrations. It is the traditionalists who will form the subject of this study. It is their religious beliefs and practices that we designate as "African."

Modernization has had a disruptive and weakening effect on African life and thus on African religion. At the same time it is evident that the missionary religions together with modern technology have proved inadequate to our needs. Since the old appears unable to stand on its own and the new by itself is proving inadequate, we should expect some creative syncretism to develop in Africa.

A living Christian faith in Africa cannot but interact with African culture. In fact there is being developed an interpretation of Christianity and specifically of Christian theology that one may describe as African. The intention of this paper is to draw attention to the fact that the process needs to be accelerated if African Christianity is to escape being a fossilized form of nineteenth-century European Christianity.

AFRICAN RELIGIOUS BELIEFS AND PRACTICES

It is now accepted by most African Christians that it is time to study the religion of our forebears. This has arisen out of the recognition of the poverty of the liturgy and theology emanating from European and North American Christianity. They do not touch the African soul at its depths. Here we will consider various African traditional beliefs and practices, giving particular attention to those relevant to African Christian theology.

a. African belief in the divine origin of the universe is shared by Christianity. In African religion, as in Christianity, God leaves humankind in charge of the world as a *steward*. In both African and Christian myths of origins, humankind becomes the center of the universe. But human beings wantonly exploit the world's physical and human resources to an extent that even God cannot tolerate. The African recognition of the divine spirit in nature and of the community of spirit between human beings, other living creatures, and natural phenomena could reinforce the Christian doctrine of creation as well as contribute to Christian reflection on ecological problems.

b. Related to the belief that humankind is the custodian of the earth is Africa's conviction that the past, present, and future generations form *one community.* Africans therefore try to hold in tension the demands of the traditions of the elders and the necessity to build for the future. This communal sense has far-reaching implications, for example, in attitudes toward land rights. In Africa there is nothing so difficult to alienate as land; it has to be preserved for the coming generations. "I conceive that land belongs to a vast family of which many are dead, few are living, and countless members are unborn."[1] If immigrant European exploiters of Africa had understood and respected this we would not today have the horrible Bantustans in South Africa. If Africans themselves had remembered that land is the gift of God to the people, and thus in modern times to the nation, development projects involving land use would have had a better chance of success.

Africans recognize life as life-in-community. We can truly know ourselves if we remain true to our community, past and present. The concept of individual success or failure is secondary. The ethnic group, the village, the locality, are crucial in one's estimation of oneself. Our nature as beings-in-relation is a two-way relation: with God and with our fellow human beings. Expand the communal ideology of clans and ethnic groups to nations and you have a societal system in which none is left in want of basic needs. It is an extension of this belief that has led some African politicians to declare that the independence of their own countries means nothing as long as there remains on African soil one state that is still under colonial rule. This is one of the underlying principles of Pan-Africanism. We prosper or perish together as a people. Nkrumah, in concluding his autobiography, said, "Our task is not done and our own safety is not assured until the last vestige of colonialism has been swept from Africa.²

The world is in need of religious tolerance, based on a recognition of one God from whom all movements of the spirit take their origin. A belief in one God who is the source of one human race renders all racism and other types of ethnocentricity and exploitation of persons heretical and blasphemous. With its mythology based on African traditional beliefs, African Christianity may be in the vanguard of this movement. Can African Christians contribute new symbols and myths for promoting justice and reconciliation? Can covenant meals, symbols of sharing and of the acceptance of communal responsibility, begin to happen more meaningfully in the church? Can more people "break bread" together not only on their knees but in their homes, sharing in the utilization of national resources?

The role of ancestors in the life of Africans becomes important in enabling them to remember their source and history. To deny history is to deny one's roots and source of self-identity. It is to deny also the fact that we embody in ourselves both the past and the future. Ancestral cults serve the purpose of keeping people from becoming rootless and purposeless, blown about by every fickle fashion and ideology. The ancestral cults have been the custodians of the African spirit, personality, and vivid sense of community demonstrated in socioreligious festivals.

The teaching that God is the Originator of all humanity and, as a corollary, that there is one human family, is held by Christianity, but it stands in dire need of reinforcement. The movement from nationalism toward universalism will be promoted by making available to the world Africa's vision of the unity of the individual person and of humanity. Africa's contribution can enable us to utilize creatively the tension between the universal and the particular and to develop the theology of the unity of humankind.

c. A sense of *wholeness of the person* is manifested in the African attitude to life. Just as there is no separation between the sacred and the secular in communal life, neither is there a separation between the soul and the body in a person. Spiritual needs are as important for the body as bodily needs are for the soul. This is basic to African medicine and psychiatry. Moreover, for a wholesome life people not only have to be at peace with themselves, but also must be fully integrated into the community. The African contribution can help purge the Christian religion of the separation of the human being into body, soul, and spirit.

d. The International Women's Year stimulated a lot of discussion which to me was basically an inquiry into whether *women* are an integral part of humanity or merely appendages to the male. The present freedom of African women to express dissatisfaction with their secondary roles and often non-roles is said to have been brought by Christianity and Westernization. I agree that there has been some progress in economic activity and politics. But as far as the cultic aspect of religion goes, women now as before are relegated to the background. The cultic events in which women take complete charge are few and far between. The fact that women do the dancing and cooking for festivals does not, to my mind, compensate for their exclusion from the "holy of holies" in the festivals. The limitations placed on women's participation in religious practices is further aggravated by the irrational fear of blood. It is an area wide open for study. Further work on women in African religion will be a great contribution to global women's issues.

African women have a traditional belief in the benefit of sacrifice for the community. Sacrifice, taken seriously, can lead to social reforms and to lifestyles that are less wasteful and more mindful of humanity's stewardship of life and ultimate dependence on the Source-Being. But I have difficulty in understanding why it is the prerogative of only one sex to sacrifice for the well-being of the community.

e. Christianity will have to take seriously the African belief that God delegates authority to intermediary beings. In Africa there is a widespread belief in the *"divine right of kings,"* which is often sanctioned by African religions. The ruler is almost invariably a cultic person, and his or her person is considered sacred. Against this background, certain modern political leaders have instituted what have come to be known as "benevolent dictatorships." Without the sanctions that provided the checks and balances in the traditional system, these have always ended in chaos. African organization had its own constitutional processes for removing rulers who abused tradition. The divine rights of rulers worked in traditional Africa when belief in the Supreme Being was taken seriously and decision by consensus was actively pursued. The people's role in their own development is slowly being recognized by current African politicians. The days when the ruler took a unilateral decision to declare what the people needed are slowly passing—one must say rather too slowly.

f. Covenant-making is a characteristic of African life. A ruler, for example, is always a covenanted or constitutional monarch. There is always a reciprocal oath-taking between the ruler and the ruled, who are often represented in the associated ceremonies by the elders of the community.[3] There are also oaths and covenants between friends and others that bind members of exclusive clubs within the community.

When these oaths are taken seriously they are more binding than any signature made on legal documents. A person who flouts *Nsamansew* (the last will and testament of a person) is sure to be called quickly to the spirit-world to render an explanation. The process of oath-taking always contains a religious element; one always swears by a divinity who thus becomes the chief witness to the transaction. Covenantal meals seal reconciliation and purification ceremonies, since one cannot conceivably work to the disadvantage of another with whom a kolanut has been shared. We should investigate what makes African traditional oaths and covenants more binding than the Lord's Supper.

g. Africa has a realistic attitude toward the *power of evil.* If we recognize that the collective evil produced by humanity is strong enough to "materialize" into a force to reckon with, then we shall see racism and other kinds of exploitation for what they are and be able to develop the appropriate weapons to fight them. Certain humanistic claims that humanity may be educated into eschewing evil leads us down a very long road to the humanization of our societies. What is evil is to be exorcized. Here again is a possible meeting point of Christian theology and African belief.

h. Reconciliation has a central role in African religion and practice. Broken relations are never allowed to go unhealed. Sacrifices are performed and communal meals held to restore normalcy. In both African religion and Christianity, when life is sacrificed, when it is given back to God, it is made sacred and harmony is restored. This belief is embodied in the Christian doctrine of atonement. A fresh statement of this belief, which makes use of African ideas of sacrifice and covenants, will enable African religion to make another contribution to the religious development of humankind. Here again, by analyzing the theological elements of Christianity and of African religion, one can indicate areas where African religion will be supportive of Christian theology and contribute to its restatement in terms relevant to the African context.

i. Most *rites of passage* performed by Christians in Africa have been enriched by African culture. Marriage, naming ceremonies, and burials are good examples. Yearly festivals involving cleansing and the driving away of misfortune are current in Africa. There are sacrifices to cleanse or to bless the individual or group after a trauma—birth, death, disease, plague, accident, etc. These have been woven into liturgies of Christians in the form of thanksgiving services for almost any situation. On the other hand, Christians have shied away from puberty rites and other rites of initiation into adulthood because they have misgivings as to whether a Christian's allegiance to the church (and Christ) does not conflict with age-group allegiance and membership in secret societies. Initiation to adulthood, however, is initiation into full responsibility in one's community; it is the culmination of a long process of sociopolitical education. There should be further discussion about the relationship of these initiation rites to confirmation and recognition rites prevalent in some Christian denominations.

j. Other traditional African *liturgical practices* are most apparent among the African independent churches. These are the churches that have been founded by African Christians and that, not being bound by the stately liturgies and theological sensitivities of the West, have developed lively liturgies with music and prayer forms that are authentically African. Some of the older Christian congregations, both Roman Catholic and Protestant, have awakened to this and are fast renewing their liturgies along the lines that are relevant to African religiosity. Drumming, dancing, extemporaneous prayer, dramatic methods of conveying the word of God, and stunning cultic robes are being observed among African Christian congregations. More use is being made of symbols and of spiritual healing and exorcism. There is a strong sense of community among members of the independent churches, and in the urban situation they become the new "extended family." The songs that Western Christians developed in their nationalistic spirit and racial pride are dropping out of the repertoire of African Christians as they become aware of the songs' non-Christian character. For example:

> Can we, whose souls are lighted
> with wisdom from on high:
> Can we to the benighted the Lamp of life deny?

Such hymns are rarely heard in African congregations today; they are being replaced by African tunes with words that come out of the depths of the African soul or from the common source of Christianity—the Bible.

THE AFRICAN THEOLOGICAL TASK: SOTERIOLOGY

The word "syncretism" has become a bogey word, used to frighten all who would venture to do Christian theology in the context of other worldviews and religions. But is syncretism not in fact a positive and unavoidable process? Christian theology and practice have always interacted with the religious and philosophical presuppositions of the various periods. Practices like the observance of Sunday, distribution of Easter eggs, and the festival of the Nile in the medieval Coptic church are instances of the acculturation of Christianity. Evidence of this process is increasing in Africa.

Since the theme of salvation features so prominently in African religion, I would like to offer some reflections on the question of salvation for African Christianity. Both in the New Testament and in the early church, the way people interpreted the significance of Christ was closely related to what they saw as their greatest need. Christ was all things to all men, to quote Paul. The names given to Jesus of Nazareth in the Bible were all titles that held significant salvific content. He was the Son of Man who came to take up the elect of God.

He was the Son of God, the Logos who was at God's right hand in bringing order out of chaos. He was Lord but, unlike our Caesars, he was the suffering servant. To some he was a Zealot, a nationalist, but one who forgave his enemies and prayed for them. To the sick he was a doctor and to the sinful he spoke as God.

These and other titles were the responses of those who had faith in his uniqueness or at least in his significance for the development of human history.

He attracted a wide variety of people, from simple manual workers to the intellectuals of the Jewish world. It was from soteriology that Christology developed. I believe that for theology to be relevant to African culture it has to speak of salvation.

Our salvation theology has to feature the questions of racism and liberation from material need. It has to emphasize the need for communal decisions as against totalitarianism. Above all, salvation is to be seen as salvation from evil, both individual and structural. At several points our Christian theology can be aided by African religious beliefs and practices.

THE AFRICAN CONTRIBUTION

Africa's approach to the basic religious problems facing humankind—creation, survival, human relations, the existence of a spirit-world, etc.—was as meaningful and relevant to the prescientific age in Africa as were similar approaches all over the world. These approaches, which we designate primal worldviews, are at the base of all religions and effectively continue to influence the ordering of society and of individual life. African religious beliefs and practices have provided, and continue to provide, Africa with a philosophical fountainhead for the individual's life and for the ordering of society. African traditional religion emphasizes the common origin of all humanity. It is the source from which a person's sense of dignity and responsibility flow. The search for security invariably begins here and for many it is also the last resort. Far from being redundant or anachronistic, African religious beliefs and practices have shown such a remarkable ability for staying relevant that Africans have a responsibility to share their basic tenets with the rest of humanity. This will be a task of recalling the peoples of the whole world to basic principles of human community and the religious basis of life even though some think these principles have become outmoded or are a hindrance to the advancement of humanity.

We must note that since "traditional" life was permeated in all its aspects by religion, any appeal we make to traditional values and practices is ultimately religious. Also we must bear in mind that the basic element in religion does not consist of practices of cultic places and persons but the beliefs that are manifested through them. So that even when modernization has modified ceremonies and other cultic practices, human beings will continue to depend on the beliefs as a rock on which to build. So, for example, the belief in the living-dead, in the existence of spirits, and in magic and witchcraft are a part of the

Africans' recognition that life is not entirely materialistic. These beliefs are an expression of the yearning for life after life. Since the Supreme Being is believed to be the Source of Life, the search after the life-force is itself a groping for a closer and more personal relationship with Being Itself.

To contribute more effectively to the religious development of people, African Christian theologians have a duty to theologize from this context and incorporate the authentic African idiom into Christian theology. Utilizing African religious beliefs in Christian theology is not an attempt to assist Christianity to capture and domesticate the African spirit; rather it is an attempt to ensure that the African spirit revolutionizes Christianity to the benefit of all who adhere to it.

NOTES

1. Kwame Nkrumah, *Ghana* (Edinburgh: T. Nelson and Sons Ltd., 1959), p. 10.

2. Ibid., p. 240.

3. R. S. Rattray, *Ashanti Law and Constitution* (Oxford: Oxford University Press, 1929), p. 82.

20

Eugene Hillman

Polygamy Reconsidered

Eugene Hillman explains why African plural marriages must remain an open question for Christianity. This selection is taken from his Polygamy Reconsidered *(Maryknoll, N. Y.: Orbis Books, 1975), pp. 35–38 and 97–101.*

THE STATE OF THE PROBLEM

Certainly there is today among church leaders in Africa a new openness and at least a willingness to discuss the recurring suggestion that the churches may have been mistaken in their previous policies regarding plural marriage.[1] At their 1967 regional conference in Nairobi, some seventy Roman Catholic bishops of eastern Africa were asked to consider the possibility of adopting a new policy regarding polygamy.[2] The discussion was brief because it came only at the end of a crowded agenda and because most of the bishops had not had time to study the prepared paper on the subject; so there was no serious effort even to debate the issues, much less reach an agreement. It is, however, significant that the question was not simply dismissed with any negative resolutions or anathemas. Instead, the bishops wisely decided that further study was required.

This "further study" has been urged upon all church leaders in Tanzania since the government's 1969 proposal that even Christian marriages in Tanzania should be legally recognized as potentially polygamous. In their most ecumenical statement to date, the ecclesiastical leaders of Tanzania offered the government a joint reply—from the Dar es Salaam Committee of Churches: Roman Catholic, Anglican, Lutheran, Presbyterian, Baptist, Mennonite, Sal-

248

vation Army, and Assembly of God.[3] Their statement points out that monogamy is not a "Western import," that polygamy was previously "justified by historical, social, and economic situations," and that even now there is no need to make this African form of plural marriage illegal for non-Christians.[4] Their defense of monogamy is based simply on the problematical hypothesis, to be examined in chapter 3, that polygamy is actually disappearing anyway. This hypothesis is supported by the sociological conjecture that the maintaining of this custom would be socially and economically retrogressive. No biblical or theological reasons are offered in support of the traditional Christian position. Basically, therefore, the argument of these church leaders comes to this: The problem will solve itself, as the problem-people, the polygamists, gradually disappear for socioeconomic reasons. Is there nothing more to be said?

The problem surely has some other dimensions. As already noted in this chapter, there are questions of justice and charity arising from the practice of "sending away" all but one of the wives of a polygamist who would become a Christian. In areas where polygamy is a preferential and socially integrated form of marriage, missionaries have all too often been seen as persons who come to break up the natural family unity and to shatter the existing complex of marriage-related human bonds. Jesus clearly taught that marriage should be indissoluble. Yet a polygamist is told that if he would fully obey the call of Christ, the first thing he must do is to divorce the mothers of his own children. Does this approach reflect the gospel message of unity, liberation, and joy? Is there no suspicion that this traditional approach amounts to little more than a legalistic improvisation? As long as polygamy continues to exist in Africa, even though it may be diminishing generally, there are some questions to be faced by church leaders.

We cannot simply wait for the whole problem to go away, while in practice the law of monogamy remains on a level of importance with faith. What is the meaning of the Christian *kerygma* if the law of monogamy must be presented together with it, and if the external observance of this particular law, no less than faith itself in Jesus Christ, is made a condition *sine qua non* for admission into the Christian fellowship? External conformity to this legal prescription has become so overwhelmingly important and finally decisive in practice that it seems almost to have become a substitute for the real conversion of faith, which alone leads to the newness of the Christian life. The theological problem here is a very old one; and it may perhaps be formulated in the question addressed to the people of Galatia: "Was it through observance of the law that you received the Spirit, or was it through faith in what you heard?" (Gal. 3:2).

So there really is a problem. An increasing number of African church leaders have come to see this problem in its true theological and anthropological dimensions. Bishop Josiah Kibira of the Evangelical Lutheran church in Tanzania, for example, has this to say about it:

> Our greatest ethical problems are divorce and polygamy and, intertwined with them, the question of church discipline. . . . The Church should

not simply stress laws without first making certain that these rules are a help rather than a detriment to those in need. . . . The problem of polygamy is the most difficult. In this area, the Church in Africa is bogged down and badly in need of a way out of the dilemma. . . . Perhaps, by theological study we may find that we should not prevent a pagan polygamist from being baptized if he is called while in that condition.[5]

For Peter Sarpong, the Roman Catholic bishop of Kumasi in Ghana, the widespread African custom of polygamy is "certainly a pressing pastoral problem." In his opinion, "the African bishops should be conducting studies into the problem. . . . Maybe some theological leeway can be found."[6]

In December of 1973 during a meeting of some sixty-five Roman Catholic bishops of eastern African countries, gathered in Nairobi to plan for the church in the 1980s, the same point was made once again, this time by Bishop John Njenga of Eldoret in Kenya. In his formal paper on African marriage Bishop Njenga concluded his sympathetic treatment of customary polygamy with a "call for more study, research, education and even rethinking and revaluation on the part of pastors, theologians and the faithful."[7] In spite of the Apostolic Nuncio's frenzied maneuverings to terminate the subsequent discussion of polygamy, the majority of the bishops agreed that this is indeed an issue which deserves far more study. However, all references to this discussion are curiously missing from the officially published conclusions of the meeting.[8]

•

THE PREVAILING ATTITUDE

The sociological data and analysis tell us something about "the prevailing attitude of African peoples" with regard to the practice of polygamy. There are, however, a few more indications worth noting.

We might recall that most of Africa's famous public figures of the past, and some of them today, are social models associated with the traditional forms of plural marriage. Nationalistic movements, moreover, are now turning more and more for inspiration to the original cultural sources of African peoples. This search for reidentification with an authentically indigenous way of life involves much more than styles of dress.[9] And polygamy is not one of those traditions that faded away under Western colonial influence. Although members of African Christian communities may tend to abandon this custom, the fact remains that the vast majority of the African populations are not Christian, and the traditional religio-ethical values are still very much in force among most of the peoples. Because it is already more numerous to start with, the non-Christian population as a whole will naturally continue to increase more rapidly than the Christian population. Even allowing for the growth of the Christian communities through conversions as well as births, the most optimistic estimates indicate that at best Christians might become about 50 percent of the total population by the year 2000.[10] In any case, whether one takes an optimistic or a pessimistic view of church growth in Africa, it must be assumed that the stronger traditional social institutions will still be very much in force by the year 2000.

Up to now, the opponents of plural marriage have not done very well in their various efforts to introduce legislation against the custom. Indeed, very few independent African countries have enacted any legislation against polygamy; and in some of these countries, Mali, for example, the new marriage codes represent an "ingenious compromise" with customary laws.[11] In Kenya the government-appointed commission on marriage legislation has recommended that "the law should recognize two distinct types of marriage: the monogamous and the polygamous or potentially polygamous."[12] During the hearings of the commission the Kenya Minister of Health strongly supported the customary laws which permit polygamy; and at least one local branch of *Maendeleo ya Wanawake* (a society for the advancement of women) suggested that the number of wives should be limited to four.[13] "Women," they pointed out to the commission, "were normally willing to share a husband."[14] The report of the commission chairman was a surprise to few:

There is undoubtedly a considerable body of opinion in favour of retaining polygamy. Of those who oppose it, many thought it would be unwise to abolish it by law, believing it should be left to die out under the pressure of social and economic circumstances, particularly the cost of education and land shortage.[15]

A recent government "white paper" in Tanzania proposed that, with a view to eliminating any conflict between civil and religious law, even Christian marriages should be recognized as potentially polygamous.[16] An articulate and well-organized minority of Christians, who would question such a proposal, is assured of an adequate hearing. But the fact remains that the less articulate majority is made up of non-Christians who traditionally subscribe to plural marriage; and, in a religiously pluralistic society like Tanzania, Christians are not totally or even generally endogamous. In their initial reaction to this government proposal, the Roman Catholic bishops of Tanzania issued a mild statement which, while affirming that monogamy "pertains to the essence of Christian marriage," explicitly recognized that "it is not the Government's responsibility . . . to enforce religious laws as though they were the laws of the country."[17] Instead of trying to prove that Christian marriage is always and everywhere essentially monogamous, the statement was concerned simply with pointing out that monogamy is not a "foreign Western custom" standing over against "the traditional African way" of polygamy.

In any case, the problem of enforcing a new law of monogamy would be formidable in any country where traditional plural marriage is intimately bound up with the kinship systems, the norms of land tenure, inheritance regulations, social control, economic security, family continuity, notions of prestige, and so on. It must be remembered that the populations of sub-Saharan Africa are still predominantly rural and that, for economic reasons, they must continue to remain so in the foreseeable future. For economic development in this part of the world "must be based pre-eminently upon agriculture and industry associated therewith."[18] This means that the traditional social institutions and cultural values will continue to influence profoundly the lives of most people. The thinking of the relatively few educated and Christian elites in the cities, however well articulated and widely publicized, does not always reflect the thinking of the less "schooled" and non-Christian masses in the rural areas.

It is important to realize that African cities really are not, as some outside observers might imagine, melting pots that produce a homogeneous cultural pattern based on Western values and lifestyles. Exotic influences are tangible enough, to be sure. But the urban populations of Africa, especially as they tend to be grouped in ethnic (or tribal) ghettoes, are profoundly and extensively influenced by the much larger rural populations. Urbanization, first of all, is not everywhere in Africa a consequence of contact with the Western world. Particularly in parts of West Africa, city living is quite traditional. Some of the urban centers of the Yoruba, Hausa, and Mali peoples date back to the thirteenth century. The traditional towns and cities have, of course, grown rapidly during the past seventy-five years, while also many new cities have come into existence. Still, it is estimated that only about 9 percent of the population of sub-Saharan Africa is found in the urban areas.[19]

Moreover, there is a continuous flow of people, back and forth, between the urban and the rural areas. There is a considerable turnover of the city populations, as many people return to the rural villages after spending some time in the cities. "African urbanism," as William Schwab points out, "must be understood with regard to its overwhelming rural background."[20] Schwab continues:

> The average African lives in a small village and leads a life structured around personal relationships. Usually, he owes his economic, religious and social security and identity to a kin group, which controls and dominates his life. Without this kin group or lineage, the average African would be unable to satisfy his needs or be able to achieve the goals or opportunities that his cultural world provides for him. To an African his village and his kin group are the major factors controlling his behavior, and the great city is viewed as a distant and remote place of splendor and evil. . . . African cities are not only populated by village migrants, since so few are born in cities, but are islands in a sea of rurality and are surrounded by the conservative rural traditions which emanate from the villages.[21]

Whether we regard it as "fortunate" or not, all the evidence at hand suggests that the practice of polygamy is still very much "in harmony with the prevailing attitude of African peoples." As Barrett says, "it is clear that polygynous society will not disappear for some time to come."[22] Indeed, we may expect this custom to be defended, and even reaffirmed, among the 580 different peoples who accept it as a traditional social institution. "Hence," Barrett continues, "we can see that in those societies where the institution is or has been common, this factor will continue to be present as a powerful component of the Zeitgeist."[23] Another noted sociologist who shares this view is Aidan Southall:

> Africa remains a continent of polygamy. Polygamy is the undoubted goal of men in rural society, though comparatively few reach it until their later years. This is a built-in value for societies based on patrilineal descent groups. . . . Economic change has undermined the economic basis of the compound polygynous family in towns and other employment centers, but the early results of this have been that the same norms and values have found expression in new forms. The usual male reaction has been either to practice successive monogamy instead, which is certainly polygynous from the diachronic point of view, or to combine official monogamy with concubinage. . . . We are therefore justified in assuming that most Africans still consider that sexual access to a plurality of women is a male right. Islam supports this and Christian teaching has made little headway against it.[24]

Social change is inevitable always and everywhere, and the pace of change is manifestly rapid in many parts of Africa. But the vitality of traditional African cultures should not be underestimated. The old ways are not being simply obliterated in favor of a totally new culture imported from the West. What is going on may be better described as a fusion. The efforts to work out what is called "African socialism" exemplify this. What may seem to be merely an uncritical imitation should be seen, rather, as a process of borrowing and testing. There remains "a strong pulse of African life below the European clothes and forms," as Guy Hunter says, and he continues:

> Beneath the outward forms of change in marriage or Parliament or trade, there remains a world of contacts and understanding between Africans which is almost wholly hidden from European eyes. . . . Private messages that pass from man to man, the long branching channels through which social life and action flow, the unspoken assumptions, the ultimate reserves of energy and emotional force upon which an African will rely in a time of testing—these are deep currents in the stream of African life which the outside watcher sees only here and there when they break against a rock.[25]

NOTES

1. For evidence of this new openness among Anglicans, see the survey of current opinions and practices by Edward G. Newing, "The Baptism of Polygamous Families; Theory and Practice in an East African Church," *Journal of Religion in Africa* 2 (1970): 130–41. See also *The Lambeth Conference, 1968: Resolutions and Reports* (London and New York: SPCK and Seabury Press, 1968), p. 37, Resolution 23, which asks each province of the church to "re-examine its discipline" concerning polygamy and other such marriage problems.

2. See AMECEA Study Conference Record in *Pastoral Perspectives in Eastern Africa after Vatican II* (Nairobi, 1967), pp. 97–98 and appendix.

3. See "The Committee of Churches of Dar es Salaam on the Government's Proposals for a Uniform Law of Marriage," *Tanzania Standard*, November 28, 1969, pp. 4, 5, 9. This refers to the Tanzanian government's proposals, *Mapendekezo ya Serikali juu ya Sheria ya Ndoa* (Dar es Salaam: Government Printer, 1969), pp. 1–12.

4. "The Committee of Churches of Dar es Salaam," pp. 4, 5, 9.

5. Josiah Kibira, "The Church in Buhaya: Crossing Frontiers," in *The Church Crossing Frontiers: Essays on the Nature of Mission, in Honor of Bengt Sundkler* (Uppsala, Sweden: Boktryckeri Aktiebolag, 1969), p. 196. See also G. C. Oosthuizen, *Post-Christianity in Africa: A Theological and Anthropological Study* (London: C. Hurst and Co., 1968), p. 199, where the author quotes from a 1962 report prepared for the Christian Council of Nigeria: "Of all the problems that confront the Church in West Africa, polygamy is the most difficult with perhaps the least light. Like an ominous dark cloud it seems to haunt the Church in all areas."

6. Peter Sarpong, as quoted by Desmond O'Grady, "The Church in Africa: Coming into Its Own," *U.S. Catholic* 38 (February 1973): 32.

7. John Njenga, "Customary African Marriage," *African Ecclesiastical Review* 16 (1974): 120.

8. See Appendix II, under the heading "Marriage and the Christian Family," *African Ecclesiastical Review* 16 (1974): 260.

9. See Anthony Allott, "Legal Systems in Africa," in *Africa: A Handbook to the Continent*, ed. Colin Legum (New York and Washington: Praeger, 1966), p. 435.

10. See David B. Barrett, "A.D. 2000: 350 Million Christians in Africa," *International Review of Mission* 59 (January 1970): 41–47. This estimate, it must be noted, includes the expected membership of the numerous and rapidly growing African "independent" churches, many of which accept the custom of polygyny.

11. See J. F. Salacuse, "Developments in African Law," *Africa Report* 13 (March 1968): 39–40; and Allott, "Legal Systems in Africa," p. 434. According to Remi Clignet, Tunisia has also enacted legislation against polygamy, while only two sub-Saharan African countries have taken such action: Ivory Coast and Guinea (*Many Wives, Many Powers: Authority and Power in Polygynous Families* [Evanston, Ill.: Northwestern University Press [1970], p. 5).

12. Kenya Government, *Report of the Commission on the Law of Marriage and Divorce* (Nairobi: Government Printer, 1968), p. 23.

13. Kenya News Agency, report in *Daily Nation* (Nairobi), September 14, 1967, p. 4. Still, it seems reasonable to assume that an increasing number of African women, perhaps even a majority of those who pass through Western-style schools, will no longer regard polygyny as a preferential form of marriage. However, the fact that many

educated men tend to support the custom of polygyny is highly significant; cf. Aidan Southall, "The Position of Women and the Stability of Marriage," in *Social Change in Modern Africa*, ed. Aidan Southall (London: Oxford University Press, 1961), p. 53: "In general, the traditional male values persist in only slightly modified form, strengthened by Islam and to an increasing extent condoned by western secular opinion, while Christian orthodoxy has made little headway against them. The impact of female criticism of male behaviours is slight because of the political dominance of men. But male criticism of laxity in female behaviour carries considerable weight, backed by traditional values, Islamic and Christian teaching." According to Clignet, *Many Wives, Many Powers*, p. 33, the schooling of girls is the only social change that has had a negative effect on polygyny.

14. Kenya Government, *Report on the Law of Marriage*, p. 4.

15. Mr. Justice Spry, as quoted by Moya Neeld, "Many Favor Polygamy," *Daily Nation* (Nairobi), December 1, 1967, p. 1.

16. See R.W. Apple, Jr., "No. 1 Topic in Tanzania," *New York Times*, October 9, 1969, p. 18; and also "Tanzania Debates Polygamy," *Christian Science Monitor*, October 27, 1969, p. 2.

17. Catholic bishops of Tanzania, "Draft Statement" (in response to Tanzania government proposals for a uniform marriage law), *Pastoral Orientation Service*, no. 8 (Mwanza: Bukumbi Pastoral Institute, 1969), p. 4.

18. John Phillips, *Agriculture and Ecology in Africa: A Study of Actual and Potential Development in Africa South of the Sahara* (London: Faber and Faber, 1959), p. 376. See also Melville J. Herskovits, *The Human Factor in Changing Africa* (New York: Knopf, 1962), p. 148; Guy Hunter, *New Societies of Tropical Africa* (London: Oxford University Press, 1962), pp. 50–51, 59–60; and René Dumont, *False Start in Africa*, trans. Phyllis N. Ott (New York: Praeger, 1966).

19. Cf. William B. Schwab, "Urbanism, Corporate Groups and Culture Change in Africa below the Sahara," *Anthropological Quarterly* 43 (July 1970): 187.

20. Ibid., p. 190.

21. Ibid.

22. Barrett, *Schism and Renewal in Africa* (Nairobi: Oxford University Press, 1968), p. 241.

23. Ibid. See also Schwab, "Urbanism," p. 200: ". . .and polygyny, although curtailed, has not been greatly reduced as it is still preferred by men. Most children continue to be reared in the traditional compound with the socialization process of the child remaining as one of the primary functions of the lineage."

24. Southall, "Position of Women," p. 52. See also the general conclusions of Clignet's extensive study of African polygamy, *Many Wives, Many Powers*, p. 259: "that participation associated with an immediate decline in the incidence of polygynous arrangements."

25. Hunter, *New Societies*, p. 92. See also Bernard Magubane, "A Critical Look at the Indices Used in the Study of Social Change in Colonial Africa," *Current Anthropology* 12 (October-December 1971): 431: "Where two cultures, differing in their technological development, meet, adjustments are inevitable. Yet the culture that is 'inferior' in terms of technology does not simply yield to the other. The two cultures yield to one another, undergoing profound modifications."

21

Desmond Tutu

Black Theology/African Theology—
Soul Mates or Antagonists?

Desmond Tutu urges that proponents of black theology and of African theology view each other as friends, not enemies. "Black Theology/African Theology — Soul Mates or Antagonists?" is taken from Gayraud S. Wilmore and James H. Cone, eds., Black Theology. A Documentary History, 1966–1979 *(Maryknoll, N.Y.: Orbis Books, 1979), pp. 483–91. The essay was first published in 1975.*

This consultation being held at this time [1974] at the University of Ghana, Accra, between black American theologians and churchmen and their African counterparts is a welcome sequel to a similar consultation on African and black theology which was held in New York in June 1973 under the auspices of the All-Africa Conference of Churches and the Society for the Study of Black Religion. But already in August 1971 a meeting between a similar group of black Americans and East Africans had taken place sponsored by the National Conference of Black Churchmen and the Council of Churches of Tanzania in Dar es Salaam. The papers delivered at that first consultation are available in paperback.[1]

I have referred to these past occasions because the series of consultations reflects a noteworthy phenomenon—a new and deep desire for black persons to find each other, to know one another as brothers and sisters because we belong to one another. We are bound together by close bonds on three levels at least.

We are united willy nilly by our blackness (of all shades). Now some may feel

256

squeamish about this apparently excessive awareness of our skin color. But are we not in fact so bound? If anyone of us assembled here today goes into a situation where racial discrimination is practiced would he or she ever escape the humiliation and indignity that are heaped on us simply because we are black, no matter whether we are native to that situation or not? Our blackness is an intractable ontological surd. You cannot will it away. It is a brute fact of existence and it conditions that existence as surely as being male or female, only more so. But would we have it otherwise? For it is not a lamentable fact. No, far from it. It is not a lamentable fact because I believe that it affords us the glorious privilege and opportunity to further the gospel of love, forgiveness, and reconciliation—the gospel of Jesus Christ—in a way that is possible to no other group, as I hope to show later.

The second level of unity between us is this. All of us are bound to Africa by invisible but tenacious bonds. It has nurtured the deepest things in us as blacks. All of us have roots that go deep in the warm soil of Africa; so that no matter how long and traumatic our separation from our ancestral home has been, there are things we are often unable to articulate, but which we feel in our very bones, things which make us, who are different from others who have no roots in Africa. Do not most of us, for instance, find the classical arguments for the existence of God just an interesting cerebral game because Africa taught us long ago that life without belief in a supreme divine Being was just too absurd to contemplate? And do not most of us thrill as we approach the awesomeness of the transcendent when many other of our contemporaries find even the word God an embarrassment? How do you explain our shared sense of the corporateness of life, of our rejection of Hellenistic dichotomies in our insistence that life, material and spiritual, secular and sacred, that it is all of a piece? Many characteristics of our contemporary African and American music, religion, culture, and so on can be explained adequately only by reference to a common heritage and common source in the past. We cannot deny too that most of us have had an identical history of exploitation through colonialism and neocolonialism, that when we were first evangelized we often came through the process having learned to despise things black and African because these were usually condemned by others. The worst crime that can be laid at the door of the white person (who, it must be said, has done many a worthwhile and praiseworthy thing for which we are always thankful) is not our economic, social, and political exploitation, however reprehensible that might be; no, it is that the whites' policy succeeded in filling most of us with a self-disgust and self-hatred. This has been the most violent form of colonialism, our spiritual and mental enslavement when we have suffered from what can only be called a religious or spiritual schizophrenia. What I said in an unpublished paper, titled "Whither African Theology?" of the African is largely true too of the black American.

Up to fairly recently, the African Christian has suffered from a form of religious schizophrenia. With part of himself he has been compelled first to pay lip service to Christianity as understood, expressed and preached by the white man. But with an ever greater part of himself, a part he has been ashamed to acknowledge openly and which he has struggled to repress, he has felt that his Africanness has been violated. The white man's largely cerebral religion was hardly touching the depths of his African soul; he was being given answers, and often splendid answers to questions he had not asked.

Speaking about this split in the African soul, J. C. Thomas writes:

The African in fact seems to find himself living at two levels in every aspect of his life. First, there is the western influence on him from two different quarters: there is the influence inherited from the period of colonial rule; but also the inevitable influence of post colonial industrial- ization and education. Secondly, there is the influence of his traditional culture and upbringing that gives many Africans the sense that they have a unique culture of their own which gives them an identity as Africans. Yet it appears inevitable that in some areas traditional culture will be abandoned if African states are to become self-sufficient economically and so free of dependence on foreign aid and trade.[2]

The third level of unity comes through our baptism and through our membership in the body of Christ which makes us all his ambassadors and partakers in the ministry of reconciliation. As a consequence of our impera- tives of the gospel and being constrained by the love of God in Jesus Christ, we cannot but be concerned to declare the whole counsel of God as much to white people as to our own black communities. We are compelled to help the white person to correct many of the distortions that have happened to the gospel to the detriment of all. To paraphrase what Manas Buthelezi from South Africa once said: God will say to the black person: "Where were you when the white man did this to my Gospel?" We are together involved in a common task and we are engaged in a single quest. After this preamble let us return to the subject of this paper.

BLACK THEOLOGY/AFRICAN THEOLOGY— ARE THEY COMPATIBLE?

Are black theology and African theology related or are they quite distinct and even incompatible entities? John Mbiti, an outstanding theologian, is quite clear in his own mind about the answer to the question. In a recent article, Mbiti has this to say: "But Black Theology cannot and will not become African Theology."[3] He can be so categorical because, to quote from the article again: "The concerns of Black Theology differ considerably from those of African Theology. The latter grows out of our joy and experience of the Christian faith, whereas Black Theology emerges from the pains of oppression." He seems to imply at an earlier point without being explicit that black theology is perhaps not quite Christian: "One would hope that theology arises out of spontaneous joy in being a Christian, responding to life and ideas as one redeemed. Black Theology, however, is full of sorrow, bitterness, anger and hatred."[4] But is this borne out by a study of the history of Christian doctrine? Most New Testament commentators appear to agree that the Epistle to the Galatians was written when Paul was very angry and yet in the Galatians he develops the theology of justification by faith. And what would we make of the theology that occurs in the Christian Apocalypse of St. John the Divine? There was no oppression, no anger, and not even hatred of the oppressor, and yet this book has found its way, admittedly after a long struggle, into the Christian canon. Professor Mbiti is unhappy with black theology mainly because it is concerned too much with blackness and liberation. To quote again:

> Of course Black Theology addresses itself also to other themes, such as the Church, the Community, the Bible, the World, Man, Violence and Ethics. But the treatment of these topics is subservient to the overriding emphasis on blackness and liberation as they relate to Jesus Christ and God.[5]

Another African, this time a young theologian, J. Ndwiga Mugambi, writes concerning liberation and theology as follows:

> Liberation is the objective task of a contemporary African Christian theology. It is not just one of the issues, but rather, all issues are aimed at liberating Africans from all forces that hinder them from living fully as human beings.
> In the African context, and in the Bible, SALVATION as a theological concept cannot be complete without LIBERATION as a social/political concept.[6]

I will have something to say on this issue later.

I contend that there are very close similarities between African theology and black theology. Both to my way of thinking have arisen as reactions against an unacceptable state of affairs. Most people would agree that the most potent impetus for the development of an African Christian theology has come because Christianity came swathed in Western garb. Most Western missionaries in the early days found it difficult if not virtually impossible to distinguish between the Christian faith and Western civilization. No less a person than Robert Moffat could say:

> Satan has employed his agency with fatal success, in erasing every vestige of religious impression from the minds of the Bechuana, Hottentots and Bushmen; leaving them without a single ray to guide them from the dark and drab futurity, or a single link to unite them to the skies.[7]

And if this was how you felt then it was logical to pursue a policy of the root and branch condemnation of things African, which had to be supplanted by their obviously superior Western counterparts. It was as if Robertson Smith had never written as he did in his *Religion of the Semites:*

> No positive religion that has moved man has been able to start with a *tabula rasa* to express itself as if religion was beginning for the first time; in form if not in substance, the new system must be in contact along the line with the old ideas and practices which it finds in possession. A new scheme of faith can find a hearing only by appealing to a religious instinct and susceptibility that already exists in its audience and it cannot reach these without taking account of the traditional forms in which religious feeling is embodied, and without speaking a language which men accustomed to these forms can understand.

The African religious consciousness and Weltanschauung were not acknowledged as possessing much validity or value. Much the same comment could be made of the black American experience. The blacks in America had their humanity defined in the terms of the whites. To be really human blacks had to see themselves and be seen as chocolate-colored whites. Their humanity was stunted. It is against this deplorable condition that both African and black theology have reacted. They stake the claim for the personhood and humanity of the African and Afro-American, for anything less than this is blasphemy against God who created us as we are in God's own image, not to be carbon copies of others of God's creatures no matter how advanced or prosperous they might conceive themselves to be. Some might feel ashamed that the most serious enterprise in which they have engaged should be characterized as a reaction rather than resulting from their own initiative. But there is no need for such a negative response. Much of the development of Christian dogma may be shown to resemble the oscillations of a pendulum. When Hegelian idealism was the philosophy of the day, Christian theology, not remaining unaffected, moved very far in the direction of immanentism. Against this trend a reaction set in exemplified by the stress on transcendence as in the theology of Karl Barth. In its turn, this emphasis on transcendence provoked the reaction that spoke about "a beyond in our midst" as in John Robinson's *Honest to God.* Perhaps today we are beginning to discern a tentative groping towards a renewed sense of awe and mystery. And this would be as yet another reaction.

More positively we could say that African theology and black theology are an assertion that we should take the incarnation seriously. Christianity to be truly African must be incarnated in Africa. It must speak in tones that strike a responsive chord in the African breast and must convict the Africans of their peculiar African sinfulness. It must not provide them with answers to questions they have never asked. It must speak out of and to their own context. Christ came to fulfill, not to destroy. Christianity should be seen as fulfilling the highest and best in the spiritual and religious aspirations of blacks and yet stand in judgment of all that diminishes them and makes them less than what God intended them to be.

African and black theology provide a sharp critique of the way in which theology has been done mostly in the North Atlantic world. Westerners usually call for an ecumenical, a universal theology which they often identify with their brand of theologizing. Now this is thoroughly erroneous. Western theology is no more universal than other brands of theology can ever hope to be. For theology can never properly claim a universality which rightly belongs only to the eternal gospel of Jesus Christ. Theology is a human activity possessing the limitations and the particularities of those who are theologizing. It can speak relevantly only when it speaks to a particular, historically and spatio-temporally conditioned Christian community: and it must have the humility to accept the scandal of its particularity as well as its transience. Theology is not eternal nor can it ever hope to be perfect. There is no final theology. Of course the true insights of each theology must have universal relevance, but theology gets distorted if it sets out from the very beginning to speak or attempt to speak universally. Christ is the Universal Person only because He is first and foremost a real and therefore a particular Person. There must therefore of necessity be a diversity of theologies and our unity arises because ultimately we all are reflecting on the one divine activity to set mankind free from all that enslaves it. There must be a plurality of theologies because we do not all apprehend the transcendent in exactly the same way nor can we be expected to express our experience in the same way. On this point, Maurice Wiles writes:

> Theology today is inductive and empirical in approach. It is the ever changing struggle to give expression to man's response to God. It is always inadequate and provisional. Variety is to be welcomed because no one approach can ever do justice to the transcendent reality of God; our partial expressions need to be complemented by the different apprehensions of those whose traditions are other than our own. There are no fixed criteria for the determination of theological truth and error. We ought therefore to be ready to tolerate a considerable measure even of what seems to us to be error, for we cannot be certain that it is we who are right. On this view a wide range of theological difference (even including what we regard as error) is not in itself a barrier to unity.[8]

African theology has given the lie to the belief that worthwhile religion in Africa had to await the advent of the white person. Similar to African history, African theology has done a wonderful service in rehabilitating the African religious consciousness. Both African and black theology have been firm repudiations of the tacit claim that white is right, white is best. In their own ways these theologies are giving the black person a proper pride in things black and African. Only thus can we ever be able to make our distinctive contributions to the kingdom of God. We must love and serve God in our own way. We cannot do it as honorary whites. And so black and African theology have contributed to those exhilarating movements of our day, black and African consciousness. Both say we must provide our source for theologizing. They seek to be effective instruments in bringing about change not merely as academic exercises. I may be wrong, but at these levels, I see remarkable similarities between African theology and black theology and I contend that they have a great deal to learn from one another and to give to each other. But there are obvious differences.

Context

There must be differences because the two theologies arise in a sense from different contexts. African theology on the whole can probably afford to be a little more leisurely (I am not convinced of this) because Africa by and large is politically independent (but is it really free?). There is not the same kind of oppression which is the result of white racism except in southern Africa (soon it may only be South Africa the way things seem to be developing in the subcontinent, and God let the day soon come when all of Africa will be truly free). Black theology arises in the context of black suffering at the hands of rampant white racism. And consequently black theology is much concerned to make sense theologically out of the black experience whose main ingredient is the suffering in and the light of God's self-revelation in the man, Jesus Christ. It is concerned with the significance of black existence, with liberation, with a meaning of reconciliation, with humanization, with forgiveness. It is much more aggressive and abrasive in its assertions because of a burning and evangelistic zeal necessary to convert black persons out of the stupor of their subservience and obsequiousness to acceptance of the thrilling but demanding responsibility of full human personhood—to make them reach out to the glorious liberty of the sons and daughters of God. It burns to awake white persons to the degradation into which they have fallen by dehumanizing the black person and so is concerned for the liberation of the oppressor equally with that of the oppressed. I am not quite sure that I understand what Professor Mbiti in the article I have referred to means when he says that people in Southern Africa "want and need liberation, not a theology of liberation." Could we not say the same things about a theology of hope, that what people want is hope, not a theology of hope?

Black theology is more thoroughly and explicitly political than African theology is. It cannot be lulled into complacency by a doctrine of pie in the sky which is a reprehensible travesty of the gospel of the incarnation. It has an existential urgency which African theology has so far appeared to lack. African theology has tended to be more placid, to be interested still too much with what I call anthropological concerns. This has been its most important achievement in the quest for indigenization.

CONCLUSION

I myself believe I am an exponent of black theology coming as I do from South Africa. I believe I am also an exponent of African theology coming as I do from Africa. I contend that black theology is like the inner and smaller circle in a series of concentric circles. I would not care to cross swords with such a formidable person as John Mbiti, but I and others from South Africa *do* black theology, which is for us, at this point, African theology.

But I fear that African theology has failed to produce a sufficiently sharp cutting edge. It has indeed performed a good job by addressing the split in the African soul and yet it has by and large failed to speak meaningfully in the face of a plethora of contemporary problems which assail the modern African. It has seemed to advocate disengagement from the hectic business of life because very little has been offered that is pertinent, say, about the theology of power in the face of the epidemic of coups and military rule, about development, about poverty and disease and other equally urgent present-day issues. I believe this is where the abrasive black theology may have a few lessons for African theology. It may help to recall African theology to its vocation to be concerned for the poor and the oppressed, about people's need for liberation from all kinds of bondage to enter into an authentic personhood which is constantly under-mined by a pathological religiosity and by political authority which has whit-tled away much personal freedom without too much opposition from the church. In short, African theology will have to recover its prophetic calling. It can happen only when a radical spiritual decolonization occurs within each exponent of African theology. Too many of us have been brainwashed effec-tively to think that the Westerners' value system and categories are of universal validity. We are too much concerned to maintain standards which Cambridge or Harvard or Montpelier have set even when these are utterly inappropriate for our situations. We are still too docile and look to the metropolis for approval to do our theology, for instance, in a way that would meet with the approval of the West. We are still too much concerned to play the game according to white people's rules when they often are the referees as well. Why should we feel that something is amiss if our theology is too dramatic for verbalization but can express itself adequately only in the joyous song and movement of Africa's dance in the liturgy? Let us develop our insights about the corporateness of human existence in the face of excessive Western individu-alism, about the wholeness of the person when others are concerned for Hellenistic dichotomies of soul and body, about the reality of the spiritual when others are made desolate with the poverty of the material. Let African theology enthuse about the awesomeness of the transcendent when others are embar-rassed to speak about the king, high and lifted up, whose train fills the temple. It is only when African theology is true to itself that it will go on to speak relevantly to the contemporary African—surely its primary task—and also, incidentally, make its valuable contribution to the rich Christian heritage which belongs to all of us.

NOTES

1. *Black Faith and Black Solidarity: Pan Africanism and Faith in Christ*, ed. Priscilla Massie (New York: Friendship Press, 1973).

2. J. C. Thomas, "What Is African Theology?" *Ghana Bulletin of Theology* 4, no. 4 (June 1973): 15.

3. John Mbiti, "An African Views American Black Theology," in *Black Theology: A Documentary History, 1966–1979*, ed. Gayraud S. Wilmore and James H. Cone (Maryknoll, N.Y.: Orbis Books, 1979), p. 481.

4. Ibid., p. 478.

5. Ibid., p. 480.

6. J. Ndwiga Mugambi, *World Student Christian Federation Dossier*, no. 5 (June 1974): 41–42.

7. Cited in E. W. Smith, *African Ideas of God* (London: Edinburgh House, 1966), p. 83.

8. Maurice Wiles, "Theology and Unity," *Theology* 77, no. 643 (January 1974): 4.

22

Allan Boesak

Liberation Theology in South Africa

Allan Boesak maintains that liberation theology in South Africa can be understood only in its own racial and political context. "Liberation Theology in South Africa" is taken from Appiah-Kubi and Torres, eds., African Theology En Route *(Maryknoll, N.Y.: Orbis Books, 1979), pp. 169–75. The paper was presented at the Pan-African Conference of Third World Theologians in Accra, Ghana, in 1977.*

A NEW CONSCIOUSNESS

We cannot understand liberation theology, whether in South Africa, in Latin America, or in other parts of the Third World, unless we understand that it developed within a framework of a new political consciousness. People became aware, first of all, of their own situations. There was a new consciousness of themselves, of where they were, of the political, social, and economic dynamics in their situations. When people began to understand their situations, they started asking questions they had never asked before.

In the theological tradition in which I grew up, a solid Dutch Reformed tradition with its Calvinist theology, we were never given a real understanding of our situation. This tradition never gave us an understanding of ourselves, and, therefore, there was never room to ask the vital kinds of existential and theological questions that should be asked if we want to say something theologically that would make sense of our situation.

The first question that we ask when we get this new consciousness is: WHY? In asking WHY? we begin to discover that we have lived through a theological tradition that, although it was our own, was really never our own. It has always been controlled by people who also control the political parties, the economic and social situation, our very lives. In South Africa we have a particular situation that we call "apartheid." Apartheid is not only a political system; it is not only an economic and social system. It is also a theological reality. Perhaps the distinction of color is stressed, but just the same "apartheid" is a religion, just as all forms of racism become religions.

The new consciousness that I'm talking about, which gave rise to the development of a liberation theology in South Africa, is a human consciousness that we call black consciousness. Through black consciousness black people discover that they are children of God and that they have rights to exist in God's world. Black people discover that they are part of history, and they share this history with God, which means that they are responsible to act as human persons. The situation in South Africa did not happen just accidentally. It did not just come about. The situation was created by people. It is a system that is still being maintained by people through various methods. Black consciousness says to black people that they are human, that they are children of God. Black consciousness gives black people a clear realization of the situation in South Africa and of the negation of their human "beingness." When black people see clearly that they are black and are children of God, then they can be proud.

But why is it then that this very blackness is the reason for their oppression? Black people in South Africa are not being oppressed because they are Muslims, or because they are Methodists, or because they are wayward Presbyterians or Dutch Reformed; they are being oppressed because they are black, because they are not born white. Whiteness is tantamount to human "beingness." If one is not white, one is not human. Nobody has to deal with a black person on the level of a human being. Can a Christian in a Christian country with a host of Christian churches speak and preach about the sanctity of family life and about the responsibility of parents and children and at the same time vote for a government and sustain and aid a system that gives theological justification to laws that maintain that black people cannot live together as husband and wife?

In 1973, hundreds of children were sent away from their parents in Johannesburg back to some homeland, where it was claimed they ought to be, back to grandparents or to aunts or to whatever relatives they had—but away from their parents. A reporter of one of the English-speaking newspapers asked the Bantu Administration Board, "Why are you doing this? These are children you are sending away from their parents." The white officer in charge of this operation said, "Well, you know, you must try to understand that these black women are not the same as our women. They really do not feel bad when we send their children away, because, you see, they do not see things the same way as we do. They are really very happy when we relieve them of the burden of having to care for their children so that they can work uninterruptedly for the white madams they work for." That was in 1973.

Last year the government demolished the squatter homes of people where I work and live in Bellville, in Motterdam. This move rendered thirteen thousand people homeless, even if their homes had been shacks of tin and cardboard and wood. Another official of the Bantu Administration said, "Well, you see, you've got to understand black Africans to understand the action of the government. They do not value family life the same way as we Christian people do." Whiteness is equal to human beingness; blackness is less than that and therefore less than human. I could spend two or three hours reciting the different laws that would substantiate this statement.

When I discover that God has made me a human being though I am not white, it means that I have a right to be here; I have a right to exist; I am not less in God's eyes. I believe in God. God has sent the Son for me, and when the word became flesh, God became a human being. God became like me. God shared the same feelings that I share. When we begin to understand this, we begin to ask the question, What am I then? White law says that I am not a human being. What do you do when you are black and you are a Christian and the people who oppress you say that they are Christians also? They also pray and they also read the Bible. For black Christians, however, the gospel is the incomparable word of liberation, while for white Christians it is an instrument from which they derive a theological justification for the system that oppresses blacks. How is this possible?

When we begin to ask these questions, we then begin to realize that the traditional theology, or what we call "white" theology, has never really asked these questions because it could not. It has never had any room for the questions we are asking because it never had any room for the sufferings of black people.

The simple question now becomes: Whom do I obey and to what extent? What is my duty as a Christian? If you ask that in a white church, the response is: "Let every person be subject to the government authorities."

In a white church, or on the radio, it is the most natural thing in the world for a white minister to pray for our Christian government: "Thank God for the Christian government that we've got." But when we black South Africans pray about the government, our prayer is for deliverance.

A SITUATIONAL THEOLOGY

Black liberation theology is a situational theology. All theology has always been situational; it has always been theology in context. The only new thing that we have discovered is that it is theological foolishness (and I am not sure whether that is equal to sinfulness) to say that what is good for the situation in Germany as discovered by a good German Reform theologian is good also for the situation in North America and therefore good also for the situation in South Africa. Each theological concept develops within a particular context, and our theological thinking—the way we read the gospel, the way we understand the gospel, the way we interpret the gospel, the way we interpret our situation in the light of the gospel—has everything to do with what we eat and how many times a day we eat, what salary we earn, whether we own a home, whether we live happily with our family, and so on. The situation in which we live, the context in which we live, profoundly influences the way we do our theology.

Even Abram Kuyper (and there was a time when those of us who are good Reformed theologians used to swear by Abram Kuyper although some people swore at him) said in a very important essay on the Reformed Social Congress of 1899 that persons who are employers will never understand the situation and the longings and the desires of those they employ because the employers do not share the situation in which their employees live.

There is a clear line of demarcation between how blacks live in South Africa and how whites live there. Everybody knows that South Africa is not a democracy, but it is not full dictatorship either. We might become that in a few years, but now we are what I would call a "pigmentoracy," whereby people are given rights and privileges according to the color of their skin. At the very top of the social ladder in South Africa we have the white South Africans. They have everything: all the economic, social, and political privileges. They vote and they have a very high standard of living. Next there are the colored South Africans: the Asians, the Indians, and so on. This is a clear, politically recognized category in South Africa, whether one is "colored," or "Cape colored," or "other colored." At the very bottom of the social ladder is what the government calls the Bantu, the *African* people.

Black consciousness makes black people look at the situation. What is a "colored"? The law says that a colored person is one obviously not white and obviously not Bantu. This means we do not know what we are. We are people of mixed blood. My mother had white skin but my father was very, very dark with very clear African ancestry. For white South Africans that is the most terrible thing to be, of mixed blood. To be a "colored" is therefore not only a political category. It is an economic and a psychological category.

Those at the bottom of the social ladder have almost nothing in South Africa, no property rights, no rights to live with their families or children. They have to carry passbooks. But the "colored," because they have some white blood, share white people's culture to a large extent and speak their language, either Afrikaans or English. We listen to their music and we share their religious concepts. We are therefore more civilized and have more rights to more things than the Africans. I may own property in South Africa, but an African cannot. I may live with my wife and my children, but an African cannot. This special situation has been a creation of the white people, who tell us who we are and where we belong. They call us the "brown" people. Black consciousness says this is nonsense.

As Christians we identify with the least in our society. Therefore we are black South Africans also and do not speak of "coloreds." We tell the government time and again that we refuse to accept privileges that they are willing to give to us but not to the rest of the black community.

This is our situation and all the elements in it have a theological significance. If we have a theology that does not take into account this oppressive situation and the hundreds of oppressive laws then we cannot be authentic. We are not true to ourselves, not true to our situation, and ultimately not true to the gospel itself. A theology that does not take into account this situation will never be able to interpret the demands of the gospel or to say what the Spirit has to say to the people in this situation. This is why we have a black theology; that is why it is a situational theology.

Black theology, therefore, because it comes from a situation of oppression and suffering of a people that believes in God and that asks what the gospel of Jesus Christ has to say about the situation, is also a theology of liberation.

THE EXODUS THEME

The themes of liberation theology that have become so important to black and Amerindian Christians in the United States and to people in Asia and Latin America are the same themes that run through black liberation theology in South Africa. The Exodus is our model also, but we are not really saying that we expect that through some miracle God today will re-enact the Exodus as it was acted out before. God will not do that because black people in South Africa are not going anywhere. We are staying, so we have no Red Sea to cross. But neither do we want white people in South Africa to cross any sea. We want them to stay, but not as they are now. What we need is a spiritual and a political Exodus out of the situation of oppression toward a situation of liberation, out of the situation of inhumanity, darkness, and hatred toward a situation in which we, both whites and blacks, can regain our common humanity and enjoy a meaningful life, a wholeness of life that has been destroyed.

When he began his ministry Jesus Christ did not draw a thick line between the Old Testament and the New, but rather he stood squarely within the tradition of the Exodus and the prophets of the Old Testament. The theme of liberation in the Old Testament became the same theme in the New Testament proclamation of Jesus Christ, and there is no way that you can speak of the gospel without speaking of liberation. In the beginning of his ministry Jesus Christ makes that very, very clear in the temple of Nazareth. His quotation from Isaiah 61 goes back to what Old Testament scholars have called "the actualization of the Exodus" throughout the Old Testament. The Exodus became the basis of the action of God and the action that God expects from the people of God.

The Exodus is not an isolated event; it is the beginning of a movement all through history, whether it is the Israelites over against the Pharaoh and the Egyptians or the poor and the widow and the orphan over against the rich and the powerful within Israel. Jesus Christ announced and accomplished what Yahweh was doing from the very beginning. The whole book of Genesis is no more than a prologue to this central event of the Exodus that would set the tune and pace of all that Yahweh would be doing for Yahweh's people right through

Exodus

to the New Testament. And the same God who listened to the people who called upon God's name and delivered them is able and willing to do the same in our situation today if we call upon God's name and believe that God will indeed liberate us.

CONCERNS OF LIBERATION THEOLOGY IN SOUTH AFRICA

But

In conclusion let me mention just a few concerns of liberation theology in South Africa today. First, we must understand that our concern is not merely to liberate people; it is also to liberate the gospel. We have read the parable of the man who goes out and sows his seeds, and some fall on rocky ground and others on the road. The parable is essentially trying to indicate vulnerability of the word and even of the reality of the kingdom.

In a certain sense, God is made vulnerable in the word by giving the word to us and saying, "Go out there and proclaim it." Few know better than the black people what has happened to the proclamation of the word. We simply have to refer to our own history and to what is happening in my country right now. The question that black people now put to the churches and the question that we are grappling with is really this: Is the gospel of Jesus Christ indeed the gospel of liberation and hope for me, or is it to remain an instrument of oppression in the hands of white people to use over the blacks? That is why I say that one of the concerns of liberation theology in South Africa is to liberate the gospel, so that that truth might come out and people might understand it.

But

A second concern of liberation theology is the integrity of the Christian church and its ongoing witness in South Africa and all over the world. The South African Christian church is not isolated; we are bound to the other churches by sharing the same faith, the same confession, the same baptism, and the same belief in God and God's Son.

Concern (But)

A third concern of liberation theology in South Africa is that we should understand what liberation means for South Africa. One of the things that we have to fight is a long tradition of Western theological dominance in South Africa. This has introduced into African thinking and way of life a kind of dualism that we had never known and an individualism that has been very detrimental, not only to the gospel but to the church and to our very human existence. Black people must understand that when they say, "I've got Jesus, then I'm all right," they are not all right. They have to understand that when we believe in Jesus Christ it does not make us immigrants out of history. In fact it places us right back within the world, in the middle of history, and that is the place where we have to proclaim his name.

We must understand what liberation means for the African. And this means that we have got to bring back what has been a reality in African heritage and African traditional thinking for centuries, namely, the concept of the wholeness of life, which is also a biblical concept. We have to move again to the sabbatical year. One of the striking things in the passage on the sabbatical year, which is also very striking in the ministry of Jesus Christ, is the wholeness of God's liberation. It begins with the rest of the land and a renewed devotion to Yahweh, and it ends with the rest of the land. In between there are people and exiles and deaths and property; not one single aspect of the life of Israel is not touched and judged thoroughly by God's proclamation of liberation in the sabbatical year. We have to bring back this wholeness, which has been in Africa for a long, long time.

The fourth concern of liberation theology in South Africa is our own situation. We must make a proper social analysis. I believe that as real and as ugly as racism is in our country, it is neither the only question nor the ultimate question. Racism has been a tool for the oppression of people whether white, black, or whatever. But beyond the question of race lies the economic question. This is one of the things I have learned from our brothers and sisters from Latin America. If we do not take cognizance of the economic question, liberation theology will fizzle out and die before we start. We have to make a proper analysis of the realities of power and powerlessness.

The final concern of liberation theology in South Africa is the contribution that African traditional thinking and African traditional religion can make to our contemporary thinking and theology. I believe that both our traditional religion and our traditional thinking have a liberating and humanizing word to say to our situation.

23

Allan Boesak

Black and Reformed:
Contradiction or Challenge?

In this address Boesak contends that the black version of the Reformed tradition is more authentic than the Afrikaner version. "Black and Reformed: Contradiction or Challenge?" is taken from Allan Boesak, Black and Reformed *(Maryknoll, N.Y.: Orbis Books, 1984), pp. 83–99. The address was first presented in October 1981.*

The Reformed tradition in South Africa is more than three hundred years old. It was brought here by Dutch Calvinists, who were followed by French Huguenots, and still later by Scottish Presbyterians and Swiss missionaries. When our Khoi ancestors were confronted with Christianity for the first time, it was the Reformed expression of it that they experienced. It was this tradition that was to have a lasting impact on the history of South Africa and on the lives of all its citizens. When our ancestors accepted Christianity three centuries ago, they became the members of a Reformed church.

Yet this history is racked with contradictions. The Europeans who claimed this land, who scattered and killed its people, did it in the name of a Christian God whom they prayed to as Reformed Christians. When they introduced slavery and enforced it with the most vicious forms of dehumanization and violence, it was the Bible read through Reformed eyes and arguments from the Reformed tradition that gave them justification for such acts of violence and human tragedy. The God of the Reformed tradition was the God of slavery, fear, persecution, and death. Yet, for those black Christians this was the God to whom they had to turn for comfort, for justice, for peace.

It was of Reformed Christians that a Dutch pastor of the nineteenth century spoke when he wrote:

> How is it possible that there could be any religious or, let me say, human feeling in persons who force their servants, mostly children of blacks shot dead, to sleep outside without any protection whatsoever in these cold nights, so that these unhappy wretches cover themselves with ashes, thereby inflicting upon themselves terrible burns. . . ? How can there be any religious or even human feeling in persons—big strong men—who beat these children mercilessly with whips at the slightest provocation, or even without any reason at all. . . ? God knows, and I myself know, what indescribable injustices occur in these parts! What gruesome ill-treatment, oppression, murder![1]

And yet these were persons who were supposed to be brothers and sisters in Christ, persons who were supposed to form with others the one body of Christ in his church—the Reformed church.

The contradictions did not disappear as time went on. On the contrary, they multiplied. Today, three hundred years later, black Reformed Christians come together to ask the question: What does it mean to be black and Reformed in South Africa today? It is a question that not only concerns our past. It concerns our present also, and it has a direct and fundamental bearing on our future. Indeed, one can put the question in another way: Does the Reformed tradition have a future in South Africa?

APARTHEID: HERITAGE OF THE REFORMED TRADITION

Today, no less than three centuries ago, being both black and Reformed is an expression of a painful paradox. Reformed Christians have the power in this country, as they did three hundred years ago. Now, as then, they call themselves Christians, and they proudly announce that they stand within the Reformed tradition. Through the power of the gun and sheer trickery they have claimed for themselves 87 percent of this land and they call it "white South Africa." Their avarice and boundless greed have claimed the vast resources and riches of this country. The wealth with which God has blessed this land, the breathtaking natural beauty that is the work of divine artistry, the majestic mountains, the sea, the fertile valleys—on all this is carved out in brazen arrogance: "For whites only." Blacks have come to understand that even though the Bible teaches us that the earth is the Lord's and the fullness thereof, experience has taught us that here the earth belongs to whites.

These Reformed Christians have created a political, economic, and social dispensation that they call apartheid. It is based on racism and white suprem-

aparteid

acy, on economic exploitation and the misuse of political power. They have made laws that are a perversion of justice and offer no protection for the poor, the weak, and the defenseless millions of our land against the power of their oppressors. For the sake of economic privileges that they regard as their right, they deliberately put asunder what God has joined together. They despise the sanctity of marriage and family life when it comes to blacks. They treat the homeless with a callousness and brutality that stun the mind. They detain without trial. They silence the prophetic voices of the nation through arbitrary bannings. They terrorize the innocent. They are prepared to kill children in order to maintain apartheid and white supremacy.

Apartheid is unique. But its uniqueness does not lie in the inherent violence of the system, or in the inevitable brutality without which the system cannot survive, or in the dehumanization and the contempt for black personhood, or even in the tragic alienations and the incredible costs in terms of human dignity and human relationships. No, the uniqueness of apartheid lies in the fact that this system claims to be *based on Christian principles*. It is justified on the basis of the gospel of Jesus Christ. It is in the name of the liberator God and Jesus Christ, the Son of God, that apartheid is perpetuated, and it is Reformed Christians who are responsible for it. Apartheid was born out of the Reformed tradition; it is, in a very real sense, the brainchild of the Dutch Reformed churches. It is Reformed Christians who have split the church on the basis of race and color, and who now claim that racially divided churches are a true Reformed understanding of the nature of the Christian church.

It is Reformed Christians who have spent years working out the details of apartheid, as a church policy and as a political policy. It is Reformed Christians who have presented this policy to the Afrikaner as the only possible solution, as an expression of the will of God for South Africa, and as being in accord with the gospel and the Reformed tradition. It is Reformed Christians who have created Afrikaner nationalism, equating the Reformed tradition and Afrikaner ideals with the ideals of the kingdom of God. It is they who have devised the theology of apartheid, deliberately distorting the gospel to suit their racist aspirations. They present this policy as a pseudogospel that can be the salvation of all South Africans.

In this uniqueness lies the shame of the Christian church in this country. Apartheid is the grave of the dignity and the credibility of the Reformed tradition.

Today we have reached a state of affairs where many, especially blacks, have come to believe that racism is an inevitable fruit of the Reformed tradition. In the experience of millions of blacks this tradition is responsible for political oppression, economic exploitation, unbridled capitalism, social discrimination, and the total disregard for human dignity that have become the hallmark of South African society.

By the same token, being Reformed is equated with total, uncritical acceptance of the status quo, sinful silence in the face of human suffering, and manipulation of the word of God in order to justify oppression. Being Reformed is to support the intransigence of our present rulers and to expect the unconditional submission of the oppressed.

The anomaly has become more acute than ever. For black Reformed Christians who suffer much under the totalitarian rule of white Reformed Christians, the question is fundamental and decisive. We have reached a point in our history where we can no longer avoid it. Black and Reformed: is this a burden that has to be cast off as soon as possible, or is it a challenge toward the renewal of church and society? Does the Reformed tradition have a future in South Africa?

A Reform in Need of Reform

But we must ask a prior question. Is the Afrikaner version of the Reformed tradition the whole truth? Is the equation between being Reformed and being oppressive and racist justified? In this country, as Douglas Bax has shown, Reformed theology has in many instances become a curious mixture of pietism, German Romanticism and *Volkstheologie*, and the negative aspects of Kuyperianism. Is this acceptable? Is the justification of tyranny legitimately based in the Reformed tradition?

Of course, in trying to answer all these questions I must of necessity be brief and selective. My aim here cannot be to give a detailed exposé of Reformed doctrine, but rather to highlight those aspects of the tradition that are especially relevant to us in our situation and that need to be redeemed from the quagmire of political ideology and nationalistic propaganda to which they have fallen victim in South Africa.

The first thing that I should mention, then, is the principle of the supremacy of the word of God. In the Reformed tradition it is the word of God that gives life to our words. It is the word of God that shapes life and provides the church with a basis on which to stand. Scripture is the indisputable foundation of the life and witness of the church in the world, and it is the guiding principle for all our actions.

Manipulation of the word of God to suit culture, prejudices, or ideology is alien to the Reformed tradition. But the way in which Reformed Christians in this country have used the Bible to justify black oppression and white privilege, the way in which the gospel has been bypassed in establishing racially divided churches, the way in which Scripture has been used to produce a nationalistic, racist ideology is the very denial of the Reformed belief in the supremacy of Scripture. The word of God is the word that gives life. It cannot at the same time be the justification of the death that comes through oppression and inhumanity. It is the word that speaks to our total human condition and offers salvation that is total, complete. For us today this means that, although the Bible is not a handbook for politics or economics, it nonetheless reveals all we need to know about God's will for the whole of human existence, including the spiritual, political, economic, and social well-being. The church believes that the Bible provides us with the fundamental principles of justice, love, and peace that we in the making of our societies ignore or deny at our own peril. It is this word of God that is the critique of all human actions and that holds before us the norms of the kingdom of God.

The kingdom of God is inextricably bound up with the lordship of Jesus Christ—another precious principle for those who adhere to the Reformed tradition. Christ is Lord of all life, even in those situations where his lordship is not readily recognized by willful humans. We believe passionately with Abraham Kuyper that there is not a single inch of life that does not fall under the lordship of Christ. All of life is indivisible, just as God is indivisible, and in all of life—personal and public, politics and economics, sports and art, science and liturgy—the Reformed Christian seeks the lordship of Christ.

Here the Reformed tradition comes so close to the African idea of the wholeness of life that these two should combine to renew the thrust that was brought to Christian life by the followers of Calvin. Reformed piety was *never* intended to include withdrawal from the world. The admonitions of politicians and even (Reformed!) churches to black Christians to "keep out of politics" are not only unbiblical; they are also, as Max Warren called them, the "essence of paganism." He quotes a missionary from Uganda:

> Without realizing it . . . we have drifted back into the old polytheism against which the prophets of the Lord waged their great warfare. The real essence of paganism is that it divides the various concerns of a man's life into compartments. There is one god of the soil; there is another god of the desert. The god of wisdom is quite different from the god of wine. If a man wants to marry he prays at one temple; if he wants to make war, he must take his sacrifice elsewhere.
>
> All this is precisely where the modern paganism of our secular society has brought us today. Certain portions of our life we call religious. Then we are Christians. We use a special language. . . . We call that our Christianity—and there we stop.
>
> We turn to another department of our life called politics. Now we think in quite different terms. Our liturgy is the catchwords of the daily press. Our divine revelation is the nine o'clock news. Our creed is "I believe in democracy." Our incentive is the fear of—we're not sure what. But it certainly is not the fear of the Lord.[2]

This kind of religion is far from the faith that characterized Reformed Christians from the very beginning. Their faith said that Christians were responsible for their world. Their Christianity was what Calvin College philosopher Nick Wolterstorff has called, "world-formative Christianity." As Reformed Christians we see ourselves as human beings who are responsible for the world in which we find ourselves. It is a world made by us, and we are capable of making it different. More than that: we *should* make it different. It *needs* reform. Furthermore, the exercise of that responsibility is part of the discipleship to which the Lord Jesus Christ has called us. It is not an addition to this discipleship but an integral part of it. Doing what we can to reform the social world in which we live is part of our spiritual life.[3]

For us as black Reformed Christians that means that in the following of Jesus Christ the spiritual experience is never separated from the liberation struggle. In the heart of this process God is experienced as one to whom every effort and every struggle is offered. Our worship of God is what must give direction and content to our action in the world. From God come bravery and courage, truth and justice. Because God raised our Messiah from the dead to demonstrate the truth of God's word, God will give life also to those who, in the path of Jesus, give their lives for others.

In South Africa, white Reformed theology has persistently pointed out that we live in the "broken reality" of a fallen world. This is true. But in the theology of apartheid this leads to the acceptance, the idealization, and institutionalization of that brokenness, and of that kind of apathy that induces Christians to accept sinful realities such as racism.

In true Reformed theology, however, the recognition of the broken, sinful realities of our world becomes the impulse toward reformation and healing. It means we understand that human beings do not automatically seek the glory of God and the good of their neighbor. That is why it becomes a Christian's task to work actively for the good of one's neighbor. In a fallen world, the structures that we create are tainted by sin and will not automatically have a liberating, humanizing effect on human lives. They will therefore have to be changed so that they may serve the humanization of our world. This means that Reformed Christians are called on not to accept the sinful realities of the world. Rather we are called to challenge, to shape, to subvert, and to humanize history until it conforms to the norm of the kingdom of God.

Social Justice: The Reformed Tradition

What shall we say about the equation of South African oppressive society and the Reformed tradition? It is necessary that we once again refute the blasphemous claim that apartheid is Christian. We must understand that the Christian character of a government is not proven by good intentions, or by the number of times it shouts Lord, Lord! It is proven by the care of the poor, the protection of the weak and the needy, the suppression of evil, the punishment of oppressors, the equitable distribution of wealth, power, privileges, and responsibilities. As Calvin says: "The Lord recommends to us . . . that we may, insofar as everyone's resources admit, afford help to the needy, *so that there may not be some in affluence, and others in need.*"[4]

It is tragic that the reformer's concern for social justice is not reflected in the policies of all those who claim spiritual kinship with him. South African history might have been different if white Reformed Christians in South Africa had taken his word on human solidarity seriously: "The name neighbor extends indiscriminately to every man, because the whole human race is united by a sacred bond of fellowship. . . . To make any person our neighbor, it is enough that he be a man."[5]

In the area of social justice, Reformed belief was expressed magnificently by Abraham Kuyper speaking to the Christian Social Congress in 1891:

> When rich and poor stand opposed to each other, Jesus never takes his place with the wealthier, but always stands with the poorer. He is born in a stable; while foxes have holes and birds have nests, the Son of Man has nowhere to lay his head. . . . Both the Christ, and also just as much his disciples after him as the prophets before him, invariably took sides *against* those who were powerful and living in luxury, and *for* the suffering and oppressed.[6]

Unlike so many rich Calvinists and other Christians who keep on telling the poor that poverty is the will of God, Kuyper refused to believe it:

> God has not willed that one should drudge hard and yet have not bread for himself and his family. And still less has God willed that any man with hands to work and a will to work should suffer hunger or be reduced to the beggar's staff just because there is no work. If we have food and clothing then it is true the holy apostle demands that we should therewith be content. But *it can neither nor may ever be* excused in us that, while our Father in heaven wills with divine kindness that an abundance of food comes forth from the ground, through our guilt this rich bounty should be divided so unequally that while one is surfeited with bread, another goes with empty stomach to his pallet, and sometimes must even go without a pallet.[7]

Later, another Reformed theologian, Karl Barth, put it in these words:

> The human righteousness required by God and established in obedience—the righteousness which according to Amos 5:24 should pour down as a mighty stream—has necessarily the character of a vindication of right in favor of the threatened innocent, the oppressed poor, widows, orphans, and aliens. For this reason, in the relations and events in the life of people, God always takes his stand unconditionally and passionately on this side and on this side alone: against the lofty and on behalf of the lowly; against those who already enjoy right and privilege and on behalf of those who are denied and deprived of it.[8]

It is in vain that the oppressive system of apartheid and its defenders claim any Reformed legitimation. Rather, the Reformed tradition calls for resistance to so blatantly an unjust government as is the South African.

Government: The Reformed Tradition

For Reformed Christians, government is not "naturally" an enemy. We believe with Calvin that governments are instituted by God for the just and legitimate administration of the world. But note two things. First, the expectation that government is not the enemy of the people must not be read as blind acceptance of any kind of government, but is in fact a crucial criterion for judging the actions of a government. Secondly, God institutes the authority of government for the *just* and *legitimate* administration of the world. A government, then, in order to be able to claim this divine institution and in order to be legitimate, has to respond positively to the expectation that Scripture has of it: it is to be a shepherd of the people (Ezek. 34).

In terms of any modern concept of democracy, as well as in terms of Calvin's understanding of legitimacy, the South African government is neither just nor legitimate. For the Reformed tradition, a government should be obeyed because it has the authority instituted by God. But there is always one very important proviso: we obey government *insofar* as its laws and instructions are not in conflict with the word of God. Obedience to earthly authority is only obedience *in God*. On this point John Calvin is clear:

> But in that obedience which we have shown to be due to the authority of rulers, we are always to make this exception, indeed to observe it as primary, that such obedience is never to lead us away from obedience to him to whose will the desires of all kings ought to be subject, to whose decrees all their commands ought to yield, to whose majesty their scepters ought to be submitted. And how absurd would it be that in satisfying men you should incur the displeasure of him for whose sake you obey men themselves! The Lord, therefore, is King of Kings, who when he has opened his sacred mouth, must alone be heard, before all and above all men; next to him we are subject to those men who are in authority over us, but only in him. If they command anything against him, let it go unesteemed. And here let us not be concerned about all that dignity which the magistrates [government] possess; for no harm is done to it when it is humbled before that singular and truly supreme power of God.[9]

And Calvin ends with an exhortation to courage and obedience, reminding us that "we have been redeemed by Christ at so great a price as our redemption cost him, so that we would not enslave ourselves to the wicked desire of men— much less be subject to their impiety."[10] Therefore the call is: "We must obey God rather than man."

This was the spirit caught by the Scottish reformation when it formulated article 14 of the Scottish Confession:

> [It is our duty] to honor father, mother, princes, rulers, and superior powers: to love them, to support them, yes, to obey their charges *unless*

repugnant to the Word of God. To save the lives of the innocent, to repress tyranny, to defend the oppressed [emphasis added].

Commenting on article 25 of the Scottish Confession, Karl Barth says:

We can afford the state such positive cooperation only when the significance of the state as *service of God* is made clear and credible to us by the state itself, by its attitude and acts, its intervening on behalf of justice, peace, and freedom, and its conduct toward the church. That is the condition which the *Confessio Scotica* is right in constantly laying down. If that condition is not fulfilled, those who administer it make a mockery [of the service of God]. But in that case we can take no share in their responsibility, we cannot further their intentions, we cannot wish to strive with them to attain their aims. We cannot do it under any conditions or on any pretext.[11]

So when Beyers Naudé sides with the poor and the oppressed in South Africa *he* is the true representative of the Reformed tradition, not those who banned him and sought to bring dishonor to his name.

When the Presbyterian Church of Southern Africa decided to challenge the government on as fundamental an issue as Christian marriage, it is closer to the Reformed tradition than are those who vindicate an unjust law.

It is not the perpetrators of injustice, but those who resist it, who are the true representatives of the Reformed tradition.

EXIGENCIES OF A BLACK, REFORMED FUTURE

Black Christians who are Reformed have no reason to be ashamed of this tradition. Of course this is not to say that Reformed Christians have not made mistakes. We know only too well the tendency of those who adhere to this tradition to become self-righteous. We have often exhibited an arrogance that becomes self-sufficiency and gives rise to a tendency toward isolationism, because we feel we do not need anybody else. Think of how the doctrine of election has been used to foster a false sense of superiority and how often it was coupled with nationalism. Indeed, it is, as Wolterstorff says:

Sometimes one is [instead] confronted with that most insufferable of all people, the triumphalist Calvinist, the one who believes that the revolution instituting the Holy Commonwealth has already occurred and that the social order has been reformed sufficiently for its roles to serve nicely as instruments of obedience for the committed ones. Of these triumphalist Calvinists the United States and Holland have provided plenty of examples. South Africa today provides them in their purest form.[12]

It is my conviction that the Reformed tradition has a future in this country only if black Reformed Christians are willing to take it up, make it truly their own, and let this tradition once again become what it once was: a champion of the cause of the poor and the oppressed, clinging to the confession of the lordship of Christ and to the supremacy of the word of God. It will have a future when we show an evangelical openness toward the world and toward the worldwide church so that we shall be able to search with others for the attainment of the goals of the kingdom of God in South Africa. I do not mean that we should accept everything in our tradition uncritically, for I indeed believe that black Christians should formulate a Reformed confession for our time and situation in our own words.

Beginning with our own South African situation, we should accept our special responsibility to salvage this tradition from the grip of the mighty and the powerful, who have so shamelessly perverted it for their own ends, and let it speak once again for God's oppressed and suffering peoples. It is important to declare apartheid to be irreconcilable with the gospel of Jesus Christ, a sin that has to be combated on every level of our lives, a denial of the Reformed tradition, a heresy that is to the everlasting shame of the church of Jesus Christ in the world.

To accept the Reformed confession is more than a formal acknowledgment of doctrine. Churches accepting that confession thereby commit themselves to show through their daily witness and service that the gospel has indeed empowered them to live in this world as the people of God. They also commit themselves to accept in their worship and at the table of the Lord the brothers and sisters who accept and proclaim the lordship of Christ in all areas of life, and to work ceaselessly for that justice, love, and shalom that are fundamental to the kingdom of God and the kingly rule of God's Son. Confessional subscription should lead to concrete manifestation in unity of worship and cooperation in the common tasks of the church. In South Africa adherence to the Reformed tradition should be a commitment to combat the evil of apartheid in every area of our lives and to seek liberation, peace, justice, reconciliation, and wholeness for all of God's children in this torn and beloved land.

We must be clear. It is one thing when the rules and laws of unjust and oppressive governments make it impossible for the church to carry out its divine task. But it is quite another thing when churches purposely reject this unity and this struggle, as the white Reformed churches of South Africa have consistently done. Apartheid is not simply a political ideology. Its very existence has depended and still depends on a theological justification by these same white Reformed churches. This, too, is part of our task: in struggling *against* apartheid, we struggle *for* liberation; *against* an oppressive and inhuman ideology, but also *for* the sake of the gospel and the integrity of the church of Jesus Christ. Christians and churches purporting to serve the gospel by the justification of apartheid on biblical grounds do so only at the risk of blasphemy.

I am also convinced that in this struggle some Reformed expressions of faith, now centuries old, and for many redundant, can provide us with both prophetic clarity and pastoral comfort. Lord's Day I of the Heidelberg Catechism asks the question: "What is your only comfort in life and death?" The answer is:

> That I, with body and soul, both in life and death, am not my own, but belong to my faithful Savior Jesus Christ; who with his precious blood has fully satisfied for all my sins, and delivered me from all the power of the devil, and so preserves me that without the will of my heavenly Father not a hair can fall from my head; yea, that all things must be subservient to my salvation, wherefore by his Holy Spirit he also assures me to eternal life, and makes me heartily willing and ready, henceforth, to live unto him.

This is one of the most powerful statements of faith I have ever encountered. In our situation, when black personhood is thoroughly undermined, when our God-given human dignity is being trampled underfoot, when our elderly are uprooted and thrown into the utter desolation of resettlement camps, when even the meager shelter of a plastic sheet is brutally taken away and mothers and their babies are being exposed to the merciless winter of the Cape, when young children are terrorized in the early hours of the morning, when the prophetic voices of our youth are teargassed into silence, when the blood of our children flows in the streets of our townships—what *then* is our comfort in life and in death? When we are completely at the mercy of those for whom our humanity does not exist, when our powerlessness against their ruthless rule becomes a pain we can no longer bear, when the stench of our decaying hope chokes us half to death, when the broken lives and silent tears of our aged show the endlessness of our struggle, when the power of the oppressor is arrogantly flaunted in the face of the world—what *then* is our comfort in life and death? That I, with body and soul, both in life and death, am not my own, but belong unto my faithful Savior, who is Jesus the Liberator, Christ the Messiah and *Kyrios*, the Lord.

Is this excessive spiritualization? No, it is not. But it is a revolutionary spirituality without which our being Christian in the world is not complete, and without which the temptations that are part and parcel of the liberation struggle will prove too much for us. Furthermore, in the situation in which we find ourselves, it is of vital importance that we be able to resist the totalitarian claims of the powers that rule South Africa so harshly. The most frightening aspect of apartheid is the totality of control that the government seeks to exercise over human lives—from the subtle and not so subtle propaganda to the harsh, draconian laws designed to ensure the "security" of the country. Apartheid is a false god whose authoritarian audacity allows no room for the essence of meaningful humanity: freedom under God. It is of vital importance that we never forget to whom our ultimate allegiance and obedience are due.

In this country, the government will come to expect more and more unquestioning submission for the sake of "national security." More and more the government will expect the church to participate in its "total strategy." Such participation could only take the form of theological justification of the national security ideology, the sanctification of the militarization of our society, and the motivation of South African soldiers for the "holy war" against communism.[13] The church will be expected to applaud the kind of theology expounded by the state president at the centenary celebrations of the Nederduitse Gereformeerde Sendingkerk in October 1981: "The total onslaught against South Africa is a total onslaught against the kingdom of God."

Furthermore, as the situation of violence and counterviolence develops and the fear of whites that they will lose their overprivileged position grows, the courage of those who seek justice will be challenged.

So the confession that Jesus Christ is Lord of my life is not spiritual escapism. It is a confession with profound implications for the whole of life. It is a fundamental theological affirmation of the place of the Christian in this world, and it firmly sets the limits of the powers of this world. It places us within the best tradition of the Christian church through the ages, opening our eyes and ears to the inspiration of the "great cloud of witnesses on every side of us." It is a reminder, in the midst of the struggle, that our lives have meaning only when they are in the hands of the one who has given his life for the sake of all others. And although he is the Lamb who is slaughtered, for those who call him Lord he is also "Jesus Christ, the faithful witness, the firstborn from the dead, the ruler of the kings of the earth" (Rev. 1:5).

It is comfort, but it is more: it is the quiet, subversive piety that is quite indispensable for authentic Christian participation in the struggle for liberation. And in this struggle I am inspired by the words of the Belgic Confession:

> The faithful and elect shall be crowned with glory and honor; and the Son of God will confess their names before God his Father and his elect angels; all tears shall be wiped from their eyes; *and their cause, which is now condemned by many judges and magistrates as heretical and impious, will then be known to be the cause of the Son of God.*[14]

This, also, is our tradition and is worth fighting for.

NOTES

1. P. Huet, *Het tot der zwarten in Transvaal mededeelingen omtrent slavernij en wreedheden in de zuidafrikaansche republiek* (Utrecht, 1869), pp. 29–30.

2. Cited in Max Warren, *The Christian Mission* (London: SCM, 1951), p. 10.

3. For this insight I am dependent on Nicholas Wolterstorff, *Until Justice and Peace Embrace* (Grand Rapids: Eerdmans, 1983).

4. Cited in W. Fred Graham, *The Constructive Revolutionary* (Richmond: John Knox, 1971), p. 70; emphasis added.

5. Ibid.

6. Cited in Wolterstorff, *Until Justice and Peace Embrace,* p. 73.

7. Ibid., pp. 79–80.

8. Karl Barth, *Church Dogmatics,* II/I (Edinburgh: Clark, 1957), p. 386.

9. John Calvin, *Institutes of the Christian Religion* (Philadelphia: Westminster, 1960), IV, xx, 32, p. 1520.

10. Ibid., p. 1521.

11. Karl Barth, *The Knowledge of God and the Service of God according to the Teaching of the Reformation* (London: Hodder & Stoughton, 1938), pp. 227–28.

12. Wolterstorff, *Until Justice and Peace Embrace,* p. 21.

13. The thought expressed here is that of Chaplain General The Rev. Van Zyl of the Republic of South Africa.

14. Belgic Confession, art. 35; emphasis added.

PART 3

ASIA

24

Kosuke Koyama

Aristotelian Pepper and Buddhist Salt

Kosuke Koyama seeks to develop a "rice roots" theology emerging from the everyday experience of the farmers of northern Thailand. In his introductory remarks to "Aristotelian Pepper and Buddhist Salt," Koyama shapes a number of general principles and questions about the relationship among Buddhism, Aristotelianism, and Christianity. Then in a letter addressed to Dr. Daniel McGilvary (1828–1911), a pioneer Christian missionary who served in northern Thailand for over half a century, Koyama attempts to resolve the issues he has raised. The following selection is taken from Koyama's Waterbuffalo Theology *(Maryknoll, N.Y.: Orbis Books, 1974), pp. 78–88.*

1. In the process of appropriation of the gospel by the Christian people of Thailand one discerns that Aristotelian philosophy (West) and Buddhism (East) season the gospel and make it palatable for the Thai.

2. The Buddhist psychological principle of "dependent origination" has prepared the Thai mind for the Aristotelian worldview of scientific causality. Aristotle has a fascination for those brought up in the Buddhistic culture, hence the Aristotle-inspired cosmological proof of the existence of God is a favorite subject in their "theological" discussions.

3. The Buddhist philosophy and the lifestyle of detachment season the religion of God's attachment to humankind. Thus, sometimes one is confronted by an "Asokanized Christ."

4. Yet Christ will become a genuinely "tasty" Christ not in the outright rejection of both Aristotelian pepper and Buddhist salt, but rather in using them. The question is, *What kind of use?* By what theological principles do we engage in this dangerous (and unavoidable) task? How

can one use Aristotle and the Buddha (the two great sages!) to articulate Jesus Christ biblically in Thailand?

•

Dear Dr. McGilvary,

This is my sixth year in northern Thailand. About one tenth the length of your ministry here! Your old teakwood mission house still stands by the Ping River, overlooking your town, Chiengmai. The residence of one of the Chiengmai princes, a house which you frequented, is now occupied by the American Consulate.

My letter to you is in the nature of an inquiry. I want to know the nature and place of my ministry in the context of the history of the church in northern Thailand. To what kind of spiritual and theological heritage am I heir? This question is of immediate concern for me, for how can I make my witness meaningful to my neighbors if I fail to understand where they are and where I am in the continuing story of the Christian church here? How can I engage in meaningful theological thinking if I do not understand the story of the development of theology in northern Thailand? Whenever I undertake the study of the church's past in northern Thailand, you are there, the dedicated pioneer missionary, whose immense spiritual and intellectual influence upon the Thai is still visible in those churches spread over the countryside, stamped with your own Christian piety. So I have studied your message.

I have read your book, *A Half Century among the Siamese and the Lao,*[1] with intense interest and eagerness. At certain points in your book you give some clues to the contents of your message:

> Why do we worship Jehovah Jesus? Because he is our sovereign Lord. The Buddha groaned under his own load of guilt, and was oppressed by the sad and universal consequences of sin among men. The Christ challenged his enemies to convince him of sin, and his enemies to this day have confessed that they find no sin in him. Buddhists believe that Buddha reached Nirvana after having himself passed through every form of being in the universe—having been in turn every animal in the seas, on the earth, and in the air. He did this by an inexorable law that he and every other being is subject to, and cannot evade. Our Jehovah-Jesus, as our Scriptures teach, is the only self-existent being in the universe, and himself the cause of all other beings. An infinite Spirit and invisible, he manifested himself to the world by descending from heaven, becoming man, taking on our nature in unison with his holy nature, but with no taint of sin. He did this out of infinite love and pity for our race after it had sinned. He saw there was no other able to save, and he became our Savior.[2]

> The sacred books of the Princes teach that there is no creator. Everything, as the Siamese say, *"pen eng,"* comes to be of itself. All this

complicated universe became what it is by a fortuitous concurrence of atoms, which atoms themselves had no creator. We come as honest seekers for truth. We look around, above, beneath. Everything seems to imply the contrivance of mind.[3]

We pressed home the thought, new to them, that there must be a maker of the world and of all creatures in it. We told them the old, old story of the infinite love of God, our Father, and of Christ, his Son, who suffered and died to save us, and of pardon freely promised to all who believe in him. This is the final argument that wins these people.[4]

And then, before that motley crowd, drinking with them their native tea from an earthen teapot, the men seated close around, or reclining as they smoke their pipes, the women and children walking about or sitting on the ground—we tell of God, the great Spirit, the creator and Father of all—the Bible, his message to men—the incarnation, life, and death of Christ, and redemption through his blood.[5]

Then our religion was explained in its two leading ideas—rejection of the spirit-cult and acceptance of Jesus for the pardon of sin and the life eternal. Questions were asked, and answered.[6]

These accounts, although brief and written for the English-speaking reader, allow me to sense the content of the message you preached and the theological approach you employed when you proclaimed Christ to the Thai. You spoke simply, forcefully, and straightforwardly to the listening Thai. When Paul proclaimed Jesus Christ in Athens, some Epicurean and Stoic philosophers remarked: "What is this cock-sparrow trying to say?" And Athenians asked: "May we know what this new teaching of yours really is? You talk of matters which sound strange to our ears and we should like to know what they mean" (Acts 17:18ff.). While you were preaching, some Buddhist monks or Chiengmaians might have been thinking, "What is this cock-sparrow trying to say?" But it may be that the oriental Chiengmaians are more courteous than Mediterranean Athenians, and they did not say it out loud. There is, however, something more significant involved than the issue of cultural modesty. I think that both in Athens and in Chiengmai the story of Jesus Christ is a story that "sounds strange to our ears." But the basic character of "strangeness," the cultural-historical context in which the "strangeness" manifests itself, and the degree of intensity with which the "strangeness" disturbs "our ears" are definitely quite different. My rough guess is that Paul in Athens had an easier assignment than McGilvary in Chiengmai. The nineteenth-century North American McGilvary, speaking in the northern Thai dialect to Thai peasants, encountered more difficulties than the Mediterranean Paul speaking in Greek to the Mediterranean audience.

In the light of this brief observation, I have become very curious to know whether your audience understood your preaching or not, if you will pardon me for asking. In my ministry here today I am forced to see how thoroughly strange and unrealistic—how "Western"—is the Christian vocabulary to the ears of my Thai neighbors. How did you explain the thoughts such as "Buddha groaned under his load of *guilt*," "Our Jehovah Jesus is the *only self-existent being* in the universe," "He did this out of *infinite love* and pity for our race after it had *sinned*," "Everything seems to imply the *contrivance of mind*," and "Christ . . . *suffered and died to save us*"? How did you explain such concepts as "the *incarnation*, life, and death of Christ and *redemption through his blood*" and "life eternal"? Don't you think, Dr. McGilvary, that you spoke *too* directly or inflexibly to your audience? Each one of these terms invites cultural resistance, psychological antipathy, and emotional reaction! Maybe your audience was not listening to your words but was only watching your magnificent long white beard; however, as a theological student, I am interested in you beyond my unlimited admiration of your beard. I am interested in your own mission theology.

My observation is that upon accepting the gospel, the Thai season the Christian ingredients—whether they be "infinite love," "sin," "incarnation," "redemption through his blood," or "life eternal"—with their own Buddhist salt. Why *Buddhist* salt? Very briefly, it is because the Thai culture is permeated with the strong influence of Theravada Buddhism, as Phra Anuman Rajadhon observes in his careful study of Thai life.[7] If you had said "Buddha groaned under his own load of *dukkha*," "Our Jehovah Jesus is the only *arahant* in the universe," "He did this out of *infinite mercy* for our race after it is caught by 'craving,' " "Everything seems to imply the highest value of the *Nirvanic Mind*," "Christ suffered and died to *instruct* the way out from *samsara*," "Christ offers to humankind salvation through the *dharmma* to *Nirvana*," then your audience might have accepted your message without much distaste, and consequently, they might not have added their own seasoning to the ingredients. It is pretty well seasoned already! But of course you cannot say that Jesus Christ is an *arahant*. This would be candy-coated poison. It might go down the throat without irritation, but when it reached the stomach it would paralyze the vital organs. Suppose you wanted to say that "Jesus is an *arahant*," then you would have to do it with endless conditional sentences and explanatory paragraphs. This would require too much labor and only invite misunderstanding. There are, of course, certain key words which can be "baptized" and used more effectively in our communication of the gospeel. Paul dared to use such loaded words as *logos* (word), *soter* (savior), *mysterion* (mystery), *metamorphosis* (transformation) for his own evangelistic purpose. He was confident that these "heathen" words could be employed as faithful servants when they are placed in the strong *kerygma* context.

Our dilemma is this: if we say "salvation through the blood of Jesus," our Thai audience is completely lost. If we say "salvation through the *dharmma*," they would see no difference between the Christian faith and Buddhism.

Perhaps the best possible way to avoid the difficulty and reach our goal is to explain that the *content* of the *dharmma* is the sacrificial death of Christ. Of course, once again this raises the question "Why such a sanguine *dharmma*?" How can the *dharmma* be *dharmma* when it has "warm blood"? The concept of the *dharmma* and "blood" are mutually incompatible!

While we are baffled by these difficulties, Thai "Christian theological thinking" is at work. The dish prepared with the flavor of Buddhist salt has, inevitably, a strange "ambiguous" taste to me. But for them I think the taste has been well "adjusted" to their liking.

Then, too, I have discovered that the seasoning takes place in the Thai theological kitchen, not in the broad living room into which missionaries have access. Thai theological activity goes on while the people squat on the dirt ground, and not while sipping tea with missionary friends in the teak-floored shiny living room. When I peep into the kitchen of their theology, the theological situation I see there is unique. No books have been written about this situation and no references are available in the best stocked theological libraries! I must confess my incompetence in grasping the details of the daring activities of this kitchen theology. My experience in peeping into the kitchen is sometimes like watching a great Chinese chef throwing six different ingredients into a heated oiled kwali. I can smell a most delicious aroma and I can see smoke, but I cannot identify the ingredients! Free theologizing is going on. No authorized "theological commission" is watching over the activity. Terribly fragmentary use of the Bible, not acceptable in any "accredited theological school," suddenly explodes with enormous energy and answers their theological needs. This process, I realize, is going on unconsciously, unintentionally, and almost semiautomatically so far as those in the kitchen are concerned. It is wrong to say that we must produce an indigenous theology. It is not necessary to produce one. It is there! Perhaps what we must do is to improve this indigenous theology by injecting more biblical information and helpful insights from the current ecumenical theological discussion.

Let me illustrate what I mean by kitchen-produced theology. The Christian message is based on the "infinite love" of God, as you say. According to ingrained Thai emotion and psychology, the word "love" *(khwamrak)* denotes humankind's attachment to things, persons, or supernatural beings. Attachment *inevitably* produces sorrow and trouble. Detachment *inevitably* creates tranquility, honesty, and genuine happiness.

Christianity teaches attachment. "So God was *attached* to the world. . . ." What a doctrine! This doctrine makes our Thai friends think about the whole thing in a completely different perspective and with a different feeling! This is great! This Christianity has something new to say to us! The kitchen becomes an exciting theological forum. The difference between attachment and detachment has been grasped, but not without much difficulty. But the hard-won difference between attachment and detachment is under the blight of *inevitability*. The old equation of inevitability: attachment produces sorrow and detachment happiness *inevitably* cripples the Christian concept of love. The basic distinction is won, but it does not show its creative newness since it is blighted. The Christian doctrine of "love" and the idea of "inevitability" are antithetical. "Love" is the least "inevitable" thing one can think of!

One of my students told me that the idea of *good* in Thai culture can be portrayed as clothing washed, neatly ironed, and placed in a closed, undisturbed drawer. Don't wear it! It will get dirty! The clothing must stay "detached" from the dirty world. Several times, both on the university campus and at rural meetings, I have encountered violent objection to Jesus' censure of the servant who carefully wrapped his one talent and gave it back to the master when he returned. What is wrong about this "honest" servant who kept what was entrusted to him in a "tranquil drawer?" Jesus' blame is unreasonable and outrageous! The sense of commitment to a "tranquil drawer" (noninvolvement) is in the very roots of Thai psychology.

By these two illustrations I am trying to point out how difficult it is for our Thai friends to break through the philosophy of detachment. In the philosophy of detachment, I sense their desire to pay respect to the great principle of "inevitability" taught by the Wise, the Buddha.

In the Buddhist doctrine of the dependent origination *(paticca samuppada'),* if you wear clothing it will inevitably get dirty. If you give one talent to someone, you will inevitably get one talent back. This is the inevitable rule of life. That attachment can be creative is a great message for Thai people. But if "love" is bound up with the general concept of "inevitability," then the Christian concept of love is sadly blurred. It is like a two-hundred-volt electric bulb operating on a hundred-volt current. I call this dimness a state of "chronic Asokanization of the gospel."[8] An Asokanized Christ is a "dim" Christ.

Here I must refer again to the question: "Why such a sanguine *dharmma*?" The idea of a "warm-blooded" *dharmma* constitutes a terrible stumbling-block in the Thai culture. If it is "warm-blooded," it cannot be a dependable *dharmma*. Jesus Christ becomes a stumbling block in this way.

My letter to you is getting to be a long one. I did not intend it to be so. So far I have tried to outline the "kitchenized Christ" who is seasoned by the Buddhist salt. Relying on your patience, let me make one more point. I am interested in your statement: "We come as honest seekers for truth. We look around, above, beneath. Everything seems to imply the contrivance of mind." You seem to be pursuing, if I am not mistaken, the traditional "cosmological proof" of the existence of the intelligent God. The remarkable design one discerns in the universe compels one to acknowledge that this universe is not self-explanatory but must be explained in reference to Someone beyond it. This Someone is the cause of all other causes. The crucial point, which the users of this argument often overlook, is the question of what kind of mind it is that exists behind the universe. Is it a good mind or a bad mind? A redemptive mind or a destructive mind? A *Nirvanic* mind or a mind concerned with history? Isn't it true that if one speaks of orderliness in the universe, another can speak of disorderliness (accident, confusion) in the universe with the same vigor?

It has been made clear to me in my rural ministry here that this important question of the cosmological argument—*what kind of mind?*—is intensified if in my congregation there is one person who is born crippled or made blind by accident. People say to me that there may certainly be a mind behind the universe, but if that mind can produce such cruel irregularities as cripples and blindness, it must be capricious and erratic! (It may be that the mind is "warm blooded," that would explain these troubles!) Where, then, I ask myself, is the distinction between the God understood through recognition of design in the universe and the varieties of spirits my neighbors worship?

My Thai friends and I may come to an agreement, although not without much difficulty, that "in the beginning was the Word" (John 1.1). But it is not self-evident what kind of word this is even when "we come as honest seekers for truth." Honest seekers may find some objective religious truth, but the God of revelation is a hidden God even to the most honest of seekers (John 1:13; Matt. 16:17). May I quote from Kierkegaard: "Now Spirit is the denial of direct immediacy. If Christ be very God, he must be unknown, for to be known directly is the characteristic mark of an idol." Gradually I have come to see that the medicine of the cosmological argument, which has been widely prescribed in Thailand to be used at the levels of pre-evangelization, evangelism, and even mature Christianity, has proved to be a paralyzing tranquilizer. And it has, in reality, hampered my parishioners' way to the presence of the "undomesticated God" of the Bible, as Luther called him. This Aristotelian argument may be useful at the level of pre-evangelization (although I am not really sure!), but it produces unwanted and even destructive effects when it is incorporated into the substance of the Christian message.

I notice that on the dinner table of Thai theology, Buddhist salt and Aristotelian pepper go nicely together, since Aristotelian pepper has a flavor of *dharmma,* tracing one cause to another cause. Thus Aristotelian pepper plays a role of wife to the husband Buddhist salt, to *dharmma*-ize the *kerygma* of Jesus Christ. Why am I so concerned about Aristotelian pepper? I must confess to you that one uneasy look cast on me by a leper while I was happily discoursing on this "proof" for the existence of God in a leper colony outside Chiengmai shook me. The leper boy, through his very existence, challenged and rebelled against Aristotelian pepper—so I understood. The God theorized under the influence of the over-anxious rationality of the West is, I must conclude, as dim as the "Asokanized Christ."

Sometimes an interesting situation occurs in the Thai theological scene. The Aristotelian Christ is put in dialogue, or even in heated argument, with the Asokanized Christ. This is a theological traffic between the two "dim" Christs. By a remarkable development of discussion and insights, the Asokanized Christ sometimes comes out on top of the Aristotelian Christ, and at other times the reverse occurs. Of course all this hot theological debate takes place in the "kitchen."

Let me come to my concluding remark. I admit that what I have written here is oversimplified. And the problems I raise would involve many thorny theological, historical, and cultural questions which would defy any easy schematic handling. Yet a persistent question comes to me every day: "Where is the sharp edge of the love *(khwamrak)* of Christ in our churches in northern Thailand? From what source did the blurring of Christ come?" I wonder if the "doubly blurred" situation, caused by the two distinctive blurring agents of East and West, have contributed to a very significant degree to the emergence of the Thai "dim" Christ.

As soon as I say this, however, a chain of questions comes into my mind. I ask myself, Why have we been so incompetent in understanding the development of "kitchen theology"? Why have we kept the "living room theology" more or less at a distance from the hot "kitchen theology"? Why have we been so unprepared to present a Christ who can be "bright" in the kitchen? Or is the "dim" Christ more salvific than the "bright" Christ to the Thai? Is Christ *supposed to be* seasoned by those elements in order to become a palatable Christ to the Thai? In order to become the neighbor of the Thai? Is it possible to have an unseasoned and raw Christ? Isn't it true that the incarnation of the Son of God means his "in-culture-ation"? Wasn't he a Palestinian Jew? Doesn't this mean that imagining an unseasoned and raw Christ is as absurd and impossible as a de-Hebraized Yahweh? Does this then mean that one must not simply reject the "pepper and salt" of any culture, but attempt to see *what kind of* pepper and salt is seasoning Christ, and try to present a well-seasoned Christ in *cooperation* with the local pepper and salt? What are the theological rules by which we should launch this *cooperation?*

Many questions indeed! I am asking all of them. I honestly do not know how I can manage them. And . . . the weather is too hot here and mosquitoes bother me. But, dear Dr. McGilvary, what should I do with the Aristotelian pepper and Buddhist salt?

Sincerely yours,

Kosuke Koyama

Chiengmai
Thailand

NOTES

1. Daniel McGilvary, *A Half Century among the Siamese and the Lao* (New York: Fleming H. Revell, 1912).
2. Ibid., pp. 181f.
3. Ibid., p. 182.
4. Ibid., p. 328.
5. Ibid., p. 342.
6. Ibid., p. 344.
7. Phra Anuman Rajadhon, *Essays on Thai Folklore* (Bangkok, 1968).
8. Asoka was a great Buddhist king in India. He died in 323 B.C. after having been instrumental in strengthening and spreading Buddhism wisely, contributing eventually to its strong pervasiveness in Thailand today.

25

C. S. Song

Theology and Asian Culture

C. S. Song explains that Christians in Asia see Christ through Asian eyes. A central image for Song is the "third eye," a concept which he borrows from the Japanese Zen master Daisetz Suzuki. Song argues that seeing with the third eye of Asian spirituality will enlighten Christianity throughout the world. "Theology and Asian Culture" is taken from C. S. Song, Third-Eye Theology *(Maryknoll, N.Y.: Orbis Books, 1979), pp. 10–13.*

The Christian gospel that seeks to lead people to the God of love manifested in Jesus Christ must find its echoes and responses from within their spirituality. By spirituality I do not mean merely something derived from a religious faith or belief. This is spirituality in a narrow sense. What I mean by spirituality is much broader. Spirituality is the totality of being that expresses itself in ways of life, modes of thinking, patterns of behavior and conduct, and attitudes toward the mystery that surrounds our immediate world and that beckons us on to the height beyond heights, to the depth below depths, and to the light beyond lights. Such spirituality is present both in the East and the West. And the discovery of such spirituality in the essence of Asian cultures will open the eyes of Christians to see something new in their understanding of the gospel. It will enable them to discover fresh insights into how God is at work in nations and peoples alien to Western Christian culture.

Doing theology with an Asian spirituality thus may bring about a conversion in Christians as well as in people of other faiths. This should prove to be an enrichment to the churches within the Western cultural tradition. To quote R. H. S. Boyd:

> The Indian Church has been strongly influenced by this same tradition [i.e., the Greco-Roman tradition] inherited from western missionaries, yet today it is emerging with its own distinct and fascinating cultural identity. Has this Indian Church anything to say to the West which will enable the West to rediscover its faith in a wider and richer context? Can the western Church break out of its bondage to Greek philosophy, to the Latin language, and to Roman structures?[1]

This reference to the church in India can be applied equally to other churches in the Third World. A new theological era is in the making. It makes doing theology more difficult yet more exciting, more complicated yet more enriching.

I propose to call such a theological effort "doing theology with a third eye." The term "third eye" is derived from Buddhism. According to the great Japanese Zen master Daisetz Suzuki:

> Zen . . . wants us to open a "third eye," as Buddhists call it, to the hitherto unheard-of region shut away from us through our own ignorance. When the cloud of ignorance disappears, the infinity of heavens is manifested where we see for the first time into the nature of our own being.[2]

The theology with which we are familiar and in which most of us are brought up is a first- or a second-eye theology—a two-dimensional theology that is not capable of a third-dimensional insight. Because of its two dimensionality it is a flat theology. It canvasses a long stretch of terrain, which is the two thousand years of church history colored strongly by Western thought forms and life styles.

It was Seeberg, a great German historian of the development of Christian dogmas, who observed that the Reformation represents "Christianity in the understanding of the German spirit."[3] He was right. The faith of the Reformation is the faith seen through German eyes. However definitive, influential, and far-reaching the Reformation faith may have been, there is no reason why Christians who are not heirs to the German spirit must see and interpret Christian faith through German eyes. Those who are not endowed with German eyes should not be prevented from seeing Christ differently. They must train themselves to see Christ through Chinese eyes, Japanese eyes, Asian eyes, African eyes, Latin American eyes.

This is what I mean by doing theology with a third eye. In fact, my concept is not innovative. Consider, for example, the Christian artists throughout the centuries who have tried to portray Christ. Each portrait of Christ expresses the artist's concept of Christ under the strong influence of his or her own cultural and religious background. Indeed, the effort of the religious mind to capture the face of Christ "has been influenced by the great art movements and by national and individual characteristics."[4] Accordingly, the face of Christ in art can be a typological study of the cultural, national, and ethnic influences on the different artists.[5] Compare, for example, Guido Reni's *Ecce Homo* of the decadent period of the sixteenth and the seventeenth centuries with the *Christ on the Cross* by Donatello (1386–1466), who was an artist of the early Renaissance. For Donatello and his peers of the fourteenth and the fifteenth centuries, art was to serve faith, not the other way around. In the treatment of the face of Christ, "it is not beauty they aim at but holiness."[6] The face of Donatello's Christ is

> marred by excruciating pain, but the spiritual majesty of the Sufferer remains; there is no heart-rending appeal to emotionalism, no effort to impress by exaggeration of physical suffering, and yet it is all there—the loneliness, the abandonment, the anguish, and above and within all the victory of that voluntary sacrifice which atones for the sins of the world.[7]

Guido Reni's face of Christ poses a striking contrast. It is the physical suffering that dominates Christ's facial expression. His sorrow, anguish, and pain come out so forcefully that the hope of salvation seems subsumed under them:

> This sense of anguish and suffering is expressed by Guido Reni with a power and pathos which profoundly moves the heart, but it displays an exaggeration of sentiment, which began to characterize the art of this epoch, and which was one of the evil effects of the Counter-Reformation.[8]

When we turn to Japanese artists, we seem to breathe a different atmosphere. In looking at the works of Japanese Christian artists, we should consider the Japanese characteristic of *sibui*.[9] Let us take, for example, the *Cross of Christ* by Giichro Hayakawa.[10] On the cross Christ's outstretched arms and folded feet are nailed. But from his face we can hardly sense the kind of pain and anguish he is going through in his body and spirit. The whole picture is a paragon of tranquility in the midst of a raging storm. The closed eyes almost shut out external intrusions into the mind of the sufferer. Christ is in deep contemplation with himself and with God. It is a profound silence that we see in Christ's face, and yet what a powerful silence! Here is Christ oblivious of his physical pain, bearing the sins of the world in his single-minded concentration on saving humankind. It is a *sibui* Christ that we encounter here, a Christ who does not show internal emotion and passion, a Christ who faces death with equanimity. Is this not a *sibui* spirituality that is seen in the savior of the world?

Be that as it may, each portrait of Christ expresses the artist's comprehension of Christ. It portrays Christ in accord with Christ's meaning to each artist in his or her particular personal, historical, and cultural context. No artist has been able to capture the *whole* Christ, the *true* Christ, Christ as he was and is. Thus each portrait of Christ is at once a representation and a misrepresentation. This is not a surprise, for even the disciples who sat at the feet of Christ, ate with him, followed him, and lived with him formed different views of him. Some thought of him as a prophet; others regarded him as Elijah; and still others expected him to be their political liberator. No view of Christ, no picture of him, therefore, is free from falsification. Likewise, no tradition of the church is free of error, no teaching of the church by the theologians and spiritual leaders can claim to be infallible. Even the creeds of the early ecumenical councils have no absolutely binding power over members of the church in succeeding generations. In the Christian art forms we have considered here, we find one Christ in many Christs. It is the Christ of the gospels who inspires artists of all ages to portray him, and yet no one portrait of Christ is the same as all the others. Nonetheless, the Christs in these portraits have inspired Christians of different eras to turn to the one Christ as their savior. Thus in the history of Christian art we are impressed with the power of the incarnation residing in Christ. He was made a man of Jewish flesh but did not become captive to that flesh. He became a man of Greek flesh, of Roman flesh, of Germanic flesh, and of Anglo-Saxon flesh. This same Christ—through the works of Japanese artists, Chinese painters, or Indonesian sculptors—is beginning to assume Asian flesh as well.

Just as with art, so it is with theology. If Christian art can be thought of as a kind of visual theology, Christian theology as we normally understand it is basically a written art. If we can speak of Christian art with a third eye, we must also be able to speak of theology with a third eye. Until Christian theology has acquired this third-dimensional formulation of Christian faith, it will remain a stranger outside the Western world. Black theology in the United States and Africa and liberation theology in Latin America have forcefully demonstrated this fact. Without this third dimensionality Christian theology will remain incomplete, underdeveloped, and impoverished. Fortunately although somewhat belatedly, Christian theology is now entering the era of third dimensionality. Doing theology with Asian spirituality is meant to be a contribution to the anguish and joy, to the frustration and excitement of this new theological era.

NOTES

1. R. H. S. Boyd, *India and the Latin Captivity of the Church* (London: Cambridge University Press, 1974), p. xiii.

2. Daisetz Suzuki, *Essays in Zen Buddhism,* First Series (London: Luzac & Company, 1927), p. 1.

3. Quoted by Kazo Kitamori in his *Theology of the Pain of God* (Richmond, Va.: John Knox Press, 1965), p. 130.

4. James Burns, *The Christ Face in Art* (New York: E. P. Dutton & Co., 1907), p. 3.

5. In *The Christ Face in Art,* James Burns distinguishes more than a dozen types of artistic works on the Christ face, such as the Tuscan, North Italian, Venetian, Flemish, Spanish, etc.

6. Ibid., p. 16.

7. Ibid., p. 30.

8. Ibid., p. 110.

9. *Sibui* is a distinctly Japanese national characteristic that has no exact equivalent in English. It can be described as a kind of quality that conveys a controlled reserve toward life and the world. It is a quality that comes from contemplating our own destiny with Stoic composure. It is exactly the opposite of being glamorous and exhibitionistic. *Sibui* is eloquent in silence, aggressive in resignation, forceful in reserve. It emanates a kind of spiritual power that enables us to cross the boundary of life and death without fear. The formation of *sibui* spirituality comes as a result of the long years of assimilation into the fabric of Japanese society of the spirit of Chinese Confucianism and Buddhism. Perhaps it is in the practice of Zen that this *sibui* quality becomes most evident. Zen is more a way of moral and physical discipline than a system of metaphysics. It is a spirituality that permeates Japanese society and the Japanese people, not a system of philosophy monopolized by thinkers and philosophers. In Zen is summed up the spirituality known as *sibui*.

10. See Masao Takenaka, *Creation and Redemption through Japanese Art* (Osaka, Japan: Segensha, 1966), plate 71. See also his more recent work, *Christian Art in Asia* (Tokyo: Kyo Bun Kwan in association with Christian Conference of Asia, 1975).

26

C. S. Song

The Cross and the Lotus

In this article Song compares and contrasts the essential symbols of Buddhism (the lotus) and Christianity (the cross), both of which he views as pointing to distinct but intersecting and intercommunicating ways to "the deepest aspect of reality" and to deliverance from suffering. These symbols intersect in the people and in the struggle to liberate them from oppression and suffering. "The Cross and the Lotus" is from Song's Third-Eye Theology *(Maryknoll, N.Y.: Orbis Books, 1979), pp. 101–23.*

Suffering touches the heart of God as well as the hearts of human beings. In the suffering of humanity we see and experience the suffering of God. God and human beings are bound together in suffering. That is why theology begins with God's heartache which is caused by human suffering and pain. In the suffering everyone of us has to go through at various stages of life, God suffers. Jesus Christ is the God-human in suffering. And it is this same Christ who is the love of the God-human in action. The cross, from the standpoint of Christian faith, is the supreme symbol of God's suffering love. It has not been surpassed even after two thousand years. In the cross we realize that suffering is not merely physical, institutional, impersonal, or secular. It is religious and human, and thus divine. Suffering is the cross God has to bear with all God's creation.

Another religious symbol that over the centuries has become the focus of the religious devotion and spiritual aspirations of a vast number of people under the influence of Buddhist spirituality is the lotus.[1] The image of Buddha or Bodhisattva seated cross-legged on the lotus has been to the masses a source of

300

comfort and peace. It stills the troubled mind and gives assurance that suffering is not the last word. It helps to maintain serenity in the midst of a turbulent life of bitterness. And it promises a life of bliss when all births cease. The lotus is to Buddhists as a religious symbol what the cross is to Christians. Radically different in every way, these two symbols point to a crucial quest of human life—deliverance.

THE POWER OF SYMBOLS

Both the cross and the lotus are powerful symbols. Without the cross the faith inculcated by the humble carpenter from Nazareth would have dissipated soon after his death. By the same token, without the lotus and what it tries to communicate, the lofty teachings of Buddhism would have probably failed to captivate the devotion of the masses. As it turned out, the spirituality of the cross and the spirituality of the lotus went on to conquer the realms of human life in the West and in the East respectively. In time two distinctive religions were born—the religion of the cross and the religion of the lotus. In addition, out of these two religions two distinct cultures came into being—the culture of the cross and the culture of the lotus. They took separate roads of development for centuries until the dawn of the modern era. But their paths were destined to cross. First through the missionary expansion of the Western churches and then through the translation of Buddhist texts into the European languages, the two religions and cultures met on the crossroad of human history. For missionary Christianity the spirituality of the lotus was atheistic in its teaching and idolatrous in its practice—the object of divine wrath and missionary castigation. However, in Europe itself, the heartland of Christianity, Buddhism fared much better. The philosopher of pessimism, Schopenhauer, for example, found in it a striking echo of his own pessimism. He called the Hegelians who built a grandiose structure of history on ideas "simple realists, optimists, eudaemonists, shallow fellows, Philistines incarnate, bad Christians" and similar things. Then he went on to say:

> The true spirit and kernel of Christianity, as of Brahmanism and Buddhism also, is the knowledge of the vanity of all earthly happiness, complete contempt for it, and the turning away to an existence of quite a different, indeed an opposite, kind. This, I say, is the spirit and purpose of Christianity. . . . Therefore, atheistic Buddhism is much more closely akin to Christianity than are optimistic Judaism and its variety, Islam.[2]

Perhaps Buddhism owes to Schopenhauer more than anybody else its reputation in the West as solely a pessimistic religion.

More recently, the encounter of these two religions and cultures took a sinister turn as they collided on the battlefields of Vietnam. The cross and the lotus quivered and groaned as the tranquility of Indochina was shattered by gunners and bombers, by demonic forces parasitic on the womb of culture. An open letter written by a group of Vietnamese to the American ambassador in 1963 affirmed that "opposition to Ngo Dinh Diem had become for many intellectuals opposition to Christianity." This expression was indicative of the religious and cultural crisis inherent in the political struggle in South Vietnam. The letter in part stated:

> For us Vietnamese, to embrace Christianity means that we would be forbidden to worship our Ancestors, our deceased Parents, when this has been the most important thing in our style of life for thousands of years. . . . The Christians are hybrids, they are eccentric to Vietnamese society, they are absurd with regard to Vietnamese thought. Nor is their language even Vietnamese. . . . The young Vietnamese want to know why there are so many differences between Christianity and their culture, why this religion is so contrary to their *Volksgeist,* why so many monstrous contradictions, why so many absurd superstitions, why this severity and cruelty of the Almighty God who unceasingly curses and threatens men with such horrible words while he ought to be saving them.[3]

It is no consolation for Protestant Christians to know that these questions were directed to the Catholic church, the main body of Christianity in Vietnam that counted the ruling family of Diem among its members. What we see here is the agony of the spirituality of the lotus versus the spirituality of the cross that had been distorted in its cultural forms and misrepresented and abused by those in power.

At any rate, in the cross and the lotus we encounter two powerful religious symbols representing two different ways in which we grasp the world of reality behind the world of phenomena. They are the portals through which we may enter the depth of human spirituality in search of what is ultimate in life. They are pregnant with meanings that concern us in this world and in the world to come. Although life as a whole is saturated with symbols, it is in the religious realm that the symbolic character of life is intensified. For this reason religious symbols embody in themselves human spirituality in communion with the reality from which human life is derived ultimately. As Tillich well expressed the situation:

> The language of faith is the language of symbols. . . . But faith, understood as the state of being ultimately concerned, has no language other than symbols. When saying this I always expect the question: Only a symbol? He who asks this question has not understood . . . the power of symbolic language. One should never say, "only a symbol," but one should say "not less than a symbol."[4]

Thus Tillich speaks of the power of symbols. In fact, life as a whole is under the spell and power of symbols. This is readily seen at a political rally in which the audience is transfixed under the spell of a powerful orator. Political demagogues in particular know almost instinctively the power of symbols and use them skillfully to sway people to their side. A leader like Hitler, for example, was able to exploit in a demonic fashion the power of symbols embodied in a political language to create a fanatical faith in despotism.

In religious symbols we have to do with the experience of revelation. What is revealed cannot be communicated or expressed literally. Literal communication cannot be applied to revelation. In fact, it drives revelation out of human experience. There is thus a basic contradiction in a literal interpretation of scriptures. Scriptures as the communication of divine revelation are highly symbolic in that they try to express what defies the normal means of human communication. Human language has to be stretched beyond its normal logic to capture something that transcends human rationality. Scriptures can thus be interpreted symbolically. This applies not only to the legends and myths of the Bible but also to its historical sections. Literal interpretations of history reveal little of the meaning which transcends history and informs the latter with revelatory significance. The Exodus in the Bible, for example, does not only refer to a historical event—the escape of a group of Hebrews from Egypt—but also to the redemption of life even for those who never participated in the historical Exodus. Therefore a literal interpretation of the Bible kills revelation. Revelation loses its meaning and power under the literalists who insist on regarding the Bible as a verbatim correspondence between what is written down and what transcends history while working within history. What Mircea Eliade, a historian of religion, has to say about symbols is very much to the point. He puts it this way:

> The symbol reveals certain aspects of reality—the deepest aspects— which defy any other means of knowledge. Images, symbols and myths are not irresponsible creations of the psyche; they respond to a need and fulfill a function, that of bringing to light the most hidden modalities of being.[5]

The deepest aspect of reality defies the conventional means of knowledge. That is why revelation must be interpreted symbolically, not literally.

It is important to bear this in mind when Christians approach other religions, including primal religions. The stereotyped judgment of other religions passed by Christians is almost invariably related to idolatry. When Western missionaries went to the world beyond the West, they found themselves surrounded by idols and people who worshiped them. Forgetting entirely the place images and ikons played in certain powerful traditions of Christianity, they launched crusades against the idols and their worshipers. They did not realize that idols were powerful religious symbols that stand for humanity's search for "the deepest aspect of reality." In other words, they interpreted idols literally, not symbolically. A literal interpretation of the meaning of idols resulted more often than not in a literal destruction of the idols. The burning of idols became therefore a necessary part of the conversion process. It was regarded as the manifestation of a genuine conversion from the worship of idols to the worship of the one true God. The following account is typical of the ritual of idol burning formerly carried out after the preacher or the missionary was reasonably sure that a genuine conversion had taken place. This account had as its background a small town in Korea in the early part of this century. The convert was a young Korean man, Chin Pai, for whom the time had come to demonstrate his confession of the Christian faith by burning the idols worshiped in his parents' household:

> The six Christians, including Chin Pai's mother, gathered for the burning of the idols. They piled them all up in the courtyard, first the guest-room guard spirit, then the rags tied to the ceiling beam in the kitchen and the picture of the kitchen god, then the bunch of old straw shoes under the gate, and the rags and straw rope under the rice hulling room. . . .
>
> From the yard they took the site god, an earthenware jar covered with a hood of thatch. They smashed the jar and burned the thatch. . . . Last of all they brought out the ancestral tablets, five of them, representing five generations. . . . Chin Pai touched a match to the pile, and as it burned, they sang one of the newly learned songs of praise.[6]

This was a bonfire celebrating a Christian victory over pagan idolatry. A clean break was made not only with the converts' religious past but with their ancestral roots also, for not even the ancestral tablets could be spared in the ritual. This was not unlike the iconoclasm that took place during the Reformation as a result of the extreme aversion Protestant Christianity felt for religious images. But if we do away with all images and symbols, then the ultimate reality they stand for is also liable to disappear from the religious consciousness of the people. This can be partly shown in the worship service of a Protestant church, especially a church that belongs to the Reformed tradition. The worship is bare and unadorned. The experience of being in a presence of a *mysterium tremendum et fascinosum* is, of course, not obtained easily.[7]

JEWISH AND CHRISTIAN REACTIONS TO THE SYMBOLS OF OTHER FAITHS

What missionary Christianity tended to miss was the symbolic meaning of idols and images in other religions. It seldom occurred to the zealous preachers of the gospel that the idols and images "provide 'openings' into a transhistorical world. . . . Thanks to them, the different 'histories' can intercommunicate."[8] I believe this observation by a historian of religions is relevant for Christian theology. But the fact is that the meaning and spirituality behind idols and symbols used in one religious and cultural milieu tend to elude the grasp of those brought up in another religious and cultural milieu. A statue of Buddha, in a museum in, say, London or New York, is to most Western viewers no more than an object of aesthetic curiosity. For them it is not something to which they express veneration and devotion. On the other hand, a crucifix to people in a remote village in the Orient who have never come into contact with Christianity cannot appear as a symbol representing God's love in Jesus Christ for the world. It is therefore evident that idols, images, and religious symbols are incomprehensible to outsiders without interpretation. Consequently, they are bound to suffer at the hands of militant missionary religions.

It is in this connection that the treatment of idols in the Bible, especially in the Old Testament, needs to be reconsidered and reinterpreted. This is important because in most cases the Christian denunciation of idols and images takes its cue directly from the Bible. Jeremiah, for example, mocks idols in a language at once derisive and amusing:

> Do not fall into the ways of the nations,
> do not be awed by signs in the heavens;
> it is the nations who go in awe of these.
> For the carved images of the nations are a sham,
> they are nothing but timber cut from the forest,
> worked with his chisel by a craftsman;
> he adorns it with silver and gold,
> fastening them on with hammer and nails
> so that they do not fall apart.
> They can no more speak than a scarecrow in a plot of cucumbers,
> they must be carried, for they cannot walk.
> Do not be afraid of them: they can do no harm,
> and they have no power to do good [Jer. 10:1–5].

This was a prophet's version of demythologizing idols! Jeremiah exposed the false nature of idols. Idols were things fashioned by human hands. There was no life in them. They could neither move for themselves nor do harm or good. There was thus no reason to be afraid of them. If one was still in doubt as to whether idols have no power over human beings, one was shown how they were constructed out of materials imported from various countries. Thus Jeremiah went on to say:

> The beaten silver is brought from Tarshish
> and the gold from Ophir;
> all are the work of craftsmen and goldsmiths.
> They are draped in violet and purple,
> all the work of skilled men [Jer. 10:9]. [9]

Idols were completely demythologized. People were exhorted to worship the one true God, the creator.

This, however, does not mean that the religious elements contained in the worship of foreign idols were entirely rejected and excluded from the religion of Israel. In fact, there are strong indications that the people of Israel adopted foreign religious feelings and beliefs into their own religion, adapting them to their needs. Thus John Gray, an Old Testament scholar, cautions us against a too-sweeping judgment on the idolatrous practices of the Canaanite religions. "In considering the condemnation of idolatry in Israel," he writes, "we must bear in mind the varying degrees in which Israel assimilated the culture of Canaan." Then he goes on to illustrate his observation by referring to the Feast of Tabernacles, which is closely related to the agricultural life of the people. He points out that the Feast of Tabernacles was associated with the New Year festival, which "was the chief seasonal festival in the peasants' year," and that "from Zech. 14:16 it is apparent that the kingship of God was a prominent theme of that festival. Psalms and passages in the prophets on this theme reveal a striking affinity in imagery and subject matter with the Ras Shamra myth of the kingship of Baal. Here the Hebrews seized upon the Canaanite expression of faith in Providence in nature and adapted it to their own peculiar ethos as the expression of their faith in Providence in history and the moral order."[10]

It seems that such religious leaders of Israel as the prophets and priests were more astute religiously than we care to believe. On the one hand, they attacked idol worship with great vehemence. They were objects of terror (Jer. 50:38), a cause of trembling (1 Kings 15:13; 2 Chron. 15:16), and an abomination to the people of Israel (2 Chron. 15:8). At the same time, idols were vanity (Isa. 66:3) and a nonentity (Lev. 19:4; Pss. 96:5; 97:7; Isa. 2:8; 18:20; Hab. 2:18; Zech. 11:17).[11] But this was not the whole story. For even a very central part of the worship of Baal related to the question of providence was incorporated into the faith of Israel in the God whose providence was at work in history and the moral order of the universe. What the prophets condemned was the "preoccupation with the material fruits of creation rather than with the nature and will of the Creator himself in idolatry in the general sense."[12] Defined in this way, idolatry, we must admit, can be said to be present in all religions implicitly or explicitly. For no religion is entirely free from the human propensity to rely on something finite as an expression of what is infinite. Being finite themselves, human beings are bound to finite objects in which the infinite is believed to be present. Thus care must be taken to distinguish between idols and images that have become the ultimate objects of worship and devotion, and idols and images through which human beings seek to grasp and express the spiritual reality on which they depend for the power and meaning of life.[13] Granted that the distinction is not always easy to make, that is still no reason for Christian believers to vent their iconoclastic zeal on the idols and images of other religions at the expense of the spiritual reality these images seek to represent. Idols and images can be, in the words of Eliade quoted earlier, "openings into a trans-historical world."

As Eliade points out, this is what happened during the Christianization of Europe. Because of its importance for our discussion here, let me quote his observation in full in the hope that it will help us grasp the theological meaning of other religions from the Christian point of view:

Much has been said about the unification of Europe by Christianity: and it is never better attested than when we see how Christianity co-ordinated the popular religious traditions. It was by means of Christian hagiography that the local cults—from Thrace to Scandinavia and from the Tagus to the Dnieper—were brought under a "common denominator." By the fact of their Christianization, the gods and the sacred places of the whole of Europe not only received common names but rediscovered, in a sense, their own archetypes and therefore their universal valencies: a fountain in Gaul, regarded as sacred ever since prehistoric times, but sanctioned by the presence of a divine or regional figure, became sacred *for Christianity as a whole* after its consecration to the Virgin Mary. All the slayers of dragons were assimilated to Saint George or to some other Christian hero; all the Gods of the storm to holy Elijah. . . . For, by Christianizing the ancient European religious heritage, it [Christianity] not only purified the latter, but took up, into the new spiritual dispensation of mankind, all that deserved to be "saved" of the old practices, beliefs and hopes of pre-Christian man. Even today, in popular Christianity, there are rites and beliefs surviving from the neo-lithic: the boiled grain in honour of the dead, for instance (the *coliva* of Eastern and Aegean Europe). The Christianization of the peasant levels of Europe was effected thanks above all to the images: everywhere they were rediscovered, and had only to be revalorized, reintegrated and given new names.[14]

Religion, like any other cultural phenomenon, is a highly complex affair. Its history is, in a sense, a history of growth through intercommunication, integration, and assimilation among diverse religious practices and beliefs. This indicates that human spirituality, despite differences in its forms and expressions, shares some basic aspirations and characteristics. Christian theology has not taken this fact seriously. Its assertion of uniqueness is often made without taking into account the very complex history of Christianity on the one hand and the contributions of other faiths and religions on the other.

Furthermore, Eliade's observation quoted above helps us to realize that human spirituality, although closely associated with a particular cultural and historical context, is capable of transcending that context. It is at once bound to it and can be freed from it. In fact, human spirituality at its deepest level transcends its own cultural and historical particularity and intercommunicates with other spiritualities. The Christianization of Europe as discussed by Eliade is a case in point. The conversion of Asia to Buddhism is another remarkable example. Joseph Kitagawa calls it the "Pan-Asianness of Buddhism." As he puts it:

Buddhism continued to grow in India's immediate neighbors and also in other areas where indigenous religions and cultures had been established. In both cases the genius of Buddhism enabled it to maintain and express its *Lebensgefühl*, which is distinct and unmistakable. Eventually, Buddhism developed into a Pan-Asian religion, closely identified with various cultures of Asia.[15]

As it made its way into other parts of Asia, Buddhism was able to transcend the "Indianness" within which it had been conceived and born. And in the course of its expansion and development throughout Asia, Buddhism has remained the religion identifiable through the symbol of the lotus just as the cross has become the symbol of the Christian faith since its inception two thousand years ago.

CONTRAST BETWEEN THE CROSS AND THE LOTUS

The question we must now ask is: What has the cross to do with the lotus? As early as the third century, Tertullian raised this question in relation to Jerusalem and Athens: What has Jerusalem to do with Athens? His answer was negative. Jerusalem—the city of the holy temple, the place where Jesus was crucified, the symbol of salvation revealed to the world in Christ in Tertullian's mind—had nothing to do with Athens. Athens stood for reason whereas Jerusalem was the embodiment of the sacred. Athens was a "secular" city in contrast to Jerusalem, a "holy" city. Furthermore, with its many gods and shrines Athens was a center of paganism in the ancient Mediterranean world. There St. Paul had delivered his famous sermon on the unknown God before the Court of Areopagus. "Men of Athens," he declared:

I see that in everything that concerns religion you are uncommonly scrupulous. For as I was going round looking at the objects of your worship, I noticed among other things an altar bearing the inscription "To an Unknown God." What you worship but do not know—this is what I now proclaim [Acts 17:22–23].

Thus it was Paul who in his missionary zeal sought to penetrate the depth of Greek spirituality which had blossomed into art, literature, and philosophy on the one hand and worship of every conceivable deity on the other. Paul's effort in Athens was a dramatic demonstration of the fact that Jerusalem had much to do with Athens. It can even be said to have foreshadowed the Hellenization of Christianity by leaps and bounds in the subsequent history of the development of Christian thought in the West. Tertullian's verdict was wrong. The history of Christian thought was in a true sense a history of how Greek philosophy, especially that of Plato and Aristotle, became integrated into the mainstream of Christian faith. As has been pointed out, ". . . through the whole history of Christianity in the West there runs the dynamic of the Gospel's course from the Jew to the Greek, from the Greek to the barbarian."[16]

However that may be, the cross and the lotus seem to have little in common, at first sight at any rate. The lotus springs from the surface of the water. When the wind blows and the water moves, the lotus also moves. It seems in perfect harmony with nature around it. In short, it gives the appearance of being at peace with itself.[17] In contrast, the cross strikes out powerfully, painfully, and defiantly from the earth. It penetrates space and is incongruous with nature. The lotus appeals to our aesthetic feelings, whereas the cross is revolting to the eyes of the beholder. The lotus is soft in texture and graceful in shape, while the cross is hard and harsh. The lotus moves with nature, whereas the cross stands ruggedly and tragically out of the barren earth. The lotus distinguishes itself in gentleness, while the cross is the epitome of human brutality. The lotus beckons and the cross repels. Indeed, what has the cross to do with the lotus? They represent two entirely different spiritualities which seem to be totally incompatible. They seem to have nothing in common.

But the contrast between the cross and the lotus may be deceptive. Essentially, they are two different answers to some basic questions about life and death. They seek to unravel problems and difficulties that beset us in our earthly pilgrimage. They also try to point to the fulfillment of human destiny in the eternal and blissful presence of the divine. They are not primarily concerned with a metaphysical solution to these very important problems, but with practical, day-to-day struggles in the harsh reality of society. Neither the cross nor the lotus, fundamentally speaking, is a system of thought, a set of rituals, or an institution of devotion. Originally they sprang out of the midst of the daily life of the people. They are religions of the people, but theologians— both in Christianity and Buddhism— have taken them away from the people and turned them into theological systems and religious principles bearing little relationship to the genuine fears and aspirations of the people. It is thus not surprising that the cross and the lotus do not intersect in their theological systems or ecclesiastical structures. In fact, these systems and structures only pull the two spiritualities further apart. The place for the cross and the lotus to intersect and intercommunicate is the people—the people who have to fight both spiritual and physical fears, the people who have to live and die without knowing why. Then and only then can the cross and the lotus begin to intercommunicate; they can then begin to point to the mystery that surrounds human destiny. Thus intercommunication and intercommunion of different spiritualities should begin with the people, and with the ways in which they try to cope with the problems of life and the world in sociopolitical and religious terms.

This can be illustrated, first of all, by the way Jesus and Buddha tried to communicate their message through stories and parables. Jesus gave the following reason for using parables to his disciples: "It has been granted to you to know the secrets of the kingdom of Heaven; but to those others it has not been granted" (Matt. 13:11). Then he went on to explain the meaning of the parable of the sower.[18] An abstruse mystery should not remain the monopoly of a few. Jesus mingled with the crowd and took pains to communicate the message of the gospel to them. He definitely broke away from the religious elitism of his day and brought religion back to the people. In a sense he was the leader of a new religious movement around which the farmers and workers, the illiterate and the oppressed, could gather. He thus posed a threat to the official religion consolidated on hierarchical structures of religious orders and teachings not readily accessible or intelligable to outsiders.

In the rise of Buddhism in India we also see something of a religious reformation that returned religion from a religious elite to the people in the street. The religious and social situation of India at the time of Buddha in the sixth century B.C. was similar to that of the Jewish community in Palestine during the life of Jesus. "At the time of the Buddha," writes Kenneth Ch'en, "the dominant position in Indian society was held by the brahmans. They held the key to knowledge, and the power that went with that knowledge."[19] Brahamanism, like Judaism in Jesus' day, was the privilege of the religious leaders and the burden of the masses. As a reformer who ended up by founding a new religion, Buddha

> repudiated the brahmanical claims that the *Vedas* were the sole and infallible source of religious truth. He also rejected correct performance of the rituals as means of salvation, and he disapproved of the Upanishadic emphasis on intellectual means to attain emancipation. He also protested against the iniquities of the caste system, especially the high pretensions of the brahman class, and welcomed among his followers members from not only the four castes but also from among the outcasts.[20]

Buddha was thus the first in the history of India to revolt against the caste system as the chief misfortune of Indian society.

It is therefore not surprising that Buddha tried to communicate a message of emancipation from the suffering of the world in plain language. We can hear him saying something like this:

> I have taught the truth which is excellent in the beginning, excellent in the middle, and excellent in the end; it is glorious in its spirit and glorious in its letter. But simple as it is, the people cannot understand it. I must speak to them in their own language. I must adapt my thoughts to their thoughts. They are like unto children and love to hear tales. Therefore, I will tell them stories to explain the glory of the dharma. If they cannot grasp the truth in the abstract by which I have reached it, they may nevertheless come to understand it, if it is illustrated in parables.[21]

It is clear from this that Buddha fully grasped the dynamics of people in religion. As Buddhism spread to China, Japan, and Southeast Asia, it became a religion of the people that created popular culture and cultivated a sense of solidarity among ordinary men and women in all walks of life. To be sure, the teachings of Buddha in their high and lofty forms never filtered down to the people unadulterated. But what is important is that Buddha brought to common men and women a sense of well-being, security, and above all a sense of destiny.

In this way a religious faith can become alive and genuine if it casts aside ecclesiastical pretensions and formidable theological systems and touches the lives and hearts of the people. As previously mentioned, both Jesus and Buddha labored to bring the light of a new faith into the lives of the people. They were close to the people, used popular language, and told stories and parables that came right out of the everyday experiences of the people. No wonder that we find in the Sutra of the Lotus Flower of the Wonderful Law the story of the lost son that bears a remarkable resemblance to the parable of the prodigal son in Luke 15:11–32.

According to the Buddhist story of the lost son, a young man left his father and went to another city where he became extremely poor. He was reduced to begging for his food. In contrast, his father grew rich and moved to a big estate where he lived in great luxury. But all the time he grieved over his lost son and said to himself:

> I am old and well advanced in years, and though I have great possessions I have no son. Alas that time should do its work upon me, and that all this wealth should perish unused! . . . It would be bliss indeed if my son might enjoy all my wealth!

One day the son wandered into his father's land, and the drama of the reunion of the father and son gradually unfolded:

> Then the poor man, in search of food and clothing, came to the rich man's home. And the rich man was sitting in great pomp at the gate of his house, surrounded by a large throng of attendants. . . . When he saw him the poor man was terrified . . . for he thought that he had happened on a king or on some high officer of state, and had no business there. . . . So he quickly ran away.
>
> But the rich man . . . recognized his son as soon as he saw him and he was full of joy . . . and thought: "This is wonderful! I have found him who shall enjoy my riches. He of whom I thought constantly has come back, now that I am old and full of years!" Then, longing for his son, he sent swift messengers, telling them to go and fetch him quickly.

The story goes on to describe how the father, who lived in a highly class-conscious society, was not able to disclose his identity to his own son and take him back into his household. The poor man had to go away without realizing that he had been in his own father's house. The father then contrived to have his son hired to work in his own household as a servant. Every day he watched with compassion as his son cleared away a refuse heap. Then one day the rich man came down, took off his wreath and jewels and rich clothes, put on dirty garments, covered his body with dust, and, taking a basket in his hand, went up to his son. And he greeted him at a distance and said, "Take this basket and clear away the dust at once!" By this means he managed to speak to his son.

In this way, the old man made every attempt to make his son feel at home but did not reveal his own identity. In the meantime, the son proved to be a frugal, honest, and industrious man. Finally, knowing that his end was near, the old man

> sent for the poor man again, presented him before a gathering of his relatives, and, in the presence of the king, his officers, and the people of town and country, he said: "Listen, gentlemen! This is my son, whom I begot. . . . To him I leave all my family revenues, and my private wealth he shall have as his own."[22]

Consequently, through the father's painful and patient effort the son was reinstated in society and accepted into his father's blessing.

It goes without saying that the ethos of this Buddhist story is quite different from that of the biblical story of the prodigal son. It is Asian through and through in its emphasis on class distinctions that affect even family relations, on accumulation of wealth as a moral and social virtue, and on inheritance as a chief factor affecting the father-son relationship. These are the elements that are part and parcel of a traditional Asian society. For the people in the street such social factors provide a background against which a religious truth can be apprehended. There is in this story no reference to the son's repentance, no mention of the elder son's protest against the father's treatment of the lost son. Despite all these differences in ethos and details, the story points up the father's compassion for his son, the expression of which is very Asian in its reserve and its respect for social conventions. It stresses the acceptance of the son by the father through a ceremony in accordance with the father's social status. The resemblance of the Buddhist story of the lost son to the biblical story of the prodigal son may be accidental. But it is evidence of the fact that deep in people's spirituality is a reflection of God's love and compassion for the world. Jesus Christ, we must admit, is not merely a reflection of God's love. He is the embodiment of that love. In any case, God's compassion for the son in the Buddhist story may be seen as a reflection, however imperfect, of God's passionate love in the parable of the prodigal son.

ST. PAUL ON GOD'S REDEMPTIVE WORK IN THE WORLD

This, I believe, can lead us to speak of redemptive elements in cultures and histories outside the direct influence of Christian faith. It is basic to St. Paul's perception of God's redemptive work in the world. It is clear also in his polemic against those who turn their backs on God. As Paul sees it:

> For all that may be known of God by men lies plain before their eyes; indeed God himself has disclosed it to them. His invisible attributes, that is to say his everlasting power and deity, have been visible, ever since the world began, to the eye of reason, in the things he has made. There is therefore no possible defense for their conduct; knowing God, they have refused to honour him as God, or to render him thanks [Rom. 1:19-21].

This is a controversial passage, to say the least. It has been interpreted as a condemnation of everything "pagan." It is regarded as throwing a negative light on whatever is not compatible with Christian traditions and practices. Furthermore, it has been used as an argument against crediting a positive meaning to cultures and histories that have had little to do with the culture and history directly associated with Christianity.[23]

True, what St. Paul says here is an indictment of idol worshipers and those who rebel against the moral law of God. But the important thing for us to remember is that not all cultures and histories outside the sphere of Christian influence are corrupted totally with idolatry and impiety; they are not all works of a demonic power that sets itself against the God of Jesus Christ. Yes, there are demonic elements in them. But what culture and history are completely free from such elements? No religion, Christianity not excepted, is entirely free from it. Paul Tillich has put it well when he says:

> Demonization of the holy occurs in all religions day by day, even in the religion which is based on the self-negation of the finite in the Cross of Christ. The quest for unambiguous life is, therefore, most radically directed against the ambiguity of the holy and the demonic in the religious realm.[24]

If we think of the corruption in the highest circles of the Christian church, of the horrible deeds of the Inquisition in the name of God, of the tragedy of the Crusades, of the disunity of the church through the centuries—if we think of all these and other evil events in the history of Christianity, we realize that Tillich is not exaggerating. Perhaps the conscience of the Christian church should have taught its members to be able to say: since even the church with its intense concentration on God's redeeming love in Jesus Christ has not been free of what Tillich calls demonization, how much more difficult has it been for other religions that have no direct knowledge of God's salvation in Jesus Christ! We therefore must admit that the Christian attitude toward other religions has in general been opposed to an open dialogue. This often results in a wholesale condemnation of other expressions of human spirituality as if they were objects of divine judgment.

Thus we should look at St. Paul's words quoted above from a different perspective. To be sure, he does not condone in the least despicable practices that debase human nature and show scorn for divine creation. That is why he condemns immorality, infidelity, and all kinds of depravity. But this does not cancel out the fact that God's love and power have been at work in the world since the beginning of creation. Human sin does not destroy God's work of creation. How could it? Otherwise sin would be stronger than the power of God. The history of the Christian church is an eloquent proof of this. The church continues to exist despite a demonizing tendency within it. The message of salvation continues to be proclaimed in spite of demonic distortions of God's love within the church. And people continue to rally to Christ, even though the church is often divided and its pettiness as an institution is revealed. God is above all these human failures and sins. And at times God works through them. It is a source of consolation and encouragement that the truth of God has never abandoned the church in spite of the church's failure to measure up to the glory of God. If this is true with the Christian church, it must also be true with the whole of creation. The idolatry and impiety we see in cultures and histories outside Christianity really do help conceal God's truth. But there are moments and events that still disclose God's continuing presence in a society that has not been shaped by Christianity. These are what I call redemptive moments and redemptive events. While fragmentary and imperfect, they are nonetheless genuine. They reflect in some way God's redeeming love and power that have become incarnate in Jesus Christ.

To avoid any misunderstanding, let me stress that Buddha, for example, is not Jesus Christ. For that matter neither is Jesus Christ a Bodhisattva. As historical personalities Buddha and Jesus have little to do with one another. The cultural and religious contexts in which each of them carried out his mission were vastly different. But the ultimate difference from the Christian point of view comes from our faith in Jesus Christ as the direct and complete embodiment of God's saving love. The affirmation of such a faith, however, should not blind Christians to God's continuing presence and work outside Christianity. In fact, it should open our eyes to perceive a redemptive quality in moments and events in other cultures and histories that have to be considered substantively related to the work of Jesus Christ.

These redemptive moments and events, in my view, result from what St. Paul regards as God's self-disclosure in creation since the world began. Christian faith in God's redemption in and through Jesus Christ must embrace this global dimension. And the best way to appreciate the global dimension of redemptive interactions between faith in Jesus Christ and other faiths is not theoretical or doctrinal. When we realize how ordinary men and women must struggle to cope with the stresses and pressures of life and to find an ultimate meaning in our finite existence, we can begin to discern redemptive events and moments in their lives and to relate them to what God has done in Jesus Christ. Viewed in this perspective, religions and cultures outside Christianity cease to be merely objects of Christian condemnation; they begin to acquire an internal relationship with what Christians believe and do.

According to a legend, after attaining enlightenment Gautama said to a mendicant he met by chance on the road:

> Having myself crossed the ocean of suffering, I must help others to cross it. Freed myself, I must set others free. This is the vow which I made in the past when I saw all that lives in distress.[25]

Compare this vow of Buddha with Jesus' announcement at the beginning of his mission. According to Luke's Gospel, Jesus quoted the book of Isaiah and said:

> The Spirit of the Lord is upon me because he has anointed me;
> he has sent me to announce good news to the poor,
> to proclaim release for prisoners and recovery of sight for the
>   blind;
> to let the broken victims go free,
> to proclaim the year of the Lord's favor [Luke 4:18–19].

At first we are struck by the fundamental differences between Buddha's vow and Jesus' announcement. Buddha is a self-appointed herald of the good news he had experienced and understood after a long search that culminated in his enlightenment under the bo-tree. Jesus Christ is conscious of having been appointed and sent by God. In his vow Buddha does not claim any special relationship with a deity, but for Jesus the Spirit of the Lord is present and working in him. Again the main tenet of Buddha's vow consists of emancipation from the world, which is an ocean of suffering and distress. In contrast, Jesus' announcement is filled with an active concern for the social and political conditions that victimize the innocent, the powerless, and the poor.

What we see, in other words, are two drastically different ways of understanding and appropriating the providence of God, and these ways are not to be confused or identified. But this should not hinder us from realizing that the expression of Buddha's compassion for the masses in his vow and the way he toiled unselfishly for their emancipation from pain and suffering are not without redemptive significance. Can we not say that Buddha's way is also a part of the drama of salvation which God has acted out fully in the person and work of Jesus Christ? The histories of nations and peoples that are not under the direct impact of Christianity are not just "natural" histories running their course in complete separation from God's redemptive love and power. In this sense, there is no "natural" history. The history of a nation and the dynamics of its rise and fall cannot be explained entirely by natural forces or sociopolitical factors. There are redemptive elements in all nations that condemn human corruption and encourage what is noble and holy. Our evaluation of the history of a nation is not complete until such redemptive elements are properly recognized. From the Christian point of view, the redemptive elements in human history are witnesses to the presence in the world of the God who, in St. Paul's words, "sent forth his Son, born of woman, born under the law, to redeem those who were under the law, so that they might receive adoption as sons" (Gal. 4:4). Here is a mystery the profundity of which cannot be measured or explained by the simplistic logic of a heaven and a hell brandished by zealous Christians. In my view Christian faith should at least include a readiness to acknowledge that God somehow uses the redemptive elements outside Christianity to prevent human history from going completely bankrupt, to sustain a world that often verges on destruction through such human cruelty as we witnessed in World War II in which the "Christian" West was brutally and demonically involved. Our acknowledgement of this fact should be accompanied by thankfulness to God for not leaving the world to its own destructive devices and meaningless chaos.

THE BODHISATTVA AND SUFFERING HUMANITY

The Buddhist concept of a Bodhisattva takes on, in this connection, an important theological meaning. A Bodhisattva occupies a place of great importance in Mahayana Buddhism as a person who follows the footsteps of Buddha and for the sake of suffering humanity refuses to enter into Buddhahood. Buddha's "prime purpose was to save mankind. He was extroverted to his fellows' needs, and his own were of no importance. He was the dedicated servant of all men, and so long as the least of them lacked enlightenment he vowed to refuse for himself that guerdon of a thousand lives."[26] The difficulty for Christians lies in the fact that a Bodhisattva is a human being. Theologically speaking, for a human being to save other human beings is a religious presumption that contradicts the basic meaning of the cross. For Christians salvation is the work of God, not of humanity. But this should not close our mind to the redemptive quality evident in a Bodhisattva, that is, the quality of putting the spiritual needs of others before our own, the readiness to enter into the suffering of our fellow human beings, and the goal toward which the human spirit should strive.

Bodhisattvas in areas under Buddhist influence perform the function of a spiritual catharsis similar to that accomplished by the prophets of ancient Israel. The crucial question is not whether Bodhisattvas are redeemers in the sense that Jesus Christ is our redeemer, for they are not. But because of them and through them people may see something of God's redemption at work in the world. Because of them and through them the world is not entirely lost. To put it positively, perhaps because of them and through them God gives hope to the world and shows a readiness to save people from destruction. The story in the Old Testament of Abraham pleading with God to save Sodom and Gomorrah can be cited as an example of my meaning. After knowing God's resolve to destroy the two wicked cities, Abraham interceded for them, asking God if God would still carry out the plan of destruction if some righteous people could be found in them. God's answer was a clear no. If there were fifty good people, thirty, even as few as ten in these cities, said God, "I will pardon the whole place for their sake" (Gen. 18:16–33). These few people constituted what I call redemptive elements for Sodom and Gomorrah. Because of them the cities would be spared and forgiven.

Let us expand this biblical story to cover historical experiences outside the biblical tradition. What redeems history—any history!—from utter nonsense and despair is the few good people we can find, even in corrupt cities like Sodom and Gomorrah, or Bodhisattvas in a society and culture like India that is outwardly and totally uninformed by a faith in Jesus Christ. The Bodhisattvas themselves are not redemptive from the viewpoint of Christian faith, but they are evidence of God's redemptive power and of humanity's hope in the future. They are witnesses to the fact that God has not forsaken the world, that the power of God's love has not been overcome by the demonic power of destruction.

At this point we recall the scene of the last judgment in chapter 25 of Matthew's Gospel. The king of the judgment seat says to the sheep standing at his right hand:

> You have my Father's blessings; come, enter and possess the kingdom that has been ready for you since the world was made. For when I was hungry, you gave me food; when thirsty, you gave me drink; when I was a stranger you took me into your home, when naked you clothed me; when I was ill you came to my help, when in prison you visited me [Matt. 25:34–36].

For the righteous these words of approval come as a complete surprise, and they do not conceal their bewilderment. They quickly reply that they have never seen the king in such misery or deprivation. They are then told that "anything you did for one of my brothers here, however humble, you did it to me" (Matt. 25:40). A conclusion we may draw is that throughout human history there are men and women who have gone about doing the king's business without being aware that they are in the king's service. Through what they are and what they do, they bring hope to those in despair, transmit light in the midst of darkness, point to life when people are threatened with death, and bring freedom to imprisoned bodies and spirits. In so doing, they knowingly or unknowingly mediate God's redemptive power to those with whom they come into contact.

It is a cause for Christians to rejoice if they are able to set aside their preconceived ideas and prejudices. They should see the mission of the church as consisting not of conquering members of other faiths but of growing with them in the knowledge and experience of God's saving work in the world. For one thing, we Christians must humbly admit that institutional Christianity alone cannot save the world. This is a historical fact as well as a theological truth that can hardly be refuted. The institutional church in Asia, with few exceptions, is a minority entity and will remain so. Its missionary work came to an end in communist China, which has about a quarter of the world's population. Furthermore, India—the Asian nation with the second largest population in the world—is largely under the influence of Hinduism. In Indonesia the

Christian church has made significant progress in terms of membership. Despite the part the church has played in building Indonesia as a nation, Islam continues to exert a dominant influence over the lives of the people.[27]

This does not mean that the churches in Asia can forego their mission and retreat into the inner sanctuaries of a Christian community sheltered from external forces at work in society and among the people. But it does mean that the mission of the Christian church in Asia can no longer be conceived of only in terms of the territorial expansion of the institutional church or a statistical increase in membership. The mission of the church is the more fundamental task of informing the Asian spirituality shaped by Asian cultures and religions with the love and compassion of God in Jesus Christ. In addition, Asian Christians together with people of other faiths and ideologies must seek to transform Asian society on the basis of freedom, justice, and equality. Socio-political conditions in Asia in recent decades have created a situation that not only makes such a mission of the Christian church possible but also necessary. For religions like Buddhism that are traditionally known as world-denying have been forced by external social and political events to take an active part in the life of the nations where they find themselves. This is another illustration of the way in which different cultural and religious spiritualities must seek to meet and find one another—not in the heat of theoretical and doctrinal disputes but in the very life of the nations where people live, suffer, and die.

The involvement of Vietnamese Buddhists in the tragic war that ravaged their country and ended with communist domination of the entire nation offers an illuminating example of how the "Christian" part of the world failed to work with redemptive elements in Vietnam to create a new society of freedom and hope for the people. In memory let us return to a hot summer day—the 11th of June, 1963—when a Buddhist monk, Thich Quang-Duc, burned himself to death on Phan-dingh-Phung Street in Saigon "to call the attention of the world public to the sufferings of the Vietnamese people under Ngo-Dinh-Diem's oppressive regime."[28] In the years that followed, the self-immolation of monks continued as a protest against the cruel war and as a sacrifice for the restoration of peace. This was literally "the lotus in the sea of fire." The world was shocked by these acts of self-destruction and could not understand their meaning. The Vietnamese monk and scholar Thich Nhat Hanh recounts his conversation with an American doctor to whom he was able to explain the meaning of self-immolation by his fellow monks. "She [the American doctor] saw self-immolation as an act of savagery, violence and fanaticism, requiring a condition of mental unbalance. When I explained to her that the venerable Thich Quang-Duc was over seventy, that I had lived with him for nearly one year at Long-Vinh pagoda and found him a very kind and lucid person and that he was calm and in full possession of his mental faculties when he burned himself, she could not believe it. She could not understand because she was unable, though not unwilling, to look at the act of self-burning from any angle but her own."[29]

The inability to understand the spirit of other cultures and religions bedevils human relations, blocks intercultural communication, and creates and perpetuates the tragedy of human conflict and war. Catholicism—the dominant form of Christianity in Vietnam—was in no position to understand its Buddhist compatriots. "Certainly," writes Frances FitzGerald,

> . . . the French had always shown great favoritism towards the Catholics, turning them into a self-conscious elitist minority without necessarily imparting to them a greater degree of French culture. Vietnamese Catholicism was harsh and medieval, a product of the strict patriarchate of the Vietnamese village rather than of the liberal French Church. Its churches stood like fortresses in the center of each Catholic village, manifesting the permanent defensive posture of the Catholics towards all other Vietnamese.[30]

Thus to the Christian world, both inside and outside Vietnam, the Buddhist involvement was regarded either as part of a communist conspiracy or as a way to gain self-salvation in a region of eternal bliss. The cross did not seem to meet the lotus in the sea of fire raging over Vietnam.

In his June 1965 letter to Martin Luther King, Jr., Thich Nhat Hanh further explained what it meant for a monk to immolate himself as an expression of religious faith and of social and political concern. Thich Nhat Hanh's statement has much bearing on our affirmation of the redemptive elements outside the Christian church. The letter in part reported:

> What the monks said in the letters they left before burning themselves aimed only at alarming, at moving the hearts of the oppressors and at calling the attention of the world to the suffering endured then by the Vietnamese. To burn oneself by fire is to prove that what one is saying is of the utmost importance. There is nothing more painful than burning oneself. . . . During the ceremony of ordination, as practised in the Mahayana tradition, the monk candidate is required to burn one, or more, small spots on his body in taking the vow to observe the 250 rules of a bhikshu, to live the life of a monk, to attain enlightenment and to devote his life to the salvation of all beings. . . . When the words are uttered while kneeling before the community of sangha and experiencing this kind of pain, they will express all the seriousness of one's heart and mind, and carry much greater weight.[31]

The pain of suffering must accompany an act of love and compassion for others. The pain of self-immolation is a radical consequence of the symbolic pain a monk has to go through at his ordination. In this pain is included the pain of his neighbors, friends, and compatriots. And surely in this pain is reflected the pain of God who must have been present in the extreme suffering and pain of the Vietnamese people. The self-immolation of monks, if carried out in the spirit described by Thich Nhat Hanh, was a painful expression of the redemptive elements at war with destruction and inhumanity. Thich Nhat Hanh went on to say in the same letter:

> In the Buddhist belief, life is not confined to a period of 60 or 80 or 100 years: life is eternal. Life is not confined to this body: life is universal. To express will by burning oneself, therefore, is not to commit an act of destruction but to perform an act of construction, i.e., to suffer and to die for the sake of one's people.[32]

Such a statement can be translated into the language of Christian eschatology. The moment of death of the monk in the act of self-immolation was an eschatological moment for him personally and for his nation. If we accept Thich Nhat Hanh's interpretation of the death of a self-immolated monk as not a destruction of life but a construction of life in the Buddhist sense, death for the monk was both the fulfillment of his religious faith in the search for eternal life and a powerful impact on the people of Vietnam to work for the transformation of society.

The eschatological moment for the monk, therefore, did not come at the end of time in an indefinite future. It came at the midstream of history. Before it were both the struggle for freedom and peace for the country devastated by war and life in the presence of the eternal God. This is not to extol death as a means to salvation or social transformation. Death as a part of the Buddhist teaching regarding the extinction of self as a way to Nirvana does not seem to play an essential role in these particular instances of self-immolation in the busy streets of Saigon in the midst of a national crisis. If Thich Nhat Hanh's interpretation is right, I am inclined to believe that the death of these monks may have had a redemptive significance. Again I must stress that the death of a self-immolated monk is not to be identified with the death of Christ on the cross. The redemptive nature of Christ's death cannot be reproduced by the death of another person. As St. Paul says, ". . . in dying as Christ did, he died to sin, once for all" (Rom. 6:10). Christ's death is for all time and cannot be repeated. It was a historical event that took place under Pontius Pilate, but its redemptive power transcended its historical framework and became effective and operative throughout history. Furthermore, Christ's death was for all of humanity. As Matthew's Gospel states: the Christ came "to give up his life as a ransom for many" (Matt. 20:28).

The death of a Vietnamese monk did not have such a transcendent power. It was a sacrifice offered in a hope that the agony and suffering of the people of Vietnam might come to an end. But insofar as it was a sacrifice, it partook of the redeeming power of God in Vietnam. At least, it was a part of that love of which the author of John's Gospel spoke when he wrote: "There is no greater love than this, that a man should lay down his life for his friends" (John 15:13). This great love can only come from God and is made possible through God. The monk who practiced this kind of love must have been close to the heart of God. This is the kind of love that heals wounds in old relationships and creates a possibility for new relationships. Without this kind of sacrificial love, the human community is doomed to fail and die. But the power of such a love brings hope to a community that otherwise is subject to exploitation and inhumanity. This love is therefore redemptive in nature, although it is not redemption itself as was the love of Christ on the cross. Perhaps we can say that all genuine love that contributes to the healing of human relations, transformation of society on the basis of justice and freedom, and the consolidation of whatever makes men and women truly human, is redemptive in nature. I believe this is not an oversimplification. As long as this kind of love remains at work in human society, it is possible for us to see, feel, and experience God's love not in abstract theory but in the actual lives of people. In this sense, the love and compassion of the Vietnamese monks who set themselves on fire give us a glimpse into the depths of God's agony in the face of human tragedy as well as into the power of God's redeeming love in a seemingly senseless and demonic situation.

This example from Vietnam demonstrates that Buddhism in Asia has come a long way in its sense of responsibility toward the world. The lotus still looks as peaceful as ever. But it symbolizes peace in the midst of unrest and fear. It still appears as tranquil as ever, but its tranquility is surrounded by the fire of destruction. It still looks toward Nirvana as the destination of human striving, but its Nirvana is forced to take history seriously. Here the cross can and must meet the lotus. What the cross encounters here is the lotus in the sea of fire of a political and military struggle that has destroyed Vietnam. If the cross cannot meet the lotus's thrust into a sea of suffering, how can we say the cross is God's redemption for people in all places and at all times? An observer stated:

> The monks who were daring to defy both General Hguyen Cao Ky and his United States protectors were neither dupes of the Communists nor ambitious would-be office holders themselves. . . . Rather . . . they had been driven to take the stand they had by their profound compassion for their suffering people, and by the fact that there literally was no one else who could speak for the war-weary people and their longing for peace. Far from being a departure from their religious faith, their actions were impelled by it.[33]

The truth of the matter is that the Buddhist involvement in the struggle for peace in Vietnam was basically not different from the Christian concern for social justice, freedom, and peace that has come to be considered increasingly as an integral part of faith. In this common cause—whether at a local level or on a global stage—the cross and the lotus should be comrades in arms. Asian Buddhists enter human suffering through the lotus, and Christians through the cross. Whether they will meet before the throne of God's salvation and glory is not for mortals to judge. But at least they have a common entry into the ultimate question of life, which is suffering, and they share a common duty to go together through suffering with faith and hope in the salvation of all humanity.

NOTES

1. "The symbolism of the lotus-flower was borrowed by the Buddhists directly from the parent religion Brahmanism. Primarily, the lotus-flower appears to have symbolized for the Aryans from remote times the idea of superhuman or divine birth, and secondarily, the creative force and instrumentality. The traditional Indian and Buddhist explanation of it is that the glorious lotus-flower appears to spring not from the solid earth but from the surface of the water, and is always pure and unsullied, no matter how impure may be the water of the lake" (*Encyclopedia of Religion and Ethics,* James Hastings, ed. [Edinburgh: T. & T. Clark, 1975], 8:144).

2. Arthur Schopenhauer, *The World as Will and Representation* (The Falem's Wing Press, 1945), 2:443–44. Quoted by O Hyun Park in *Oriental Ideas in Recent Religious Thought* (Lakemont, Ga.: CSA Press, 1974), p. 116.

3. See Piero Gheddo, *The Cross and the Bo-tree: Catholics and Buddhists in Vietnam* (New York: Sheed & Ward, 1970), pp. 242–43.

4. Paul Tillich, *Dynamics of Faith* (New York: Harper and Brothers, Publishers, 1957), p. 45.

5. Mircea Eliade, *Images and Symbols: Studies in Religious Symbolism*, trans. Philip Mairet (New York: Sheed & Ward, 1952), p. 12.

6. Charles Allen Clarke, *First Fruits in Korea* (New York: Fleming H. Revell Company, 1921), p. 101.

7. Tillich's following remark concerning sexual rites and symbols is very much to the point: "In judging the sexual rites and symbols of many religions, one should remember that it is not the sexual in itself which is revealing but the mystery of being which through the medium of the sexual manifests its relation to us in a special way. This explains and justifies the rich use of sexual symbols in classical Christianity. Protestantism, rightly aware of the danger of a demonization of these symbols, has developed an extreme distrust of them, often forgetting the mediating character of sex in revelatory experiences. But the goddesses of love are in the first place goddesses, displaying divine power and dignity, and only in the second place do they represent the sexual realm in its ultimate meaning. Protestantism, in rejecting sexual symbolism, is in danger of losing much symbolic wealth but also of cutting off the sexual realm from the ground of being and meaning in which it is rooted and from which it gets its consecration." See Tillich, *Systematic Theology* (Chicago: University of Chicago Press, 1951), 1:119, note 4.

8. Eliade, *Images and Symbols*, p. 174.

9. See also Isaiah 40:18–20.

10. See *The Interpreter's Dictionary of the Bible*, 2:676.

11. Ibid., p. 673.

12. Ibid., p. 676.

13. Protestant Christianity has not been able to make a fine distinction here and tended to play down the visual aspect of religious devotion in favor of the aural aspect. It has always appealed to the ear to the exclusion of the eye. Tillich's historical observation on this point is very important. He writes: "If we look at the history of Protestantism, we find that it has continued and often surpassed the achievement of the early and medieval churches with respect to religious music and hymnical poetry but that it has fallen very short of their creative power in all the visual arts. . . . This is related to the turn in the late Middle Ages from the emphasis on the eye to the emphasis on the ear. . . . The background of this rejection of arts of the eye is the fear—and even

horror—of a relapse into idolatry. From early biblical times up to the present day, a stream of iconoclastic fear and passion runs through the Western and Islamic world, and there can be no doubt that the arts of the eye are more open to idolatrous demonization than the arts of the ear. But the difference is relative, and the very nature of the Spirit stands against the exclusion of the eye from the experience of its presence" (*Systematic Theology* [Chicago: University of Chicago Press, 1963], 3:200).

14. Eliade, *Images and Symbols*, pp. 174–75.

15. Joseph M. Kitagawa, *Religions of the East* (Philadelphia: The Westminster Press, 1968), p. 210.

16. Arend T. van Leeuwen, *Christianity in World History* (London: Edinburgh House Press, 1965), p. 146.

17. For the origin and meaning of the symbolism of the lotus, see note 1 above.

18. It is certain that Jesus did not use parables to hide the truth about the kingdom of God from the people. As is pointed out, "for those who came to Jesus expecting or demanding either a revolutionary or a wonder-worker a different approach was necessary." Thus the parables provided an alternate approach. See W. F. Albright and C. S. Mann, eds., *Matthew: The Anchor Bible* (New York: Doubleday and Company, 1971), p. cxlii.

19. Kenneth K. S. Ch'en, *Buddhism: The Light of Asia* (New York: Barron's Educational Series, 1968), p. 11.

20. Ibid., pp. 11–12.

21. See Paul Carus, *The Gospel of Buddha* (Chicago: The Open Court Publishing Company, 1894), p. 159.

22. See William Theodore de Bary, ed., *The Buddhist Traditions in India, China, and Japan* (New York: Vintage Books, 1972), pp. 89–90.

23. John Knox, for example, says in his exegesis on Romans 1:19–23: "It now becomes apparent that Paul is to speak first to the Gentiles; and that the first and most important item in his indictment of the Gentile world is its idolatry." See *The Interpreter's Bible*, 9:398.

24. Paul Tillich, *Systematic Theology*, 3:102.

25. Edward Conze, comp. and trans., *Buddhist Scriptures* (Baltimore: Penguin Books, 1959), p. 54.

26. Christmas Humphreys, *Exploring Buddhism* (London: George Allen and Unwin, 1974), p. 89.

27. The population of Indonesia is made up of the following elements: Muslims 85 percent; Christians 6.3 percent; Hindu-Bali 2 percent; Buddhists 0.9 percent; and others 5.9 percent. See Frank L. Cooley, *Indonesia: Church and Society* (New York: Friendship Press, 1968), p. 125.

28. Thich Nhat Hanh, *The Lotus in the Sea of Fire* (London: SCM, 1967), p. 9.

29. Ibid.

30. Frances FitzGerald, *Fire in the Lake: The Vietnamese and Americans in Vietnam* (Boston: Little, Brown and Company, 1972), p. 81.

31. Thich Nhat Hanh, *Lotus*, p. 118.

32. Ibid.

33. "Afterword" by Alfred Hassler in Thich Nhat Hanh, *Lotus*, pp. 109–10.

27

Tissa Balasuriya

Why Planetary Theology?

Tissa Balasuriya believes that current liberation theologies are too contextual and limited; he points the way to a liberation theology which might embrace all cultures, religions, and societies. "Why Planetary Theology?" is taken from Tissa Balasuriya, Planetary Theology *(Maryknoll, N.Y.: Orbis Books, 1984), pp. 1–16.*

It puzzles and saddens me that so many who call themselves Christian are so little concerned about the immense human misery and suffering in almost all parts of the world. Sometimes we are even the cause of this suffering and we seem not to realize it. Our going regularly to church and attending prayer services seem to leave us uninterested in the fate of our sisters and brothers. On the contrary, our being considered good Christians may be what makes us insensitive to them.

Why is it that most of the Christians who attend Sunday worship in the city of Colombo, Sri Lanka, hardly ever reflect seriously on the utterly inhuman conditions of the one hundred fifty thousand shantytowners who "live" in our beautiful city? The roof of their hovel cannot prevent the rain from drenching their one-room dwelling. The floor on which they sleep is damp. They have no clean water. There is one toilet for about every hundred persons. No schooling for children; no jobs for adults. They live in filthy conditions. Infant mortality is high; malnutrition is standard. And this continues from generation to generation; if anything, the situation worsens. The rich prosper, and many of them are Christians and consider themselves good Christians.

How was it possible for an American bishop to visit the U.S. forces in

Vietnam at Christmas and encourage them to fight the poor Vietnamese . . . in the name of the Prince of Peace? Did he not know that more bombs were dropped by the U.S.A. on Vietnam than all the bombs dropped in World War II? How was it possible that Western missionaries could accompany European and American traders, gunboaters, and soldiers into China in the nineteenth century? How could good Christians allow themselves to be slave traders and slave owners in the New World, which they occupied after killing or driving away the aboriginal inhabitants?

These are not questions only of the past. How is it that good Christians in Europe and North America still are not aware that their countries have abundance partly at the expense of the poor of the Third World? How is it that $1 million is spent each minute on armaments by governments, mainly of countries that think of themselves as Christian, when over 500 billion human beings have not enough food to satisfy their hunger? Why is it that the urgent appeals of Popes John XXIII, Paul VI, and John Paul II for justice and sharing fall on deaf ears even among their own faithful? Why is it that the World Council of Churches' Program to Combat Racism in South Africa is not only unheeded by many Christians, but is even viewed as suspect by many of them?

A simple response to these questions would be to say that unfortunately persons and countries paid no attention to the Christian message, or that sin is a commonplace in human history. However, we can go a step further and ask whether *a world system of unjust relationships* has come to be set up in the past few centuries. And we can ask whether the teaching, motivations, and actions of organized Christian churches contributed toward it. Has a distorted social order in turn influenced the churches? Has the prevalent Christian theology lent a religious justification to unjust attitudes and approaches?

TRADITIONAL THEOLOGY

It seems to me that dominant groups—based on race, class, sex, or religion—were encouraged in their convictions of superiority by the theology that prevailed in the Christian churches during the five hundred years from about 1450 to about 1950. And similar theological perspectives still prevail, by and large, within the mainstream thinking of the churches, with some adaptation to modern times.

This is not a problem peculiar to theology. It seems to affect human knowledge as such. Our understanding of history, and even of right and wrong, is conditioned by our environment, interests, information, and field of awareness. I write mainly from a consciousness arising from an Asian context, though I have had the good fortune of having been in or visited very many other parts of the world.

Reflecting on these issues, I cannot escape the conclusion that the traditional Western theology, which claimed a certain universality, was very much determined by dominant world powers and groups. European—and later, North

American—capitalist-oriented, adult, male, clerical groups determined the method, contentual boundaries, and application of theology. They read the gospel and human history in a manner suited to their dominant situation. Many of the concerns that preoccupied Western theologians over the centuries were irrelevant to Third World peoples or even detrimental. Instance divisions of North Atlantic Christians solidified into Catholic and Protestant positions on rather marginal issues and exported to rural villages in Bolivia, Sierra Leone, or the Philippines. The approach toward other religions also began with a Western prejudice against them—as if they could not be from God and salvific, unless they could somehow be considered "Christian in disguise." Again, the close link between Christian missionary activity and Western colonial expansion unduly affected both theology and pastoral practice all over the world. Following is a sketch of some of the major traits that traditional theology accrued from its North Atlantic conditioning.

A Culture-Bound Theology

Traditional Christian theology was in fact profoundly culture-bound throughout its development. It was implicitly ethnocentric: arising from and directed toward concerns of the West. It was a handmaid of Western expansion, an unwitting ally in the exploitation of peoples of other continents, first by Europeans and later by North Americans. The symbiosis of the "sacred duty" of civilizing, baptizing, and saving pagans and the North Atlantic quest for military, economic, political, and cultural domination was disastrous for Christianity itself. It not only made many aspects of Christian theology unacceptable to the rest of humankind, but it also dehumanized the content of Western theology and blinded its practitioners to the cultural implications of what they—and others—were creating.

The attitude of many Westerners toward nature is one aspect of this cultural impact on Christian theology. African, Amerindian, and Eastern peoples have had a respectful attitude toward nature, almost to the point of overdoing it. Indian culture respects life in all forms, including plants and animals. Chinese culture attaches a high value to the harmony of all things: the heavens and the earth, nature and humanity, society and the inner person. Western Christianity, in its emphasis on possession and work, has largely neglected this respect for nature. Nature becomes an appropriate object for human exploitation. Although this has fostered an extraordinary development of science and technology, it has been harmful for the conservation of nature and the dignity of humankind. The quality of human life has in fact been lowered in the process, and now nature itself is being irreparably damaged and threatened with global devastation.

A Church-Centered Theology

Traditional theology has been very largely church-centered, tending to equate the universal kingdom of God and the common human good with the expansion of the church. The divine claims of the church made all else seem faulty, in need of submission to and remediation by the church. The good of the church became the ultimate value according to which other priorities were gauged and issues resolved. The church was regarded as the indispensable vehicle of salvation. The main focus of interest of theology was life within the institutional churches. That life was very much dominated by the more power-ful Western churches, and among Catholics particularly by the church in Rome.

A Male-Dominated Theology

The clergy teaching in seminaries and universities has maintained a virtual monopoly over theology. Theological preoccupations were very much those of persons within church institutions and dependent on them. Thus theology pursued many interests of concern to adult, male clerics and, in the case of Catholics, celibates. They tended to read the Scriptures through an adult-male (celibate) lens. They naturally were inclined to find in revelation many texts that reinforced their authority, importance, and indispensability.

The rights of women did not figure in traditional theological reflection. All rights seem to have been attributed *a priori* to males, beginning in the garden of Eden, leaving women to struggle for their rights by themselves, if at all. During the many centuries of male domination, the churches, in particular the Catho-lic church, saw God on the side of the dominating male. Even now what changes have been tolerated in the Catholic church are reformist and analgesic. Thus women are to be given functions such as the distribution of communion under exceptional circumstances. But there is no acceptance of the fundamen-tal equality of men and women in the life of the church—and this in an age when there are female heads of state, including elected prime ministers. Within the churches, real power in matters both spiritual and temporal is kept in the hands of males. The laity-clergy relationship is dominated by the (male-dominated) clergy. The theology of marriage is such that marriage is a bar to certain positions within the church. These may be disciplinary, not doctrinal, norms, but they reflect the reigning pattern of thought.

An Age-Dominated Theology

Traditional theology was also age-dominated, representing the thought of those who had spent many years studying hefty tomes of the past. The whole apparatus of church life is still age-dominated: the higher the echelon of ecclesiastical authority, the more advanced is the average age of those exercis-ing it. The young are practically excluded from having an impact on thought and action in the churches. Even the most forward-looking changes give the young only a subsidiary role. It is scarcely acknowledged that persons of eighteen to twenty-five or so years of age can be mature human beings, capable of making a significant contribution to the life of a community. Yet what youth can contribute is vitality, dynamism, freshness of approach, openness to the future, a keen sense of justice, and readiness to face risks.

A Procapitalist Theology

In its social orientation, traditional theology was procapitalist. Theological thought and ecclesiastical activity were influenced by the class composition of church personnel. The life style of most theologians and church personnel was fashioned within the framework of Western capitalism, and they benefited from it. Consciously or unconsciously, they did not deal with issues that threatened their interests and positions. Thus traditional theology had little to do with the conditions of the working classes. Even today it is largely unrelated to the issues that concern the rural poor, who form the bulk of the population in the poorer countries of the world, or the many millions of the urban poor everywhere.

Where theology or church social teachings touched on these issues, the remedies they proposed were palliatives rather than fundamental reforms of social structures themselves. Economic power was to remain with the owners of capital—with a certain softening of the exploitative process through the sedatives of recreational facilities for workers, labor laws, profit-sharing, workers' councils, and trade unions. These are good in themselves, but there was no serious intention of fundamentally altering the social system so that workers would receive a just share of the benefits of their work. There was to be no basic change of the social order to end exploitation of person by person. The attitude of many Christians was even more conservative than were official church teachings.

An Anticommunist Theology

Now that the Western world is coming to a coexistence with the Soviet Union, Eastern Europe, and China, Christian thinkers are beginning to turn from condemnation to tolerance of communism. But in the early decades of the Russian, Chinese, and Vietnamese revolutions, the Christian churches took a strong condemnatory attitude toward the new Marxist regimes. The churches saw the negative aspects of communist dictatorships, but were slow to acknowledge their achievements for the people.

This caused conflicts with the revolutionary governments and a long estrangement with them, including the expulsion of missionaries from China. From about 1950 onward, Western theology turned a blind eye to the half of Asia that is China, which was going through one of the most significant revolutions in human history.

We thus are faced with the enigma of a theology that gives a positive acceptance and evaluation of colonialism and capitalism, and a fault-finding evaluation of socialist regimes, which have been in many areas and aspects the liberators of African and Asian peoples. Once again, culture-bound preferences of the West pass for Christian theological positions. Concerning traditional Christian theology Asians are therefore in a dilemma, much deeper than merely that of being asked to adopt Western languages, rituals, and thought-patterns. It concerns a whole worldview of human reality and human history.

A Nonrevolutionary Theology

A similar evaluation can be made of the traditional thinking among church-persons concerning development, justice, and peace. Development within the present world order, with the technology of the West and its financial and economic institutions, is presupposed as normal, or qualifiedly normal. The Western, urban, technological model is implicitly accepted as the normal pattern of national development. The naked greed and insatiable thirst for profit central to this model are not seen as contrary to the spirit of the gospel. Christianity has come to terms with this legitimation of greed, neglecting nonmaterial incentives to build a just society and recast the common understanding of what the goals of human endeavor should be.

As yet the churches have not opted for a world system different from the prevailing capitalist, Western-dominated system. Except for some references in recent papal encyclicals, remedies suggested for problems are mere anodynes. The churches recommend reforms *within* the world system, such as economic cooperation through "aid," commodity agreements, currency reforms, deceleration of the arms race, and promotion of peace. These are good things in themselves, but utterly inadequate to transform a system in which 80 percent of the world's population has access to 20 percent of the world's resources. Poverty thus continues in the midst of plenty. Peace is understood as the preservation of the given status quo.

Yet, in view of the magnitude of Third World problems, totally different approaches are necessary. A revolutionary change in the world system is needed. Revolutionary change does not necessarily imply violence. It does, however, mean a radical and rapid change in the world system—a change neither marginal nor quantitative, but qualitative and all-pervasive. The world is meant for all and a qualitative change in the relationships among peoples and resources is required to ensure basic human rights to all.

Christianity lacks a revolutionary global theology. Even the Latin American theology of liberation is articulated in terms of changes within the world created by Western expansion since 1500.

A Theology Bereft of Social Analysis

Social analysis has not yet been accepted and incorporated as an essential ingredient in theological reflection. For the most part, traditional theology was drawn directly from scriptural sources; inasmuch as data from other deposits of God's revelation were largely ignored, that theology was heavily influenced by the prejudices, delusions, and preoccupations of the theologians, who were mainly used to an urban bourgeois way of life. This is a further point of methodology in need of radical remediation if there is to be any meaningful consensus among the churches concerning Christian action in society. The absence of sociopolitical power analysis lulls the churches into complacency with the fact and the consequences of the dominance of some over others.

Because a great deal of theological thinking is individualistic in orientation, the social aspects of the kingdom of God, of sin, conversion, and salvation have been neglected. Sometimes these social aspects are considered "merely" human, humanitarian, horizontal, "merely" natural—as if they were not related to the spiritual, to God. Here too basic presuppositions must be overhauled to meet the aspirations of contemporary men and women, and to be honest about reality, with its absurd extremes of towering affluence and abject poverty.

An Overly Theoretical Theology

Closely related to the absence of social analysis is the absence of action-orientation in traditional theology. When theology is only theoretical, it fails to take into account the exigencies of real situations and of the efforts required to change them. But only in action do the many dimensions of multifaceted problems become clear. When action is precluded from reflection, thought tends to be sterile, oriented to the status quo, and conservative. It is then possible to elaborate theology in a merely academic way, having but little relevance to the flow of events and forces as they develop in the world. An action-oriented theology, on the other hand, would have to assess the forces operative in a given situation, think of goals, strategies, and tactics, yields and risks, timing and alliances. All these require skills different from those of merely academic theologians. It will also have to develop a different spirituality, one that will not shun active participation in social change even in conflictual situations.

Churches have been action-oriented, mission-oriented, even when their theology was overbearingly speculative. But the action was largely church-centered in its missionary approach and conservative in its social aspirations. We need a theology that pays more attention to all aspects of the human person and is oriented toward justice in society. This demands an option in favor of the oppressed. Such a theology would also be more God-centered—that is, centered on God actively present in human history. Traditional theology neglected the dynamic nature of the kingdom of God and its impact on human history.

A theology that is action-oriented must take into account the dimension of time. Timing is of the essence. Awareness of the pace of events has to be included in the input for decision-making. There is not much use condemning the old colonialism today, except as regards Macao, Hong Kong, and the like. Today we have to deal with neocolonialism and new forms of exploitation, as in such nations as Malaysia, Chile, Afghanistan, and Poland. The churches—

like so many civil governments—have generally sided with oppressors in power, but then with liberators once they are in power. This is sheer opportunism. Prophetic timing demands that we be with the oppressed in their struggles while they are engaged in them—not only after they are successful.

Such a theology would be continually in process, not static; it would endeavor to meet the problems posed by a fast-changing world. An action-oriented theology would also be largely lay, rather than clerical. The ministerial clergy, as such, would not necessarily provide leadership in a theology requiring the skills of sociopolitical analysis, decision-making, and risk-bearing. The young would play a significant role in the growth of such a theology: they have a greater penchant for being present where the action is than do older adults, especially patriarchal academics and clerics.

Action-orientation also implies that theology be concerned with strategies of action for different places and environments. Traditional theology was largely concerned with intrachurch strategies and methods. The action called for today is very much in the field of public life. Hence the confluence of events, forces, and obstacles has to be evaluated and different strategies weighed and adopted. Risk-bearing in such situations is quite different from risk-bearing inside a cloister or in intrachurch or even interchurch issues.

A spirituality that faces up to conflictual situations requires a re-evaluation of the virtues of a Christian life and of progress in the spiritual life. Ascetic practice and mystical experience can and will have to evolve within the context of struggle against the wrongs of sociopolitical structures and the sacrifices and joys that struggle will entail. Spirituality will have to relate critically to politics, which is an essential target area for charity and justice. All these elements are only now beginning to be brought into Christian theology. They are indispensable for the building up of the kingdom of God in our world.

CONTEXTUAL THEOLOGIES

Though we may understand the traditional Western theologies of the past five centuries as being of one overall mold—from within the context of the European and North Atlantic quest for world domination—history shows many other examples of the contextualization of theology. Catholic theology has been very much conditioned by its West European and Roman matrix. The theologies of the Orthodox tradition arose from an oriental context in reaction against West European, particularly Roman, perspectives and authoritarianism. The Orthodox churches have always maintained a certain autonomy at the local level, while being linked in a wider federation. However, they have not often escaped the dominant influence of the political powers in their parts of the world.

The different schools of Protestant theology were also affirmations of an autonomy from Roman and Latin domination and related to national issues facing their peoples or political authorities. They retain differences with Catholicism and among themselves concerning matters such as the nature of grace and redemption, the sacraments, church ministry, and ecclesiastical authority. However, all of them that began in Europe or North America are within the general framework of white Western capitalist world domination.

After the Russian Revolution of 1917 and the establishment of socialist regimes throughout Eastern Europe, the Orthodox churches there have developed theological perspectives in line with a critique of capitalism and imperialism. They are developing theological orientations in keeping with the general ideological stance and social structure of their Marxist-dominated socialistic countries. They are supportive of the struggles of the oppressed peoples in other countries against capitalism and neocolonialism. But they are less energetic in articulating a theology that would voice a prophetic critique of their own societies.

The Chinese Revolution compelled the Christian churches in China to rethink their own theologies without an ongoing contact with any other Christian churches. The Protestant churches in China have thus evolved their own way of Christian life guided by the principles of the Three-Self Patriotic Movement: self-government, self-support, self-propagation. They have reread the Scriptures from a postrevolutionary perspective and see many of the gospel values better realized under the new dispensation. The Catholic church in China has set up the Catholic Patriotic Association and claims an autonomy for the church in managing its own affairs, especially in selecting its bishops. They too are supportive of the revolution. Both Protestants and Catholics affiliated with the Patriotic Association share in the public life of the country and endeavor to make a critical contribution to China's advance within the framework of the communist revolution. The Protestant churches are moving toward a postdenominational relationship among themselves: they have been on their own, cut off from denominational "mother churches," for over three decades. These experiences of the Chinese churches are very significant developments of Christian life and theology in an Asian context. They will doubtless influence Christian reflection in the future, especially inasmuch as they have to do with nearly a fourth of the human race.

With the setting up of the Vietnamese socialist government of the liberated zones from the early 1950s, most of the Christians—mainly Catholics—who remained there cooperated with the Marxist-led liberation movement. They faced together the trials of struggle and the horrors of war, especially after the United States came into the Vietnam War with over half a million soldiers and daily bombardment. After the defeat of the south and the U.S. withdrawal in 1975, many of the Christian leaders in the south also gave critical support to the unified Vietnamese revolutionary regime. All this implied a Christian theological reflection in and through a revolutionary struggle. Christians in Vietnam are going through a difficult period, intensified by the continuing conflicts throughout the nation. The Catholic church in Vietnam counts about 10 percent of the population. Its size and the evolution of both Christianity and Marxism may have helped to avoid such a sharp break as was experienced in China.

Contextual theologies are likewise being evolved in other Asian countries such as South Korea, where a theology is being developed in the face of a people's struggle against an oppressive dictatorial regime. Here the concept of the people—minjung—as cared for by God receives special attention. In the Philippines, Christians are theologizing in small groups from their experience of participation in national liberation from the procapitalist dictatorship. In India the concern for dialogue with other religions has been expressed in the ashramic movements and has led to a questioning of the major traditional theological positions of Christians concerning other religions. In India and Sri Lanka the two currents of concern for socioeconomic justice and religiocultural dialogue meet in a search for a more integral approach to liberation.

During the past decade Latin American theologians, using Marxist analytical methodology, have evolved a theology of liberation based on a critical study of their capitalistic society and a rereading of the gospel from their situation. They make a powerful critique of traditional theology and offer penetrating insights into the teaching of Jesus from the point of view of the poor and the oppressed. In more recent years they have developed an ecclesiology, related especially to grassroots Christian communities, and a spirituality in commitment to liberation even unto martyrdom. This Latin American theological evolution, clearly demanding a Christian option in favor of the oppressed in the harsh world of socioeconomic reality, is one of the most significant developments in theology in recent centuries.

The African Christian experience is quite varied from Ethiopia and Egypt to black peoples' liberation struggles in southern Africa. All these are providing a base for contextual theologies. African culture is seen as a basis for a people's integral approach to life, community, and God.

In the United States black theology and the theology of woman have been more strongly articulated during the past decade, and have influenced other continents as well.

The political theologies that are being developed in Europe, especially in West Germany and France, have the advantage of posing sociopolitical problems in the perspective of the ultimate goal of the church. They emphasize the eschatological nature of the kingdom of God. Yet few of them present a clear analysis of the contradictions of the capitalist form of society, on which the quest for Western dominance over the world has been built. They have not yet moved theology into the sphere of political conflict. These trends may develop as the process of politicization continues. The political change in France in favor of a prosocialist government had the support of many Christian reflection/action groups. In Portugal, Spain, and Italy there is now a more serious critique of the capitalist system, influenced by their intermediate position in world capitalism and by Latin American thinking.

THEOLOGY: CONTEXTUAL AND GLOBAL

Contextual theologies arise because the earlier theologies, which claimed universality, did not take local contexts seriously, and because they are articulations of insights from different situations. Contextual theologies arise from a new consciousness of groupings—a class, an ethnic kinship, a sex, a culture—or an overall social or religious environment. They are a valid and necessary contribution to the evolution of Christian life and theology. They can lead to deeper scriptural insights and a better understanding of the sufferings and aspirations of different groups.

Contextual theologies by their very nature tend to be partial, being rooted in local situations and experience. They may, however, have a permanent value insofar as a microhuman experience may embody a universal value. By deepening the analysis of a particular context, we can arrive at more universal perceptions. A contextual theology related to one group, nation, or region may be too narrow to respond to all the aspects of even a local problem. Thus, a black theology may not be open to the values of an Asian people, and so may not be able to analyze or absorb the significance of the Chinese Revolution under Mao Tse-tung. A Latin American theology may neglect the problems of marginalized racial groups within that continent, as well as the issues relating Latin America to the whole world. Latin American theologians do not look upon Brazil and Argentina as vast underinhabited lands in a land-hungry world. They may not understand the tragedies caused by overpopulation in India and Bangladesh, and the impact of Latin American anti-Asian immigration laws on famine and starvation in other parts of the world. Hence even the best of contextual theologies, related to a limited group or region, must be counterbalanced by more universal perspectives relating to the world as a whole.

The action-orientation of contextual theologies may lead to liberation struggles that are necessary but only partial. They may sidestep the problems of global domination within the world. What is needed, therefore, is a dialectical interchange between local struggles and the world situation, between local theologies and a theology that tries to read the significance of global realities. Even local liberation struggles, such as those in El Salvador, Namibia, and Poland dare not be fought in isolation, for the enemies of human liberation are organized globally.

The universal approach will be very valuable in the development of a global strategy for bringing about social change. Only a universal approach can help us to respect human beings everywhere, whatever be their ethnic inheritance, color, creed, sex, or social class.

Rejection of the false universalisms of the past should not dissuade us from at least trying to evolve the general outlines of a truly universal theology grounded in the basic elements of the human condition and the overall world situation. Such a theology would recognize the global implications of many of our local or regional problems and proceed accordingly. Reflection on the Asian context seems especially recommendable in the search for a global theology inasmuch as Asia's population is more than half of the world population.

By extension, the whole planet earth, as an entirety, must also be seen as a context for theology. The human search for meaning and fulness of life takes place on this planet, with all its potentialities and limitations. Today the destinies of all peoples are closely interrelated and linked to the future of the earth: the land, the seas, the atmosphere, and outer space.

The world system that humankind has built up especially in the past few centuries is increasingly global in communications, economy, polity, culture, and way of life. The major power blocs would gladly have the whole world as the arena of their interests and operations. Some groupings based on class, color, sex, religion, ideology, and culture are also global in many aspects. The efforts of world bodies such as the United Nations further highlight planetary interdependence for peace, human rights, justice, the resolution of international conflicts—even food and employment.

REORIENTING THEOLOGY

Some of the approaches required to reorient theology are already being developed in the political theology of Europe, in the practical, issue-oriented theology of North America, in the theology of liberation in Latin America, and by the action/reflection dynamism evident in Asian and African churches, the socialist countries, and women's movements. Their reflection would be broadened by a keener awareness of Asian contexts. It could lead to a sharpening of strategies, thanks to a better understanding of the demands of Asian revolutionary processes.

We have to take a fresh look at the central core of the Christian message. This requires a direct return to the sources of revelation—the Scriptures—especially to the person of Jesus Christ as we see him in the gospels. We must purify our minds of the restrictive Christendom-centered theologies that have blurred the universality of Jesus Christ. We must ask ourselves how we are to understand the Gospels in our times.

Another point of departure must be socioeconomic and political reflection on the contemporary world in diverse contexts. We should try also to relate them to the basic yearnings of the human person for freedom and personal fulfillment. The de facto world system of order and disorder can be one starting point for the growth of a planetary theology, for the world system affects the life of each person and group within it. This impact grows rapidly as human global interdependence increases.

28

Francisco F. Claver

Two Letters to the People of Bukidnon

In the following pastoral letters, entitled "The Violence of the Meek" and "The Stones Will Cry Out," Francisco F. Claver, who at the time the letters were written was the Bishop of Bukidnon, Philippines, speaks to his people of the growing violations of their political and human rights. He asks them to use Jesus as their model and act with determined perseverance and love against their oppressors and for their liberation. The letters are taken from Claver's The Stones Will Cry Out *(Maryknoll, N. Y.: Orbis Books, 1978), pp. 20–22 and 41–43. The notes for Claver's book were prepared by Mary Heffron and Rev. Thomas J. Marti, M. M.*

February 19, 1977

THE VIOLENCE OF THE MEEK

"The Lord put you in my power, but I would not raise my hand" (1 Sam. 26:23). Thus did David do violence to his persecutor Saul: the violence of the meek. He could have used the other kind of violence—the killing, hurting kind. He did not. And it made Saul think. It made Saul persecute David less.

As we noted last week, we live under violence. And the communist urging is to counter this violence with violence—the same kind of violence, the violence that kills.

This is where we as Christians differ most, I would think, from communists, even if we may be one with them in our desire to right injustice, to uplift the downtrodden, to give power to the masses. It is not that the Christian must

336

avoid at all costs armed violence. Under very restricted circumstances—as a last resort—violence can be moral. This is ordinary Catholic teaching. Violence in self-defense, for instance. And that self can be individual. It can be collective too.

But as an equally *ordinary* means of redressing wrongs, I doubt violence is Christian. "Put your sword back in your scabbard. Turn the other cheek." These are hard sayings of Christ, but they do point, I believe, to something that is at the core of Christianity: not repaying evil with evil. But does this mean, when we suffer violence, that we must meekly give in? Allow ourselves to be trampled upon? Have no thought for our dignity as children of God? Just so long as we survive?

I doubt this is Christian either. So what is Christian? Some act, I should think, like David's toward Saul—the violence of the meek. This is not just a nice phrase, a clever paradox. For the action it connotes comes from strength. It also comes from gentleness, the strength and gentleness of Christ.

To be concrete: one of many acts that the government insists on calling subversive is *civil disobedience*. The boycott of the referendum is one very clear example.[1] Speaking out critically about the present government we have is another, and still another is striking for better wages in industries that enjoy special favor these days. These are all against certain decrees or government policies, but decrees and policies that in one way or another infringe on human rights and hence by the very fact are acts of violence, unjust, immoral.

Citizens can acquiesce meekly to this violence, or they can oppose it. And this they can do violently, even unto blood, or nonviolently, but nonetheless effectively.

Thus, in the case of the referendum, the boycotters are protesting the indignity done them in its farcical nature; in the case of criticism of government, citizens are exercising their right to the free expression and pursuit of the truth; and in the case of a strike, the laborers assert their right to freely associate with others in working to achieve a just wage. The main intent is to correct an unjust law by opposing it, by disobeying it—nonviolently.

But is this kind of disobedience to law disruptive of the general order? It is indeed. But if that same order is based on unjust laws, it deserves to be disrupted precisely in order to set it right again—not violently unless that were the *only* way, but peacefully. This means—and here we bring in an essential aspect of civil disobedience—citizens who choose the way of civil disobedience to protest what they in conscience believe to be an unjust law must be ready to suffer the penalties imposed by the state for their disobedience.

This is the violence of the meek. Christ practiced it even unto Calvary. He violated the Sabbath law to correct its unjust man-made prescriptions. He criticized public authorities openly for their twisted interpretations of the law. He gathered the people together against the wishes of those in power and spoke to them of *the* kingdom that was to come. And for all this he was visited with violence. And the charge leveled at him? *Subversion and rebellion.*

"The Lord put you in my power, but I would not raise my hand." Do these words mean anything to our living of Christianity today?

•

April 2, 1977

THE STONES WILL CRY OUT

It is Holy Week once again. And we start our sorrowful commemoration of the Passion of Christ with a re-enactment of his triumphal entry into the city of his death. Life and death, glory and shame, light and darkness: these are interlocking themes of the mysteries we will be recalling this week of weeks. We see these themes even now in the procession of the palms. They are meant for our instruction. They are meant for our salvation.

So we watch the powers of darkness close in on Christ even in his hour of triumph—precisely, in fact, *because of* his triumph: surpassing glory today, hosannas and blessings; insults and imprecations tomorrow, and deepest shame—from the same crowd.

We are *that* crowd. Today we are his. Today we are not afraid to proclaim him Lord, Redeemer, God. And we will not be silenced. On Friday we will probably flee when he needs us most—in fear, in shameless and selfish cowardice. We will probably deny him too, like Peter, or betray him, like Judas, or condemn him, like the mob.

But then we could also stand by him, unafraid, like his mother, like Mary of Magdala, like John, the apostle. Strange, but in the drama of the passion, every character is *us,* every role is *ours*.

Today we are the crowd. We are the people, glorying in him, triumphing with him. We are totally his, loyal and faithful, ready to follow him wherever he leads. We live the day all over again, as we must, every day of our life, live his passion and, we hope, his resurrection.

The re-enactment is not mere make-believe, as in a play, as in a dramatic presentation. It is for real, not only for each one, individually, but for all of us too, as a community, as a people.

The reality of the passion of Christ in our life as church and as individuals was heavily underscored for us last Saturday here in Malaybalay. More than twenty-five men and women were hauled before a military tribunal at the Philippine Constabulary (PC) pelota court,[2] some as witnesses, most as respondents, for a preliminary investigation on a blanket charge of "inciting to sedition." All the accused, as we noted two weeks ago, are church workers.

We could draw many parallels between the investigations at the pelota court at the PC camp of Malaybalay and the interrogation of Christ before Pilate's court at the Praetorium of Jerusalem. I will draw only one: the part truth played in both judicial proceedings, the way truth was made out to be seditious, subversive, destructive of the peace.

Christ spoke the truth, did the truth. So he was put on trial. The respondents in the Malaybalay hearing, too, each in his or her own little way, tried to speak the truth, to do the truth. So they are on trial. Truth was on trial then, truth was the issue—its preaching, its doing. So it is now. So it has ever been under martial law. So it will always be wherever, whenever Christians try to take their faith seriously, to act on it, to live it—and governments look at the truth as criminal. This is what we mean by the living re-enactment of Christ's passion and death, Christ's life and resurrection. This is what we meant, in last week's pastoral letter, by "the pain of Christianity."

Is this inevitable pain reason therefore to keep our peace, to be silent? Or should it not be reason, rather, for the direct contrary: to cry out all the more strongly? Christ's enemies could not stomach the loud hosannas the people proclaimed for him, the Lord of truth. And they demanded that he bid them be silent.

> If they keep silence,
> the stones will cry out!

That was Christ's answer. It will have to be ours too, for it is as impossible for stones to cry out as for real believers to be silent about the truth. And I thank God that there are thousands of real believers in Bukidnon today. I thank God that there are still many who take their task of proclaiming the truth seriously. They came by the hundreds last Saturday, in token delegations from parishes and barrios, from farms and hills, to show their solidarity with the respondents. Their support is most highly appreciated indeed—as is that of people who could not come but wrote nonetheless to express their unity with them. Their message, we trust, will not be lost on the Pilates and the Herods, the suborned witnesses and the Palace Guards of Bukidnon.

The passion of the church of Bukidnon continues. We look ahead with the supreme confidence of faith to the final triumph of the resurrection, for there will be a resurrection.

So, my brothers and sisters in the truth of Christ, we cry out all the more today despite attempts at hushing our voice:

> Hosanna to the Son of David!
> Glory and honor to the King of truth!

He said the truth will make us free. And we will be free in him, through him. In these times of great unfreedom and untruth, we have to be all the stronger. We have to be all the louder. Or the stones will cry out.

NOTES

1. The referendum was held on April 17, 1977. The background of it is complex, but it may help to offer here a brief explanation. Following a meeting in Tripoli between

Imelda Marcos (the president's wife) and Muammar Kaddaif (common knowledge had it that his government was supplying the Muslims in Mindanao with arms and money), Marcos agreed that thirteen provinces of Mindanao would be declared autonomous (including the island of Palawan, the Sulu Archipelago, and about half of Mindanao). This area would be placed under a provisional government that would include representation of the Moro National Liberation Front, and a referendum would be held to determine "administrative arrangements." In fact, the referendum greatly modified the initial grant of autonomy. The referendum was confusing for conscientious Christians and Muslims alike, as Bishop Claver explains. It was formally rejected by the Moro National Liberation Front. They claimed it contradicted the letter and the spirit of the Tripoli agreement. Observers reported that voting was not heavy (at best 50–60 percent turnout, in some places only 20 percent of those registered showed up to vote). Yet the government Commission on Elections said that 95 percent of the area's 3 million voters had voted against merging the thirteen provinces into an autonomous Muslim region.

2. The pelota court on the Philippine Constabulary (PC) compound in Malaybalay and the pelota court in Davao City were both scenes of hearings involving church workers who had been arrested on charges of "subversion." Pelota is a Spanish game, played with a short-handled racket on a court similar to a handball court. The Philippine Constabulary is the part of the Philippines armed forces responsible for internal peace and security in the country. It functions like a national police force.

29

Geevarghese Mar Osthathios

The Reality of Sin and Class War

Geevarghese Mar Osthathios contends that "any true Christian theology is a theology of a classless society." "The Reality of Sin and Class War" is taken from his Theology of a Classless Society *(Maryknoll, N.Y.: Orbis Books, 1980), pp. 71–79.*

Dr. Robert MacAfee Brown was attacked by many when he produced the thesis at the Nairobi Assembly [Fifth Assembly of the World Council of Churches, 1975] that Jesus Christ divides before he unites. The theme of the assembly, "Jesus Christ frees and unites," could have been dealt with by him saying that "sin divides and Christ unites." Slavery and divisions are not the work of Christ but the work of Satan. The passage which Dr. Brown took as the basis for his thesis that Christ divides before he unites—"do not think that I have come to bring peace on earth; I have not come to bring peace, but a sword. For I have come to set a man against his father, and a daughter against her mother . . ." (Matt. 10:34f.)—needs interpretation in the light of the person and work of Christ as God and human being.

"God is light and in him there is no darkness at all." Darkness, divisions, hatred, sin, and so on cannot come from God directly. We have the promise of the master—"Peace I leave with you, my peace I give to you" (John 14:27); this promise must be seen as the work of Christ, and the sword he spoke of as what he permits in a sinful order. Class war in a family takes place when the members who take the discipleship of Christ are hated and persecuted by those who would not follow him. "Let no one say when he is tempted, 'I am tempted by God'; for God cannot be tempted with evil and he himself tempts no one; but each person is tempted when he is lured and enticed by his own desire" (James 1:13f.). The Lord who created everything and found everything to be very good could not have created Satan directly. Hence the ancient churches have the theory of fallen angels to show that the misuse of freedom by the good angels made them devils and God did not create the devils. The possibility of ascent and descent is given to humankind with the image of God, as to the angels. Misuse of freedom makes people satanic and good use of divine freedom to do the will of God makes them divine. In the fallen order in which we live, God permits class war to create a classless society since the freedom God has given to human beings has to be honored even when that freedom is not submitted to the will of God.

POWER AND POWERLESSNESS

The Magnificat is a song of high revolution. It shows how the power of humankind is checked by God in history when God gave power to the powerless. "He has put down the mighty from their thrones, and exalted those of a low degree" (Luke 1:52). The moneyed class does not remain as the highest stratum of society forever; nor do the rulers remain rulers forever. Parliamentary democracy has acted as a mighty weapon for dethroning corrupt governments by a peaceful revolution through the ballot box. The books of Judges and Kings are full of incidents of the overthrow of the powerful by the powerless, strengthened and guided by the presence of God through the ark of the covenant. When the Israelites become powerful and proud, they are also punished by being subjected to the persecution of powerful nations. World history is a history of wars between one class and another or between one nation and another or between allies and allies, and the end result is often the overthrow of the arrogant and the powerful by the powerless, as occurred in the Vietnam War. History is the story of God's wonderful actions in the world.

James Cone and the proponents of black theology and liberation theology have a point in saying that God is on the side of the oppressed and not on the side of the oppressor. God gives power to the powerless, which is mightier than the power of the powerful. The dictatorship of the proletariat of which Karl Marx speaks is not to be seen as the natural flow of history but as the providential hand of God, who chooses the weak to confound the strong and uses the foolish to confound the wise. Power and might belong to God. The pale Galilean is conquering the world. The meek are inheriting the earth again and again though the powerful capture it for a short time. When some king wanted a clear proof for the existence of God, the wise minister answered, "The Jews, my Lord." There has been no people in history who have become so powerless and so powerful time and again. They were chosen by God to be a blessing for all the families of the earth (Gen. 12:3), but they wanted to be an exclusive powerful class and so were hated by all classes of people.

The Christian church should learn a lesson from the old Israel and share its power with the powerless lest it lose its God-given powers, whether that is the power of the Spirit or of matter. The powerlessness of the cross was able to conquer the power of the Roman Empire and continues to conquer the world by the power of service. "For the word of the cross is folly to those who are perishing, but to us who are being saved it is the power of God. . . . We preach Christ crucified, a stumbling block to Jews and folly to Gentiles, but to those who are called, both Jews and Greeks, Christ the power of God and the wisdom of God. For the foolishness of God is wiser than men, and the weakness of God is stronger than men" (1 Cor. 1:18–25).

Sin makes the powerful selfish, oppressive, and exploitative. On the other hand, if we have the mind of Christ, we will not want to hold on to power but to empty ourselves of our power and stoop down to the lowest level of powerlessness to give power to the powerless (Phil. 2:5–11). As humanity at large cannot be expected to have the mind of Christ, the power of the powerful will not be parted with voluntarily. Hence the powerless must be aided by those who stand for a classless society to consolidate their power in such a way that they can exert power on the powerful through collective bargaining, strikes, and so on. The government which stands for justice can help also in the creation of a classless society through laws that would raise the standard of living for the poor and bring down the salary of the highly paid. Trade union leaders are often so corrupt that they take bribes from the rich owners of estates and factories and use their power for their own advantage without using it for the powerless. The leaders of the church are also guilty of identifying themselves with the moneyed class and perpetuating the class structures of the society and the churches. The church, following in the footsteps of the Nazarene, must become poor and preach the gospel to the poor, not only in words, but also in liberating them from the oppression of the mighty.

CLASS AND CLASSLESSNESS

The richest and the poorest are the least concerned for God in the class-structured society. The former are too busy and the latter too indifferent. Human beings are social beings and so create class structures for security, combat, and prestige. A classless society as a world community can only remain an ideal on account of cultural differences, pride of nationalism, and ethnic identities. Karl Marx's theory that class war would lead to a classless society and a utopia on earth fails to take seriously the sin of humankind. The state will not wither away as prophesied by Marx. A perfect classless society is only an eschatological possibility.

It is the image of God in humankind that desires a world fellowship, a sharing of resources, world government, jobs for all, equality of opportunity, eradication of poverty and exploitation, all of which are the marks of a classless society. The fallenness, frailty, and sin of human beings, on the other hand, make them desire their own prosperity, class formation for narrow ends, fights between classes, colossal waste of money for armaments of the most sophisticated type, and a using of the lower classes for their own higher class comforts and luxuries. The human being is an amphibian, living and moving towards the heights of heaven in ideas and drifting towards the depth of hell in practice. The impracticability of the theology of a classless society is a result of the beast in the human. Its practicability, however, is constantly hoped for since we know that the image of God is not completely lost. If humankind is a lump of sin as taught by Augustine, it is impossible even to dream of a classless society. But God is still on the throne and God is already bringing about some sort of a socialism all over the world, whether it is through benevolent capitalism or Russian communism or Chinese communism or through the thinking of the intelligentsia.

THE SEAT OF SIN

Is private property the root of all evil? Is it not because of the selfishness of humankind that primitive communism did not last long and that slavery, feudalism, and capitalism emerged in history? Sin is not to be pinpointed in the individual alone or in society alone, but in the cosmic evil at work in both. Sin will not disappear from the world when the whole world is brought under communism as Marx expected. All economic, cultural, social, political, and even religious orders are tainted with sin. Structural injustice forces the individual to acquiesce to the injustice. The reality of sin has to be discovered by introspection and by sociological studies. No "ism" is free of sin and the possibility of corruption. The advantage of a classless society is that endemic injustice will be less there than in a capitalistic society. The inevitability of the class war was taught by Marx.

Will the dictatorship of the proletarian class, achieved by class struggle, usher in the classless society we envisage? The classless society we dream of is not the dictatorship of any class, but a democratic, socialistic rule based on a parliamentary system in which, when the party in power becomes corrupted by sin and selfishness, the opposition party can come into power. The destiny of humanity cannot be entrusted to any one single party forever as every person is a sinner. As Lord Acton said, "Power tends to corrupt and absolute power corrupts absolutely." "Jesus did not trust himself to them because he knew all men and needed no one to bear witness of man; for he himself knew what was in man" (John 2:24f.). Democracy is possible because of the dignity of humankind, but it must be democracy with an opposition party because of the frailty of humankind. Sin necessitates mutual correctives in every human situation. The universality of sin gives us the warning that the renewal of humanity is indispensable even in the days of the world government and classless society.

Anything outside and rebelling against the sovereignty of God is liable to corruption and decay. That all human beings are children of God is not merely a slogan, but rather it is the basic principle of life, on the basis of which all the resources of the earth should be shared by all God's children everywhere. Sin is that which does not take seriously God's role as Parent to humankind. "If any one says, 'I love God,' and hates his brother, he is a liar; for he who does not love his brother whom he has seen, cannot love God whom he has not seen" (1 John 4:20). The lack of love, justice, and holiness is the seat of sin. Sin is Godlessness and the absence of human solidarity. Therefore, even class war should not be out of hatred, but out of the burning desire to bring down the mighty from their thrones and exalt those of a low degree.

PRIORITY OF SOUL?

In Hinduism what is all important is the supreme self (*paramatman*) and the personal self (*atman*). Thinkers of eminence like Plato, Sankara, Soren Kierkegaard, and A. N. Whitehead have all subscribed to this theory in one way or another. K. Guru Dutt, a spokesman for conservative Hinduism, concludes his critical review of *Man and the Universe of Faiths* by M. M. Thomas thus, "Kierkegaard stressed that religion was the concern of the 'single one.' In our own times A. N. Whitehead has said, 'Religion is what a man does with his solitariness.' Social activity is necessary but not primary. Today it looks as if the tail is trying to wag the dog" (*Religion and Society,* Bangalore, September 1976).

My contention in this book is that the personal and the social are inseparable and neither has priority over the other. The soul exists in body and mind and there is no priority for a disembodied soul if it exists as a separate monad. The social is not the tail and the person the dog; nor is the individual the tail and the social activity the dog. Sociology, which stresses the importance of sociological pressure on each individual, and individualistic psychology, which emphasizes the power of the mind, are two complementary truths to be taken together. God does not exist as a monad because God is eternal love. The solution of the human predicament is not in *advaita,* where love has no ontological nature; it is not in *dwaita,* which sees two entities as two eternal separate realities; rather it is in the Trinity, in which love is ontological, eternal, equalizing fellowship. No person in isolation from God and from fellow human beings can do anything.

Even Sankara does not see any salvation for *jivatma* apart from identity with *paramatma.* We must go on to say that *jivatma* has an identity with distinction with other souls as well as with God, the triune. "No man is an island." Would any person learn a language if there were no other persons to communicate with? Every person is a sociological reality, a co-being being, just as God is triune. If Martin Luther had said, "Here we stand" instead of "Here I stand" and had had a concern for the church equal to his concern for the freedom of the Christian, capitalism would not have come into existence. Personal dignity and human rights, about which we hear so much, are only one side of the coin. Why should the rich alone have dignity and right without extending the same to the millions of slum-dwellers and the downtrodden? Any dignity, right, or freedom I want for myself without wanting it for my neighbor is shallow, superficial, and transient. In Christian theology and ethics, I as a soul do not exist without my body and soul. Hence the Christian hope of resurrection of the body is the transformation of the carnal body to a spiritual body. We do not believe in the immortal soul but in the resurrection of the person and the new humanity. Sin exists in the person and in the class together.

ON TAMING THE CLASS WAR

There are thinkers who teach that a world government can never come into existence unless a world conqueror comes forward and conquers the whole world. There are also prophets of gloom who discard the whole idea as wishful thinking. More in number are the prophets of doom who expect a third or fourth world war destroying life on our tiny earth. Fundamentalistic Christian sects do not have any optimism about our world except in the apocalyptic second coming of Christ and the millennium of peace he would inaugurate on earth. Some of us, however, believe that the Holy Spirit is a present reality, not only in the church, but also in the world, "convincing the world of sin and of righteousness and of judgment" (John 16:8). It is the same Holy Spirit who is telling the world through the scientists that the resources of the world must be used with a sense of stewardship and that a sacramental view of nature is indispensable. The rich nations of the world are becoming more and more convinced that at least a part of their wealth has come from the markets of the poor and developing Third World and that they themselves cannot make any progress unless they take the developing world along with them. The United Nations Conference on Trade and Development and other United Nations agencies are asking for better "trade and aid" rules to bridge the gulf between the haves and the have-nots. The enlightened consciences of the rich countries of the world are also clamoring for a world government, international economic order, a cutting short of the arms race, and the rechanneling of military expenses for the clearing of slums and the creations of employment opportunities. The wrath of many has been turned against the unpardonable exploitation of the wealth of the poor countries by the international corporations and indeed against the whole capitalistic system itself.

If we are to create a classless society, three levels of force must be brought to bear—the moral, the legal, and the military. Many say that the first will take a long time to take effect; the preaching of Christian love for the past 2,000 years and of Hinduism for 7,000 years and of Buddhism and Jainism for 2,500 years has not created a just world with social justice. Also, the legal machinery of each country is not moving fast to create a new society. Thus many young people are impatient and are asking for a bloody revolution, military intervention, and the aggravation of the class war. Religious and moral forces therefore have to be strengthened through word as well as deed. Sermons and books alone will not be sufficient. Classless communities of sharing work and reward must grow up in large numbers all over the world. Such communities must inspire governments to create quickly rules favoring a classless society. Bloody class war will become inevitable if these two forces do not act well and act quickly. Sharing communities can tame the class war that is in the offing.

Political action for a classless society must be stepped up. The church and good people must identify themselves with the oppressed, the downtrodden, and the lowest strata of society and hasten the conscientization process to give them a sense of dignity and worth.

We cannot have infinite material progress in a finite world. Let us therefore be satisfied with the minimum comforts and live simply so that the poor may simply live. This alone will tame class war.

30

Samuel Rayan

The Justice of God

Samuel Rayan asserts that the purpose of the church is to champion a new social order based on God's justice. "The Justice of God" is taken from John C. England, ed., Living Theology in Asia *(Maryknoll, N.Y.: Orbis Books, 1982), pp. 211–20. The essay was first published in 1979.*

THE JUSTICE OF GOD

That God loves us is the whole gospel. That God loves us, loves our world, and loves all men and women unconditionally is the basic affirmation on which everything else is built, the source—reality from which everything else flows. God's love means that God gives us our own selves, gives us life, the earth, the sun, the rain, crops, fruits, food, and happiness. God's love is faithful and just, and God's justice consists in the fidelity and care with which God makes abundant provision for our life, growth, and wholeness as men and women in the human community. In God's love and justice God provides for the fulfilment of every man and woman.

An aspect of God's providence is that we freely become providence one to another. We are, one to another, the concrete presence and experience of God's love and justice. It is the privileged vocation of each one of us to be our sister's and brother's keeper, to be the place of God's provident justice for our fellow human beings, to be a sacrament of God's love. So also this earth with all its riches and resources, as well as all the wealth of any kind we produce and create, is meant to be God's justice and love and providence to one and all.

Four important conclusions follow. *One:* wherever a person is found without the means required to meet human needs, without resources for creative action and participative life in society, there injustice has been operative. *Two:* where people do not care and share but seek to dominate and oppress and where some have plenty while others do not have enough, there is injustice. *Three:* where there is injustice, the sign of God is abolished, and God's personal experience is impeded, which amounts to a divine blackout leading to a progressive crystallizaton of atheism. *Four:* in all such circumstances it is the privilege and task of the churches to "gospel" people and situations with that divine love and justice which they have experienced in joyful faith. To neglect to do so and to choose to stay within the security of a ritual and legal religion unsoiled by proximity to the dust and sweat of real life would be disloyalty to the core of the gospel of Jesus and refusal to be his church.

Our response to God's unconditional love is obedience to God's commandments: "If you love me you will keep my commandments. If anyone loves me he will keep my word" (John 14:15, 23). And God's commandment is that we should love one another: "I give you a new commandment: love one another" (John 13:34; 15:17). We must here take note of the very special grammar of the thought of Jesus which gives to the Christian faith its characteristic structure. Love is never a returning love completing the circle, but a new and creative love reaching out further to ever-widening horizons. "As the Father has loved me, so have I loved (not the Father, but) you. Just as I have loved you, so you must love (not me, but) one another. If I . . . have washed your feet, you should wash (not my, but) each other's feet" (John 15:9; 13:34; 13:14). We are here at the heart of the gospel and in touch with the specificity of the faith. The only adequate response to God's unconditional love in Jesus Christ is to make our own God's concern for people and to give all we have for their total liberation and wholeness as God gave the Son for the world's salvation. Now, love is something concrete; it is deeds, not words. It means securing bread for the breadless, recognition for the marginated, dignity for the despised, liberation for captives, and freedom for the downtrodden. It means making ourselves responsible for all who are dispossessed, stripped, broken, and discarded on the roadside by a competitive society propelled by the single idea of grabbing ever fatter profits (see Luke 10:29–37; 4:18–19; Matt. 25:31–46; 11:1–4; I John 3:16–18). In the face of these imperatives of the faith, the churches stand summoned to prove themselves neighbors in solidarity with victims of actual and structural injustice, not merely at the individual level but especially at the level of groups and whole masses of marginated and downtrodden people.

For people are sacred. Women and men are made in the image of God. Men and women, not simply as individuals, but as community, are the only image and symbol capable of pointing to the mystery of the divine with any relevance and meaningfulness. It is in respecting, loving, serving, cultivating, liberating, and waiting upon the mystery of this image that we come to discover and experience the divine with an ever-deepening, creative sense of the real. Communities of men and women are the only places of life-giving encounter and communion with God. That is why other than this human image, which God has placed on the earth, no other image may be made. Attempts to put up other images are escapist tricks: images of our making can be manipulated whether they be rubrics or laws, liturgies or authorities, establishments or dogmas. But men and women, brothers and sisters, neighbors whom God has placed here as God's own image, make demands on us, and apart from meeting these demands there is no meeting with God. If then we are true and brave enough to follow up the consistency of biblical thought, we shall find that humankind has in our faith a surprisingly central place. Everything is for humankind: the earth and the Sabbath; all sabbaths, sacraments, laws, and institutions, whether sacred or secular; all authorities, parliaments, economic and political arrangements; all sciences and technological devices. Where therefore injury is done to people as individuals or groups, where their rights and freedoms are abridged, their creativity and growth are impeded, or they are denied due voice and place in society, the most sacred reality on earth is being insulted and profaned, the image of God is being humiliated and discarded, the face of God is being wiped out and atheism built, the future of our earth marred, and the humanity of all impoverished. The question therefore of injustice, misery, and oppression cannot but become a central human and Christian concern.

A MISSION OF LIBERATION

Hence we see Jesus defining his mission as well as his own identity in terms of people, of needy people and of services rendered to them; of captive people and their liberation; of dead people and people not allowed to live and their uprising. Jesus' basic redemptive service was a service of liberation, freeing people and enabling them to be themselves first, and then build their destiny and their future. He liberated people from ritual religion and ritual morality; he liberated them from the meshes of legalistic religion and legalistic morality and the shallowness of externalism. He liberated them from every sort of fear of gods and demons, of the powers that be, of one another, of themselves, and summoned them to live in love. He led them out of the depressing sense of guilt and the prisons of yesterdays by proclaiming God's universal and unconditional forgiveness, and by calling on them to make it their own personally by sharing it generously. He liberated them from burdensome traditions and from all oppressive powers symbolized in Satan and detailed in temple, priest, scribe, and Pharisee, in Herod and Caesar, and in the arrogance of the rich. He liberated them from isolation and individualism by educating them to life as a sharing fellowship patterned on the table-fellowship he enjoyed and recommended. In place therefore of the old exploitative, divisive, and classist society, Jesus initiated a movement of justice and love, of freedom and fellowship, and of celebration of humankind and God. Today the movement is us. In us it seeks to be alive and active. We surely want to be the Jesus movement, but we are it only in the measure in which we as churches are a real fellowship and a home of freedom, in the measure in which we are a voice raised against injustice and a hand working to end the degradation and exploitation of the majority of men and women, in the measure in which we are good news to the wretched of the earth.

Jesus was rejected by the political and religious leaders of his nation and his church. They had him killed. They started plotting against his life the moment they discovered that he was no preacher of innocuous pieties, no dealer in religious platitudes, no traditionalist mouthing old words or quoting ancient authorities. They were upset and angry because Jesus spoke in God's name about the people and their problems, about the poor, the downtrodden, and the working class, about the masses that labored and were heavily burdened and were allowed no rest; they were angry because Jesus moved among these, ate and slept with them, and championed their cause and their right to dignity and a fair deal. Jesus' words and deeds and lifestyle, his relationships and demands, the models he projected and the course he followed were all subversive of established systems, of interests and value-sets of religion, of social life, of the economic set-up, of political power structures. When the powerful ones saw that Jesus was out to affirm people, to let the lower classes feel that they were not low and need not remain low, that their squalor and servitude were not part of God's plan, that they could serve God and be God's children only by throwing away the yokes imposed on them, they opposed him and finally got rid of him.

That means the church has a stake in the real world of men and women, in the world of "the vast majority," the world's poor. It has to get involved in areas where the life of the people is made or unmade, in social, political, and economic affairs, not for the gain and power of its leaders, or for the prestige of a minority community, but for the sake of humanity, of the image of God on earth, of justice, of the quality of human life on earth. It also means that the church, when it takes up the cause of justice, must be ready to take the consequences of its conviction and pay the price.

AMBIGUITY OF CHURCH PRACTICE

Turn now from this ideal and call of the church to its practice in the matter of justice and sensitivity to the condition of the poor, and we meet with many a perplexing ambiguity. Other persons and I in India have been very vocal about the poor justice meted out to Christians of Scheduled Caste Origin, and there is a thirty-year history of our "fight." But I guess we do not pretend that this is the only or the biggest case of injustice we have come across in this country. Is not this rather a small sector of a vast system of injustice in which the masses of the people are held captive? Have there not been cases of enormous atrocities perpetrated on the poor, the small farmer, the landless worker, the Harijan, the Adivasi? And we have chosen most of the time to keep silent. Our silence perhaps is not an example of ambiguity: it is an example of support for the status quo which has mechanisms of oppression built into itself. We have not only been silent, we are deeply involved in the system itself which is a system of individualism and competition with a view to maximization of profit that can swell capital to be invested with accelerated competition for fatter profits. We are involved in this system and are supportive of it though perhaps unwittingly. We have not adequately questioned the moral basis and the human consequences of capitalism, landlordism, the big industry with sophisticated technology, an export-oriented economy, and so on. We have rather supported it with investments, or by letting ourselves be drawn into its dynamics by developing services that have to depend upon it continually. We have rarely stopped to ask what critical judgment our faith has to pass on the system.

All our churches seem to have accepted without question the classist pattern of social structuring. We have settled down to the fact that rich and poor exist within the churches. There are places where the priest, the sisters, the lay teachers, and the orphan students eat in four different places and not together; and the quality and quantity of food go on diminishing as the classes descend from priest to orphan. The intricate questions of justice and Christian fellowship implied in the situation are never raised. Nor is attention paid to the social models implicit in and proposed by our eucharistic celebrations, or our faith in a creator, or in the Trinity, or the Lord's Prayer, which we say together but have not yet begun to live. If we really take these things seriously, then we should share all the resources of the Christian community in order to make sure, as the early Christian communities made sure, that nobody among us is left in want and that no classes and divisions exist in our midst. Can we demand fair distribution of national resources before making sure of fair distribution of Christian resources, which are considerable? Can we point to government's duty without fulfilling our own within the churches?

We spend an undue proportion of our resources, which are by no means small, in the service of a minority of the wealthy and the well-to-do, be these Christian or non-Christian. Usually it is the representatives of this minority that control the levels of decision-making, policy-making, and priority-setting in the churches, just as in the government it is often non-Christians and nonscheduled caste people who settle the affairs of Christians of Scheduled Caste Origin (SCO). We go out of our way to secure enormous funds to run colleges, special schools, medical colleges, and excellent hospitals, all of which we know only the richer classses can afford. Aid goes to the poor mainly in relief or in emergency cases. While thus we serve the rich of all sections we want the government to care for our own poor. The churches seem to be saying something like this: "I am a rich Christian. So many (how many?) millions of rupees come into my hands every year from funding agencies abroad. With this I serve my class, the upper class, irrespective of religion. Now here are the poor Christians. Government, you, please, take care of them. You must if you are just."

There are Christians of SCO who are well off economically, and there are needy Christians who are not of SCO. This is true also of all the non-Christian sectors of the nation. Should the churches then seek a liberal interpretation of the provisions of the Constitution of India and a wider application of this interpretation, or should it bring a gospel critique to bear upon the very provisions themselves and the socioeconomic presuppositions of these provisions? Thirty years of experience has shown that an approach of privileges and paternalism does not improve the lot of long-oppressed sections of the people. Some of the groups tend to enjoy being privileged and protected. But that is not redemption, and we with our gospel culture should be among the first to detect the falseness of the situation and cease being preoccupied with laying claims to our share in the cake of privileges.

There is another, greater, ambiguity which clouds the question in hand. We Christians are a casteless community. We are strictly egalitarian. We do not accept the idea that some are low-born while others are high-born, for all are born of God through Jesus Christ in the Holy Spirit. Those who have accepted Jesus in faith have received the power to become God's children; their birth is free of the stains and chains of the willfulness and instincts of human selfishness, the breeding ground of class and caste and outcaste. Our faith is that all men and women are created in the image of God and are being renewed in the image of the creator, "and in that image there is no room for distinction between Greek and Jew, between the circumcized and the uncircumcized, or between barbarian and Scythian, slave or free man. There is only Christ: he is everything and he is in everything" (Col. 3:11; Gal. 3:27–28). Theologically, therefore, nobody is, nobody may be, marginated in the Christian community, and there are no caste distinctions. Theologically, then, what could be the meaning of the term "Scheduled Caste Christians"? It is perhaps an awareness of the incongruity of the term and its contradiction on Christian lips that leads us to grope for other phrases and to come out with "Christians of Scheduled Caste Origin." But our thought betrays us and the contradiction remains. It is ungracious (and the gospel is all grace) to keep harping back to distant origins and carnal divisions when Christ has abolished all divisions and united us into the New Woman and Man through the grace of his cross. If the correction of inadequate terminology was ever theologically or religiously necessary, it is necessary here. We know Christians recognize no caste linkage, for God has redeemed us from all such bondage into the fellowship of the Son. Is it right on our part to make that from which God has saved us the basis of claims to social and economic advantages?

When in the Indian Constituent Assembly Christians through their leaders declined reservations, separate electorates, and special privileges, they were at once overcoming the temptations of a minority situation and caste awareness and underlining the redemptive universalism of the Christian fellowship. And if the government cannot see caste distinctions in the Christian ranks, is it doing us an injury about which we should complain, or paying us a compliment over which we should rejoice? Is it impossible for us to understand the government as saying, "You, Christian churches, have solved in your measure the big problem of casteism and communalism with which we are still wrestling. You have such spiritual resources." We could then press forward to try to solve the problem in a still larger measure! The government is saying that in its view the Christian community does not marginate sections of itself; those who converted have escaped from the meshes of the caste system and the prisons of a closed society into the situation of openness and hope which characterizes the Christian fellowship. But if caste has followed them into the churches what difference has conversion made? It depends on us whether we take up or decline the challenge of this stance, whether we turn it into grounds for anger or for hope.

THE TASK AHEAD

The basis and scope of our struggle, therefore, need to broaden out. From concern for certain privileges for a particular group within a denominational minority community, we should move to the larger, catholic issue of justice for all the deprived, dispossessed, and downtrodden masses of the people of the subcontinent. It will be more consonant with our faith to take up or to join those who have taken up the cause of all the underprivileged and exploited. The basis of the struggle will be the rights of the millions who belong to that class which has been working the hardest for generations and centuries and has remained the poorest, also for centuries and generations. The fight will be against those social and political mechanisms by which the fruit of the toil of these millions is siphoned off and enjoyed by the few at the top rungs of the social ladder. The fight will be against a conception of life and of humankind which acquiesces in the existence of very rich and very poor in the same national or ecclesial community. The stand will be for a redistribution of resources in order to give some substance to the ideals of equality, freedom, and democracy. For in a landlordist-capitalist system of high productivity and cheap labor, these words are but hollow ideological gimmicks. In sponsoring the "rights" of Christians of SCO, the church is only tackling symptoms and not causes. It will do well to devote its energies to detecting the causes of widespread misery and wretchedness, to attacking these causes, and to promoting action for the implementation of such directive principles of the Constitution of India as call for distribution of the national community's resources to subserve the common good, and for prevention of concentration of wealth and means of production to the common detriment.

The concern of the church is not Christians but the poor; its struggle is not for itself but for the liberation of all men and women who are held captive. Not that its care for Christians of SCO is unjustifiable: it is natural, it is perhaps the concretization and focal point of the church's universal concern. The New Testament too has such sectarian perspectives. Paul tells us to do good to all, and especially to our brothers and sisters in the faith (Gal. 6:10; James 2:15). This is an attitude evolved in the early Christian community. The passages that directly reflect the mind of Jesus are universal in scope as in Matthew 25:31–46, or in the story of the good samaritan. It is such love and concern for the neediest, irrespective of religious affiliation, that can be the finest witness to the unconditional love that God has disclosed and given to the world in Jesus Christ. Every particular concern of the church must be seen as a symbol that seeks fulfillment, that is, transcendent realization, a realization always larger than itself on a higher or deeper plane.

The task of the church is to champion a whole new social order of true and not merely nominal freedom and equality and people's power. It will begin with itself becoming the new reality, an egalitarian, socialist society based on freedom and animated by love and realized in shared resources as indicated in the celebration of its Eucharist. It will go on to identify with the poor and suffering and dispossessed masses of men and women everywhere, help awaken their humanity and dignity, help them organize themselves for effective action to bring about a total revolution in structures of the heart as well as in structures of society so as to forge towards the creation of the new earth of God's dreams and God's promises. It will organize the poor rather than go claiming privileges or begging for benefits. It will take an open stand for justice and try to establish its credibility after too long a silence which has become an embarrassment to its members and its friends. Its call for a redistribution of national resources will be heralded by a reallocation of its own resources with a clear partiality for the poor and the downtrodden which marks the entire history of God's action on our earth. It will take upon itself afresh its responsibility for its poor, but as a concrete sign of its involvement with the plight of all the poor of this land. And finally it will try to make sure that all its ranks, especially those who have come into its freedom from an oppressive past, become catalysts of social change and not seekers of social security, become leaders of liberation movements in favor of all the oppressed of our country and not enjoyers of a separate paradise.

31

Henriette Marianne Katoppo

Asian Theology: An Asian Woman's Perspective

Henriette Marianne Katoppo is an Asian Christian woman who has found her experience of the Other to be alienating. She calls Mary the fully liberated human being. "Asian Theology: An Asian Woman's Perspective" is taken from Virginia Fabella, ed., Asia's Struggle for Full Humanity *(Maryknoll, N.Y.: Orbis Books, 1980), pp. 140–51. The paper was given at the Asian Theological Conference in 1979.*

INTRODUCTION

For a long time, Asians were denied the right to theologize. Asian experience was denied validity. Asian expression was denounced as pagan.

We can relate this to the fact that Christianity had been the "white man's burden" for so long that European and North American theologians did not accept independent Asian thinking. At the moment (January 1979), numerically the majority of Christians is still found in the so-called First World. However, the balance is shifting so rapidly that by May 1979, the majority of Christians will be in the Third World. Having grown so "strong in number" in relation to our First World Christian brothers and sisters, perhaps we can assert our right to be different, our right to be the Other.

In Asia's struggle for full humanity, woman are especially concerned in moving towards a relevant theology. A relevant theology for Asian women considers the Asian women's perspective about God, for theology, whether it is seen as a discipline or a critical reflection, is primarily about God. Done from a woman's perspective, this reflective process might be termed women's theology. I do not use the term feminist theology because the word "feminist" has become so loaded that it will take a long time before people will say "feminist is beautiful." Those who are eager to put everything in categories might say of women's theology that it is process theology (or more accurately, *theologia viatorum*) and that its methodology is inductive. In doing theology, however, an Asian woman has additional odds to overcome in order to assert her right to be different, her right to be the Other.

BEING THE OTHER

In order to clarify my position and to provide the context from which I speak, I should like to begin with my personal experience of being the Other and the problem of alienation that it entails.

Personal Experience

First of all, I am Asian. More specifically, I am Indonesian, from the Minahassa (Northern Sulawesi), which is about two thousand kilometers from Jakarta, Java. Ethnically, linguistically, and culturally, there are very great differences between the Minahassans and the Javanese. Furthermore, the Minahassans are 99 percent Christian, while the Javanese are predominantly Muslim (90 percent).

Historically, the Minahassa has had its own peculiarites. Four hundred years ago, the Minahassa was under the Bishop of Manila, as Spain was in control of that entire region at the time. Two hundred years later, the Minahassa chieftains concluded a treaty with the Dutch against the Spaniards.[1] Around the turn of the nineteenth century, the Dutch seriously considered making the Minahassa "the twelfth province" of the Netherlands, the kingdom having eleven provinces at the time. Though this plan was never realized, it gave the Minahassa an image of being different, of being Westernized, an image that prevails until now.

After independence from the Dutch in 1945, the Minahassa first became part of the state of East Indonesia (Timor); then in 1950, when the United States of Indonesia was dissolved, Minahassa formally joined the present Republic (Republic Indonesia Serikat).

Secondly, I am a Protestant of the Evangelical (i.e., Presbyterian) Church of Minahassa. Together with six other churches of Eastern Indonesia, our church is a member of the Federation of the Protestant Churches of Indonesia (GPI).[2] One should bear in mind, however, that in Indonesia the Protestant churches are not so much determined by denominational as by ethnic factors. Hence we have the Minahassa church, the Molucca church, the Timor church, rather than the Presbyterian church, the Methodist church, and so on. Protestant

Christianity is one of the six accepted religions in Indonesia, the others being Islam, Roman Catholicism, Hinduism, Buddhism, and Confucianism. Protestants and Catholics together constitute about 10 percent of the population,[3] the ratio being seven to three.

In the third place, I am a woman. Numerically, women are not a minority. Almost anywhere in the world, "women hold up half the sky." In Sri Lanka, for instance, women are 52 percent of the population; in Indonesia, 51 percent. However, in decision-making, and the like, women are definitely treated as a minority in most areas in Indonesia. Minahassa is the exception; women are raised in a more egalitarian atmosphere, *egalitarian* meaning less traditionally feudal and less sexist. However, since I moved to Jakarta as a child, I have continuously experienced being the Other: a Christian among Muslims, a "Westernized" Minahassa who was unfamiliar with the proper speech and behavior in a Javanese society, a girl raised to look upon boys as equals and not superior, a girl taught to think and not to cook.

To be the Other is an alienating experience in a society which is subconsciously still strongly influenced by concepts of cosmic balance, by the importance of ties of kinship and soil, and so on. In such a society, the Other is the discordant note, the threat to harmony. Fortunately, Indonesia is now moving towards the Great Society, where national consciousness is supreme as opposed to the divisive regional chauvinist consciousness. In such a context, to be the Other can also be a liberating experience. One's "Other-ness" might be used positively to enrich national culture, as has been evident in the revival of many traditional tribal elements.

Philosophy and Theology of the Other

There is both a philosophy and a theology of the Other, the finer points of which I will not go into here. A few remarks are necessary and at the same time sufficient.

God is the absolute Other. Since God is eschatological, the divine self is not given entirely to us in history, but only at the end of history.[4]

People tend to worship idols of their own making, not only from nature, such as stones, trees, animals, or even human beings, but also systems and structures, capital, products, power. The prophets, in order to affirm God the creator, had first to lash out against idols or gods that people had created for themselves.

Sin, all sin, is by nature an all-encompassing absolute. When we sin, we think we are all there is and are therefore divine. We deny the Other and believe that our own totalized order is the kingdom of heaven. We become, as the old Malays put it, "like the frog under the coconut shell, which cannot conceive of a world of light and vast open space beyond its world of darkness and limitations."

I must state that I find the theology and philosophy of the Other useful and relevant only inasmuch as they reinforce or help or develop my own.

Woman's Image of Herself

It has been established that, on the whole, the Asian woman's self-image is unsatisfactory. This can be attributed to culture and education. From an early age woman is conditioned to a subservient, submissive role. Her status is "derived"; instead of being a person in her own right, she is "daughter of," "wife of," or "mother of" a man.

In the case of Christian women, their poor self-image is the result of the church's tendency "to give male chauvinism . . . a theological and quasi-divine legitimation."[5] There are Christian churches where women have no awareness of having been created in God's image (*imago Dei*) because they are taught that woman was created to be a "helper" unto man. These churches have conveniently overlooked the implications of the Hebrew *eser* (which is translated as "helper"). In the Old Testament, *eser* is otherwise used only in reference to God, the help of the helpless (cf. Ps. 107).[6]

Many Christian women are likewise unaware of the feminine aspects of divinity, which I will discuss in more detail later. There is need to emphasize these feminine qualities as well as the need to raise our awareness about them, if women are to improve their self-image.

The Liberation of Woman Is Also the Liberation of Man

From my personal experience as the Other, I came to realize that not only in society but in the church in general, woman is the Other.

If women are at all admitted to male-dominated institutions of higher theological education and to patriarchal church structures, they are expected to theologize by proxy: faithfully to relay the ideas fabricated in male chauvinist, white supremacist contexts. A woman's own experiences are denied validity, and her personal encounter with God is denounced as heretical or hysterical. In the first case one is figuratively burnt at the stake; in the second, people hasten to find her a husband.

To get ahead in patriarchal society, woman is expected to become a man and hence to cease being the threatening Other. In politics, whether of church or state, we often find that the few women who "reach the top" have often become so "man-ly" that they do the woman's cause far more harm than good. Some have become such dictators that some men self-righteously claim that this only goes to prove that women should never be given the chance to wield power, failing to recognize the underlying psychological process.

Many men are antagonistic to women's liberation, since they fail to perceive that it is also human liberation. Actually, this indicates how deeply ingrained is their belief that woman is the Other. Man, being the norm, is human. Woman, being the "deviation," is therefore not human.

There is the saying: "Men of quality are not threatened by women's call for equality." They realize that their worth as human beings is in no way threatened by women also asking to be recognized as human beings.

Men who feel threatened are those who fail to realize that women's liberation is concerned with the liberation of all people to become full participants in human society. They are not aware that their reaction is not rational, but emotional. It is caused by fear—fear of loss of status, fear of what will happen when patriarchal structures mutate, but, basically, fear of the Other.

And this fear will prevail as long as the church gives male chauvinism not only a practical expression but a theological legitimation. I am claiming the right for a woman to be the Other, to be a human being in her own right, not as an afterthought, a derivation, a deviation, a subordinate in reference to man.

Only recently have Asians been "granted" the right to their own perspective of history. We may hope that Asians will formulate their own theology (with the caveat that there will never be a pure Asian theology). Why is it so difficult, then, to accept the fact that Asian women may have their own insights to contribute to the richness of Asian theology?

When will Asian churches learn that, unless they admit the right of their women to be the Other and use this Other-ness positively, they will alienate them totally?

The Other

I am—You are.
I am free—You are free.
But where I am, what I am, you cannot be.
Where you are, what you are, I cannot be.
Am I encroaching on your freedom?
Are you intruding on mine?
Have I the right to be what I am?
Can we be fully human, you and I, each in our own way?
Can we enrich another, by being the Other?

SOCIOPOLITICAL REALITIES

The Exploitation of "Nonpersons"

Women are members of the same sexual caste, whether they live in Sweden or Saudi Arabia.[7] Women are used as objects in many different ways. A look at almost any advertisement confirms this fact. Whether it is to sell cars or cameras or bathroom tiles or inexpensive tours abroad, women are prominently displayed. When one is conditioned to think of categories or groups of people as "nonpersons," then one subconsciously sees them as objects to be used or disposed of as one pleases. Sexism, racism, imperialism, and exploitation are all expressions of the same attitude, which denies the Other (nonpersons, objects, etc.) the right to exist. The rape of women, of races, of any human or natural resource therefore becomes justified for the mode of existence of a few. Conquest is the watchword when it is far better to strive for conviviality!

Women in the Rural Areas

The nutritional situation in the underdeveloped countries has generally not improved since before World War II; in many countries, it may even have deteriorated. In Southeast Asia, people spend two-thirds or more of their income on foodstuffs, yet the U.N. Food and Agriculture Organization has pointed out that the majority of people in those countries suffer from undernutrition or malnutrition. I shall not discuss here the roots of this situation. It is well known throughout Asia that power and especially economic power is ordinarily held by a very small section of the population, and the rest of the population is simply the "nonpersons" who serve the interests of this upper class.

In Indonesia, women as "nonpersons" are doubly exploited from the very start of their lives. Statistics show that 85 percent of all female children under five in Indonesia are undernourished. In the rural areas, people often live at subsistence levels. Seen in the overall context of poverty, the undernourishment of female children may not be surprising. There are in fact entire villages where children are cretins because of the malnutrition. However, the undernourishment of female children can also be attributed to the fact that they are often the ones who get the least food, fathers and brothers getting first priority.

Women in the Urban Areas

If the female child survives her early struggles, her plight is unlikely to be brighter as a young woman. Many young women of the rural areas are lured to the big cities with promises of work in the factories or as domestic servants. Once in the urban centers, their dignity is continuously insulted and these women, having come from conditions of the most abject poverty, are easily driven to prostitution. Once forced into this way of life, they are ashamed to return to their homes. It becomes almost impossible to get away.

It has been estimated that 60 percent of the women in certain areas are prostitutes. Where prostitution is not legalized, it is localized.

At Kramat Tunggak, Jakarta, there is a localized prostitution complex surrounded by a high fence. There are about one hundred houses, with at least eight women in each. The total number of prostitutes in Jakarta has been estimated at three thousand, including five hundred Christians. Some Ursuline nuns started a program for Bible study and general knowledge lessons for the prostitutes, held at an office across the road. Before the Department of Social Service intervened, the madame used to charge the women who attended the nuns' program for "being away from work."

The hotel industry is also involved in the prostitution racket. Tourism and prostitution almost always go together. I find it interesting that in the tribal societies of old, prostitution was not known. It came with increased mobility and commercialization. Does this not indicate the degree of alienation a person has to experience to start treating sex as a commodity?

Prostitution has not only been commercialized or legalized; it has even received ideological support through the Indonesian language itself.

In Bahasa Indonesia, the national language which evolved from the commercial Malay (the *lingua franca* of the archipelago), the word for prostitute was *pelaour,* which means "a person who sells him/herself." A few years ago, the trend was to use complicated Sanskrit words, even when there were perfectly good words in Malay. Hence "prostitute" became *Wanita tuna susila,* "woman without morals." Interestingly enough, there is no corresponding *pria tuna susila,* "man without morals."

Is there any significance in the fact that the risen Christ first appeared to Mary Magdalene who, according to tradition, was a prostitute?

The Dowry

A further exploitation of women is the dowry system still practiced in some areas in Indonesia. In these areas, dowry means "brideprice," that is, the amount the man's family has to pay for the bride. It is in this very sense that in the U.N. Declaration against the Discrimination of Women "dowry" is especially mentioned as "one of the forms of slavery" still to be combatted.

Some Indonesian churches, for example, the Nias church, have condemned the practice of giving dowry or accepting it. Those members who still do it are refused Holy Communion.

In my opinion, however, the abolition of dowry should not be imposed "from above," but should come from the grassroots level through a proper understanding of "personhood." Admittedly this will be difficult in a tribal society which attaches great importance to cosmic balance. Here it is the tribe, not the person, which is important. The *adat,* or customary law which was orginally intended to preserve the tribe from all evil, often has become itself an evil, insofar as it oppresses the people instead of protecting them. The church does not always take a clear stance here, failing to realize that the *adat* has become a manifestation of the Anti-God.

The Political Participation of Women

There is a growing awareness of women's exploitation and status in Indonesian society, and it began prior to the country's independence. Women's movements and organizations began to be formed. In their early days, the burning issues for women were coeducation and marriage, the latter covering polygamy or polygny, child marriage, and a woman's lack of voice in her own marriage.

However, women's concerns and activities went beyond mere social protest. They were as active as the men in Indonesia's struggle for independence. Political parties and youth organizations began to have women's units and, in some cases, to accept women as full members. In fact, one of Indonesia's great statesmen said in 1939: "The women's movement was born in the twentieth century as a full sibling *(adik kandung)* of the Indonesian nationalist movement."[8]

In these different organizations, men began to realize that women were good comrades-in-arms, possessing equal capabilities as well as rights and responsibilities. Another positive effect of the inclusion of women in the organization was the overcoming of regional chauvinism as well as the breaking down of male chauvinism. Members began to consider themselves as Indonesians rather than Javanese or Sumatrans or Amboinese, reflecting the words of the *Sumpah Pemuda* (Oath of the Youth) of 1928, which said: "We, the sons and daughters of Indonesia, vow to have one motherland, one nation, one language—Indonesia."[9]

Partnership of Men and Women in Society

What is actually emerging is the growing consciousness of the indispensability of a partnership between women and men in the process of liberation and change. This partnership is an important point in Asian culture which we need to rediscover and to recover. In the agricultural societies of the past, great value was attached to this partnership, but as societies moved towards industrialization, the partnership tended to become obscured. We must seriously ask ourselves whether development takes place only at the expense of others or the Other. Are both consumerism and the commercialization of women the inevitable product of development? Should not our struggle for full humanity be motivated by love for life, for the Other? It is in this challenge that we shall encounter the absolute Other—God.

THEOLOGICAL MOTIFS

The Concept of God from the Feminist Perspective

If our theology is to be relevant, then our concept of God has to be relevant. For this we must learn to read the Bible again. For so long, masculine imagery has dominated the text; the feminine images have been conveniently overlooked. The text which has come to us has indeed been the product "of a society driven to choose male metaphors by virtue of patriarchal structures predicated upon sexual inequality."[10] We have further flattered ourselves into thinking that while patriarchal structures have remained, we no longer have sexual inequality.

If that were really true, then why is the name of God, Yahweh—which is a verb, not a noun—still consistently translated as Lord? To quote Hanson again, "This masculinization does seem to be a conspiracy spanning three millennia."[11] It is a fact that where the original texts make no indication of gender it has been supplied gratuitously by the translators, who were usually male. The Dutch theologian Maria de Groot, also a linguist, draws our attention to the way in which the domination of the male hyperboles and male symbols has gravely impaired our understanding of revelation. Most of us do not really take Genesis 1:27 seriously. It is not really accepted that woman is created in God's image; nor is it accepted that it is just as valid to ascribe feminine qualities to God as it is to ascribe masculine qualities.

In the Old Testament, the word *rahamin* is used for God's mercy, compassion (cf. Exod. 3:6). Literally it means "movements of the womb." Yet some male theologians will perform the most extraordinary contortions exegetically in order to avoid relating this to the motherliness of God. Isaiah 49:15 is another example of the motherliness of God. So is Hosea 11:1-4.[12]

When we call God "Father" this does not necessarily limit God to being male. *Father* is intended to express the loving concern of God. Clement of Alexandria sings:

> God is love
> God can only be perceived in love
> Father is his inexpressible being
> Mother is his compassionate pity for us
> In his love for us
> The Father became woman
> The great sign for us is this:
> He who was born.

Clement has the deep insight of the ecstatic love for Christ in the early church, when (as Karl Rahner remarked somewhat wistfully) theologians were still poets and able to see the greater context. We must point out, however, that it is not quite right to say that only "in his love for us, God became woman"; God is Father and Mother in all eternity.[13]

Anselm of Canterbury sings of Mother Jesus: "And Thou, Sweet Lord, art Thou not a mother, who tasted death in order to give life to us?" Even Pope John Paul I referred to God as our Father-Mother. There is nothing new or strange in acknowledging the feminine aspects of divinity. Yet why do so many still recoil from the thought?

In the tradition of the ecclesiastical West, the Holy Spirit is conceived of as he. This is due to the fact that the feminine *ruach* of the Hebrew was first effectively neutered in Greek, then made masculine in Latin. Is it coincidence that the symbol for the Holy Spirit is the dove (*peristera* in Greek: "Bird of Istar")? The battle between Yahweh and Istar, "the Great Mother," seems to be going on still.[14]

In view of the quality and the function of the Spirit as God who creates, who comforts, it is not surprising that in the Gnostic writings (such as the Gospel of the Hebrews) the Holy Spirit was explicitly called "Mother of Jesus" or (in the Acts of Thomas) "Mother of all creatures."

Some people do not feel that it is oppression to force people to relate to an all-male Trinity. Yet they would laugh at those who are still firmly convinced that "God is an Englishman."

For a more relevant theology, perhaps we could do some more reflection on the significance of other feminine aspects of the divine besides *ruach,* such as *hokmah* (wisdom) and *shekinah* (presence). We will confine ourselves to *hokmah,* which had the good fortune to remain feminine in the "sacred" languages (Greek: *sophia*; Latin: *sapientia*). Since "wisdom" is feminine in most languages, it is interesting to note that women are often accused of lacking wisdom.

Postexilic literature show how *hokmah* (as eventually *shekinah*) was almost personified: "A female form of great refinement and beauty, whose utterances were most profound and radiant."

She inspired love. She was love. In Proverbs, the Book of Wisdom, and Ecclesiasticus (Ben Sira), whenever Hokmah was the subject, even the most desiccated hagiographer would wax lyrical in praise of her.

In the light of the New Covenant, rather than personifying wisdom, should we not see Hokmah as God's personal inclination to the world? As a form in which God is with us, and wants to be sought by us?

And it is interesting that in the early church there seems to have been an identification of Hokmah with Jesus.

Mary: The Fully Liberated Human Being

I would like to devote this last portion of the theological section to Mary, the Mother of Jesus. To me, Mary was the fully liberated human being. It might be startling that I, a Protestant, should make this claim. Protestantism, especially the Calvinist variety, has not displayed any great interest in Mary. Except for children's pageants at Christmas and Easter, Mary is invisible in the Protestant church.

Many feminists, including feminist theologians, have rejected the model of Mary. One can readily agree with that if one looks at the standard portrayal of Mary: sugar sweet, fragile, with eyes downcast or turned up to heaven, not quite here-and-now. This is in line with her supposed submissiveness. After all, did she not say: "I am the Lord's servant; may it happen to me as you have said"?

We fail to realize that Mary's submission to the will of God is in no way the abject submission of the slave who has no choice. Rather, it is the receptive submission of the truly liberated human being who put the will of God first. It is the creative submission of the fully liberated human being who, not being subjected to any other human being, is free to serve.

This, too, is the deepest meaning of virginity. It is a positive stance.[15]

"Virginity" represents the state in which the human being is responsive to God and allows God to take the initiative.

In women's theology, "virgin" can be the symbol for the autonomy of woman. Virgin then would not primarily mean a woman who abstains from sexual intercourse, but a woman who does not lead a "derived" life (as "mother of," "wife of," daughter of"), a woman who matures to wholeness within herself as complete person, who is subject of herself, and who is open for others, for God. Through this maturing process, she is fertile, she gives life. Not only "Virgin," but also "Mother," attains a new power of imagery, and this may liberate women from the previous concept of Virgin-Mother, a biological impossibility which was held up to them as model. It is no coincidence that lately more importance is being given to Mary, both in Catholic dogma and in Protestant thinking.

Asian Catholics, for example, are beginning to see Mary no longer as "the fairy queen oozing out sweet piety," to quote Aloysius Pieris, S.J., "but as the peasant mother who cheerfully wore herself out to feed and clothe her carpenter son; the worker's wife wearing holy furrows on her face, an image reflected in millions of Asian village mothers today."

Protestants, who have learned to overcome their initial fear of "Mariolatry," might find their sign of hope in her as the first fully liberated human being, whose Magnificat is central in the theology of liberation.[16]

In my opinion, it speaks for itself that Gutiérrez, the famous liberation theologian, for example, makes little mention of Mary, although the Magnificat is generally attributed to her. Is this perhaps an example of the way women are constantly eclipsed in history—this occurring so often and so naturally that we simply forget that things should be different?

The thanksgiving and the joy in the Magnificat are addressed to God, but "true liberation will be the work of the oppressed themselves; in them God saves history."[17] Human liberation often seems a grim and joyless struggle. The Magnificat shows otherwise. And I exult in the fact that this Asian woman, this Mary, upon her encounter with God bursts out in this great song of thanksgiving and joy. Mary is the truly liberated, fully liberated human being, subject to no other human being, submitting only to God. Receptive to God's action and creative inasmuch as she shares in bringing the good news of salvation to the world, she is the model not only for woman, but also for man. She is the new human being (man-woman), receptive before God, who calls him/her to be *imago Dei:* compassionate and free.

NOTES

1. One of the most interesting clauses of the treaty is the solemn undertaking of the chieftains "to abolish the abominable practice of headhunting."
2. The Federation of the Protestant Churches of Indonesia (GPI), together with

forty-two other churches, forms the Indonesian National Council of Churches.

3. The population of Indonesia in 1979 was 144 million, making it the fifth largest country in the world.

4. Enrique Dussel, *Ethics and the Theology of Liberation* (Maryknoll, N.Y.: Orbis Books, 1978), p. 13.

5. Tissa Balasuriya, *The Eucharist and Human Liberation* (Maryknoll, N.Y.: Orbis Books, 1979), p. 52.

6. See also Pss. 10:14; 30:10; 54:4; 71:12; 94:17.

7. Mary Daly, *Beyond God the Father: Toward a Philosophy of Women* (Boston: Beacon Press, 1973), p. 2.

8. Adinegoro, "Soal Ibu," *Keutamaan Istri,* April 21, 1939.

9. The Indonesian *tumpah darad,* which I have translated as "motherland," literally means "bloodshed," obviously in its context referring to the process of childbirth.

10. Paul Hanson, "Masculine Metaphors for God and Sex Discrimination in the Old Testament," *The Ecumenical Review* 27 (October 1975).

11. Ibid.

12. See D. Preman Niles, "Old Testament: Man and the Holy," in *The Human and the Holy,* ed. Emerito P. Nacpil and Douglas J. Elwood (Quezon City, Philippines: New Day Publishers, 1978; Maryknoll, N.Y.: Orbis Books, 1980), p. 18.

13. Eulogia Würz, "Das Mutterliche in Gott," *Una Sancta* 32 (1977): 268–69.

14. Gerhard Voss, "Maria in der Feier des Kirchenjahres," *Una Sancta* 32 (1977): 308–9.

15. Catharina Halkes, "Eine, andere-Maria," *Una Sancta* 32 (1977): 323–37.

16. Gustavo Gutiérrez, *A Theology of Liberation* (Maryknoll, N.Y.: Orbis Books, 1973), pp. 207–8.

17. Ibid., p. 208.

32

Albert Widjaja

Beggarly Theology: A Search for a Perspective toward Indigenous Theology

Albert Widjaja makes an important distinction between "theological begging" and "beggarly theology." "Beggarly Theology" is taken from John England, ed., Living Theology in Asia *(Maryknoll, N.Y.: Orbis Books, 1982), pp. 154–59.*

INTRODUCTION

The term "beggarly theology" in the discussion below will be distinguished from "theological begging." The latter term refers to a theological pursuit which more or less imitates, borrows, and transfers from other theological work. Theologians engaged in such pursuits try to explore and interpret the meaning of Christian existence through the structure and content of a borrowed theology. They have the profession of receiving. Theological pursuit thus described is found among the theologians or church leaders of the Third World (or of the "younger churches"). They believe that the theology of Martin Luther, Karl Barth, Rudolf Bultmann, Billy Graham, Paul Tillich, Gerhard von Rad, or Reinhold Niebuhr are "the theology" indispensable for the development of Christian faith. Any deviation from these systems of theology is considered shallow, untheological, and even perhaps sinful or secular. The theology of these great men often receives a special status, almost equal to the Scripture. The practice of theological begging has been one of the major outcomes of the Western missionary endeavor. And it has been promoted by the Western seminary theologians, who educated the church leaders of the Third World. Most problematic of all, we Third World churchpersons tend to perpetuate such practice.

"Beggarly theology," however, is different in the sense of the spirit of the beggar, not in the sense of the profession described above. The true spirit of beggars can be discovered when they encounter a garbage container. They face the garbage with a sense of anticipation. They believe that something will be invaluable, even though the garbage as a whole is considered junk by the society. They have an attitude of respect to the things which society rejects or depreciates. Similarly, beggarly theology takes its own experience and native culture seriously, even though such cultural experience is considered pagan, secular, and inferior by the Western missionary theology. These beggars have an independent spirit which is not motivated by rebellion or national pride, but by a desire of being sincere to their Christian commitment. They realize that to be true and faithful to Jesus Christ one has to be detached from the demand of conformity to human-made theology. They want to be genuine in their Christian life and witness. But such genuineness requires uninhibited acceptance of the demand of the gospel and whole-hearted encounter with the challenges of their culture and society. Beggarly theology hungers after the righteousness of the kingdom of God, not the wisdom of Western theology. In his Sermon on the Mount, Jesus said: "Blessed are the poor in spirit for theirs is the kingdom of God. Blessed are those who hunger and thirst for righteousness, for they shall be satisfied" (Matt. 5:3, 6). Beggarly theologians seek a new orientation because they want to be genuine in their commitment to Christ and far-reaching in their witness.

The term "beggarly theology" may be confusing for many people. It may be charged with being emotional, indecent, and unscholarly terminology. These charges may be made by those who forget that the majority of the Third World people are poor. These charges may come out of pride, for they are often made by those who identify with Western theology, which often substitutes cultural cleanliness for holiness. The confidence in the power of the gospel is replaced by the complacency of the power of wealth. Freedom in Christ is replaced by conformity to the existing social order. Even with such opposition, the beggarly theology continues its work because it is not designed for the Western world. It is for the Third World whose true problem has often been ignored.

The beggarly attitude is an attitude of identification with the struggle of the dispossessed, of the lost, of the disintegrated ones who are caught in the modernization process. The beggarly attitude seeks to accompany those whose "souls hunger after the living bread, and their spirits thirst for the living water." The beggarly theology does not seek, however, to bring revolution or to tear down the social order; it seeks the path of gradual but decisive transformation of human hearts and human relations as done by the early church.

The beggarly theology does not say that culture is more authoritative than the gospel. On the contrary, it does say that on the one hand the beggarly theology rejects any form of conformity; and on the other hand it maintains serious confrontation between the gospel and the culture in which it lives. It does not flee from its society. Yet it wants to move beyond the trivialities of the society in the light of the gospel. Realizing its poverty in theology, in culture, and so on, the beggarly theology gives special attention to its relation with God who promises: "For the needy shall not always be forgotten, and the hope of the poor shall not perish forever" (Ps. 4:8). The beggarly theology emphasizes the need of repentance when it is confronted by Christ. It is by this experience that a new and substantial theology can be gained.

In short, the beggarly theology offered here basically reflects a search for fundamental perspectives through which a truly indigenous theology is to be developed. The beggarly theology, however, is not "the" indigenous theology! It is one among many approaches to indigenous theology. Yet it is indispensable for an indigenous theology. It does not stand in false hope because it seeks to be a disciple of Christ who is our hope. As Paul says: "Though he was rich, yet for your sake he becomes poor, so that by his poverty you may become rich" (2 Cor. 8:9; cf. Phil. 2:5–6; Rev. 2:9). An indigenous theology from a poor church is indeed possible. The resources are right "here," not "there" in overseas places.

A PERSPECTIVE FOR INDIGENOUS THEOLOGY

The current discussion about indigenous theology may be a fad for some and fruitless for others. Yet it is deeply significant for the Third World churches. It reflects a constant struggle to free themselves from the letter of the "law" and a constant quest to live with the gospel in a deeper way.

Indigenous theology is not a theology which merely adjusts Western theology into the thought-form of the indigenous culture. Nor is it a ramification and elaboration of certain fundamental aspects of Western theology to meet the presuppositions of the native culture. Indigenous theology is a theology which seeks to be genuine in its commitment to the demand of the gospel, seeks to be original in its perception of the challenges of the world in the light of the gospel. It attempts to be relevant to the society, yet faithful to its God.

Theology is a tool of the church. It serves to deepen and clarify the church's faith in Christ. At the same time theology serves to shed light upon the consequences of that faith for the church's responsibility in society, both in evangelism and social witness. As Christ himself came to the world with a task to accomplish, so the church has the task to continue his work. Thus theology has to keep its perspective in tension between the world and the gospel, not in a peaceful continuation as upheld by the Western liberals or in arbitrary friendship and hostility as perpetuated by the evangelicals. . . .

Our point here is that we are deeply entangled in the ways of the world in which we live. We try to perpetuate the status quo and cannot go beyond it. The common sense and the traditional theological reason often control our reason in its attempt to understand the illumination of the Holy Spirit in intuition. In that case, reason cannot grasp the newness of the gospel. Theological endeavor then only repeats or elaborates the things which have been said by others. Or, it merely conforms to the norms of the culture. If reason wants to grasp the novelty of God's revelation, and if reason wants to do justice to God's ways which are different from humankind's ways, then reason should not allow common sense and the traditional theological reasoning to dominate its work. This is not to say, however, that we ought to suppress or to feel as if our reason and experience are empty. What it says is that reason has to develop a critical attitude toward the status quo. Persons have to be aware and willing to admit that they have been deeply socialized by their culture and religious background. Then, at the same time they need to be critical of these forces. This critical attitude means that we have to question what is obvious, final, and popular; scrutinize what is simple and assumptive; juxtapose what is contradictory and paradoxical; and probe what is unfamiliar and profound. Only by a critical attitude can people open themselves to the new revelation of God. They will allow God to judge and transform their lives and faith. They will no longer be at peace with their old stereotypical faith. By such self-criticism, they can shake their hang-up with Western theology. At the same time, they can develop an indigenous theology without blindly conforming to their culture.

THE RELEVANCY OF BEGGARLY THEOLOGY AS INDIGENOUS THEOLOGY

When the Protestant Reformation abolished the monasteries and established the concept of the priesthood of believers, it tried to recast the nature of the dynamic relationship between the gospel and the world, the contemporary historical experience of the society. It tried to place Christianity in its true calling; that is, to identify with the world and yet to transform it for the sake of God's kingdom. To do so requires a new perception of the ways of God and a thorough-going involvement in the experiences of the society. Beggarly theology's emphasis is to give the society a special place in its theological endeavor. It identifies with the people of all walks of life. It goes to all the streets of its own society, and not to Geneva, New York, Oostgeest, Barmen, Harvard, or Heidelberg. Beggarly theology does not pretend to be holier, wealthier, or more civilized than thou toward its own society. It wants to live deeply with the agony of the world in which it lives. It moves out of the pietistic ghettoism. It tries to bring the message of God in the most intelligible, concrete, and dynamic way. It also provides a basis for the church to be involved in the development program of the society.

The pursuit of an indigenous theology is also a sign of a mature church. A church is mature when it realizes that it is fully responsible for its own life and task in the world. A mature chuch is a church which does not need to go to "mother church" to ask an explanation of what God wants to say to the church. A mature church makes for dialogue and mutual admonition. A mature church can meet God directly, without human mediacy. In arriving at such consciousness, the church feels the need to be equipped with a thoroughly developed Christian faith which is rooted in its environment. Such is the indigenous theology which is seeking a genuine and comprehensive faith. Indigenous theology is a search for an authentic path of a mature church, a path of true servanthood to Jesus Christ.

33

Kim Yong-Bok

Messiah and Minjung: Discerning Messianic Politics over against Political Messianism

---

Kim Yong-Bok is a leading spokesperson for Korean minjung theology. "Messiah and Minjung: Discerning Messianic Politics over against Political Messianism," written in 1979, is taken from the Commission on Theological Concerns of the Christian Conference of Asia, ed., Minjung Theology: People as the Subjects of History *(Maryknoll, N.Y.: Orbis Books, 1983), pp. 183–93.*

In this essay we intend to use the category of messianism as a conceptual tool to determine the relation between minjung and power. We shall first define the term "minjung" as the subject of history and clarify an approach to historical reality.[1] In the context of such an understanding of history, the relationship between the people and power will be clarified. To do this we will do three things. First, we will trace messianic traditions in Korea. Second, we will use messianic categories to analyze Japanese colonial power in Korea, the Korean Communist regime, and the present government of Korea. Finally, we will seek to shed light on the messianic politics of the minjung in terms of the liberation of the minjung.

The minjung are the permanent reality of history. Kingdoms, dynasties and states rise and fall; but the minjung remain as a concrete reality in history, experiencing the comings and goings of political powers. Although the minjung understand themselves in relation to the power which is in command, they are not confined by that power. The minjung transcend the power structures which attempt to confine them through the suppression of their stories. Power has its basis in the minjung. But power as it expresses itself in political powers does not belong to the minjung. These powers seek to maintain themselves, and they rule the minjung.

When we view minjung in relation to power, we define the minjung in political terms. The political definition of minjung also includes the socioeconomic determination. The political and socioeconomic conditions of the minjung are not just objective realities for socioeconomic analysis. Rather, we have in mind the total subjective experiences of the minjung—their aspirations and sufferings, their struggles and defeats, which form their social biography. Therefore, our reflection on the minjung involves not only objective socioeconomic analysis, but also an empathy for their expressive language and culture.

The identity and reality of the minjung is known not by a philosophical or scientific definition of their essence or nature, but rather through their own stories—their social biographies which the minjung themselves create and therefore can tell best. This story of the minjung or their social biography is told vis-à-vis the power structure that rules the people; and therefore power is the antagonist in the story, while the people are the subjects. The minjung themselves are the protagonists. Thus the story of the minjung entails a historical understanding which regards them as subjects—not as objects—of their own story and destiny.

In discussions of the minjung as the subjects of history there have arisen several questions. The first is about the unclearness of the concept of the minjung. The second is about the social determination or definition of the minjung; the third is whether or not the minjung have been "glorified" into an ideal notion.

We have an obligation to clarify these questions, but before we do so we should indicate our basic position. "Minjung" is not a concept or object which can be easily explained or defined. "Minjung" signifies a living reality which is dynamic, changing, and complex. This living reality defines its own existence and generates new acts and dramas in history; and it refuses in principle to be defined conceptually.

One of the issues involved in the above questions is the difference between the minjung and the Marxist proletariat. The proletariat is defined socioeconomically, while the minjung is known politically. Politics as power relations is understood comprehensively and thus includes socioeconomic relations. Philosophically speaking, the proletariat is "confined" to socioeconomic (materialistic) determination, so that it is bound to historical possibilities and the internal logic of history. The minjung suffers these limitations in reality; yet the minjung as historical subject transcends the socioeconomic determination of history and unfolds its stories beyond mere historical possibilities to historical novelty—a new drama beyond the present history to a new and transformed history.

This difference between the minjung and the proletariat entails different views of history. Minjung history has a strong transcendental or transcending dimension—a beyond history—which is often expressed in religious form. There is a close relationship between religion and the minjung's perception of history. Even if minjung history does not involve religious elements in an explicit manner, its folklore or cultural elements play a transcending function similar to religion in the perception of history.

In scope too there is a difference between the minjung and the proletariat. The former is a dynamic, changing concept. Woman belongs to minjung when she is politically dominated by man. An ethnic group is a minjung group when it is politically dominated by another group. A race is minjung when it is dominated by another powerful ruling race. When intellectuals are suppressed by the military power elite, they belong to minjung. Of course, the same applies to the workers and farmers. However, the proletariat is rigidly defined in socioeconomic terms in all political circumstances. It is even a name through which a totalitarian political dictatorship is justified.

Historically, the minjung is always in the condition of being ruled, a situation which it seeks to overcome. Therefore, minjung history will never permit the glorification of the minjung so that its name may be used to justify any kind of political dictatorship, especially the totalitarian kind. In many ways, the minjung view of history has an affinity with the cultural values of Western democracy; but the constituency of the minjung is the poor and the suppressed who are alienated in their political and socioeconomic condition.

Often we are asked about the difference between the idea of minjung and the Maoist notion of *inmin*. Here, we should recognize the fact that the Maoist notion upholds the supremacy of the proletariat, and that total dictatorship—which is antagonistic to the minjung and therefore contrary to minjung politics—is an integral part of Maoism.

The minjung is not a self-contained or completely defined concept, but a living entity, which has an ever-unfolding drama and story. The minjung has a social and political biography. The minjung reality is known only through its biography, its story, its hope, and its sufferings. The sociopolitical biography of the minjung is the key historical point of reference for minjung theology in addition to references of biblical stories. The problem with philosophical and ideological views of history is that they reduce the total sociopolitical biography (the record of sociopolitical experiences) of the minjung to an appendix to their systems or concepts. Rather than coopt the story of the minjung into their systems, philosophy and ideology should serve to clarify the story of the minjung, in which the pain and suffering of the people as well as their hopes and aspirations are expressed.

The next question we need to clarify concerns the historical subjecthood or subjectivity of the minjung. The minjung is the protagonist in the historical drama. It is the subject and its sociopolitical biography is the predicate. In the Korean context, one may suspect that the notion of the subjecthood from North Korean Communism has sneaked into minjung theology. Once again, we should not mistake the fact that in North Korea the notion of *juche* refers to the autonomy of the national totalitarian dictatorship which uses the name of the proletariat. It is a sort of "realized" subjecthood in the form of a dictatorial state. But in minjung theology, the subjecthood of the minjung in between the times of the "not yet " and the "already."

The minjung are not yet fully the subjects of history. However, their subjectivity is being realized through their struggles against oppressive powers and repressive social structures. In so doing, the minjung have risen up to be subjects of their own destiny, refusing to be condemned to the fate of being objects of manipulation and suppression. The minjung have their own stories to tell over against the stories or the dominant ideologies of the rulers. When we say that the minjung are the subjects of history, we are not exalting them in political terms but are affirming as authentic their identification of themselves as the masters of their own history which is told in their sociopolitical biography. We should neither glorify nor absolutize the minjung, for they suffer under their historical predicament. In traditional theological terms we may say that they are under and in a state of sin.

Up to now, historical writings have usually centered on the ruling power. A typical example of this is Confucian historiography. It is the chronicle of the king as the ruler. Here the people do not appear as actors in history.[2] Our proposal is that we read history from below, from the point of view of the minjung, rather than from the point of view of the ruling power. History is the process in which the minjung realize their own destiny to be the free subjects of history and to participate in the messianic kingdom. This theological notion of messianic kingdom has been chosen to develop a minjung perspective on history.

The messianic aspirations of the people arise out of the historical confrontation between the people and the powers. The messianic kingdom is not an illusory or utopian dream, but is the core of the history for which the suffering people, the poor and oppressed, struggle. It is therefore concrete. Herein lies the origin and the basis of messianic language. It does not come from a dreamlike world. When we talk about messianism, we are implying a messiah who is of the people and whom the people feel to be theirs. Both terms, "messianism" and "messiah," are often used to indicate a certain "fanaticism" or to describe a hero or elitist cult. Although these negative qualities exist in the history of messiahs and messianisms, they are external to the essence of true messianism. Here, the Messiah emerges from the suffering people and identifies with the suffering people.

Theologically, the messianic expectation of the people is based upon theodicy, which is the victory of the justice of God over evil in history. The Messiah and the people actualize the justice of God in history. This historical process is a radical transformation, in which the new one arrives as the old one departs. Messianism is an eschatological phenomenon closely linked to an apocalyptic perception of history.

From our point of view, the focal point of messianism is the general resurrection of all the people (the minjung) for historical judgment against evil and its followers. The general resurrections of all the people is a concrete vision of history in which the people realize their corporate subjectivity in participating in the messianic kingdom. The content of the messianic kingdom may be viewed as *justice, koinonia* (participation),and *shalom* (peace or becoming whole). *Justice* is a faithful relation or a faithful interweaving of the stories of the people and power so that there is no contradiction between them; *koinonia* is the content of the creative interaction that will take place among the people; and *shalom* is the wholesome development of humanity and its well-being. These messianic categories which we have described briefly can be developed into a social philosophy which takes into account the story of the minjung and operates with a messianic view of history.

In a brief paper it is not possible to enter into a discussion of all aspects of the large and complex issue of messianism. In this paper we will concentrate on the conceptual difference between power-messianism and Jesus-messianism, or ruler-messianism and minjung-messianism, or political messianism and messianic servanthood. Jesus-messianism or messianic servanthood is a radical challenge to all forms of political-, royal-, and power-messianisms. It is concerned with saving and transforming the minjung so that its subjecthood may be realized. Hence, all powers must be under the rule of Jesus the Messiah, who came to be the servant of the minjung, who died for them, and who rose from the dead so that the minjung may rise from the power of death historically and not just at the end of time.

With this conceptual background we will turn very briefly to an examination of Korean messianic movements. The oldest significant instance of messianism in Korea came with the introduction of Buddhism, particularly the Maitreya Buddhist tradition. The Maitreya Buddha is known as the Messianic Buddha who comes from the West Paradise to rescue the people from suffering. As yet there has been no substantial study of the Maitreya Messianic Buddha movement although there are several indications of its influence in Korean history. The first such indication is the commentary of Won Hyo, a Silla scholar-monk, on the scriptures concerning the Maitreya Buddha. Won Hyo's famous doctrine that "the ordinary person is Buddha" indicates a strong influence of the popular egalitarian ethics of messianism. Recent archaeological discoveries suggest that the Maitreya formed a decisive ideological backbone for the Unified Silla Dynasty of the Three Kingdoms Period. Toward the end of that dynasty, Maitreya Messianic Buddhism influenced the popular resistance movements against dynastic regimes. One may conclude that the people in Korea have been under the strong influence of the messianic movement and ideology of Maitreya Buddhism throughout much of history.[3] Even during the Yi Dynasty, which was dominated by neo-Confucian orthodox ideology, the idea of the Maitreya Buddha was *alive* among the people.

Recently the question has come up about the role Buddhism, especially Maitreya Buddhism, played in undergirding the ideology of the state. It is a question in the area of political messianism, which attributes to the state a redemptive messianic role. The historical facts which will answer this question have yet to be determined; but Maitreya Buddhism seems to have played two rather contradictory roles during the time of the Silla dynasty.

The second messianic tradition in Korea is the tale of Hon Kil-Dong.[4] Ho Kyun, a chungin (member of the social class between the ruling yangban class and the commoners), wrote this popular novel in the vernacular language of Korea so that the common people could read it easily. The story was told and retold and was most popular during the Yi Dynasty, when the ruling power was making the people suffer most.

The scenario is as follows: The alienated social hero, Hong Kil-Dong, like the author a chungin, leaves home and joins a group of bandits, because he cannot fulfill his life's ambitions and goals in the existing society. Collecting a gang around him he calls it "hwalbindang" (party to rescue the poor). The hero of the story attacks the rich and distributes wealth to the poor. This creates great social disturbances. Finally, the hero is persuaded by his father to leave the country, and he goes off to an island called Yuldo—his paradise, which is characterized by the absence of social division and contradiction between the yangban class and the common people. With its picture of a messianic kingdom, the novel prompted much social imagination among the people. This novel seems to have been heavily influenced by Maitreya Messianic Buddhist ideas.

The third is the famous Donghak messianic movement. This movement emerged in the middle of the nineteenth century, when the Yi Dynasty was progressively becoming decadent and the suffering of the people reached extreme proportions. During this time the ruling yangban population increased but agricultural production decreased at an alarming rate. The Japanese invasion under Hideyoshi caused many disruptions, and not much land was put under cultivation. There was also a decrease in the number of common people, the productive base of society. The exploitation of the poor peasants by the yangban was extremely severe.

In this historical context, the Donghak religious movement manifested itself as a messianic religion among the common people. This was a truly indigenous minjung messianic religion. It played a powerful role in the Donghak Peasant Rebellion of 1895, and in the March First Independence Movement of 1919.

In 1860, Choe Je-U (Choe Messiah or Choe Jesus) founded the Donghak religious movement. Although he was disillusioned and alienated from society, he was a religiously sensitive person. His basic teaching or doctrine was that humanity is heaven. On this basis he advocated egalitarian ethical practice. He believed that there will be a second apocalypse when the whole world will be destroyed and a new era will emerge. This hope led his believers to revolutionary actions. This movement may owe something to Catholic literature which was appearing in the early nineteenth century when Catholics were being severely persecuted. However, there is no doubt that the messianism in Donghak is unmistakably indigenous. It played a powerful role in people's movements in the late nineteenth and early twentieth centuries.

The fourth is the Christian movement in Korea. Although to start with it was a western missionary movement, it soon became a Korean Christian movement among the suffering people of Korea.

The messianic impact of Christianity upon the Korean people took place during the Great Revival of 1907. Here the messianic dynamic of this Korean Christianity unfolded in the successive actions of the national liberation movement against Japanese colonial rule. Korean Christians were agents of messianism in the people's movement. Christians struggled against the Japanese Imperial Education Rescript; and they participated in the March First Independence Movement of 1919. The next historical expression of the Korean Christian messianic movement was when it confronted the Japanese imperial authority and Japan's ultranationalism over the issue of Jinja worship. The story of martydom of Pastor Chu Ki-chol, a devout Christian nationalist, reveals the nature of this struggle.

The most dramatic manifestation of minjung messianism in Korea was the March First Independence Movement of 1919. Korean historians have carefully documented this movement and show the minjung to be its motive power.[5] They also show that the messianic traditions of Buddhism, Donghak religion, and Christianity joined together to form a minjung messianic religious foundation which became the backbone and the dynamic of the movement. This movement produced an axial transformation in the history of modern Korean people; and it has become the paradigmatic or root experience of the Korean people. It supplies the motivation, scope, and direction for the minjung to create their own new future.[6]

The Christian messianic movement of the people can be understood more clearly when we see it against the background of *political messianism* in Korea during the last fifty years or so.

Basically, there are five types of political messianism in Korea. Two are traditional, namely, Buddhist political messianism, an example being the Unified Silla Dynasty, and Confucian orthodox political ideology, which found expression in the Yi Dynasty. One may dispute the messianic character of Confucianism, but the ideology itself contains definite messianic characteristics.

The next three experiences of political messianism by the Korean people were: Japanese ultranationalism in its colonial form; the North Korean Communist movement; and the emerging modern technocracy in Korea.[7] One might argue that modern technocracy should not be classified as messianic, but as we will show, it has strong messianic tendencies.

For the sake of brevity, we will deal with these three cases of political messianism in a schematic manner.

These three political regimes are totalitarian in different ways and to different degrees on the political level; and at the same time on the religious level each claims absolute authority in different ways by assuming divine and messianic roles *for* the people.

According to the polity of Japanese ultranationalism, all values and institutions come under the imperial authority of the emperor. Hence, the government, the military, business, all truth, beauty, and morality belong to the institution of emperor. The infamous Education Rescript was an open declaration of the fact that the Japanese state, being a religious, spiritual, and moral entity, claimed the right to determine all values. This was the spirit of Japanese national polity which was combined with the doctrine of the divinity of the emperor. This messianic motive, championed by the Japanese military which was the holy army of the emperor, launched the mission to bring the "light of the emperor" to the eight corners of the world.

With regard to the Communist political messianism in North Korea, we do not have all the information we need to deal with it fully. However, it seems clear that the personal messianic or cultic role of Kim Il-Sung is very much emphasized. Communism is a secularized form of messianism. Its messianic role, understood in terms of the dictatorship of the proletariat, is in fact assumed by the political leader and finds expression in a totalitarian political structure.

Finally, modern technocracy, in its Korean form, is being experienced as another form of national messianism. There seems to be a conviction that technology and science, organized into the capitalist system, can solve all the human problems of the Korean people; the political regime integrates and contols all the economic, military, and cultural institutions. While doing this, the regime places itself and its authority above the law and criticism and claims the loyalty of the people by emphasizing filial piety, which was formerly a cardinal virtue of Japanese ultranationalism. It is not yet totalitarian and absolutist in the classical sense, but such tendencies are unmistakably present.

These three manifestations of political messianism have common characteristics, not only in their totalitarian and absolutist character, but also in sharing a common theory of contradiction. Their view of history is that there are two powers which are struggling against each other, and that one must destroy the other. One is absolutely good and the other is absolutely evil. The justice of God (theodicy) is alleged to be immanent in the established political regime, be it that of the emperor, a Communist leader, or the military technocracy.

The theodicy immanent in Japanese ultranationalism was seldom obvious or well-defined and thus had an air of mystery about it. It showed itself, however, in opposing its internal enemies, which included liberal, political, and intellectual movements. It also waged a holy way on the so-called Western barbarians and attempted to expand the realm of the emperor. Proponents of Communism believe that its manifest destiny is to bring about the victory of the international proletariat, with imperialism (the United States) as its chief enemy. The military technocracy sees irrationality, traditionalism, and chaos (instability) as characteristics of its internal enemies, who oppose its messianic claims, and it suppresses them. It has Communist North Korea as its external enemy.

In claiming absolute authority, these three kinds of political messianism advocate radical reforms in society. However, these are to be carried out from the top working toward the bottom. For instance, the North Korean regime was not established by the process of a popular revolution, but rather was imposed from the outside by the Soviet Union against the popular will of the Korean people.

These so-called radical reforms—all in the name of an earthly millennium—are undertaken with a great deal of social and political cost which has to be borne by the minjung. Indeed, the sufferings of the Korean people under these three political messianisms were and are extreme. The free subjectivity of the people is reduced to nothing in history. Socioeconomic and cultural analyses of the Korean people's sufferings under these conditions bear witness to the fact that political messianism is antagonistic to the people (the minjung). They experience it as a contradiction.

Therefore, besides making and maintaining false claims to messianism, political messianism sets itself up against the minjung, who face it as a contradiction.

As we have already shown, messianism is a political process or a history in which the minjung join with the Messiah in realizing his messianic role. While political messianism attempts to make the minjung a historical nothing or an object of its messianic claims, the messianic politics of Jesus are the politics that will realize for the minjung their historical subjectivity, thus making them masters of their own historical destiny. Fundamentally, messianic politics must be understood as that of the minjung, not that of the leader, especially not that of the ruling power. The relationship between the minjung and the Messiah should be understood as a relation between the minjung as the subject and the Messiah as their function. However, the messianic function of the people should not be understood in terms of an elite who are at the top of a political hierarchy but in terms of the Suffering Servant.

To be sure, there are many images or models in the Bible which will help to illuminate this notion of messianic politics. For instance, there is the model of King David; there is the figure of the Son of Man in apocalyptic literature; and there are other kingly ("the anointed") images of the Messiah. However, all of these have a corrupting influence, for we see the Messiah as a power personality (political messianism) who embodies self-righteousness and triumphalism. In contrast, the most appropriate and convincing of all messianic images is that of Jesus as the Suffering Servant, in the light of which we must examine and reshape other images like that of David, the Son of Man, and so on. What is noteworthy about the figure of the Suffering Servant is that it provides the two messianic qualities of identification with the suffering people and functioning as servant to the aspiration of the people for liberation.

Such an understanding of messianic politics will provide the means for purging Christian confessions and theologies of elements of political messianism which have come from the ideology of Christendom. The claims of Christendom did not serve the messianic politics of the people to be subjects of history; this was deliberate. It may be one of the critical tasks especially of Third World theologians to purge elements of political messianism from our Christian confessions, proclamations, and theologies.

Furthermore, to expose the reality of political messianisms in the modern state, no matter how secular they claim to be, is one of the fundamental political tasks of the Christian community today. This task needs to be performed while the Christian community seeks to serve the suffering people as Jesus the Messiah did and while Christians in Korea seek to realize the hope expressed through his resurrection and his promise of the general resurrection of all the minjung. This task needs to be done in this context because the struggle to realize the messianic aspirations of the minjung is not just a religious or spiritual matter isolated from the political arena. In fact, the political field is the center stage on which the messianic struggle is carried out. Therefore, the confession that Jesus is the Messiah of the people entails political service to the people.

On the basis of the analyses given above, several further tasks emerge in the Korean situation.

The first is to expose the long history of political messianism which has enslaved us and to struggle against it. This involves critical evaluations of political values, political structures, and political leadership.

The second is to rediscover the popular messianic traditions inherent in Maitreya Messianic Buddhism and Donghak religion, both through a research of extant literature and through dialogue with Buddhist and Donghak leaders who have concerns similar to ours. In undertaking this task we must remember that messianic traditions are not immune to influences from political messianism once they are linked to the ruling power. We know of the process in the history of Christianity, which has justified absolute power like that of the divine right of kings.

The third is to evolve in a concrete way a Christian political perspective based on the following ideas: (1) The general resurrection of the people (bodily as well as spiritually) understood in terms of the messianic subjectivity of the people. (2) *Shalom* in relation to the unification of Korea. (3) *Koinonia* and justice in relation to the social and political development of the Korean people. In order to do all this we need a general understanding of Korean history and we should dialogue with secular intellectuals who seek to serve the people.

The fourth is to tackle the issue of the use of power in a political struggle. It is not simply a question of the use of violence. The issue concerns the nature and use of power in politics. Although there can be no general rule on the use of power, including force and violence, in the process of realizing the messianic hope of the people, a few general things can be said.

1. Ultimately, power, as we know it, has no ontological status in the framework of the messianic kingdom. Jesus not only did not use power as we know it, but he could not use power, because he himself was the embodiment and reality of the messianic kingdom, which is the powerless status of Jesus the Messiah and the people.

2. However, as we have indicated, history shows the continuous contradiction between political messianism and messianic politics, the power and the people. Therefore, some tamed measure of political realism should be allowed,

although an absolute political cynicism or "realpolitik" should never be permitted.

In considering a realistic posture on the part of Christians, the notion of people's power should be taken into account. It is infinitely creative; and various forms of it are evident especially at the grassroots level, where identification and participation with people are easiest.

The people will be the subjects of their own historical destiny. Jesus the Messiah died to expose Roman political messianism and its historical antecedents and descendants; and Jesus the Messiah was resurrected as a foretaste and affirmation of the raising of all the dead minjung to inaugurate the messianic rule of *justice, koinonia* (participation), and *shalom.*

NOTES

1. As a preliminary and tentative approximation, we can say that the concept of "minjung" encompasses such words and groups as the masses, the people, the downtrodden, the poor, the marginalized,and the underdogs. However, see below for clarification of the definition of this complex and illusive term.

2. The traditional Korean historical books, *Samguksagi* (Historical Records of Three Kingdoms) and Royal Chronicles of Yi Korea Dynasty are typical examples of this.

3. The Korean Buddhist scholar Ko Eun recently developed this theme under Minjung Buddhism. Maitreya Buddhism had two moments, one being the royal messianic leader and the other being the leader of the suffering people (minjung).

4. "The Tale of Hong Kil-Dong" is a paradigm of the social biography of the minjung. It contains popular Buddhist and Taoist elements and is full of social imagination, humor, and satire.

5. Prof. Ahn Pyong-Jik of Seoul National University has, through socioeconomic analysis, determined the constituency of the March First Independence Movement to be the minjung.

6. For a detailed analysis, see Kim Yong-Bock, "Historical Transformation: People's Movement and Messianic *Koinonia,*" (Ph. D. diss., Princeton Theological Seminary, 1976), especially chapter 5.

7. The first draft of this paper was written in 1979. The reference is to the so-called Yushin system.

CONTRIBUTORS

Rubem Alves teaches in the department of social studies at the Campinas State University in Brazil.

Kofi Appiah-Kubi is lecturer in sociology at the University of Science and Technology, Kumasi, Ghana.

Hugo Assmann, a Brazilian, is formerly professor of journalism at the University of Costa Rica.

Tissa Balasuriya teaches at the Centre for Society and Religion in Colombo, Sri Lanka.

Allan Boesak is student chaplain at the University of the Western Cape, Peninsula Technical College, and Bellville Training College for Teachers in South Africa.

Leonardo Boff teaches at the Petrópolis Institute for Philosophy and Theology in Petrópolis, Brazil.

Manas Buthelezi is bishop of the Evangelical Lutheran Church in South Africa.

Francisco F. Claver, now retired, was the bishop of Bukidnon in the Philippines.

Segundo Galilea is a Catholic priest from Santiago, Chile.

Gustavo Gutiérrez is professor of theology at the Catholic University in Lima, Peru.

Eugene Hillman has served as a priest to the Masai people of Tanzania.

Henriette Marianne Katoppo is active in the Indonesian Student Christian Movement.

Kim Yong-Bok is Co-director of research at the Christian Institute for the Study of Justice and Development, Seoul, Korea.

Kosuke Koyama, who is from Japan, is professor of ecumenics and world Christianity at Union Theological Seminary in New York City.

J. B. Libânio is a professor of theology at the Pontifical Catholic University in Rio de Janeiro, Brazil.

John Mbiti, a Kenyan, is the former director of the Ecumenical Institute of the World Council of Churches, Bossey, Switzerland.

José Miranda teaches at the Universidad Metropolitana Tztapalapa in Mexico City.

Mercy Amba Oduyoye is a lecturer at the University of Ibadan, Nigeria.

Geervarghese Mar Osthathios is the metropolitan of the Orthodox church in Kerala, India.

385

Samuel Rayan is dean of the faculty of theology of the Vidyajyoti Institute in Delhi, India.

Lamin Sanneh taught at the University of Ibadan, Nigeria, and now teaches at Harvard University.

Juan Luis Segundo is chaplain to various reflection groups in his native Uruguay.

Jon Sobrino is a professor of philosophy and theology at the Universidad José Simeón Cañas in El Salvador.

C. S. Song, who is from Taiwan, is associate director of the secretariat of the Faith and Order Commission of the World Council of Churches.

Elsa Tamez is a professor of biblical studies at the Seminario Bíblico Latino-americano in San José, Costa Rica.

Desmond Tutu is the Anglican bishop of Johannesburg, South Africa.

Albert Widjaja, an Indonesian, is associate general secretary to the Christian Conference of Asia, Singapore.

Other Orbis Titles . . .

A PLACE IN THE SUN
Liberation Theology in the Third World
by Theo Witvliet

Liberation theology is often perceived simply as a Latin American phenomenon. In this insightful study by Dutch theologian Theo Witvliet, however, the sundry manifestations of liberation theology throughout the Third World are explored, revealing a richly diverse and truly global theological development.

   With its detailed surveys of African, Asian, Latin American, and Caribbean liberation theologies, as well as of the black theologies emerging in the U.S. and South Africa, this work provides a thorough, intelligent introduction for students and scholars interested in the sources and scope of liberation theology.

   Theo Witvliet is Lecturer in Ecumenism on the Theological Faculty of Amsterdam University.

no. 404-6   208pp. pbk. $8.95

CHRISTIANITY WITHOUT FETISHES
An African Critique and Recapture of Christianity
by F. Eboussi Boulaga

From one of the leading theologians in West Africa, a penetrating analysis of the inculturation of Christianity in Africa. Eboussi Boulaga rejects as a fetish manufactured in the west the Christianity imposed upon and adopted by the African churches. He mounts a constructive and comprehensive African alternative. Essential reading for academics, ecumenists, and missioners.

   "Once the depth of Eboussi's critique begins to sink in, once one realizes that inculturation has precious little to do with liturgical vestments and musical instruments but rather with very basic worldviews, with basic human values and indeed with the sharing of power, then the significance of this book begins to dawn. This is a threatening book. It cuts to the quick."   *Simon E. Smith, S.J., Jesuit Refugee Service, Nairobi*

   Eboussi is professor of philosophy at the National University of the Ivory Coast.

no. 432-1   256pp. pbk. $11.95

FAREWELL TO INNOCENCE
A Socio-Ethical Study on
Black Theology and Black Power
by Allan Boesak

Farewell to Innocence relates the black South African experience of oppression and the theology that has emerged from it to liberation movements and theologies in North America, Latin America, Asia, and the rest of Africa. Boesak provides an excellent introduction to the main themes of black theology and critiques the works of black theologians such as James Cone, Martin Luther King, Jr., Preston Williams, and Deotis Roberts.

no. 130-6   **197pp. pbk.**   **$6.95**

WE DRINK FROM OUR OWN WELLS
by Gustavo Gutiérrez

"Gustavo Gutiérrez develops a spirituality which grows out of the lived experience of the Latin American people. Rooted in the reality of oppression and repression, this book calls forth a conversion from self-complacency and self sufficiency to that of solidarity with the poor." *Catholic New Times*

". . . it powerfully and beautifully provides a guide for 'the spiritual journey of a people,' a people of whom we too are a part." *Robert McAfee Brown*

no. 707-X   **176pp. pbk.**   **$7.95**

FACES OF JESUS
Latin American Christologies
edited by José Míguez-Bonino

The most extensive part of this book is devoted to describing and analyzing the christologies that have been present in Latin America throughout history. A fascinating picture emerges of how Jesus functions within establishment, traditional peasant, and revolutionary sectors of the population. Boff, Casalis, Segundo, Croatto, Assmann, and others contribute to this ecumenical effort.

"If one thinks, or is tempted to think, that Christian theology is boring, stale, repeating the eternal, unchanging truths, then this book will shatter the myth." *America*

no. 129-2   **192pp. pbk.**   **$10.95**

FRONTIERS OF THEOLOGY IN LATIN AMERICA
edited by Rosino Gibellini

Rosino Gibellini invited thirteen of the most prominent Latin American theologians to contribute to this comprehensive survey of liberation theology in the Southern hemisphere. The authors represented are: Alves, Assmann, Boff, Bonino, Comblin, de Valle, Dussel, Galilea, Gutiérrez, Muñoz, Scannone, Segundo, and Vidales. Includes extensive biographical information about the contributors.

"If there is any one college textbook best suited to introduce students to Latin American liberation theology, this is it." *Religious Studies Review*

no. 144-6   **333pp. pbk.**   **$10.95**

THE TRUE CHURCH AND THE POOR
by Jon Sobrino

This unusual scholarly venture into ecclesiology focuses on the poor as the channel through which God's spirit is manifesting itself today. For Jon Sobrino, the shift in Latin

American churches to a mission centered on the poor has led to vicious persecution but also to hope, and hence, to "a recovery by the Church of the memory of Jesus."

". . . a challenging and controversial book."   *Sojourners*

Jesuit priest Jon Sobrino is professor of philosophy and theology at the Universidad José Simeón Cañas in El Salvador.

no. 513-1   **384pp. pbk.**   **$13.95**

GALILEAN JOURNEY
The Mexican-American Promise
by Virgilio Elizondo

In *Galilean Journey*, a liberation theology emerging from the experience of the Chicano population in the Southwest, Virgilio Elizondo penetrates the dynamics that govern the life and death of Mexican-Americans. He elaborates the parallel between the experience and mission of Mexican-Americans as a conquered and despised, mixed-race people and that of the historical Jesus as a Galilean, a member of a similarly oppressed group.

"*Galilean Journey* will provide a double revelation, disclosing new dimensions of the uniqueness of Mexican-Americans and of the universality of Christian faith and experience."   *National Catholic Reporter*

Virgilio Elizondo is founder and president of the Mexican-American Cultural Center in San Antonio, Texas.

no. 151-9   **158pp. pbk.**   **$7.95**

HERALDS OF A NEW REFORMATION
The Poor of South and North America
by Richard Shaull
Foreword by Paul Lehmann

Richard Shaull interprets Latin American liberation theology for first world Christians and shows how it relates to our situation. The one-time Princeton Professor of Ecumenics includes a moving account of how his own life plan and faith have been altered by his encounter with the poor of the Americas over four decades.

"For those of us in the 'First World,' living as we do 'in a society deeply troubled because it can dream of no future beyond the continuation of what it is now—and is in danger of losing,' this book is a timely and renewing account of the vision of the people of the 'Third World,' and of the new future which their vision can offer to us as well."   *Paul Lehmann*, from the Foreword

no. 345-7   **160pp. pbk.**   **$8.95**

SALVATION AND LIBERATION
In Search of a Balance Between Faith and Politics
by Leonardo and Clodovis Boff

After an introduction to the basic propositions of liberation theology, the authors discuss their stance on the relationship between faith and politics, salvation and liberation. The expositional chapters are rounded out by a lively, imaginary "conversation" among a parish priest, a theologian, and a Christian activist confronting the challenges posed by the present social reality in Latin America.

"The book serves well to introduce the reader to the theology of liberation while at the same time being self-critical and adopting a needed historical perspective. Recommended for undergraduate and graduate libraries that desire to stay abreast of one of the century's most significant religious and theological movements." *Choice*

no. 451-8   **128pp. pbk.**   **$6.95**

THE IDOLS OF DEATH AND THE GOD OF LIFE
A Theology
by Pablo Richard, et. al.

Ten Latin Americans look at the biblical, economic, and ideological implications of a liberating, life-giving God in contrast to "the false gods of the system," which through militarism, oppression, and economic exploitation deny life and usher in death. Richard, Croatto, Pixley, Sobrino, Araya, Casanas, Limon, Betto, Hinkelammert, and Assmann contribute to this ecumenical endeavor.

"Even where their way is not our way, we need to listen to what they have learned. These essays make an excellent listening post."

Walter Wink, Auburn Theological Seminary

no. 048-2   **240pp. pbk.**   **$12.95**

MOUNT FUJI AND MOUNT SINAI
A Critique of Idols
by Kosuke Koyama

This is the work toward which Kosuke Koyama's previous books, from *Waterbuffalo Theology* to *Three Mile an Hour God*, have been leading. It is a report of his personal pilgrimage, showing how his historical experience as a Japanese and his confession of Christian faith have led to a profoundly Asian theology of the cross.

Kosuke Koyama is Professor of Ecumenics and World Christianity at Union Theological Seminary, New York.

no. 353-8   **288pp. pbk.**   **$12.95**

THE COMPASSIONATE GOD
by C. S. Song

A proposal for a *transpositional* theology which "crosses the boundaries of cultures, religions, and histories in order to have deeper contacts with the strange and mysterious ways and thoughts of God in creation." C.S. Song moves toward developing this theology first by analyzing biblical themes and texts, providing an interpretation vastly different from the traditional Western interpretation, and then by journeying into an examination of particular incidents in Asiatic history to show the ways of God in the Asian world.

". . . rewarding reading."   *International Bulletin of Missionary Research*

C.S. Song is the Associate Director of the Secretariat of the Faith and Order Commission of the World Council of Churches, Geneva.

no. 095-4   **284pp. pbk.**   **$12.95**